Alexa Soba

EMPLOYER'S GUIDE TO

WORKERS' COMPENSATION

D1417707

Alexa Baba

Other BNA Books of Interest:

Employer's Guide to The Americans With Disabilities Act
Employer's Guide to Workplace Torts
Employer's Guide to Using Independent Contractors
Human Resources and the Law
Employment-Labor Law Audit

EMPLOYER'S GUIDE TO
WORKERS' COMPENSATION

Edward M. Welch

The Bureau of National Affairs, Inc., Washington, D.C.

Copyright © 1994
The Bureau of National Affairs, Inc.

Library of Congress Cataloging-in-Publication Data

Welch, Edward M.
　Employer's guide to workers' compensation / Edward M. Welch.
　　p.　cm.
　Includes bibliographical references (p.　　).
　ISBN 0-87179-710-0
　1. Workers' compensation—United States—States. 2. Workers'
compensation—Law and legislation—United States—States.
3. Workers' compensation—United States.　　I. Title.
HD7103.65.U6W45　1994
658.3'254—dc20　　　　　　　　　　　　　　　　　　94-29492
　　　　　　　　　　　　　　　　　　　　　　　　　　　　CIP

Authorization to photocopy items for internal or personal use, or the internal or personal
use of specific clients, is granted by BNA Books for libraries and other users registered with
the Copyright Clearance Center (CCC) Transactional Reporting Service, provided that $1.00
per page is paid directly to CCC, 27 Congress St., Salem, MA 01970. 0-8179-710-0/94/$0
+ 1.00.

Published by BNA Books, 1250 23rd St., N.W.
Washington, D.C. 20037

Printed in the United States of America
International Standard Book Number 0-87179-710-0

Dedication

The workers' compensation system works well most of the time. We hear many complaints about the problems, but about 80 percent of the time the system works just the way it is supposed to. The reason it works as well as it does is that people make it work. The workers' compensation system is made up of thousands of men and women. They include employees and officials of state agencies, those who handle workers' compensation cases on behalf of employers, those who work for insurance companies and service companies, doctors, lawyers, rehabilitation counselors, therapists of many kinds, union officials, and a variety of others. This book is dedicated to them, the people who make the system work.

Acknowledgments

Kimberly Ernzer, Elizabeth A. Hubler, Valarie A. King, Nancy L. Scott, Denise E. Shonds, Susan E. Straffon, and Katherine J. Welch assisted in preparing the manuscript of this book. Their help in overcoming my difficulties with typing and spelling is greatly appreciated. I also want to thank Camille D. Christie at BNA for her help in preparing and editing this manuscript.

A great many people contributed ideas that are included in Part 3. Among them are Roger Fries and Mark Hogle from the Accident Fund of Michigan; Alan Strohmaier, Daniel J. Osborne, Philip J. Monaghan, Jr., William P. Kelly, Richard D. Webster, Richard L. Bade, and Arthur L. Schott from General Motors Corporation; Paul Mattera, John Antonakes, and others from Liberty Mutual Insurance Company; Libby Child from Steelcase Corporation; Glenn Whittington from the U.S. Department of Labor; and John P. Miron, Ervin Vahration, and Bruno Czyrka from the Michigan Bureau of Workers' Disability Compensation.

My wife, Rosemary, has been extremely patient and supportive as I have worked on this project. This is just one of the many things for which I am extremely grateful to her.

Contents

Part 1

Introduction

Chapter 1

Introduction

1.1 Organization

This book is divided into four parts. It begins and ends with rather short, two-chapter parts. The bulk of the book is contained in Parts 2 and 3. Part 1 includes this introduction and a chapter reviewing current topics.

Part 2 deals with what I call *macro*workers' compensation, the laws, the system. It is intended to give the reader a basic understanding of how the system works. The part begins with chapter 3, which includes an overview of how the system works, a quick history of workers' compensation, and a brief discussion of some economic issues. Part 2 then goes on to discuss the legal issues relating to which employers and which injuries are covered, how disability is defined, and what benefits are available. It includes a review of how state workers' compensation systems are administered, insurance requirements, and concludes with some data comparing state systems.

Part 3 turns to *micro*workers' compensation. It is intended to show employers the things that they can do to control their own workers' compensation experience. It views workers' compensation from the firm level and reviews topics such as claims handling, safety, and disability management. Part 3 begins with chapter 16, which includes a discussion of research that documents the importance of employer-level approaches and explains how the information for this part of the book was developed. Most of Part 3 is in a question and answer format that can be used by an employer to inventory its workers' compensation system. Section 16.3 explains how the approach was developed.

Part 4 includes chapters 28 and 29, which are written by physicians and deal with back injuries and repetitive trauma disorders of the hands and arms. These problems are so common and important to workers' compensation that anyone dealing in this area should have a basic understanding of the medical principles involved. Accordingly, we have included two chapters dealing specifically with these medical issues.

1.2 Purpose and Limitations

The goal of Parts 3 and 4 is to provide employers with specific ideas that they can use in dealing with workers' compensation on a day-to-day basis. By necessity Part 2 is a bit more general. It is intended to provide an overview of how the system works and an understanding of the issues involved.

There is a tremendous diversity in the ways in which the states deal with workers' compensation, especially with regard to matters such as permanent partial disability and procedures. There is no publication that catalogs how all the states deal with many of these issues. The statutes and appellate court decisions are helpful, but they do not tell us how the systems operate on a day-to-day basis. Accordingly, this book is not able to provide readers with specific information on how each state handles each issue involved in workers' compensation. Instead it will describe the issues, and where possible, indicate the approach taken by most states as well as any trends.

The reader will have to research the specifics of how the issues are handled in each of the states in which he or she operates. Appendix A lists the addresses of state workers' compensation agencies. This should be of some help in obtaining information. In a few states, such as Michigan, there is a legal treatise that describes in detail how the system works. In some others, the state agency publishes rather detailed guides for employers and workers. In many states, however, there is simply no good source for this information other than experienced attorneys and claims managers.

The above caveat having been stated, it must also be said that the place to start is a basic understanding of the issues and alternatives. This book will provide that.

1.3 Terminology and References

I believe strongly in inclusive language and have tried to use it in this book. As a former English teacher, however, I lived for several years in fear that I would have to deal with *workpersons'* compensation. Fortunately someone came up with the idea of *workers'* compensation. During the 1970s, most states amended their statutes to use this more inclusive term, accordingly this book uses *workers'* compensation. The previous term was *workmen's* compensation, the plural possessive. It must be noted, however, that some statutes and insurance policies use other forms such as the singular possessive, *worker's,* or the simple plural, *workers.* I will occasionally refer to publications or organizations that predated the use of inclusive language. In those cases I will use the original form of their name.

This book will deal with 53 workers' compensation laws. They are the laws of the 50 states, the District of Columbia, and two laws that are administered by the federal government (see section 3.2). With apologies to my friends in the District and the federal government, I will use the term *states* to refer collectively to all of these jurisdictions. (Actually there are more than 53 workers' compensation laws in the United States. Several territories and the Navajo Nation have their own workers' compensation laws, but they are beyond the scope of this book.)

When an employer purchases insurance, the insurer agrees to carry out the employer's responsibilities under the workers' compensation law. They are, however, originally and ultimately the responsibilities of the employer. Accordingly, and for the sake of convenience, I will often speak of the rights and responsibilities of the *employer,* even in cases where those rights and responsibilities are delegated to an insurer. Thus, I will say "the employer must pay 30 weeks of benefits," even though in many cases the benefits will actually be paid by an insurance company.

I will include within the term *carrier*, an insurance company or a self-insured employer, but not an insured employer. Unless otherwise indicated, I will generally intend to include *state funds* (see section 14.4) when referring to insurers, insurance companies, or carriers.

Section 3.5 describes some important organizations and resources. A few of them will be referred to so frequently that I will use shortened titles to refer to them. Thus I will use *National Commission* for the National Commission on State Workmen's Compensation Laws and its 1972 report,[1] *Larson* for the *Workmen's Compensation Law*,[2] written by the late Arthur Larson, and *NCCI* for the National Council on Compensation Insurance.

Notes

1. Report of the National Commission on State Workmen's Compensation Laws (Washington, D.C.: GPO, 1972).
2. Larson, Arthur, *Larson's Workmen's Compensation Law* (New York: Matthew Bender, 1952, with supplements to date).

Chapter 2

Current Topics

2.1 Introduction

A number of topics are of particular interest at the time this is being written. For the most part, they are dealt with in other parts of this book. Because of their currency, however, they will be explored here with references to the other chapters where they are considered.

2.2 Fraud

Recently, there have been many articles on TV and in the popular press about workers' compensation fraud.[1] Some of these have included sensationally high estimates for how much of the workers' compensation dollar goes to fraudulent claims. Most of the articles and TV exposés have focused on fraud by claimants, although a few have acknowledged that there can be fraud by health care providers, employers, and insurers.

In order to talk reasonably about the fraud problem, we need to define what we mean by "fraud." If Mr. A is injured at home on Saturday, goes into work on Monday, and claims to have been hurt there, that is clearly fraud. If Ms. B is receiving benefits and lies in saying that she is not working, when in fact she has a part-time job, that too is clearly fraud.

But what about Mr. C? We know he was really injured, we saw it happen. The doctor confirmed that he had a muscle strain. The problem is, he is not getting better. Most people with a similar

7

strain get better in six weeks. He has been off six months and there is no sign of improvement. His doctor says he is still "disabled," but the company doctor cannot find much wrong with him. He has been known to go bowling. He does not do as well as he used to, and in fact he often is unable to finish a game, but if he cannot work, it does not seem like he should be bowling. Is this fraud? I do not call Mr. C's situation "fraud." It is, nevertheless, a very big problem for workers' compensation.

Some of the reports in the popular media have talked about fraud equaling 20 percent of workers' compensation costs. There is absolutely no data to back up this claim. I know of no research that yielded such results.

If we are talking about hard-core fraud (Mr. A and Ms. B), I would guess that it involves no more than 1 or 2 percent of the cases nationwide. (Although, it certainly may be higher in some parts of the country.) I would emphasize, however, that this is only a guess. What about Mr. C and other similar cases? How big of a problem are they? Cases like these may well account for 20 percent of the workers' compensation dollars. We could argue all night about whether we should call it "fraud," but there is no question that it is a big problem.

Dealing with hard-core fraud is fairly straightforward. It requires some time and resources, but most experts agree about what should be done. The claims handling practices discussed in chapters 20 and 21 will catch most of these individuals. This should begin with a thorough investigation of each injury. The worker's description of what happened should be put in writing and signed. All witnesses and potential witnesses should be interviewed. The reports from the worker and all witnesses should be compared with each other and with the history given at the emergency room and the histories given to doctors. The scene should be carefully observed to determine if it is compatible with the story.

In addition to providing details about past incidents, a thorough investigation will have a deterrent effect. If fellow workers see that every injury claim is treated as a serious event that must be carefully documented, they will think twice before making a false claim. They will also be more careful and pay more attention to safety practices, which should result in an overall reduction in injuries.

Diligence, of course, cannot stop with the initial investigation of the accident. There should be continual follow-up. If a worker is claiming a long-term disability, there should be an "activities check" at least once a year. Some would say every six months. Common sense would suggest an investigation more often under certain circumstances. If, for example, Mr. D wants his checks sent to a post office box, it might be a reason for concern. If Ms. E never answers the phone between 8:00 a.m. and 5:00 p.m., it is time to check up on her. These are routine things that a claims person should be sensitive to.

An "activities check" usually starts with someone talking with people in the neighborhood. If they all say, "Oh, poor old Joe, he can't do anything at all," it can stop there. If, however, they say, "Joe? We didn't know there was anything wrong with him," further investigation is in order. This usually means that someone gets out a van and a video camera and follows Joe around for a few days.

I want to emphasize that this is not new or unusual. This is routine. Insurance companies have been doing this kind of investigation for years. An employer should expect it as part of the claims adjusting service.

Who pays for and does all of this investigation? Generally, the initial investigation of the injury is done by the employer. I think it would be reasonable, however, to ask an insurance company or service company to help an employer set up a program or even to assist with the investigations. The follow-up investigations of on-going claims should be provided as a routine part of claims adjusting. An insurance company should be expected to do it without additional cost, and it should be part of the service that a service company contracts to perform.

Except in a few parts of the country, the procedure outlined above will do a very good job of controlling what I call "hard-core fraud," those cases in which the worker is clearly and consciously lying. What about Mr. C whom we described above? What about the person who is not lying but who simply does not get well? This is a much more difficult problem. Return to work programs are one tool, but they are only one of many. It is impossible to describe in a few paragraphs how to deal with these cases. In fact, one of the primary goals of Part 3 of this book is to help employers deal with those situations. In particular, chapters 19 and 25 should help employers structure the environment to eliminate the cause of some of these problems and provide an arsenal of weapons for dealing with them when they do arise.

We have focused here solely on fraud by workers. There are also many problems caused by the inappropriate actions of employers, doctors, lawyers, and insurers. Employers frequently are found to be underreporting their payroll in order to lower premiums. Doctors sometimes present false bills. Lawyers sometimes either alone or in conjunction with others solicit and present false claims. And insurers sometimes use inappropriate means to deny or minimize claims. A detailed discussion of all of these is beyond the scope of this book. The system, however, needs to be adjusted to reduce and punish inappropriate behavior by all parties.

One of the problems is that the system does not have incentives to deter fraud. If a worker claims benefits that he or she does not deserve, the worst that usually happens is that he or she is denied those benefits. If an insurance company denies benefits that it clearly should have paid, in most cases all that happens is that it is required to pay them. If an employer lies about its payroll and is caught, the punishment is usually that it is required to pay the premiums it should have paid in the first place. We need a system the will reward the honest players and punish the cheats on all fronts.

2.3 Mental Stress Cases

Mental stress cases have received a lot of attention lately. It is true that they are a serious problem in a few places such as Southern California, and they are very disturbing for employers when they happen. I do not believe, however, that they represent a serious threat to the system overall.

A recent study, "Workers' Compensation Paranoia: Mental Stress Claims" done by N. Mike Helvacian, Ph.D., of NCCI, shows that the number of mental stress claims is relatively small.[2] Only 1.4 of every 1,000 cases is a stress claim. The study also shows that after a brief increase, the frequency of these claims appears to be declining.

There is great diversity in the way that the states treat mental stress cases, and this situation is currently in considerable flux as states attempt to tighten their rules in this regard. While a state by state listing is beyond the scope of this book, it may be helpful to look at the some of the ways in which the issue is being defined.

One of the most frequent approaches is to categorize cases as physical-mental, mental-physical, and mental-mental. In physical-mental cases, a mental disability follows from a physical injury, the shell-shocked soldier. In mental-physical cases, a physical injury is caused by mental stress, a heart attack following intense negotiations at work. Finally, mental-mental cases involve mental disability caused by mental stress, a teacher becomes despondent and depressed after dealing with unruly students for many years. These latter cases are compensable in only a minority of states.

Some states apply a higher standard of causation in mental stress cases. As discussed in section 6.5, most disabilities are compensable if the work merely aggravated the condition; it need not be the sole or even the primary cause. There has been a trend to apply a higher standard in mental stress cases. In California, for example, the law has recently been amended to require that the work be the preponderant cause of a mental disability in order for it to be compensable. Other states, such as Oregon, require that the stress be unusual or that the events be objectively stressful. Finally many states exclude mental stress claims that result from ordinary personnel transactions.

Why should stress cases be treated differently? Advocates for workers would argue that they should not be. In an enlightened society, they would say, we should treat all disabilities the same. Employers respond that it is too easy to fake emotional disabilities and too difficult to evaluate them objectively. Because of this they must be treated differently. Employers also worry that too broad a definition of the compensability of stress cases will lead to compensating everyone who does not feel good about his or her job. The data cited at the beginning of this section suggest that we are far from doing that. That may be, however, because of the stringent rules we have applied. Some strategies for preventing on-the-job stress are discussed in section 18.4.

2.4 The Americans with Disabilities Act

The Americans with Disabilities Act (ADA) prohibits discrimination by employers against workers with a disability. Further, it requires that employers take affirmative action to accommodate individuals with a disability unless the accommodation is unreasonable or would cause an undue hardship.

This has several implications for workers' compensation. The Equal Employment Opportunity Commission (EEOC), which is charged with enforcing the ADA, has attempted to assure employers that there should be little conflict between the ADA and workers' compensation cases by claiming that most injured workers will not qualify for coverage under the ADA. In its *Technical Assistance Manual* (section 9.2) the EEOC tells us:

> Clearly, not every employee injured on the job will meet the ADA definition [of an individual with a disability]. Work-related injuries do not always cause physical or mental impairments severe enough to "substantially limit" a major life activity. Also, many on-the-job injuries cause non-chronic impairments which heal within a short period of time with little or no long-term or permanent impact. Such injuries, in most circumstances, are not considered disabilities under the ADA.
>
> The fact that an employee is awarded workers' compensation benefits, or is assigned a high workers' compensation disability rating, does not automatically establish that this person is protected by the ADA. . . .
>
> Thus, many injured workers who qualify for benefits under workers' compensation or other disability benefits laws may not be protected by the ADA.

The EEOC cites as an example a person with a broken leg that could be expected to heal within a few months and suggests that there is no need to accommodate such a person.

I question the value of such advice on both legal and practical grounds. In formulating the above advice, the EEOC relies on that part of the Act which defines a disability as "a physical or mental impairment that substantially limits one or more of the major life activities," and contends that a six-week disability is not "substantial." But the Act goes on to also include in the definition of disability "being regarded as having such an impairment." An attorney for a worker with a broken leg who was refused an accommodation could argue that the employer regarded the worker as having a disability. The reason it refused to accommodate was because it views all impaired workers the same, or because it was afraid the disability would last longer than expected.

Why invite such problems? If the disability is only going to last six weeks and the accommodation would cost $6,000, it is clear that the employer is not required to accommodate. This would be unreasonable and an undue hardship and is not required under any circumstances. If, however, the accommodation will only cost $60, just do it! The answer is to approach these matters from a practical, not a technical, point of view. In each case, consideration should be given to whether the necessary accommodation is reasonable under all the circumstances.

The ADA does require employers to attempt to accommodate injured workers who want to return to work, but as discussed in section 19.2, employers should have return to work programs that aggressively seek to bring injured employees back to the job as fast as possible. Such a program will usually exceed all the requirements of the ADA. In fact, the ADA may heighten the awareness of managers, supervisors, and workers to the idea of accommodation and make it easier to implement return to work programs.

"But what if he or she gets hurt again?" employers always ask. Of course, a worker should not return to a situation that is dangerous considering his or her physical condition. I believe, however, that employers worry about this too much. If the worker wants to come back and the employer can reasonably make an accommodation, the worker should be allowed to give it a try. The employer already has a compensation claim, and a return to work might solve the problem. If at the end the employer still has a claim, it is no worse off.

What if the first injury occurred away from the job? In this situation a new injury will create a compensation case where none existed before. That is a much more complicated matter, one which is beyond the scope of this book.

Subsection 18.2.1 talks about some implications of the ADA in disability prevention programs. Subsection 19.2.8 deals with the ADA and return to work programs. Subsection 21.6.9 suggests some ADA considerations in settling cases. And subsections 25.4.6 and .7 talk about the ADA and unions.

A few good sources of information about the ADA include the *Technical Assistance Manual,* which is available free of charge from the EEOC,[3] *Employer's Guide to the Americans with Disabilities Act,* and *BNA's Americans with Disabilities Act Manual.*[4]

2.5 The Safety Trend

Over the years, there have been certain trends that legislatures seem to have followed in reforming their workers' compensation laws. During the 1970s, in response to the National Commission report, the primary trend was to increase the level of benefits. During the 1980s, the trends focused on vocational rehabilitation. In the early eighties, it was popular to emphasize or mandate vocational rehabilitation. The late eighties, however, saw a backing away from this approach.

In the early to mid 1990s, the most popular legislative trends seem to involve a new emphasis on safety and programs that bring "managed care" to workers' compensation. In addition, as discussed in chapter 16, there appears to be more emphasis recently on the things that can be done at the employer level to deal with workers' compensation.

Oregon was one of the first states to emphasize safety in workers' compensation reform. In 1987, it increased its penalties, expanded the consultative efforts of its safety agency, and required insurers and self-insurers to provide safety and loss prevention programs. In 1989, it developed a grant program, and in 1990, it required that all employers with 10 or more employees establish a safety and health committee and that employers with 10 or fewer employees establish safety committees if they had a high incidence of injuries. Gary Weeks, Oregon's director of insurance and finance, gives its safety program much credit for the dramatic reductions in workers' compensation premiums in Oregon.

Texas, in its 1990 amendments, required the workers' compensation commission to identify "extra hazardous employers." These employers were required to obtain a safety consultation, develop an accident prevention plan, and pass a six-month follow-up inspection. The commission in Texas has had some difficulty in implementing this program, because there have been various challenges to its methods for identifying extra hazardous employers. As a result, it is not yet clear how successful the Texas approach will be.

A number of other states have put an emphasis on safety as part of their workers' compensation reform. California has passed a law that increases assessments on insured and self-insured employers with bad safety records and requires insurers to take more aggressive action in helping insured employers improve their safety record. Nebraska adopted a bill that calls for mandatory safety consultations for employers with high injury rates, and Nevada passed a reform bill that requires its exclusive state fund to adopt a plan for reviewing and penalizing employers with excessive losses.

As discussed in chapter 17, safety is the approach to the workers' compensation problem that is most likely to yield significant long-lasting solutions. Legislators' increased awareness of the connection between safety and workers' compensation costs is a significant sign that we are moving in the right direction and that we may be able to really solve this problem by reducing injuries.

Programs, such as the one in Oregon, that emphasize consultation and education, are the most likely to be successful. Many of the new statutes provide for identifying the worst employers in the state. They should go a step further and identify the best employers as well, study what those employers do to prevent injuries, and use the results as an educational tool.

2.6 Managed Care

Since the late 1980s, there has been an increasing awareness that the fastest growing component of workers' compensation costs involves health care. As discussed in chapters 10 and 24, numerous approaches to controlling these costs have been attempted, including fee schedules and requirements for utilization review. Most recently, attention has focused on the use of managed care organizations.

Under these arrangements, an employer or insurer enters into a contract with a group of health care providers, including physicians, hospitals, and others. It agrees to send those providers a certain volume of business in return for a reduction in costs. The agreement may also include provisions concerning the quality and nature of care provided and reports to be sent to the employers.

In states in which employers are allowed to select the treating physician, employers are free to implement such plans. Most states, however, give the workers at least some say in the choice of physician. In those jurisdictions, the employer cannot guarantee that it will send all of its cases to the managed care organization, and accordingly, cannot bargain quite so effectively concerning cost reduction. The most recent round of statutory amendments have been designed to give employers more power to use managed care organizations in states that previously gave the employee great latitude in choosing his or her physician.

In 1991, Connecticut amended its law to allow employers and insurers to contract with managed care organizations. Employees are free to go to physicians outside the managed care organization, but the employer is only required to pay those physicians the amount it would have paid had the employee gone to a physician within the managed care organization. Recent California legislation gives employers significant increased control over the choice of physician if they offer treatment through a managed care organization. New Jersey allows premium discounts to employers who use managed care organizations; and a bill passed in Ohio allows employers to require injured workers to treat with physicians and hospitals within a managed care network.

There is more controversy over managed care than there is over safety. The legislative debate about managed care is usually focused on controlling health care costs, but control over the case may be the real issue. The treating physician has great control over how soon the individual returns to work, and in many states, his or her opinion is given special importance in determining the extent of disability. Advocates for workers point to research that questions whether controlling the choice of provider really saves money and charge that employers are really using the managed care approach to gain control over the choice of physician.[5]

As discussed in chapter 24, in the long run the success of this approach will depend on how insurers and self-insured employers implement their new rights to use managed care organizations. If they simply shop for the cheapest doctors in town, workers will not recover as quickly, they will be dissatisfied with the system, they will seek help more frequently from attorneys, and there will be more litigation and higher costs. If, on the other hand, employers consider quality as well as costs, they will choose the providers who offer the best care, who do the most to help the worker to a prompt and complete recovery, and who treat the worker with dignity and respect. This will reduce indemnity benefits, reduce the dissatisfaction and turmoil that many workers experience, reduce their need to resort to attorneys, and make the system better for everyone.

The future of managed care will also depend on developments related to 24-hour coverage and national health care reform, discussed below.

2.7 Twenty-Four Hour Coverage

Recently, legislatures and workers' compensation "experts" all across the country have been talking about "24-hour coverage" as a way to deal with problems in state workers' compensation systems. Generally, this means that to some extent, the worker will receive the same benefits, regardless of whether the injury occurred on or off the job. New Zealand has had such a system for many years. Accident victims receive compensation under this system for any accident, whether work-related or not. That, however, is not the model people have in mind for the United States.

Instead, most of the recent initiatives are much more limited. They propose only to combine the health care part of workers' compensation with other health care coverage provided by the employer. Florida law was amended to allow such arrangements in 1990. Oregon has received grants to experiment with such programs, and California has designated certain counties for pilot programs. To date, however, implementation of such programs has been very limited.

Advocates for 24-hour coverage point out that it will avoid disputes over whether an injury comes under the workers' compensation system. If, however, the 24-hour approach only covers medical costs, there will still be disputes over coverage when disability benefits are involved. "Medical-only" cases, while very numerous, usually do not involve large amounts of money. At present, there is actually very little litigation over these cases. Accordingly, it is questionable whether combining workers' compensation health care with some other system would have any significant effect on the number of disputes or the amount of litigation.

As discussed in section 10.6, there is a growing body of evidence that the cost of health care for injured workers is higher than the cost of the same treatment provided under other systems. Workers' compensation costs seem to be higher for several reasons. For one thing, injured workers may receive more aggressive treatment. Since a prompt return to work is important to the employer who is paying the bill, this may be desirable. However, costs are also higher for less desirable reasons. It appears, for example, that some health care providers simply charge more when the payer is part of the workers' compensation system. One study found that in some circumstances, providers charged twice as much when the case involved workers' compensation.[6] Also, the workers' compensation system is only now beginning to apply many cost control strategies that have been used by other payers for many years.

Some advocates of 24-hour coverage assume that if the systems are combined, the costs of workers' compensation health care will come down to the level of other systems. Can we be certain, however, that the costs of other systems will not come up to the level of workers' compensation? In fact, this seems unlikely to happen. Workers' compensation represents only about 2 or 3 percent of all health care expenditures. If a leveling process were to occur, it seems likely that other expenditures would increase by only a very small amount, and workers' compensation costs would come down substantially. It may be possible, however, to achieve the same savings by simply applying to workers' compensation the techniques that are widely used in other areas.

Most health care systems, other than workers' compensation, require the patient to pay part of the costs through co-pays and deductibles. Some experts claim that these are very important tools for controlling health care costs. They argue that bringing co-pays and deductibles to the workers' compensation system might be the principal "advantage" of 24-hour coverage. Advocates for workers oppose this approach. They question whether co-pays and deductibles really save costs, suggesting that instead they merely shift part of the cost to the worker. They also argue that this is a breach of the original compromise under which workers gave up their right to sue employers in return for certain benefits including health care coverage.

I would suggest that co-pays and deductibles are an issue that should be debated separately from 24-hour coverage. We can have them with or without 24-hour coverage, and we can have 24-hour coverage with or without co-pays and deductibles. We should not use 24-hour coverage as a way to bring co-pays and deductibles into the system.

To the extent that 24-hour coverage is a good idea, employers should simply start doing it on their own. When a worker is injured on the job, they should send the worker to the same doctor or hospital that the worker would go to under his or her group health care coverage. In fact, some employers are doing this either directly or with the help of a vendor who sets up a system for them. The ability to do this, of course, depends on the state workers' compensation law. In states where the employer has the choice of physician, this is very easy to do. In states where the worker has the choice of physician, it is somewhat more difficult. Nevertheless, even in those states, many workers will voluntarily go to the doctor or hospital suggested by the employer, even though they are not required to do so.

There are some clear advantages to this informal approach. Employers are able to negotiate reduced fees from providers in return for sending them a larger volume of patients. Workers are likely to have greater faith and trust in the "company doctor" if he or she is also the family physician. Finally, there may be some administrative savings by combining the systems in this manner.

There are, on the other hand, certain limitations to this employer-level approach. In states where workers have a choice of physician, employers will not be able to negotiate as effectively with providers since they cannot guarantee that all injured workers will go to those providers. In addition, to the extent that there are differences in the systems, such as the maximum fee schedules and the presence or absence of co-pays and/or deductibles, there will be administrative costs in sorting out the differences.

As discussed at the beginning of this section, some state workers' compensation laws have been amended to allow employers or insurers to create systems of 24-hour coverage under which workers could be required to seek care from health maintenance organizations (HMOs) or preferred provider organizations (PPOs) and under which all administrative rules would be the same, regardless of where the injury occurred.

There are a number of problems with this approach. For one thing, organized labor generally opposes these moves if they result in a restriction of the worker's choice of provider. One way to avoid this is to allow workers or workers' representatives to have some role in choosing the managed care organization. Another solution is to stipulate that the worker can be required to go to the selected provider for work-related injuries only if he or she is already seeing that provider as a family doctor, or in the alternative, if he or she does not have a family doctor.

Another problem involves the question of *occurrence* versus *claims-made* coverage. Health care insurance is generally written as a claims-made coverage. In other words, the company that is insuring the risk at the time the person needs care pays the provider. Workers' compensation, on the other hand, is generally an occurrence type of policy. The insurer on the risk at the date of injury pays for health care related to that injury indefinitely in the future. Remembering that many workers move from job to job, it is difficult to reconcile these approaches in a 24-hour system.

There is one trend in state law changes that may have an indirect effect on the possibility of 24-hour coverage. As discussed above, a number of states have recently changed their laws to allow employers to use managed care organizations similar to HMOs or PPOs in workers' compensation. These changes in the laws may make it easier to implement 24-hour coverage at the employer level.

The Employee Retirement Income Security Act (ERISA) is probably the biggest obstacle to the implementation of 24-hour coverage at the state level. This federal law governs the provision of fringe benefits by employers to their workers. It also pre-empts state action in this area. In other words, it says that only Congress, and not state legislatures, can pass laws concerning employee benefits such as group health care. ERISA contains a specific exemption for workers' compensation and unemployment compensation. In most proposals for 24-hour coverage, state legislatures desire to provide controls and limitations on the health insurance provided for both work-related and non-work-related injuries. While it has not been definitively decided by the courts, it would appear that ERISA prevents state legislatures from passing such laws.

While ERISA prevents state legislatures from enacting laws concerning employee benefits, it does not prevent Congress from doing so. In fact, it appears quite likely that the most significant move toward 24-hour coverage will come in the form of national health care reform as discussed below.

2.8 National Health Care Reform

As this is being written Congress is considering proposals for reform of the nation's health care system. This is bound to have a significant impact on workers' compensation. The proposal advanced by the Clinton administration would begin with a partial integration of workers' compensation (treatment would be provided through the national health care system but costs would be charged back through the current workers' compensation system). The proposal includes a commission to study the complete merger of workers' compensation health care into a larger system.

Integration into national health care raises questions similar to those discussed above regarding 24-hour coverage. Will the safety incentive be reduced if we combine the costs of the two systems? Will the management of medical care be coordinated with the management of return to work? Will there be co-pays and deductibles? If there are co-pays on the health side and not on the workers' compensation side, will this create an incentive for workers and providers to classify conditions as compensable? Who will control choice of provider? Will we allow or encourage more aggressive treatment of work-related injuries?

The insurance industry is especially concerned about the possibility of a complete merger of workers' compensation health care into a national plan. It makes a profit by insuring risk. Currently about 40 percent of the risk in workers' compensation is for health care. If that is merged into some other system, insurance companies will lose 40 percent of the business that they do.

The alternative may be even more frightening. If at some time in the near future everyone in this country reaches an agreement on how to reform health care, do we want workers' compensation to be left out? As discussed in section 10.6, it appears that there is already cost shifting to workers' compensation from other areas. To whatever degree national health care reform results in a leveling of payments, it will most likely reduce the costs to workers' compensation.

It is too early to tell how this will all work out. A proper partial integration into a national health care system could lower workers' compensation health care costs without disturbing other aspects of the system. If done poorly, integration has the potential to greatly disrupt the way cases are managed and increase overall costs.

Notes

1. For example, Kerr, P., "Vast Amount of Fraud Discovered in Workers' Compensation System," *The New York Times* (December 29, 1991), 1, 14.
2. Helvacian, N. Mike, "Workers' Compensation Paranoia: Mental Stress Claims" (National Council on Compensation Insurance, Inc.: 1993), 3.
3. Equal Employment Opportunity Commission, Office of Public Information, 1801 L Street, N.W., Washington, D.C. 20507.
4. Frierson, James G., *Employer's Guide to the Americans with Disabilities Act* (Washington, D.C.: BNA Books, 1992); *BNA's Americans with Disabilities Act Manual*, a two-binder monthly information service from The Bureau of National Affairs, Inc.
5. Pozzebon, Silvana, "Do Traditional Health Care Cost Containment Practices Really Work?" *John Burton's Workers' Compensation Monitor*, Vol. 6, No. 3 (May/June 1993), 17–22.
6. Baker, Lawrence C., and Krueger, Alan B. "Twenty-Four-Hour Coverage and Workers' Compensation Insurance," *Health Affairs* (1993).

Part 2

Macroworkers' Compensation

Chapter 3

The Workers' Compensation System

3.1 Introduction

Part 2 of this book is a description of the fundamentals of the workers' compensation system. Chapters 4 through 13 review the various legal issues related to the rights and responsibilities of workers and employers. Chapter 14 deals with insurance and self-insurance, which is sometimes referred to as the means by which employers provide security for workers' compensation. Finally, chapter 15 reviews a few of the methods available to make comparisons between state workers' compensation systems.

This chapter will begin with a quick overview of the workers' compensation system. This review of important issues includes references to the more detailed discussions contained in subsequent chapters. This is followed by a brief summary of the history of workers' compensation. Next we present a discussion of some of the economic issues, specifically, a discussion of who ultimately pays the cost of workers' compensation and whether the system provides the incentives that are intended. The chapter ends with a listing of some important organizations and resources.

3.2 Overview

3.2.1 The Tradeoff

Workers' compensation is the system used to provide compensation to individuals who are injured while at work. Prior to its introduction in about 1911, a person injured on the job could only be compensated if he or she could show that the employer was in some way negligent or at fault and that the worker was completely free from fault. If the worker could prove this, however, he or she could recover whatever damages a jury would grant including compensation for pain and suffering and loss of enjoyment of life.

The new system is a tradeoff. Under it, workers do not need to prove that the employer was at fault or that they were free from fault. If they are injured on the job, benefits are paid regardless of who was to blame. Today we refer to such an approach as a "no-fault" system. At the same time, workers are now limited in the damages that they can receive. They can recover a fixed amount for lost earnings, payment of their medical expenses, and usually some form of vocational rehabilitation. They receive this and nothing more. (See also section 3.3 for a further discussion of the historical tradeoff.)

3.2.2 Coverage and Insurance

With some exceptions, almost all employees in the United States are covered by workers' compensation. Most are covered under state laws but some, such as railroad workers and employees of the federal government, are covered under special federal laws. Self-employed workers are not "employees" of anyone and thus are usually not covered. Disputes often arise over whether a person is an employee covered under workers' compensation or an independent contractor who is not covered. These and similar issues are discussed in chapter 5.

If a worker is covered, then workers' compensation benefits are the only damages the worker can receive from his or her employer. With only a few exceptions, he or she cannot sue the employer in a civil action. Workers' compensation is the exclusive remedy the worker has against the employer. If, however, someone else, a third party, was responsible for the injury, that person can be sued. These issues are discussed in chapter 4.

All states require employers to provide some assurance that they can pay the benefits that they might owe to their workers. Most often this is in the form of an insurance policy. Usually the insurance can be purchased from a number of private insurance companies but a few states have an exclusive state fund that is, in effect, the only insurance company allowed to write this kind of policy. All but two states (North Dakota and Wyoming) also allow companies to be self-insured if they can convince the state that they are financially sound and large enough to undertake this risk. See chapter 14.

3.2.3 Eligibility for Benefits

For a specific injury or disease to be covered it must *arise out of* and *in the course of* the employment. *In the course of* means that the injury must have happened while the employee was at work as opposed to at home or while recreating. Generally if the worker was going to or coming from work, an injury will not be covered unless he or she was on the premises when it happened. Injuries that occur during lunch hours, when traveling, and while engaged in horseplay are troublesome and may or may not be covered. The *arise out of* requirement means that the work must have, in some sense, caused the disability. Usually the work does not have to be the sole cause of the disability. It is enough if the work contributed to the problem or aggravated a preexisting condition, but an ordinary disease of life is not compensable. The laws in many states require that to be compensable an injury must in some way have been an accident. It is usually enough that either the cause of the injury or the result of the event was unexpected. Thus, if a worker is injured as the result of an ordinary lifting incident, it might be said that although the lift was not an accident, the injury was an accidental result of the lift. These issues are covered in chapter 6.

How do you determine if, and to what degree, a person is disabled? This is one of the most troublesome questions in workers' compensation. If the disability period is short, the worker receives what are called *temporary total* benefits. If the injury is extremely severe, the worker is paid *permanent total* benefits. Temporary total are by far the most frequent type of benefit, but the cost of these cases is relatively small. The permanent total type of case is very costly but relatively rare.

In between are claims for *permanent partial* benefits. These involve people who have some long-term residual effect of their injury but who are not totally disabled. There is great diversity among the states in how they approach this problem. One alternative is to pay these benefits based entirely on the extent of the physical injury. Another is to base payment entirely on the wage loss that results from the injury. In between these extremes is an approach that estimates the loss of wage-earning capacity that results from the injury. In practice most states use some combination of these choices. Disability is the topic of chapter 8.

To encourage employers to hire workers with a missing limb or the loss of sight in an eye most states have set up a *second injury fund*. If a worker with one lost member loses a second, the worker receives the usual benefits payable to a person with two lost members, but the fund helps the employer pay the cost. Over the years the special funds have been assigned a variety of different responsibilities. These are discussed in chapter 13.

Some work-related disabilities do not in any way result from an injury or accident. They are the result of an occupational disease. These are nearly all now covered by workers' compensation, but this was not always the case, and under many circumstances they receive special treatment. See chapter 7.

3.2.4 Benefits

If a worker is found to be entitled to benefits, how much does he or she receive? The calculation of the amount of benefits starts with the worker's preinjury wages. Most often the rate is 66⅔ percent of that amount. Some states have a minimum level of benefits, and all have a maximum that is usually set as a percentage of the state's average weekly wage. The duration of benefits usually depends upon the severity of the disability. Benefits are discussed in chapter 9.

Under most circumstances an injured worker is entitled to have all of his or her medical expenses paid by the employer. Rules vary as to whether the employer or the worker can choose the doctor. In rare instances benefits can be terminated for refusal to accept reasonable medical care. Recently there has been much emphasis on efforts to control the cost of medical benefits. Chapter 10 discusses medical benefits.

Nearly everyone agrees that vocational rehabilitation is a good thing, but there is a great deal of controversy over how it should be done and when it is appropriate. In some states it is mandatory; in some it is optional. Sometimes vocational rehabilitation involves nothing more than having the worker make phone calls to prospective employers. Sometimes it can lead to a college education. These issues are covered in chapter 11.

3.2.5 Administration and Procedures

All states have a commission, bureau, or other agency that is responsible for the administration of workers' compensation. There is variation as to how active the agency is. In some cases it must approve the payments in virtually every case. In others, the agency only becomes involved if there is a dispute.

There are time limits within which a worker must report an injury (frequently 30 to 90 days) and before which he or she must file a claim (most often 2 years). These are often interpreted quite liberally.

Unfortunately, workers' compensation is an area that results in many controversies. In some states attorneys are involved in a large percentage of cases. In some cases the worker and employer must agree on the outcome of a case or it is automatically reviewed by the state agency. In others, it is up to the worker to file a dispute if he or she is not satisfied with what the employer pays. In nearly all states, workers' compensation cases are heard by special judges without a jury. There is a right to appeal to the courts, but this may be limited to legal and not factual disputes. Recently many states have begun emphasizing mediation and other forms of alternate dispute resolution. Procedures are covered in chapter 12.

3.3 A Brief History

It is customary to begin histories of the workers' compensation system by reference to certain documents that are attributable to bands of pirates, which provided that a mate should receive so many pieces of gold for a lost eye, so many for a lost leg, and claim that workers' compensation originated with pirates. It is possible,

however, to see the following quotation from Exodus as an even
earlier incarnation of a workers' compensation law.

> If men quarrel and one strikes the other a blow with stone or fist so
> that the man, though he does not die, must keep his bed, the one
> who struck the blow shall not be liable provided the other gets up
> and can go about, even with a stick. He must compensate him,
> however, for his enforced inactivity, and care for him until he is
> completely cured. Exodus 21:18-19.

I would prefer to think that workers' compensation originated
with the Bible rather than with the pirates.

More immediately, the workers' compensation laws in the
United States came from Germany via England. The first modern
workers' compensation law was enacted in Bismarck's Germany in
1884. An English version was adopted in 1897. These laws formed
the basis for the acts eventually passed in the United States.

The first workers' compensation law in this country was the
Federal Employers' Compensation Act, which was passed in 1908
and covered some employees of the federal government. New York
was the first state to adopt a workers' compensation law, in 1910.
Its law was based on a report of a commission on employers' liability,
better known as the Wainewright Commission. New York's law,
however, was held unconstitutional. The unconstitutional defect
was later remedied, but Wisconsin was able to claim its law, enacted
in 1911, as the first constitutional state workers' compensation law.

Other states followed suit almost immediately. By 1920, 42
states had adopted workers' compensation laws. It was not until
1949, however, that Mississippi, the last of the then 48 states,
joined the ranks.

It is the conventional wisdom that workers' compensation laws
were enacted to help employees.[1] Prior to their enactment, workers
could receive benefits only if they could prove that their employers'
negligence had caused the disability. In addition employers had
three defenses, each of which served as a complete bar to recovery
by the worker:

1. The worker could not recover benefits if he or she was in
   any way *contributorily negligent*. Even if the employer was
   negligent, if the worker was also negligent, this contributory
   negligence was a bar to recovery.

2. The *fellow employee rule* prevented recovery by the worker if the negligence of a fellow employee contributed in any way to the injury.
3. Recovery was also barred if the employee in some way knew of and *assumed the risk*.

As a result of these factors, it was, prior to 1911, very difficult for workers to win lawsuits against their employers. It is generally suggested that society determined in the first part of this century that it should be easier for workers to obtain some recovery and thus workers' compensation laws were adopted. Some authors, however, question this and suggest instead that workers were beginning to win cases occasionally and that employers were concerned that if the trend continued, they might be subject to a growing number of very costly lawsuits.[2] Accordingly, a system was adopted that limited the recovery workers could receive.

The workers' compensation laws then adopted were "no-fault" systems in the sense that the worker no longer needed to prove negligence on the part of the employer. In addition, the three defenses discussed above were eliminated. In return for these concessions to workers, however, the amount of recovery was strictly limited. Workers were allowed to recover certain specified wage-loss benefits and payment for their medical expenses, but nothing more. Their right to recovery for pain and suffering, loss of enjoyment of life, and other damages that a jury might award, which were available under the earlier system, were eliminated by the workers' compensation system.

The law evolved rather gradually from 1911 until the early 1970s. In the late 1960s, organized labor and others sought the establishment of a national workers' compensation law or at least national standards for state laws. They were unable, however, to pass such provisions through Congress. The Occupational Safety and Health Act (OSHA) was enacted in 1970 and it contained provisions for the creation of a National Commission on State Workmen's Compensation Laws (National Commission). The report of the National Commission, issued in 1972, was a watershed in the history of workers' compensation. Its most significant finding was that in many respects the benefit levels paid to injured workers were too low. It pointed out that in many cases the benefits then paid resulted in an income significantly below what was considered the poverty level. In response to this report, many states amended their laws during the 1970s to substantially increase the level of benefits paid.

From 1972 until at least 1980, there was a clear trend across the country to raise the level of benefits and to expand the availability of benefits to injured workers. During the 1980s however, employers became increasingly outraged over the cost of workers' compensation. In response to this, a countertrend developed in the 1980s and early 1990s. As a result of this trend, legislatures have acted to restrict the availability of benefits and in some cases to reduce the level of benefits paid.[3]

The two trends just discussed are most apparent in legislative enactments. While it is much more difficult to document, I would suggest that there has been a similar trend in the ways in which courts interpret workers' compensation statutes. Through the 1970s and into the early 1980s, courts were inclined to apply a very liberal interpretation to workers' compensation laws and to expand the eligibility requirements of those statutes. During the late 1980s and into the 1990s, I believe the courts have responded to societal attitudes and now are tending to give a much more restricted interpretation to the workers' compensation laws.[4]

As discussed in chapter 16, the early 1990s have seen another trend that bodes well for the future. It is a trend to emphasize strategies that help both workers and employers at the same time. Employers are now becoming more aware that they can control their own workers' compensation experience, reduce the frequency of injuries, and decrease the severity of injuries that do occur through safety and prevention programs, through disability management, and through good human relations procedures. This is especially significant since these strategies not only reduce employers' cost, but help workers at the same time.

3.4 Economic Issues

3.4.1 Who Bears the Loss?

It is often said that workers' compensation is a system for shifting or spreading the cost of on the job injuries. It is the conventional wisdom that the loss is shifted to consumers.[5] A few people complain about this, but most consider it appropriate. It is said that if a certain number of people are hurt for every car that is manufactured, then the cost of those injuries should be passed on to the people who buy the cars. This assumption is widely held by lawyers, administrators, and politicians. There are, however, both practical and theoretical reasons to doubt the validity of this assumption.

A great deal of the cost is borne by the worker. There is a part of the cost that can never be passed on whatever the system. If a man or woman loses a hand or loses the productive value of a year of his or her life, there is no monetary award that really makes up for it. Few people would trade their arm for a million dollars, much less the few thousand that most compensation laws pay. Some would suggest that there is no way for an economist to put a value on the loss of self-esteem that is experienced when a child asks a parent why he or she now stays home instead of going to work every day like other people. As a matter of fact, however, economists do attempt to put a value on these items. Moore and Viscusi estimate that the total value to workers of a lost work day accident is between $39,000 and $47,000 and that of this amount, between $18,500 and $28,500 is attributable to the "non-monetary health losses associated with accidents."[6]

In addition, we do not attempt to fully compensate workers for their monetary losses. As discussed in subsection 3.2.1, in return for a right to certain benefits without regard to who was at fault, workers gave up their right to damages for pain and suffering, loss of enjoyment of life, and other damages that are ordinarily awarded in civil trials. In addition, even the wage loss benefits we do provide are deliberately set at less than the full amount of the loss, usually two-thirds of gross wages. This is done to create an incentive for the individual to return to work. Karen DeVol Roberts, now of Michigan State University, reported in a study for the Workers' Compensation Research Institute (WCRI) that over the long-run our systems usually provide the worker with much less than the nominal amount of wage replacement.[7]

Economists also question whether employers are able to pass on to their customers the costs levied on them by the system. A business cannot necessarily raise its prices every time its workers' compensation costs go up. Much will depend on the marketplace and the prices charged by competitors.

Economists insist that to understand fully the costs related to injuries, we must take into consideration the *compensating wage differential*.[8] According to economic theory, workers must be paid more to perform more dangerous jobs. Thus iron workers who work at a great height are paid more than laborers who work on the ground. If, however, a worker receives higher benefits in the form of workers' compensation when he or she is injured, the financial consequences of the injury are less severe and the compensating wage differential does not need to be as great. Thus as workers' compensation benefits go up, the risk of financial loss associated with the dangers of doing a job go down, the necessity of a compensating wage differential also goes down, and therefore, the wages for the job go down.

This has some very interesting implications. It means, for one thing, that if labor unions go to a state legislature and lobby successfully for increased benefits, they will in the long run pay for the benefits at least partially by receiving reduced wages in the future. In other words, to the extent this principle operates, the cost of workers' compensation benefits are not paid by employers or consumers, but by fellow workers.

How big is the offset? Moore and Viscusi suggest that it is complete. "In terms of the level of net costs (that is, premiums less wage reductions), workers' compensation more than pays for itself."[9] They suggest that the cost of workers' compensation is more than offset by reductions in wages. This would mean that employers really do not pay anything for workers' compensation, that the cost is more than made up in reduced pay. Does this mean that employers should lobby for increased benefits so they can have even lower wages? Even Moore and Viscusi would not go this far. They point out that as benefits go up, the tradeoff in wages diminishes. Accordingly, while the system more than pays for itself at the present level, increases in benefits would not necessarily pay for themselves.

Is this theory plausible? Certainly it is true at least to some extent. I have met many employers who told me, "I sat down at the bargaining table and told the union 'I can't give you any raises this year because workers' compensation costs are too high,'" or "'you can't have a raise unless you help me reduce workers' compensation costs.'"

Does it happen to the extent that Moore and Viscusi suggest? Although I am not an economist and cannot question their results from that perspective, I suspect that a large part of the burden, as discussed above, is borne by the injured worker. Another significant portion is borne by fellow employees in the form of lower wages. I believe, however, that some of it is also borne by employers through reduced profits and by consumers through increased prices.

3.4.2 Incentives

Incentives are another issue raised by economists. What incentives are built into the system and do they work? We pay workers less than their actual wage loss so that there will be an inducement to return to work. We charge employers with their workers' compensation losses so that they will be encouraged to adopt safety practices. What happens in practice? There have been a number of studies that touch on these questions.[10]

A number of these studies have focused on the effect of increased benefits. The National Council on Compensation Insurance (NCCI) assists insurance companies in setting rates. Naturally, it needs to predict how much a given increase in benefits will affect losses. Its economists and others have conducted a number of studies on this topic. Most, though not all, of the researchers conclude that as benefits go up there is a disproportionate increase in costs.[11] There are three possible components to the increase in costs: an increase in the number of claims, an increase in the length or seriousness of claims, and an increase in the number of actual injuries.

Economists refer to the increase in the number of actual accidents as the *moral hazard*. This concept is the hardest to accept. Perhaps more people file claims when benefits are higher or choose to stay away from work longer when the loss is smaller. People do not intentionally injure themselves, however, and workers do not make a conscious, rational, economic decision about whether they will get hurt.

Economists do not claim that workers intentionally injure themselves. They claim, rather, that under certain circumstances workers take more risks. As discussed above, there is, they claim, a "wage differential" for certain jobs. Workers will ordinarily only do more dangerous work if they are paid a higher wage. If, however, the disability benefits paid to an injured worker increase, then the loss that results from an injury is less severe and workers are willing to take more risks for a given wage.

Edward Yelin of the University of California, San Francisco, has suggested that much of this research is flawed because it fails to account for the nature of the work that is being performed. His data suggest that factors such as whether the worker has discretion in the way the job is performed and the psychological demands of the job are much more important than benefit levels in determining whether a given injury will result in permanent disability.[12]

What about the safety incentives? Do higher benefit costs induce employers to improve safety practices? There is no question that there is a safety incentive. Increased workers' compensation costs encourage employers to make efforts to reduce the frequency of injuries. The questions concern how strong this incentive is. Richard B. Victor of the WCRI points out that success of safety incentives depends on the degree to which employers, as opposed to insurers, bear the costs of an increased number of injuries. He points out the relationshiop between cost and the insurance arrangement. His analysis suggests that experience-rated insured employers may bear an exaggerated share of the increased costs. Non-experience-rated insured employers may bear none of the increased costs and self-insured employers appear to bear the actual cost.[13]

In addition to the cost of workers' compensation, the compensating wage differential discussed above also provides a safety incentive. To whatever extent an employer must pay higher wages because a job is dangerous, there is an incentive to remove the dangers.

The problem that economists see is that there are countervailing incentives. As benefits rise, the cost to a worker of an injury decreases; accordingly, workers have less incentive to be careful. On the other hand, as the cost of workers' compensation goes up, employers have a greater safety incentive. Which effect predominates?

Most of the studies cited above by economists reach the conclusion that the incentive on workers is greater than the incentive on employers, and that if benefits are increased, there will be a disproportionate increase in costs. In fact, WCRI routinely takes the position that on average, a 20 percent increase in benefits yields at least an additional 10 percent increase in costs due to increased utilization.[14] Not all of the studies, however, have reached this conclusion.[15] In addition, while this position is generally accepted by economists, it is generally not accepted by actuaries. When they calculate rates necessary to cover benefit changes, they often do not include this factor.

Moore and Viscusi provide a comprehensive analysis of this issue from an economic point of view. They conclude that "[w]orkers' compensation is more successful in promoting its intended objectives than previously believed."[16]

They break down their analysis between fatalities and injuries. They reach the conclusion that, with respect to fatalities, the safety incentive predominates and that without the workers' compensation program, the rate of fatalities in this country could double. They also conclude that workers' compensation benefits exert a downward pressure on injury rates. This effect, however, diminishes as benefits rise. They conclude that the incentive for employers to reduce injuries continues to dominate up to a weekly benefit maximum of $450 in 1988 prices. Above that rate the incentive for workers to take risks becomes dominant.

This brief summary does not do justice to a very complicated topic. More, however, would be beyond the scope of this book. It should suffice to say that practitioners and policy makers do not and probably should not take the statements of economists at face value without further questioning. At the same time, we would be foolish to ignore what they are saying. Additional research may give us more answers.

3.5 Some Important Organizations and Resources

When OSHA was being considered by Congress in 1970, thought was given to adopting national standards for state workers' compensation laws. There was, however, insufficient support for this, and as a compromise the law created a National Commission on State Workmen's Compensation Laws. Its report, issued in 1972, became a watershed in workers' compensation. It is the most widely recognized standard against which most parts of a state workers' compensation law can be evaluated.

The report includes a series of recommendations for state workers' compensation laws, 19 of which were denominated as essential recommendations. These had a profound effect on legislative enactments over the next decade. The recommendations are discussed in more detail in section 15.3.

Several members of the staff of the National Commission continue to be prominent today as scholars and advisors concerning workers' compensation. John Burton was the chair of the commission. He is now at Rutgers and continues to teach, write, and consult concerning workers' compensation. The general counsel for the commission was John Lewis. He is now a consultant working in Florida. Peter Barth was the executive director. He now teaches, writes, and consults at the University of Connecticut. Monroe Berkowitz was a consultant. He is now professor emeritus at Rutgers and continues to be recognized as an outstanding scholar in the area of workers' compensation.

Arthur Larson was considered by all to be the leading legal authority on workers' compensation. He passed away in the spring of 1993, but his 11-volume treatise, *Larson's Workmen's Compensation Law*, is frequently relied on by the courts. It is published by Matthew Bender and as noted above is cited frequently here as Larson §____.

The International Association of Industrial Accident Boards and Commissions (IAIABC) is an association of workers' compensation agencies in the United States, Canada, and other countries. It holds a meeting in the fall of each year at which administrators, judges, and commission members from all around the word share ideas about workers' compensation. The association includes about 600 associate members, including employers, insurance companies, attorneys, union representatives, and others who also participate in its activities. There are committees covering adjudication, administration, legislation, medical issues, rehabilitation, safety, self-insurance, and statistics that carry on much of the work of the association and often publish reports that either summarize the current situation or contain recommendations for the future.

Each spring the association sponsors a workers' compensation college. The course is a comprehensive review of workers' compensation taught by the leading experts in the field and is open to any interested party.

The association publishes the *IAIABC Journal*. The address of the IAIABC is 1575 Aviation Parkway, Suite 519, Daytona Beach, FL 32114, (904) 252-2915.

In addition to the international association, there are several regional associations.

The National Council on Compensation Insurance (NCCI) is an organization funded primarily by the insurance industry and gathers data about workers' compensation losses in order to assist carriers and state insurance commissioners in setting workers' compensation rates. It issues numerous publications including, among others, the *NCCI Digest* and *Annual Statistical Report*. NCCI's address is 750 Park of Commerce Drive, Boca Raton, FL 33487, (407) 997-1000.

The Workers' Compensation Research Institute (WCRI) was founded in 1983 for the purpose of conducting research concerning workers' compensation. Since that time, it has probably conducted more research concerning workers' compensation than all other sources combined. The Institute has published many books on topics such as medical costs, the causes of litigation in a state system, the adequacy and equity of benefits, mental stress claims, and rehabilitation. It also publishes a monthly newsletter *Research Briefs*. The Institute is funded primarily by insurance companies and employers but it seeks to ensure objectivity by applying the academic review process to its research and publications. Information is available from the Workers' Compensation Research Institute, 245 First Street, Suite 1402, Cambridge, MA 02141, (617) 494-1240.

California has its own research organization. The California Workers' Compensation Institute is sponsored by the insurance industry in California and conducts valuable research concerning workers' compensation in that state. It is located at 120 Montgomery Street, San Francisco, CA 94104, (415) 981-2107.

The Office of Workers' Compensation Programs of the U.S. Department of Labor is an important source of information about workers' compensation in the United States. Among other things, it publishes two important surveys of state workers' compensation programs: *State Workers' Compensation: Administrative Profiles* and *State Workers' Compensation Laws*. The former is a detailed profile of the program in each state. The latter is a compilation of information such as the maximum rate for all the U.S. jurisdictions.

Organized labor is often a key player when changes to workers' compensation laws are made in state legislatures. Very often, however, the union representatives do not have expertise in workers' compensation and must rely on the trial bar for advice. In recent years James Ellenberger, assistant director of the AFL-CIO's Department of Occupational Safety and Health in Washington, D.C., has been active in this area, acting as national coordinator for organized labor concerning workers' compensation.

There are three organizations that represent the insurance industry. They are the Alliance of American Insurers, the American Insurance Association, and the National Association of Independent Insurers.

The National Council of Self-Insurers (NCSI) is an organization of self-insured employers. It publishes a newsletter and other documents relative to self-insurance. It holds an annual meeting in the spring and also sponsors a program in conjunction with the IAIABC fall meeting. The executive director is Douglas F. Stevenson, 10 South Riverside Plaza, Suite 1530, Chicago, IL 60606, (312) 454-5110.

The National Foundation for Unemployment Compensation and Workers' Compensation publishes a newsletter that includes information about workers' compensation. The foundation was established by UBA, Inc., an organization that is seen as having a very conservative point of view. The research conducted by the Foundation appears, however, to be quite objective. Each year the Foundation publishes a study of benefit costs by states. Information is gathered by the Social Security Administration concerning the amount of benefits paid in each state each year. The Foundation then analyzes this information and compares it to information concerning the number of workers and wage rates in each state.

In recent years, a number of publishers have started periodicals related to workers' compensation. Admitting that we are not without bias in this area, we would highlight three here.

The Bureau of National Affairs, Inc. (BNA), publisher of this book, publishes *BNA's Workers' Compensation Report*. It is published biweekly and is the most up-to-date and exhaustive source of current information about workers' compensation. Information is available from BNA Customer Relations at (800) 372-1033.

John Burton's Workers' Compensation Monitor is published by LRP Publications six times a year. It features longer articles and a deeper analysis of issues related to the workers' compensation systems. It is one of the best sources of data about workers' compensation. LRP can be reached at (800) 341-7874.

On Workers' Compensation is published by Ed Welch, the author of this book. This is more in the nature of a magazine and is published 10 times a year. It includes articles covering both the overall system and employer-level approaches to workers' compensation. More information is available from *On Workers' Compensation*, 2875 Northwind Drive, Suite 210-A, East Lansing, MI 48823, (517) 332-5266, fax (517) 332-5273.

Notes

1. See, for example, Journal of American Insurance, "Workers' Compensation: 75 Years of Helping the Injured Worker," *J. of American Ins.* (Second Quarter, 1986), and Chelius, James R., "Workers' Compensation and Injury Prevention," *Worklife* (Spring 1989), 33–36.
2. White, L., *Human Debris* (New York: Seaview/Putnam, 1983), 59–73; Bureau of Statistics, Wage and Labor Standards Admin., U.S. Dep't of Labor, "Insurance Arrangements Under Workmen's Compensation," Bulletin No. 317 (1969), 7; Friedman, Lawrence M., and Ledinsky, Jack, "Social Change and the Law of Industrial Accidents," *Colum. L. Rev.* Vol. 67 (1967), 50, 67–69.
3. This has been the case, for example, in Connecticut, Florida, Massachusetts, and Michigan.
4. See, for example, *Thomas v. Certified Refrigeration, Inc.,* 392 Mich. 623, 221 N.W.2d 378 (1974), and *Petrie v. General Motors Corp.,* 187 Mich. App. 198, 466 N.W.2d 714 (1991).
5. See, for example, Larson §3.20.
6. Moore, Michael J., and Viscusi, W. Kipp, *Compensation Mechanisms for Job Risks* (Princeton: Princeton University Press, 1990), 49.
7. DeVol Roberts, Karen, *Income Replacement for Long-Term Disability* (Cambridge: Workers' Compensation Research Institute, 1986).
8. Worrall, John D., ed., *Safety and the Work Force: Incentives and Disincentives in Workers' Compensation* (Ithaca, N.Y.: ILR Press, 1983), 61–86; Worrall, John D., and Appel, David, eds., *Workers' Compensation Benefits: Adequacy, Equity, and Efficiency* (Ithaca, N.Y.: ILR Press, 1985); Berkowitz, Monroe, and Hill, M. Anne, eds.,

Disability and the Labor Market: Economic Problems, Policies, and Programs (Ithaca, N.Y.: ILR Press, 1986).

9. Moore and Viscusi, *supra* note 6, at 68.
10. Gardner, John A., *Return to Work Incentives: Lessons for Policy Makers from Economic Studies* (Cambridge: Workers' Compensation Research Institute, 1989); Worrall, John D., ed., *Safety and the Work Force: Incentives and Disincentives in Workers' Compensation* (Ithaca, N.Y.: ILR Press, 1983), 61–86; Worrall, John D., and Appel, David, eds., *Workers' Compensation Benefits: Adequacy, Equity, and Efficiency* (Ithaca, N.Y.: ILR Press, 1985), Berkowitz and Hill, *supra* note 8.
11. Krueger, Alan B., and Burton, John F., Jr., "The Employer's Costs of Workers' Compensation Insurance: Magnitudes, Determinants, and Public Policy," *Rev. of Economics and Statistics*, Vol. 62 (May 1990), 228–40 (finding no disproportionate increase in costs).
12. Yelin, Edward, "The Myth of Malingering: Why Individuals Withdraw from Work in the Presence of Illness," *The Milbank Q.*, Vol. 64, No. 4 (1986), 622–49.
13. Victor, Richard B., "Experience Rating and Workplace Safety," *Workers' Compensation Benefits: Adequacy, Equity, and Efficiency*, in Worrall, John D., and Appel, David, eds. (Ithaca, N.Y.: ILR Press, 1985), 71–88.
14. Gardner, John A., *Benefit Increases and System Utilization: The Connecticut Experience* (Cambridge: Workers' Compensation Research Institute, 1991) and *Return to Work Incentives: Lessons for Policy Makers from Economic Studies* (Cambridge: Workers' Compensation Research Institute, 1989).
15. Krueger and Burton, *supra* note 11, at 228–40.
16. Moore and Viscusi, *supra* note 6, at 135.

Chapter 4

The Exclusive Remedy (Civil Lawsuits)

4.1 In General

As mentioned in subsection 3.2.1, it is the basic principle of workers' compensation that workers trade the possibility of a civil lawsuit for an assurance of certain benefits. Thus, workers are guaranteed certain wage loss and medical benefits if they are injured on the job, regardless of who was at fault. In return, they are ordinarily not allowed to sue their employers in a civil action even if the employer was clearly at fault and the worker was completely free from blame. Thus we say that workers' compensation is the *exclusive remedy* for injuries that occur at work.

The exclusive remedy provision is the protection that employers receive in the workers' compensation tradeoff. This is illustrated by a recent Michigan case.[1] Patrick Burns was an employee of the Waterfront Inn, a resort in Northern Michigan. After finishing his shift, Mr. Burns took a sailboat owned by his employer and sailed on the bay for about an hour. While returning to his employer's dock, he fell into the water, hit his head on a rock, and was seriously injured. Mr. Burns did not file a claim for workers' compensation benefits. Instead, he filed a civil action against his employer alleging negligence in allowing a dangerous condition at the dock.

It might have been possible for Mr. Burns to argue that he was still in the course of his employment when he was injured. He might have claimed that he never left the employer's "premises," or that he was using the employer's "tools." He chose not to do that, however, because the potential civil damages from his severe injury were much greater than he could have hoped to receive under workers' compensation.

The employer, however, filed a petition with the Michigan Bureau of Workers' Disability Compensation in which the employer sought a ruling that Mr. Burns was in the course of his employment when he was injured. The employer actually sought a determination that it was required to pay workers' compensation benefits to Mr. Burns. Had the employer received such a determination, it would have been required to pay workers' compensation benefits, but Mr. Burns would have been prevented from pursuing his civil lawsuit.

The Bureau eventually ruled that Mr. Burns was not in the course of his employment when he was injured. This case illustrates the value of the exclusive remedy portion of the workers' compensation system to employers. It is their protection from civil lawsuits.

Generally, workers' compensation is the employee's exclusive remedy if the injury is covered by workers' compensation regardless of whether the worker actually files a claim. A worker is not given the option of refusing workers' compensation benefits and filing a civil lawsuit.

Some states (see section 9.10) do not provide compensation for disfigurement under their workers' compensation acts, and no state provides compensation for pain and suffering. Nevertheless, if an injury is covered by the act, the worker cannot sue the employer to recover damages for either pain and suffering or disfigurement. Extreme cases have occurred where a worker suffers severe damage to his or her sexual organs but suffers little or no wage loss. Most states would grant these individuals relatively little in terms of workers' compensation. See Larson §65.21. Generally, however, the courts have held that it is all the workers can receive. If the injury is covered by the workers' compensation act, a worker may not sue the employer in a civil action.

In most U.S. jurisdictions, the exclusive remedy provision also means that the worker cannot sue his or her co-workers. Some U.S. jurisdictions (such as Alabama, Arkansas, Maryland, Minnesota,

Missouri, New Hampshire, Rhode Island, South Dakota, and Vermont) allow suits against co-workers, and such suits are permitted under the Federal Employees Compensation Act. See Larson §72.11. As will be discussed later, lawsuits are permitted against parties who were not the worker's employer or co-workers. These are generally referred to as "third-party cases." (See section 4.3.)

Assume that Mr. A is an employee of the XYZ Manufacturing Company and that he is injured while operating a machine purchased by his employer from ABC Company. He is entitled to workers' compensation benefits from the XYZ Manufacturing Company regardless of who was at fault for the injury. He is prohibited, however, from suing XYZ Manufacturing Company for negligence, even if he can prove that the company was at fault. In addition, if he could show that he was injured because of the negligent behavior of a co-worker, most states would not allow him to sue that worker. As discussed later, if he can show that the reason for his injury was the fact that the ABC Company negligently manufactured a dangerous machine, he can file a lawsuit against ABC Company.

In most states, the exclusive remedy provision applies not only to the worker, but to the spouse and children of an injured worker as well. A few states such as Massachusetts, however, apply the exclusive remedy provision only to the worker.

4.2 Exceptions (Suing Your Own Employer)

There are certain exceptions to the exclusive remedy provision. Under some conditions, workers are allowed to sue their employers. These exceptions are discussed below.

4.2.1 Injuries Outside the Coverage of the Act

If the injury cannot be covered by the workers' compensation act, the employee can sue his employer. In the example in section 4.1, Patrick Burns was found not to be in the course of his employment when he was injured. He was thus permitted to proceed with his civil lawsuit.

Workers' compensation acts do not prevent suits based on contracts. If Mr. B entered into a contract with his employer, which provided that he was employed for a specific period of time, and the employer attempted to fire him without good reason before the expiration of that time period, the workers' compensation act would not prevent a civil lawsuit to enforce the contract.

Federal and many state civil rights laws give workers a right to sue their employer on the basis of illegal discrimination. In general, the exclusive remedy provision of the workers' compensation statute does not prevent such a claim. In some instances, however, this right to sue may depend upon the type of damage suffered. Some courts have held that if the discrimination resulted in a personal injury, workers' compensation may be the exclusive remedy. For example, if Ms. C claimed that her employer treated her differently because she was a woman and as a result she suffered a nervous breakdown, some courts might hold that this was a personal injury and her only claim was for workers' compensation. On the other hand, if she claimed that she was denied a promotion because she was a woman, the workers' compensation act would provide no remedy and thus would not be a bar to recovery in her civil rights action. Thus, if a worker has a right to sue his or her employer based upon some other specific law, the exclusive remedy provision ordinarily does not prevent such a lawsuit.

4.2.2 Misconduct by the Employer

There are several situations under which a worker is allowed to sue his or her employer if the injury resulted from conduct by the employer that is considered seriously wrong. A common and recently troublesome category of this type is *intentional torts*. It is the general rule that if the employer intentionally injures the worker, it should not have the protection of the exclusive remedy provision. This applies only to situations in which there was a conscious and determined intent by the employer to injure the worker.

In addition, the person having this intent must be what the law refers to as "the alter ego" of the employer. For example, if Mr. D is the sole owner of a small business and he deliberately hits Mr. E over the head, Mr. E can file a civil action against him.

On the other hand, if Mr. D is a foreman in a huge multinational enterprise and he hits Mr. E over the head, Mr. E is probably precluded from suing the corporation on the basis of an intentional injury. If, however, the board of directors of the corporation sat at a meeting and decided to continue with a dangerous process even though it clearly knew that a substantial number of its workers would be injured as a result of that process, then those injured workers could file a civil action against the corporation.

In recent years the courts in a few states, such as West Virginia, Ohio, and Michigan, have handed down what some thought to be a rather liberal interpretation of what constituted an intentional tort. In most states where this has occurred, the legislature has attempted to respond by changing the statute to incorporate a more restrictive definition of an intentional tort.[2]

Another example of misconduct that causes an employer to lose the protection of the exclusive remedy provision is the failure of an employer to purchase workers' compensation insurance. If an employer is covered by a state's workers' compensation act and fails to provide insurance according to that law, then the worker is entitled to file a civil damage action against the employer.

4.2.3 Retaliation

In some states if a worker is fired or in other ways discriminated against in retaliation for having filed a workers' compensation claim, the worker is allowed to file a civil action against the employer.

4.2.4 Bad Faith Claims Handling

Courts in some states, as in Arizona and Michigan, have allowed workers to sue a workers' compensation insurance company for bad faith claims handling. In Arizona, this was followed by an amendment to the Workers' Compensation Act that forbids such suits, but provides an administrative remedy in their place.

4.3 Third-Party Cases

Although workers' compensation is the exclusive remedy against the injured worker's employer, the worker is permitted to file an action against third parties if he or she can show that the third party was responsible for the injury.

The typical example would be a situation in which an employee of XYZ Company was injured while operating a machine manufactured by the ABC Company. If the injury occurred because the ABC Company negligently designed or manufactured the machine, then a civil action may be brought against the ABC Company. As another example, if a worker is injured on the job and the injury is aggravated by the malpractice of a treating physician, an action may be brought against the physician. (This assumes that the physician is not a plant doctor working for the same employer. If the physician is on the payroll of the employer, he or she is thus a co-employee of the worker and most states would prevent such an action.)

Third parties usually include everyone except the employer and co-employees. As mentioned above, a few states do not include co-employees in the exclusive remedy provision.[3] In those states co-employees may be subject to a third-party action.

Nearly all jurisdictions provide for subrogation. Exceptions that do not are Georgia, Ohio, and West Virginia. Larson §74.11. This means that if a worker receives both workers' compensation benefits and a recovery from the third party, the employer is entitled to be reimbursed out of the third-party recovery for the workers' compensation benefits that have been paid. In other words, if Ms. F receives $30,000 in workers' compensation benefits and $100,000 in a civil lawsuit against a third party, Ms. F would actually receive only $70,000 from the third-party suit and $30,000 would go to repay the employer or workers' compensation insurance carrier.

Actually, neither Ms. F nor the insurance carrier would receive quite that much. In order to recover the $100,000 against the third party, there would have been substantial legal fees and costs. In most jurisdictions the worker and employer share the costs in proportion to the amount of recovery they receive. See Larson §74.40.

There is considerable variation among the states concerning the specifics of the subrogation rights. In some states, for example, the worker must file the third-party case and reimburse the employer out of the proceeds, while in other states it is the employer that has the right to bring the third-party case and it pays the excess recovery to the worker. See Larson §74.10.

Notes

1. *Netherlands Ins. Co. v. Bringman*, 153 Mich. App. 234, 395 N.W.2d 49 (1986).
2. For example, Michigan and Ohio.
3. They are Alabama, Arkansas, Maryland, Minnesota, Missouri, New Hampshire, Rhode Island, South Dakota, and Vermont.

Chapter 5

Coverage of Employers and Workers

5.1 Introduction

Workers' compensation coverage is now nearly universal, covering the vast majority of workers and employers. Coverage is so widespread, in fact, that it is appropriate to describe it by listing the exceptions. These are discussed below.

5.2 Federal Coverage

Certain workers are covered by federal and not state laws. Employees of the federal government are covered by the Federal Employees' Compensation Act (FECA). This applies, for example, to postal workers and employees of the Veterans Administration, among others. Seamen injured on navigable waters are covered by the Merchant Marine Act (sometimes called the Jones Act). Persons loading and unloading vessels and some construction workers working above or near navigable waters are covered under the Longshore and Harbor Workers' Compensation Act (LHWCA), and workers on interstate railroads are covered by the Federal Employees Liability Act (FELA).

FECA and LHWCA are federal forms of a workers' compensation program. The FELA and the Merchant Marine Act are more like tort systems in that, at least theoretically, a worker must show negligence on the part of the employer and a court may grant a damage award not limited by statutory provisions such as those found in workers' compensation laws.

5.3 Exceptions for Workers

For some of the exceptions discussed below, clear policy reasons are obvious. For others, the reasons are less clear. In some cases there is a historical reason; in others the only explanation is political compromise.

When workers' compensation laws were first passed, there was some question as to their constitutionality. To avoid this problem some acts were voluntary or elective. Their voluntary nature was, however, somewhat elusive. The employer was usually assumed to be subject to the act unless it took some action to exempt itself, and if it was exempted, it could not take advantage of the exclusive remedy provision or the traditional defenses on which employers had previously relied. Accordingly, there was a very strong incentive to accept workers' compensation even in systems that were nominally voluntary. As of 1993, only two states, South Carolina and Texas, have *elective* or *voluntary* workers' compensation laws. The National Commission recommended that coverage be mandatory and universal.

Under a few clearly delimited circumstances, states allow workers to waive their rights on an individual basis. There is a serious danger in allowing such waivers. Workers' compensation was designed to relieve injured workers of the need to resort to civil litigation. Given the opportunity, some unscrupulous employers might take advantage of any means to avoid the costs of workers' compensation. (This is probably unwise for the employer since it may then be exposed to civil liability. See section 5.7.) If the law allowed workers and employers to opt out of the system on an individual basis, marginal workers would be in a position where they had to bargain for the right to be covered by workers' compensation. This is contrary to the basic intent of the program. Accordingly, most allowed exceptions are limited to closely defined circumstances. Nevertheless, 24 states allow some sort of waiver. (See Table 5.1.)

Table 5.1. Insurance Requirements for Private Employment

Jurisdiction	Waivers Permitted	Numerical Exemptions	Notes
Alabama	No	5	
Alaska	Yes	None	
Arizona	Yes	None	
Arkansas	Yes	3	1
California	No	None	
Colorado	Yes	None	
Connecticut	Yes	None	
Delaware	No	None	
District of Columbia	No	None	
Florida	Yes	4	2
Georgia	Yes	3	
Hawaii	No	None	
Idaho	No	None	
Illinois	No	None	3
Indiana	No	None	
Iowa	Yes	None	
Kansas	Yes	None	4
Kentucky	Yes	None	
Louisiana	Yes	None	
Maine	Yes	None	
Maryland	Yes	None	
Massachusetts	No	None	
Michigan	Yes	3	5
Minnesota	No	None	
Mississippi	No	5	
Missouri	No	5	
Montana	Yes	None	
Nebraska	Yes	None	
Nevada	No	None	
New Hampshire	No	None	
New Jersey	No	None	
New Mexico	Yes	3	
New York	No	None	
North Carolina	Yes	3	6
North Dakota	No	None	
Ohio	Yes	None	
Oklahoma	No	None	
Oregon	No	None	
Pennsylvania	No	None	
Rhode Island	No	4	
South Carolina	Yes	4	7
South Dakota	Yes	None	
Tennessee	Yes	5	
Texas	No	None	
Utah	No	None	
Vermont	Yes	None	

continued

Table 5.1—*continued*

Jurisdiction	Waivers Permitted	Numerical Exemptions	Notes
Virginia	Yes	3	
Washington	No	None	
West Virginia	No	None	
Wisconsin	No	3	8
Wyoming	No	None	
FECA	No	None	
LHWCA	No	None	

FECA=Federal Employees' Compensation Act
LHWCA=Longshore and Harbor Workers' Compensation Act

[1] *Arkansas*: A contractor engaged in building or building repair work is covered if he or she employs two or more employees at one time. If a contractor subcontracts any portion of the work, the numerical exemption requirement applies. Any corporate officer or self-employed employer who elects to be exempt from coverage is required to cover his/her employees, regardless of whether the number of employees in the business is reduced to less than three.

[2] *Florida*: Employers in the construction industry are excluded from the numerical exemption applicable to other private employment, since coverage is required even if one or more employees are employed by the same employer in the construction industry.

[3] *Illinois*: A numerical exemption of two or less employees is applicable to "carriage by land, water, or aerial service and loading or unloading in connection therewith. . . ."

[4] *Kansas*: Employers are exempt if they have a total gross annual payroll in the preceding year of less than $10,000, and anticipate the same or lower payroll expenses for the current year.

[5] *Michigan*: A numerical exception of two or less employees applies, unless at least one employee is employed by the same employer for 35 hours per week for 13 weeks or longer during the preceding 52 weeks.

[6] *North Carolina*: The Act exempts individual sawmill and logging operators with less than 10 employees, operating less than 60 days in six consecutive months, and whose principal business is unrelated to sawmills.

[7] *South Carolina*: Numerical exemption does not apply if employer has a total annual payroll during the previous calendar year of less than $3,000.

[8] *Wisconsin*: Employers, other than farmers, who usually have less than three employees but who have paid wages of $500 or more in any calendar quarter for work performed within the State are covered the first day of the next calendar year.

Source: State Workers' Compensation Laws, U.S. Department of Labor, Office of Workers' Compensation Programs, January 1994, Tables 1 and 2.

A number of states also exempt small employers from workers' compensation by way of numerical exemptions that provide if a business has less than a certain number of workers, it is exempt. (See Table 5.1.)

The majority of jurisdictions have some limitation on the coverage of agricultural workers. The nature of the exemptions depends on such factors as the number of workers, the total payroll paid by the employer, and the length of employment of the workers. In most of these states voluntary coverage is available. "Domestic servants" have also traditionally been excluded from coverage under workers' compensation.

Based on the language of the original statutes, most jurisdictions exempt work that is casual and not in the course of the employer's trade, business, or profession. In most instances the work must be both casual (brief and irregular) and different in nature from the work regularly done by this business. Most often this issue is presented in terms of whether the worker was an independent contractor rather than an employee of the business. This issue is discussed in section 5.5.

Public employees are generally covered by workers' compensation laws. A few states exclude employees of charitable or religious employers[1] and a few others exempt or limit the coverage of professional athletes.

5.4 Exemptions for Business Owners

Businesses usually take one of three forms: corporations, partnerships, or sole proprietorships. The first two are defined through formal agreements; corporations must be registered with a state government.

Generally, all employees of a corporation are covered, but a few states, such as Michigan, allow corporate officers to be excluded if it is a very small, closely held corporation. In a business that is formed as a partnership, partners are ordinarily not covered, but some states allow them to elect coverage.[2] Obviously, the election must take place before an injury occurs.

If Ms. A simply starts a business without any formal action, and she is the owner of the business, she is *self-employed* and the business is a *sole proprietorship*. The owner of such a business is not an employee. Thus, if Ms. A sets up a hot dog stand where she works alone, she is the owner and not an employee of the business. If she is injured, she will not ordinarily be able to collect workers' compensation benefits. If the business prospers and she hires several people to work for her, they will be employees and covered by workers' compensation, but as the owner she will still not ordinarily be covered. A few states, such as Missouri, allow sole proprietors to voluntarily elect to be covered, but they are the exceptions.

5.5 Exceptions for Independent Contractors

One of the most frequent problems concerning coverage involves determining whether an individual is an employee or an independent contractor. Assume that Company X is in the business of building houses and that Mr. B is a carpet layer. Assume further that Mr. B advertises in the yellow pages and lays carpets for many different entities including several builders and individual home owners. If Company X hires Mr. B to lay the carpets in a few of its houses, he is probably not its employee and not entitled to workers' compensation from X if he is injured.

Assume, however, that Y is a very big company and that it builds so many houses that it has several people including Mr. C who are kept busy full time laying carpet in its houses. Assume also that these people never work for anyone but Y. Under these circumstances they are most likely employees of Y and entitled to benefits from it if they are injured.

These are examples of fairly clear-cut situations. It is harder to distinguish between independent contractors and employees in ambiguous situations or when employers attempt to avoid the law by disguising the nature of their employees. As an example of an ambiguous situation, assume that Z is a medium size company and that Mr. D was the only carpet layer that it uses. Assume that he is kept busy 80 percent of his time by Company Z and that the rest of the time he works for individual home owners usually referred by friends. Once in a while he works for another builder. While working for Z, is he an employee or independent contractor?

There is no easy answer. The right to control the individual in the performance of his or her job is most often cited as the primary test to determine if the worker is an employee or an independent contractor. Larson argues that a more appropriate test is gaining acceptance.[3] He claims that we should look at the nature of the claimant's work in relation to the regular business of the employer. If the work is an integral part of the company's business, the worker should be considered an employee. Thus, for a home builder, a lawyer would ordinarily be an independent contractor, and a carpenter an employee. The carpet layer, however, might still be an ambiguous case.

Other factors that have been considered in determining whether a worker is an employee or an independent contractor include: control over the details of the work, whether the worker is engaged in a distinct occupation or business, whether the worker works for others, whether the worker holds himself or herself out to the general public as available to perform services, whether this kind of work is usually done by independent contractors, the amount of skill involved, who supplies the tools, the length of time involved, the method of payment, the right to fire, and what kind of arrangement the parties believed they were creating when they entered into the relationship.

With respect to the issue of what the parties believed they were creating when they entered into the relationship, it is important to note that this is only one of many factors that will be considered. The parties cannot change the status of the worker by simply entering into an agreement, even a written contract, saying that the individual is an independent contractor.

As an example of a deceptive situation, imagine that Company W employs several carpet layers, all of whom work full time for it and never work for anyone else. Assume that Ms. E, owner of W, decides that the company's insurance premiums are too high. To reduce them, she decides to change the status of the carpet layers. She could turn to a nationwide carpet laying firm, but she is not certain that such a firm will lay the carpet in just the way she likes. Instead, she calls in the carpet layers and tells them that they are no longer employees. If they wish, however, they can continue to work just as they have in the past. All they have to do is sign a paper saying that they are now independent contractors. This will be good for them because they now own their own businesses. Furthermore, W will no longer withhold taxes from their paychecks; they can report their earnings as they please. The work, however, will continue to be performed and supervised just as it was before.

If a carpet layer is injured under these circumstances, it is most likely that the worker will be found to be an employee and W will be responsible for workers' compensation benefits. In addition, when the company providing insurance to Company W audits the company's records, it will in all likelihood charge a premium based upon the wages paid to the carpet layers.

In the case of the employer that deliberately tries to avoid liability by simply calling someone an independent contractor, it can be safely said that the law is not as technical or as blind as some may think. If a dispute arises, the administrative agency or the courts will look behind the names and forms to find the real situation and hold the parties to it. In the ambiguous situation, we most often rely on either the good will of the parties or litigation to sort things out.

5.6 Statutory Employment

Most states provide that if one employer contracts with another to do work for it, and the second employer does not have workers' compensation coverage, the first employer can be held liable to provide benefits to the employees of the second. Assume that Company T is a general contractor managing the operation of a large construction site. Assume also that Ms. F is a plumbing contractor and has, in her employ, five plumbers. Assume further that Ms. F is truly an independent contractor with respect to Company T, and that the individual plumbers are employees of Ms. F. Finally, assume that Ms. F, although she is required to do so by law, fails to buy workers' compensation insurance coverage. Nearly all workers' compensation laws[4] allow employees injured under these circumstances to collect benefits from Company T, the general contractor. It is said that they are *statutory employees* of the general contractor.

The states vary in how broadly this principle is applied. It is important for an employer to research the law in its own jurisdiction, and to guard against this situation. Many employers adopt a requirement that they will not contract with anyone unless that party presents proof of insurance, usually a copy of a policy or a certification from an insurance carrier. In some states, it is possible to phone the state workers' compensation agency and determine if an individual party has workers' compensation insurance. (Appendix A includes a listing of state workers' compensation agencies.)

5.7 The Alternative to Workers' Compensation

Often it is assumed that a business is better off financially trying to exempt as much of its work force as possible from workers' compensation coverage. Excluding workers from coverage under the workers' compensation act will reduce insurance premiums and will relieve the employer of payment for many of the smaller injuries that occur. This, however, is not necessarily the best approach.

If a worker is not subject to the workers' compensation act, the employer does not receive the protection of the act's exclusive remedy provisions. As discussed more fully in chapter 4, if an individual is not an employee of a business, then he or she has a right to sue that business in civil court for any injury that may occur. If the worker can show that the company was negligent, then the company will be responsible for any damages that a jury might give. Thus, the company is open to the disastrous results that may occur from a serious injury that can be attributed to its negligence.

Notes

1. Arkansas, Mississippi, and North Dakota. *See* Larson §50.40.
2. Colorado, Florida, Michigan, Nebraska, Oregon, Tennessee, Utah, Vermont, and Virginia. Larson §54.30.
3. Larson §43.50.
4. The exceptions are Alabama, California, Delaware, Iowa, Maine, Rhode Island, and West Virginia. Larson §49.11.

Chapter 6

Coverage of Disabilities

6.1 Introduction

To what extent must a disability be related to the employment in order to come under the coverage of workers' compensation? This chapter will attempt to answer that question. Statutorily it is usually framed as a requirement that covered disabilities must "arise out of and in the course of the employment." Sometimes it is referred to as the *causation* issue.

6.2 The General Approach

6.2.1 Two Theories of Risk

Larson speaks of several theories for determining which risks are covered.[1] Two, however, are the most common. Under the *increased-risk* theory, an injury is covered only if the work increased the risk that the worker would be injured in a specific way. Under the *positional-risk* theory, a worker is covered if the work put him or her in the position where the injury occurred.

If two individuals work on an assembly line and Mr. A. contracts tuberculosis from Mr. B. simply because they work next to each other, most states would apply the increased-risk doctrine and deny compensation. They would say that there was nothing about the nature of the work that increased Mr. A's risk of contracting tuberculosis over the risk experienced by the general public. A few states, such as Michigan, however, would apply the positional-risk doctrine and say that the work put Mr. A in the position where he was exposed and would thus award benefits.

If Mr. A worked in the contagious disease ward of a hospital and contracted tuberculosis from a patient, this would be compensable even under the increased-risk theory because the work increased the risk.

A more difficult case arises if the nature of the employment did not involve any unusual exposure to the disease, but required Mr. A. and Mr. B to work in unusually close contact and to drink from the same water container. This would clearly be compensable under the positional-risk doctrine. It might also be argued that this was in fact an increased risk and compensable under that approach.

In general, acts of God, such as lightning, wind storms, and earthquakes, are said to cause compensable injuries if the employment increased the risk that the worker would be injured.[2] Under the increased-risk doctrine, a lightning strike might be considered compensable if the work required the employee to work outside around tall metal structures that increase the exposure to lightning. A few states, such as Michigan and New York, apply the positional-risk doctrine to these circumstances and hold that it is enough if the work put the person in the position where the injury occurred. Under the positional-risk doctrine, a lightning strike would be compensable if the work put the employee at the spot where the lightning struck even though there was no increased risk of lightning at that spot.

"Street risks" is another category of cases that sometimes cause difficulty. If the job requires the employee to be on the street an unusual amount of time, driving a delivery truck, for example, then injuries resulting from traffic hazards and other street risks will be compensable under the increased-risk doctrine. Most states, including California, Ohio, and Connecticut, however, would apply the positional-risk doctrine to such an injury and find it compensable if the employment required the worker to be on the street at the moment in which he or she was injured, even though the worker was not on the street an unusual amount of time.

6.2.2 *Idiopathic Injuries and Level Floor Falls*

Unexplained accidents cause particular problems for workers' compensation. These are situations in which an individual is simply walking across a level floor, falls, and suffers an injury. There is nothing about the floor that increased the risk, and likewise there is nothing about the worker that increased the risk that he or she would fall. If the walk across the floor was clearly part of the individual's employment, the courts are divided as to whether benefits should be awarded under those circumstances. These are sometimes called "idiopathic" injuries because we do not know the origin or cause of the injury.

A different situation arises if we know that the cause of the fall was personal. If an individual has epilepsy, has a seizure, falls, and is injured, is the injury compensable? The condition of the injury is not idiopathic because we know the cause. These are called "level floor fall" cases. Level floor falls are generally not compensable.

In both situations discussed above, it is assumed that the likelihood of injury was not heightened in any way by the employment. If, for example, the employment required the individual to be working at a height from which he or she fell, or in the proximity of machinery into which he or she fell, then the subsequent injury is compensable. Such an injury would be compensable even if the cause of the fall was unexplained or was a personal one such as epilepsy. In these cases, the employment at a height or near machinery would have increased the risk of injury.

To summarize, if the work increases the risk, then the injury is compensable. If the work does not increase the risk, and the injury is idiopathic (of unknown origin or cause), then compensability varies from state to state. If it is a level floor fall, and we know of a personal origin or cause, the injury is not compensable.

6.2.3 *Unexplained Deaths*

Courts have a tendency to grant benefits in the case of an unexplained death. Larson explains this with the theory that if the death occurs in the course of the employment, there is at least some probability that the work caused the death. Furthermore, since the death has removed the only possible witness who could prove causation, fairness to the dependents requires some presumption in favor of compensability.[3]

This assumes, of course, that the death is unexplained. If the death is known to result from a heart attack, for example, then attention must be turned to the question of whether or not the work caused or contributed to the heart attack.

Two states, New York and Massachusetts, actually have statutory language providing for the presumption of compensability in a case in which the individual is killed or is physically or mentally unable to testify. The presumption may be rebutted by substantial evidence to the contrary.

6.2.4 The "Accident" Requirement

Most workers' compensation laws provide, or once provided, for compensation for "an injury by accident" or an "accidental injury." Over the years, the courts have generally broadened the definition of the term "accident" and a few states no longer apply it at all.[4] The National Commission recommended that the accident requirement be dropped as a test of compensability.[5]

Even so, in many jurisdictions there must be some element of an accident or at least some part of the incident must have been unexpected. In most jurisdictions, it is enough that either the event is unexpected or the result is unexpected. Thus, an injury as a result of a fall is compensable because the fall was unexpected. A back injury that results from repeated lifting is also compensable as an accident in most jurisdictions. Even though the repeated bending was not unexpected, the resultant back injury was unexpected. A few jurisdictions, such as North Carolina, however, would require a showing that the work performed was in some way unusual. The usualness issue relates to the individual worker concerned. It is not a question of whether there are many people who usually perform these tasks, but rather a question of whether the work was unusual for this particular individual. For example, appearing in a courtroom might be considered unusual for a laborer but common for an attorney, while heavy lifting might be considered usual for a laborer but unusual for an attorney.

Sometimes the nature of the injury will influence a determination of whether it was an accident. If an event results in a breakage, rupture, or herniation, it is more likely to be considered an accident. If the result is a "generalized condition," such as a weakness or shortness of breath, it is less likely to be considered an accident. Such disabilities, however, may be compensable as occupational diseases. (See chapter 7.)

The ability to satisfy the accident requirement is also affected by whether the disability arises at a definite point in time. If the cause of the disability can be traced to a specific, reasonable amount of time, or the result of the disability materializes at a definite time, it is more likely to be seen as an accident.

6.2.5 *The Consequences of Injury*

When an injury is compensable, nearly all of the subsequent consequences related to that injury are also compensable. A subsequent event is compensable if it is the direct and natural result of the original compensable injury. Assume, for example, Ms. C suffers a compensable injury that requires complete bed rest. If, as a result of lying motionless, she develops pneumonia and dies from the pneumonia, the death is compensable. If Mr. D suffers an injury to his knee in the course of his employment and later falls and injures his back because he has a bad knee, the back injury is compensable. It must be remembered of course that there is always the possibility of factual questions. Was it really the knee problem that caused him to fall?

It is also generally held that if, in the course of receiving medical treatment for a compensable injury, the condition is worsened by the medical malpractice of the physicians, the results of the malpractice are compensable. (However, as discussed in section 4.3, the compensation carrier may be entitled to reimbursement as the result of a malpractice suit against the physicians.)

6.3 Place of Injury

6.3.1 *The Premises Rule*

Ordinarily, a worker is not covered while going to or coming from the place of employment unless he or she is on the premises of the employer. Thus, if Ms. E is involved in an auto accident on the street while on her way to work, she will not be covered by workers' compensation. If, however, she slipped on a wet floor and fell while walking down an aisle in the employer's building on the way to her work station, she would be covered. Most states include parking lots as part of the employer's premises.

The same rule generally applies during lunch hours. If the worker is on the premises, an injury is compensable, but if the worker is off the premises, an injury is not compensable.

Generally, if two parts of the employer's premises are separated and a worker is injured while traveling between them, he or she is covered. In most states this includes travel across public property from a parking lot owned by the employer to the place of work. Courts have sometimes extended the premises concept and held that injuries were compensable if they occurred very close to the employment, in some way connected with the employment, or if the employment imposed some special risk on the situation.

If an employee works at home as well as on the employer's premises and is injured traveling between these two locations, the injury may be considered compensable. (See the discussion of dual purpose trips in subsection 6.3.3.)

6.3.2 Travel

If traveling is part of the job, then an injury that occurs during that travel is compensable. If the employment requires special trips to and from work, those may be compensable. For example, where an employee is required to return to the building during his usual off-duty hours to perform some function such as turning on a heater or admitting a repair person, an injury occurring during the trip to and from work is usually considered compensable.

Many disputes arise as to whether a specified travel is sufficiently work related to be compensable. If the worker is paid for the time during which he or she travels, this is ordinarily enough to bring it within the course of the employment. It is sometimes enough that the employer pays for the expenses of the travel.

Generally, if the employee is injured while using the employer's car or other means of transportation, even if going to or from work, the injury is compensable. The theory behind this is that the risk of the employment is extended when the worker is using the employer's means of transportation. This concept is sometimes extended to include travel in the employee's own automobile when the terms of the employment required him or her to provide that means of transportation.

Generally, employees on business trips are covered during their entire trip. In most instances, if an employee dies in a hotel fire or while eating in a restaurant or is struck by a tornado in a hotel, the employee has been considered to be covered. However, if employees deviate from the employment-related trip, coverage can cease. Deviation is usually viewed geographically, but the activities can be so unusual as not to come within the course of the employment.

Thus, if Mr. F is traveling from Dallas to Los Angeles as part of his job, he will probably be covered during the entire trip. If, however, he takes a side trip to San Francisco to visit a friend, he will not be covered during that side trip. If while in Los Angeles, he eats, drinks, and sleeps in the manner one would normally expect of a traveling businessperson, he will probably be covered during all those activities. On the other hand, if he spends an evening drinking and carousing to an unreasonable extent, he may take himself out of the course of his employment.

6.3.3 Dual Purpose Trips

There has been controversy over injuries that occur during a trip that has two purposes, one of which is personal and the other business related. In general, if there is a business purpose to the trip sufficient to cause the trip to have been taken, then an injury incurred during the trip is compensable, even if there is also a personal purpose for the trip.

Assume Ms. G takes a trip from Chicago to New York for two purposes: to make a contact with a potential customer and to see a play. If she would have made the trip to see the customer regardless of the play, the trip is compensable. The fact that there was also another purpose to the trip does not take it out of the course of the employment. However, Ms. G may not be covered while she is at the theater. As discussed earlier, she would be said to have deviated from her business route.

The principle of dual purpose trips is sometimes used with the result that trips from home to work are compensable if the employee genuinely works at home and would have been required to travel from the employer's premises to his or her home for business purposes.

6.4 Type of Worker

Another way to analyze the place of injury issue is based upon the type of worker involved. The *Compendium of State Workers' Compensation Laws*, published by the National Commission, discusses "in the course of the employment" by dividing workers into three categories: (1) inside workers, (2) outside workers, and (3) resident workers who live on the premises of their employer or are on call 24 hours a day.

For "inside workers," the Commission suggests that an injury is compensable if the workers are on the employer's premises when injured. This includes a reasonable time before and after work. Almost anything that happens to inside workers while they are on the premises is compensable, including recreational activities, horseplay, and injuries during lunch hours.

For inside workers, the Commission applies a going-and-coming rule. Ordinarily, injuries suffered while going to or coming from employment are not covered. Exceptions include unusual hazards as a result of the employer's location, performing services for the employer while going to or coming from work, or while performing special errands.

For "outside workers," the course of the employment is much broader and ordinarily starts from the time the worker leaves home. There are, however, limits. If a worker strays too far from employment-related activities, he or she will no longer be covered.

For "resident" workers, who live on the premises or are on call, the *Compendium* indicates there is no clear line of authority. Most states apply to resident employees what is called "the bunkhouse rule." If an employee is required to live on the premises and is continually on call, almost any injury is likely to be compensable. If the employee is required to live on the premises, but only works during clearly defined hours, the compensability of an injury outside of those hours may depend upon whether or not living on the premises increased the risk of injury. Assume that Ms. H is a jailer and is required to live on the premises of the jail. If she is required to be on call and available at all times, she would probably be covered by workers' compensation even if she slipped and fell in the bathtub. If we changed the assumption and say that even though she lives on the premises, she works only eight hours a day and is not in any way on call when off duty, she will probably not be covered when she slips and falls in the bathtub. If, however, a prisoner burned down the jailhouse, injuries Ms. H suffered as a result of the fire would probably be covered even if she were off duty sleeping in her bed when the fire occurred.

6.5 Circumstances of Injury

6.5.1 Activities Not Related to the Employment

The preceding section dealt with the location of the employee when an injury occurred as a means of determining whether the injury was compensable, but even when the worker is on the job site during working hours when injured, questions can arise as to whether the worker's activities are covered by workers' compensation. The courts have generally held that there are a wide variety of activities that take place on the job that are covered by workers' compensation even though they are not directly a part of the work to be done. These activities include eating, washing, going to the toilet, and talking to co-workers. Unless there is something unusual about the activities, a worker is generally covered from the time he or she arrives on the premises until he or she leaves the premises. This includes normal activity in preparing for the job before the shift actually starts, lunch hours, and break periods whether paid or unpaid, and normal activity after the end of the work period.

Personal activities of a worker may not be covered if they are being carried out in an unusual or unreasonable manner, or if they were prohibited by the employer. The question should not be whether the activities were carried out in a "negligent" manner, but rather an unreasonable or unexpected manner. Since, as discussed in subsection 3.2.1, workers' compensation is a no-fault system, it is not appropriate to consider negligence. It is, however, appropriate to ask whether the personal activities took the worker out of the course of the employment; thus, while performing work in a negligent manner might not be a reason to deny benefits, performing personal activities in an unreasonable or unexpected manner may well remove the worker from the course of the employment.

6.5.2 Recreational and Social Activities

Injuries that happen during recreational and social activities are generally covered if the injury occurs on the premises during working hours or at lunch time, if the activity is required by the employment, or if the employer derives a substantial benefit from the activity. A few states have specific statutory provisions concerning this,[6] but in most jurisdictions the principle has developed through case law. Even in on-the-premises cases, a social activity must be somewhat regular. If it is spontaneous and clearly unusual, it may not be covered.

Entertainment of potential customers by a salesperson is considered in the course of the employment. If an individual is required to take part in some social activity, he or she will probably also be covered.

Company picnics and office parties often result in disputed cases. Among the factors that will be considered are (1) whether or not the employer sponsored the event, (2) the extent to which the employer encouraged or required attendance, and (3) the extent, if any, to which the employer benefited from the attendance at the event.

6.5.3 Horseplay

It is generally considered that a certain amount of "horseplay" should be anticipated in any employment. Thus, injuries that result during such horseplay may be compensable. As discussed above, however, the activity may be so different from expected behavior that it takes a worker out of the course of his or her employment.

A nonparticipating bystander is nearly always covered. Thus, if Mr. I and Mr. J stepped away from their work station and started playing catch with the parts they were supposed to be assembling and Mr. K, a bystander, was struck when J missed, K would be covered. Whether or not I and J are covered will depend on a variety of circumstances, including whether this was a brief diversion during a short lull in their work or whether they purposely left their job sites for a long period of time to engage in this activity. It may also depend upon whether or not the employer knew of and condoned the activities.

6.5.4 Misconduct

In general, workers' compensation is a no-fault system. Accordingly, misconduct by an employee is ordinarily not enough to deny workers' compensation benefits to a worker.

In some cases, however, it is said that the misconduct takes the person out of the course of his or her employment. Thus, if a worker is making something for his personal use on an employer's machine and is injured while doing so, he or she will probably be denied benefits. The court, however, will deny benefits not because the worker was engaged in misconduct, but because the activity was not in the course of the employment.

Most workers' compensation laws specifically state that an injury is not compensable if it was the result of "willful misconduct" or "intentional and willful misconduct." Generally, the courts have interpreted this quite narrowly.

In theory most states would deny benefits to workers who are injured as the result of a violation of a safety rule. Larson reports, however, that there are few cases in which employers succeed in using this defense.[7] To take advantage of this defense, the employer must show that the worker was aware of the rule and that the rule was regularly enforced by the employer. Thus, if an employer issues a rule that workers cannot perform a job unless they are wearing masks, it cannot simply put that rule in its policy manual, regularly allow employees to ignore the rule, and then deny benefits based upon it. On the other hand, if an employer announces the rule, repeatedly informs its workers of the rule, and regularly enforces the rule, it may then be able to deny benefits to a worker who suffers an injury as the result of not using the mask.

A few states have specific provisions denying benefits to a person injured while violating the law.[8] Unless there is such a provision in a state's statute, however, the fact that a worker was injured while violating a law will not necessarily result in the denial of compensation. In many cases, however, it is likely that a person violating a law will be found not to be in the course of his or her employment.

Suicide has been held to be compensable under certain circumstances. Generally, cases are decided upon how close the connection was between the suicide and the employment.

6.5.5 Use of Alcohol and Illegal Drugs

Most states have some provisions in their law that deny or limit benefits to employees who are intoxicated or using illegal drugs while injured. The exact provisions of these statutes vary greatly. Even in states that do not have such a provision, benefits may be denied to an employee whose voluntary intoxication was so severe as to take him or her out of the course of the employment.

Generally, benefits are denied if the injury was caused to some degree by the worker's use of alcohol or drugs. Texas, in theory, denies benefits to anyone who was intoxicated when injured, but in practice certain procedural requirements have made this hard to enforce. Florida has amended its law to provide that an employer may deny benefits to any worker injured while using alcohol or illegal drugs, even if such use was not a cause of the injury, if the employer has adopted an approved program for a "drug-free workplace."

6.5.6 Assaults

What happens if a person gets into a fight at work? Is this sufficient misconduct to take the injury out of the course of employment? In general, if the employment increased the risk of the fight or assault, it will be compensable. Also, if the topic of the quarrel had to do with the employment, it may also be compensable. The outcome may also be affected by whether the claimant was the aggressor in the dispute. If the fight is over a purely private topic, it is probably not compensable. Some states have accepted the idea that if the employment requires people to be in constant close contact and the strain of the contact causes a fight, the results may be compensable. Generally, assaults by outside parties, such as drunks or mistaken identity assaults, are considered compensable.

Obviously, if a police officer is assaulted by a criminal, the injury is compensable. This is generally true in other similar circumstances, such as plant guards or supervisors assaulted by workers. Also, if the job requires a person to be in a part of the city where that person is alone and subject to assault, a resulting injury is usually compensable. It is said in these cases that the employment has increased the risk of the injury.

6.6 The Causal Relationship

Assuming that an event occurs that has a sufficient nexus, or connection, to the work to be "in the course of the employment" another question must be answered: To what extent must this event be the *cause* of the disability? Problems most frequently arise when the disability is the result of a work-related event in combination with a preexisting condition.

The basic principle of law is that the presence of a preexisting weakness does not disqualify the worker from benefits. A disability is compensable if the employment "aggravated," "accelerated," "contributed to," or "combined with a preexisting condition" to cause the disability. This approach is not unique to workers' compensation. It has always been a basic principle of English and American personal injury law that "you take your victim as you find him." When workers' compensation laws were adopted early in this century, this approach was carried over into virtually all of them.

There is an economic argument that supports the application of this principle. Workers' compensation benefits should reflect the change in the person's earning capacity which results from a work-related event. Nearly all workers' compensation benefits are based upon the worker's earnings prior to the injury. If the preexisting condition affected the individual's prior earning capacity, it will be reflected in reduced wages and thus reduced benefits. If it did not affect the earning capacity, then it should not be considered in determining benefits.

A worker might put it differently. If Mr. L has been working successfully for some time and now suffers an event at work that causes him to be unable to support his family, he feels that he should be entitled to compensation even if he suffered a similar injury once before. Even if Ms. M has had continuing difficulties with her back right up to the time of her new injury, she will point out that to the extent that her prior condition caused her to miss time from work it will be reflected in a reduced average weekly wage and thus a reduced benefit.

Employers, on the other hand, often find this a particularly difficult principle to accept and in recent years a few states such as Oregon and Florida have amended their laws to limit its application. There has been special pressure to change laws with respect to disabilities caused by mental stress. (See section 2.3.)

A few states that pay benefits based primarily on the extent of physical impaiment provide that when a preexisting condition is aggravated by the employment, then compensation is payable only for the percentage of disability attributed to the employment.[9] In other words, assume that Mr. N, who engages in heavy labor and suffers a back injury in the course of his employment, had back trouble before the injury. These states would attempt to determine the extent of his preexisting disability and reduce any subsequent award by a percentage based upon that determination.

As discussed in chapter 13, some states deal with this problem to varying degrees through "second" or "subsequent injury" funds. These funds relieve the burden on the employer when a second or subsequent injury has more serious effects because of the preexisting condition. There is great variety in the way these funds operate. Some apply only to workers with a permanent total disability, while others apply to all disabling injuries. Some require that the employer knew of the disability before the worker was hired, while others do not. Some apply only to amputations or specifically listed disabilities, while others apply to all conditions.

In general, second injury funds have provided some help but no complete solution in dealing with this situation. The states in which second injury funds seem to function effectively and are accepted by employers and workers alike are usually those in which the fund only covers a limited number of situations. In states such as Missouri, where the coverage of the fund is very broad, the funds tend to be costly, cumbersome, and difficult to administer.

Allergies are a special problem. It is generally said that no one would suffer any allergy unless he or she had a preexisting disposition toward it. Consider that Mr. M may come to a tannery with no apparent allergies. After many years of work, he may eventually develop an allergy to the chemicals used so that he can no longer function in that situation. At the same time, Ms. N may come to a job and on the second day develop an allergy to a soap that, although used in her work, is not particularly unusual. In both cases, a preexisting condition has been aggravated by the employment. Allergies are particularly troublesome because, in the case of a true allergy, once a person has been sensitized to the material, they are usually permanently sensitive thereafter. Mr. M, for example, may never be able to handle anything coated with chrome, and Ms. N may not be able to do her laundry or wash dishes at home. Are all the results of both conditions to be compensable? In general, the answer is yes. Although both individuals had a preexisting condition before the injury, neither was disabled until the industrial exposure. It is that last exposure that "sensitizes" the person, or in essence turns on the allergy.

Hernias are another problem. In general, a person will not suffer a hernia unless there is some preexisting weakness. At the same time, the person will probably not suffer the hernia unless there is some strain that causes the final event. In general, hernias are held to be compensable, although many states, such as Virginia, have special requirements, for example, a specific, sudden event or prompt reporting.

The National Commission in its recommendation R 2.17 stated, "We recommend that full workmen's compensation benefits be paid for an impairment or death resulting from both work-related and non-work-related causes if the work related factor was a significant cause of the impairment or death."

Finally, it should be noted that in some cases the dispute is really factual or scientific rather than legal. For example, while lawyers might agree that a heart attack should be compensable if the work contributed to it in a significant manner, there is very little agreement among doctors as to whether or not stress actually contributes to a heart attack. For this reason the legal system has difficulty developing rules to deal with mental and physical stress cases. (See section 2.3.)

Notes

1. Larson §6.00–6.60.
2. Larson §8.00–8.52.
3. Larson §10.32.
4. California, Colorado, Iowa, Maine, Massachusetts, Michigan, Minnesota, Pennsylvania, Rhode Island, and South Dakota, United States Employees' Compensation Act. Larson §37.10.
5. National Commission Report R. 2.12.
6. For example, California, Colorado, Illinois, Massachusetts, Michgan, Nevada, New Jersey, New York, and Oregon. Larson §22.00.
7. Larson §33.10.
8. Alabama, Delaware, Georgia, Indiana, Michigan, Pennsylvania, South Dakota, Tennessee, and Washington. Larson §35.40.
9. California, Florida, Kentucky, Maryland, Mississippi, North Dakota, and South Carolina. Larson §12.24.

Chapter 7

Occupational Diseases

7.1 Defined

Occupational diseases are usually defined as conditions resulting from an inherent hazard or continuous exposure unique to or characteristic of a particular job or type of employment. Thus, occupational diseases are distinguished from "accidents" or "injuries" in that accidents are unexpected or unusual, whereas occupational diseases are, at least to some extent, common to the employment involved.

Occupational diseases are ordinarily gradual in onset, whereas accidents are usually related to a specific time. What about the situation in which a worker injures his back by repeated lifting? If this repeated difficult lifting was peculiar to and characteristic of the job, should it be considered an occupational disease? Perhaps so, but few states have chosen to treat it that way. As discussed in subsection 6.2.4 most states have found this situation compensable as an "accident" or injury and bring it within the definition of an accident by saying that it qualifies as an accident because the result was unexpected.

Occupational diseases must also be distinguished from ordinary diseases of life. Silicosis, for example, is considered an occupational disease because it is characteristic of certain employments such as mining and foundry work. While arteriosclerosis, or hardening of the arteries, is usually considered as an ordinary disease of life because it is not characteristic of any particular work. Note, however, that a myocardial infarction—a heart attack—might be compensable, not as an occupational disease, but as an accident or injury, if it occurred as the result of a sudden, dramatic event in the course of employment.

7.2 Coverage

The first workers' compensation laws did not cover occupational diseases. The coverage of these disabilities has been gradually added over the years. Typically, jurisdictions added coverage of occupational diseases by at first adopting a list of specific diseases that were covered. The list was often expanded over time by adding additional specific diseases. Later on, a provision might be added to the end of the list to provide coverage of the listed diseases and "similar diseases." Today most states provide coverage for all conditions that are characteristic of a particular job or employment. The National Commission recommended that all states provide full coverage for work-related diseases.[1]

Some diseases have been excluded from coverage because it was felt that requiring the payment of compensation for these diseases would result in the destruction of certain industries such as mining, foundries, and quarries. As discussed in section 13.3, a few states have dealt with this by creating special funds. For example, in Michigan a foundry worker suffering from silicosis receives the same benefits as any other worker. However, the employer pays only the first $25,000 in wage-loss benefits and a special fund pays benefits above that amount. All employers pay into the fund.

The payment of benefits to miners suffering from pneumoconiosis, often called black lung disease, is the subject of a special federal law with its own peculiar history. A discussion of those benefits is beyond the scope of this book, but can be found elsewhere.[2]

As medical science is gradually learning of the connection between certain medical problems and a variety of substances that we encounter in our working environment, the number of occupational diseases is increasing. There are many cases, such as the connection between benzine and leukemia, in which only a few years ago the experts saw no connection, but which today are considered by almost everyone to be causally related.

There are, of course, a great many other situations that are on the margin. We simply do not know if there is a relationship. Some researchers suspect a relationship and others doubt it. The consensus among researchers may be developing or shifting, or there may be no consensus. These cases result in difficult problems for the workers' compensation system, but that fact should not be seen as a weakness of the system. If there is no agreement among scientists concerning the relationship of a certain disease to specific chemicals, one cannot blame the workers' compensation system for having difficulty in dealing with this question.

In general, occupational disease laws require that the risk be peculiar to the employment or at least that the employment result in an increased risk. Thus, if a nurse contracts tuberculosis as a result of working in a tuberculosis ward in a hospital, this is clearly a condition which is peculiar to her employment. The employment caused not only an increased risk but a peculiar risk.

If, however, an employee contracted tuberculosis from a fellow worker in a room that was clean and where they were not required to work in close proximity and there was no reason the job attracted an unusually high number of people infected by tuberculosis, then benefits might be denied even if the worker actually contracted tuberculosis while on the job.

Problems often arise when an occupational disease clearly has two causes—one employment related and one not. A typical situation involves a worker who smokes cigarettes and also is exposed to something on the job that causes lung cancer. The legal problem is compounded by the medical situation in which the relationship between the two causes is said to be *synergistic*. If a person smokes cigarettes, that person might have 2 chances in 100 of contracting a certain form of lung cancer. If a person is exposed to certain substances at work, that person might have a 3-in-100 chance of contracting the same cancer. If, however, he or she both smokes and is exposed to these substances, the chances of contracting the cancer might be 20-in-100.

As discussed in section 6.5, the general rule is that if the work makes a significant contribution to a disability, it is considered compensable even if the employee had some preexisting condition that increased the susceptibility or contributed to the disability. There is no reason this same principle should not be applied to occupational diseases.

7.3 Special Treatment of Occupational Diseases

There have been many special requirements or limitations placed upon the compensation of occupational diseases. In general, there has been a strong trend to eliminate these differences, but some still persist. Indeed some states, such as Illinois, Indiana, and Pennsylvania, have a separate law covering occupational diseases.

Many states have shorter notices provisions or shorter statutes of limitation provisions relating to occupational diseases. In some states the notice or filing requirement runs from the last day of work.[3] This has an obvious advantage for insurance carriers and employers. The problem with this is that medical science is now teaching us that many occupational diseases have a very long latency period. Asbestosis can first appear 25 years after the last exposure to asbestos. Other statutes take an entirely different approach and provide that in the case of an occupational disease, the time limits for giving notice or filing do not start to run until a worker could reasonably have known that he or she had the disease.

7.4 Police Officers and Fire Fighters

A few states, such as Michigan, have special statutes dealing with police officers and fire fighters. Most of these establish a presumption that heart or lung disease is compensable if it occurs in these workers while they are in the active performance of their duties. Usually the presumption can be "rebutted" by showing some other cause.

Notes

1. National Commission Report R 2.13.
2. Barth, Peter S., *The Tragedy of Black Lung: Federal Compensation for Occupational Disease* (Kalamazoo, Mich.: W.E. Upjohn Institute for Employment Research, 1987); Larson §41.90.
3. Alabama, Idaho, Illinois, Indiana, Maine, Montana, Oregon, Vermont, Virginia, and Wyoming. Larson §41.81.

Chapter 8

Evaluation of Disability

8.1 Introduction

The determination of who is disabled and the extent of disability is the heart of a workers' compensation system. The study of this topic is difficult because there is great diversity among the states in how they handle this issue and because some states have evolved extremely complicated systems for making the determination.

This chapter will begin with a very brief overview of the issues. It will then turn to a discussion of benefits at the extremes—temporary benefits during short-term disability or during the first part of a long-term disability, and permanent total benefits paid to the most severely disabled workers. These extremes will be discussed first because there is greater similarity in the way they are treated among the various jurisdictions and because they are in general the easier problem to deal with. We will then turn our attention to how the various systems treat workers who have a disability which is permanent, but less than total. This situation is the most complex, the most diverse, and the most difficult. The chapter will then conclude with some suggestions on reforming the system of payments for permanent partial disabilities.

8.2 Overview

It is possible to describe workers' compensation disability benefits in very simple terms. When a worker is first injured, he or

79

she is paid *temporary total* disability benefits. In a great many cases a worker receives these benefits and returns to work without receiving any permanent benefits. Sometimes an individual may return to work at a reduced wage and receive temporary partial disability benefits. These temporary benefits continue until the worker's medical condition has stabilized. This is sometimes called the point of *maximum medical improvement.*

By the time this point is reached, most individuals have returned to work. Those who continue to be disabled are, broadly speaking, divided into two categories: the most severely disabled are characterized as having permanent total disability, and the remainder are characterized as having a permanent partial disability. Benefits for permanent total disability are generally available for longer periods of time (sometimes for life) than benefits for permanent partial disability.

States differ in how they draw the line between these two forms of disability. They also differ in how they compensate permanent partial disability. At one extreme, the assessment may be based purely on the amount of physical *impairment.* At the other extreme, the assessment may be based entirely on the amount of the worker's actual *wage loss.*

It is important to understand how these various benefits are distributed in terms of the number of cases and the dollars spent. Temporary total cases are the most frequent. They account for perhaps 70 percent of all lost-time cases. Permanent and total cases are by far the most costly. They average in the neighborhood of $180,000 each as opposed to $32,000 for permanent partial and $2,000 for temporary total cases. It is, however, permanent partial cases that account for most of the money overall. They are not the most frequent or individually the most costly but they cost enough and occur often enough to account for about 75 percent of the indemnity benefits paid in lost-time cases.

Chapter 9 will discuss in more detail the calculation of the amount of benefits paid. It should be pointed out, however, that the amount of benefits paid is usually based on the worker's preinjury earnings or *average weekly wage.* Most often, weekly benefits are paid at the rate of two-thirds of the gross earnings before the injury. Some states, however, pay benefits based on a percentage (usually 80 percent) of the after tax value of the preinjury earnings.

All states place a maximum limit on the amount of benefits (see Table 9.2 in chapter 9). Most commonly, this is equal to the average wage earned by all workers in the state during the previous year, but as discussed in section 9.2, there is considerable variation. As discussed in section 9.9, there is also variation in the extent to which other benefits may be offset or "coordinated" against workers' compensation benefits payable.

8.3 Temporary Disability

Temporary disability benefits are paid during the period immediately following an injury. This period lasts until either the worker recovers and returns to work, or the worker achieves as much recovery from the injury as can be expected. At this point it is said that the worker's condition has stabilized, and this point in time is usually called the point of maximum medical improvement.

Temporary disability benefits are ordinarily paid on the basis of the individual's wage-loss. In general, an assessment is made of the worker's average weekly wage before the injury, and the worker is paid a percentage of this amount. The payment is most often 66⅔ percent of the gross wage. In all states the benefit is subject to a maximum limit. Some jurisdictions allow for temporary partial disability benefits. If a worker is still recovering from his or her injury and returns to work at a wage that is less than he or she earned before the injury, the worker receives the appropriate percentage of the difference between the preinjury wage and the current wage.

Most jurisdictions allow temporary disability benefits to be paid for the duration of the disability. Fourteen states, however, place a limit on the number of weeks during which an individual can receive temporary total disability benefits. The limit ranges from 104 weeks in Texas to 700 weeks in New Mexico. See Table 9.5 in chapter 9.

Although temporary disability cases outnumber other claims, they are the least controversial. These are usually the cases in which there is an obvious injury, a clear period of disability, and an early return to work. More serious cases usually also involve a period of temporary total disability. Even in those cases during the temporary total disability period the parties generally agree that some disability exists that should continue to be compensated at least until maximum improvement is reached. If there is a dispute in this area, it is likely to be whether the worker has reached maximum medical improvement. In other words, whether the worker is ready to move on to another type of benefit.

8.4 Permanent Total Disability

One might think that the cases involving the most serious injuries would be the most troublesome part of the system. In general, however, this is not the case. The category of permanent total disability is reserved for workers with extremely severe injuries, and while there may be controversy as to who fits into that category, it is generally agreed that the individuals who are in this category are entitled to substantial benefits.

Permanent total disability benefits can be broken down into two categories: *conclusively presumed* total and permanent disability and *practical* total and permanent total disability. Most states offer both types of benefits. A few, such as Michigan, offer only conclusively presumed total and permanent disability benefits, and a few others, such as Missouri, offer only practical total and permanent total disability benefits.

8.4.1 Conclusively Presumed Permanent Total Disability

In most states, if a worker loses two legs, two arms, two eyes, or any combination of these members such as one leg and one eye, he or she is conclusively presumed to be permanently and totally disabled. The conclusive presumption generally implies that the worker can receive benefits during a specified period, even if he or she returns to work. Loss can generally include an amputation or a complete loss of use, such as would result from paralysis. Some states, such as California and Michigan, also include a category for "incurable insanity and imbecility." Qualification for these conclusively presumed benefits is usually very strict and the benefits are granted to only a limited number of workers.

8.4.2 *Practical Permanent Total Disability*

Most states also pay permanent total disability benefits to individuals who suffer a disability so severe that they will never be able to return to gainful employment, but who have not suffered the complete loss of two bodily members. I call this category *practical* permanent total disability. Unlike workers with a conclusively presumed permanent total disability, workers with a practical permanent total disability lose their benefits if they return to work.

One controversy that arises in this area involves the extent to which economic conditions will be considered in determining whether a person is permanently totally disabled. Suppose Mr. A lives in the woods in northern Minnesota, has very little education, and injures his back. The only work available to a person in his area with his education requires heavy lifting. He would claim that he is entitled to permanent total benefits if he has a condition that permanently prohibits him from doing the only work at which he can expect to make a living. His employer would argue, however, that if he lived in Minneapolis, or had a better education, there would be many jobs that he could do in spite of his injury, and therefore, his disability is only partial. States differ in the extent to which they consider geographical, educational, and economic factors in determining permanent total disability.

8.4.3 *Duration*

Generally, permanent total disability benefits are payable so long as the worker remains disabled. Six states, however, place a limit on the number of weeks of total permanent disability benefits a worker may receive. See Table 9.5 in chapter 9.

8.5 Permanent Partial Disability

8.5.1 *In General*

Permanent partial disability is the most difficult part of the workers' compensation system to describe. It accounts for a larger share of workers' compensation costs than any other type of disability. There is a greater diversity among states in this area than in any other part of the system. The system for compensating permanent partial disability benefits in some states is extremely complex and often controversial. Workers argue that the benefits paid are not adequate, employers argue that they are too costly, both complain that they are not delivered efficiently, and scholars point out that they are not distributed equitably.

The following discussion will attempt to describe some of the considerations in the area of permanent partial disability and provide some examples of how these benefits are paid. Monroe Berkowitz and John F. Burton, Jr., of Rutgers have written an analysis of this topic.[1] This is an excellent theoretical analysis and a good description of how 10 states have dealt with the problem. The Workers' Compensation Research Institute has conducted administrative inventories in numerous jurisdictions. These inventories provide the best across-state comparisons of how permanent partial disability is compensated.

While these publications provide an overview of the systems, neither they nor the sections that follow here are specific enough to advise a worker or an employer in a given case. For that purpose, it is necessary to consult state-specific publications where they are available or to consult with the state workers' compensation agency. A list of state agencies is found in Appendix A.

This section will begin by examining the two extreme approaches to the evaluation of permanent partial disability—*impairment rating* and *wage-loss*. We will then consider the concept of *loss of wage-earning capacity*, which is used by many states to modify these extreme alternatives. Then we will present some concrete examples of the way states apply these principles. Next we will discuss some other considerations that are applied in evaluating permanent partial disability systems. Finally we will consider some possible recommendations.

8.5.2 Impairment Rating

In a pure impairment state an assessment would be made of the extent of the worker's physical or mental impairment at the time of maximum medical improvement. The assessment would be made by physicians and would be based entirely upon the physical or functional limitations that resulted from the injury. These might include factors such as the limitation of motion in the back or a limb, or a measurable assessment of the capacity of the heart or lungs. It would not include vocational factors such as the worker's age, the type of work performed, or the education or skill of the worker.

The impairment is generally expressed as a percentage. This might be a percentage of a whole person or of a specific body part. The percentage is then most often translated into a specified number of weeks of benefits. In many states some arbitrary number of weeks is established as the value of a "whole person." Individual impairments are then assessed as a percentage of the whole person. For example, if a state sets 800 weeks as the period of payment for a whole person, the loss of an arm might be rated as 25 percent of a whole person and a worker who suffered such a loss would receive benefits for 200 weeks.

Sometimes this is stated differently. It is said that each percentage point of disability is worth so many weeks of benefits. For example, each point of disability might entitle the worker to three weeks of benefits.

Sometimes the whole person concept is applied only to injuries such as heart disease; for other injuries it is said that specified body parts are valued at a certain numbers of weeks and the losses are measured against those criteria. For example, in Missouri, the hand is rated at 175 weeks. The loss of a hand results in the payment of benefits for that number of weeks. A lesser injury that resulted in a 50 percent loss of use of a hand would result in benefits for 87.5 weeks (175 × ½).

A couple of features of an impairment system should be noted. Under such a system, Ms. B would receive the same benefits regardless of whether she was a concert pianist who now could never return to her prior work or a radio announcer who is able to return to full employment shortly following the injury.

An impairment system creates an incentive for the employee to return to work. A worker with an impairment rating can receive full workers' compensation benefits and earn full wages. There is not, however, any incentive for the employer to offer a job to the worker. The employer will have to pay impairment benefits regardless of whether the worker returns to work.

8.5.3 Wage-Loss Systems

At the opposite extreme from an impairment rating is a wage-loss system. In a pure wage-loss system, the benefits are based entirely upon the extent of the worker's wage-loss. Benefits are ordinarily paid weekly and the amount of the wage-loss is assessed retrospectively. The payment could potentially be adjusted each week. So long as there is a wage-loss related to a compensable injury, benefits are paid and no assessment is made of the degree of physical or functional impairment.

Assume Mr. D was a heavy laborer who injured his back. After a period of recovery, it is determined that he will always have some difficulty and will never be able to return to all of the duties he formerly performed. Assume further that he was earning $600 per week at the time of his injury. So long as he did not return to work, he would receive weekly benefits. In the most common situation these would be $400 per week ($600 × ⅔). In some states, such as Michigan, these benefits could continue for the rest of his life. If for a period of time he returns to work, say, earning $400 per week, his benefits would be based on his wage loss of $200 per week ($600 − $400), and would be paid at the rate of $133.33 ($200 × ⅔).

A couple of aspects of wage-loss systems should be pointed out here. Assume Ms. E and Ms. F suffer exactly the same back injury, which results in permanent limitations. Assume further that Ms. E was a heavy laborer and is never able to return to significant employment and that Ms. F is a human resource manager who returns to work after only a few weeks. Ms. E will receive life-long benefits, while Ms. F will receive benefits for only a few weeks. This will be true even though Ms. F may continue to suffer pain for the rest of her life, may be unable to play golf or go bowling, or even lift her children. Her benefits will be based entirely on her wage-loss.

A wage-loss system does not in itself create an incentive for workers to return to work. In fact, since benefits are paid only for a wage-loss there is an incentive for workers to prolong their period of disability. Wage-loss systems deal with this by providing that if a worker refuses a job offer, benefits are reduced or terminated. This in turn creates a strong incentive for employers to offer jobs to the injured worker. If the employer offers work and the worker accepts it, the employer is now receiving work in return for wages rather than paying workers' compensation benefits. If the worker refuses the offer, benefits can be terminated. Of course, there are often disputes whether the offer is reasonable and whether the work is within the worker's physical capacity. Nevertheless this incentive for return to work with the original employer is one of the strongest advantages of a wage-loss system.

8.5.4 Loss of Wage-Earning Capacity

Loss of wage-earning capacity is a concept that is used to modify the extremes of both impairment and wage-loss systems.

In an impairment system, the concept of loss of wage-earning capacity adds the consideration of vocational factors to the assessment of the degree of an impairment. Many states, such as California, start with an assessment of the amount of physical impairment, but modify this by vocational factors, such as the worker's education, skill, age, and the relationship of the particular impairment to the kind of work the person was performing. Thus, if Ms. G suffered an injury to her back that prevented her from doing heaving lifting, she would be given a higher impairment rating if she was a dock hand unloading trucks than if she was a file clerk. Virtually all impairment states give some weight to vocational factors. Some systems give more weight to these factors than others, and some do it explicitly as part of the statute or by a formula, while others include these in an informal or subjective manner.

Commentators sometimes create two categories: one termed *impairment states* and another termed *loss of wage-earning capacity states*. Ordinarily, under such a categorization, they mean that in both cases an assessment is made of the worker's disability and benefits are paid for a fixed number of weeks regardless of whether or not the individual returns to work. In one category, however, physical or mental limitations are the overriding criteria. In the other, physical limitations are explicitly modified by vocational factors.

In wage-loss states the concept of wage-earning capacity is also sometimes used to soften the extreme cases. In many wage-loss states, an employer can establish that an individual has a certain wage-earning capacity even though he or she has no actual wages. In this situation, if the worker's loss of wage-earning capacity is less than the actual wage-loss, benefits are based on the loss of wage-earning capacity.

For example, assume Mr. H was a heavy laborer earning $500 per week at the time he was injured. As a result of his injury, he now cannot perform heavy work but can perform a variety of medium and light duty jobs. In a pure wage-loss system, his benefits should be based upon a wage-loss of $500 per week unless he actually receives earnings. Suppose, however, that his employer can establish by credible testimony that Mr. H has the capacity to perform a variety of jobs which would pay $300 per week. In other words, he has a wage-earning capacity of $300 per week and a loss of wage-earning capacity of only $200 per week ($500 − $300). Many wage-loss states would hold that his benefits should be based upon a wage-loss of only $200 per week.

States vary a great deal in what factors are taken into consideration in determining the wage-earning capacity. The most difficult question here is the extent to which general economic factors will be taken into account. For example, why is it that Mr. H is not earning $300 per week? Are there actual jobs for which he would be hired or are there only a few such jobs with a great many people competing for them? Is he simply too lazy to go out and get a job, or is there some general economic downturn such that he has no real prospect of being hired? States that use loss of wage-earning capacity to limit the application of the wage-loss principle vary in the ways they answer these questions.

Some wage-loss states require that the worker demonstrate that he or she has performed a "job search." By this it is meant that the worker can obtain wage-loss benefits only if it is shown that he or she has attempted to obtain work and has been unable to do so because of the injury. States vary a great deal in how strictly they enforce this requirement.

8.6 Factors to be Considered

8.6.1 In General

In examining the operation of a state's workers' compensation system, or in comparing various systems, there are certain factors that commentators usually consider. These will be discussed below.

8.6.2 What Is It We Wish to Compensate?

As discussed earlier, there is a tradeoff in the workers' compensation system. Workers are guaranteed the right to recover some benefits regardless of who was at fault. In return, workers give up the right to some damages for which an employer might otherwise be liable. The general formulation is that we should compensate a person for the work-related consequences of an injury, but not for the personal or social consequences.

If an individual loses wages as a result of an industrial injury, there is no doubt that he or she should be compensated, at least to some extent, for that wage loss. At the same time, if a worker experiences pain and suffering as a result of an industrial injury, it is generally agreed that a workers' compensation system should not provide compensation for the pain and suffering.

The above extremes appear obvious, but there are many more subtle situations in between. Assume Mr. P is a laborer and suffers the loss of both legs. Clearly, he will be entitled to a very large payment of compensation benefits. In many states, he might receive benefits for the rest of his life. Suppose, however, that he was a clerk and that he returned to work in a few months. What should be his compensation? If we are limited to the job-related consequences of the injury, this person has suffered only a few months of wage loss and his compensation will be limited to a percentage of that loss. This, however, seems like very little compensation for such a serious injury.

One way to deal with this is by paying compensation for the physical impairment that results from the injury. The clerk in the example above suffered a serious impairment and thus should receive substantial compensation even though there was only a small wage loss. In fact, as discussed in section 8.6.7 below, nearly all states pay at least some benefits based on the physical impairment, and for many jurisdictions physical impairment is the primary means of determining compensation.

While it can be argued that it is appropriate under some circumstances, such as an amputation, to compensate a worker for the physical impairment, purists would argue that compensation should be based more directly on the work-related consequences of the injury. This leads to a conclusion that a wage-loss type of system is more appropriate because the benefits are more directly related to the worker's wage-loss.

Defenders of the impairment approach counter by saying that impairment ratings are used merely because they are a convenient way of measuring or predicting the wage loss. They argue that in an impairment-based system, the impairment rating is a "proxy" for the wage loss, which is the true basis for compensation.

8.6.3 Prospective Versus Retrospective

Ordinarily, impairment determinations are made prospectively. In a purely prospective system, an assessment of the degree of impairment is made at the time of maximum medical improvement and the person's benefits are fixed as of that date. They are usually paid in weekly installments, but the amount and duration is fixed as of a specific date.

Wage-loss systems, on the other hand, are necessarily retrospective to the extent that payment is for actual lost wages that can be determined only after the expiration of the specified period. Workers' compensation benefits are ordinarily paid weekly. It is possible in a retrospective wage-loss system that the rate of benefits would vary each week. A worker who still suffers some disability and returns to limited duty might have a varying wage rate for a number of different reasons: he or she might return to a piece-work job where the rates vary under ordinary circumstances; the remaining effects of the disability may cause the worker to become easily fatigued; the worker might not be able to work full-time and thus work a varying number of hours each week; or the light duty job created for the worker might be one that is not always available and thus the hours available to the worker might vary from week to week. In these cases the worker reports his or her earnings each week and the carrier calculates the difference between those wages and the preinjury wages and pays the appropriate percentage. It should be pointed out, however, that these cases are the exception. The majority of individuals who receive permanent partial disability benefits in a wage-loss system are, in fact, not working at all. In these cases the compensation rate is the appropriate percentage of the preinjury average weekly wage and does not vary from week to week.

As with everything else in this area, there are variations from purely prospective and purely retrospective systems. Many states have a prospective system, but allow for a "reopening" of the claims under various circumstances. Thus, the degree of impairment may be established shortly after the point of maximum medical improvement, but either of the parties may reopen a case at some time in the future. As discussed in subsection 8.6.6, to whatever extent a system allows reopenings, it is not a purely prospective system.

8.6.4 Schedules

Most states have some *schedule of impairments*. This is a listing of disabilities and the compensation payable for each. Losses on the schedule are paid accordingly, while all other losses are compensated in some other fashion as *nonscheduled losses*. A number of states provide that a person can receive both scheduled and nonscheduled benefits for the same injury.

Generally, the schedule specifies a certain number of weeks for each loss. For example, a statute might specify that the loss of an arm entitles the worker to benefits for 250 weeks. Schedules generally cover arms, hands, fingers, legs, feet, toes, sight, and sometimes hearing. California, however, has a schedule that purports to cover every possible injury.

Some states limit the application of the schedule to injuries that result in either the amputation or the total "loss of use" of the scheduled part, while others apply it to any injury to that part. The amputation of an arm would always be treated as a scheduled injury. An injury that did not cause an amputation, but which was so severe as to render an arm useless, would nearly always be treated this way also. Jurisdictions differ, however, in how they treat a worker who suffers an injury to his or her elbow, which now limits the extent to which he or she can use the arm. Some, such as Michigan, would treat this as a nonscheduled injury, while others, such as Missouri, would assess the extent to which this resulted in a loss of use of the arm.

8.6.5 Impairment Rating "Guidelines"

In states such as Missouri the parties often complain that there is a lack of consistency among the impairment ratings given by physicians. They claim that different physicians or physicians in different parts of the state give different ratings to the same injury. In order to avoid this situation, many states publish "guidelines" that are designed to standardize the way in which physicians rate impairments. The theory is that if all physicians follow the published guidelines, ratings will be fair and consistent.

Some states, such as Wisconsin, publish their own guidelines for physicians. Other states, such as Maryland, have adopted a set of *Guides to the Evaluation of Permanent Impairment*, published by the American Medical Association.[2]

A recent study by Leslie Bowden of the WCRI points out that while the AMA guides may be a step toward objectivity and consistency, they do not in themselves guarantee this result.[3]

8.6.6 Settlements and Reopenings

The degree to which a state permits settlements and reopenings can greatly affect the nature of the system. Consider a state that grants a 20 percent impairment rating to Mr. Q because he is considered severely disabled, and a 5 percent impairment rating to Ms. R because her injury is considered minor. Assume that two years later Mr. Q is in fact gainfully employed at no wage loss, and that Ms. R has a disability that is much more severe than originally thought. If the state allows Mr. Q's employer to reopen the case and terminate the payment of impairment ratings and allows Ms. R to reopen her case and have her rating adjusted upward, the state is in fact considering their actual wage loss as opposed to purely their impairment rating in determining benefits.

As discussed in subsection 8.7.6, Michigan claims to be a pure wage-loss state, but in fact a very large percentage of permanent partial disability claims are settled by the payment of a single lump-sum benefit, which in practice closely resembles impairment ratings paid in other states.

Procedures concerning reopenings and settlements are discussed in more detail in sections 12.5 and 21.6. At this point it will suffice to say that these considerations must be examined when attempting to answer the question of how a state compensates disability.

8.6.7 Variations and Combinations

No state has a pure system. Rather, all states modify the extreme approaches at least to some extent and many employ a combination of approaches. As will be seen in the examples in section 8.7, even states such as Missouri and Michigan, which in theory have rather pure impairment and wage-loss systems, respectively, allow for a softening of these approaches through compromise settlements. Other states, such as Wisconsin and New York, pay one type of benefits under some circumstances and a different type of benefit under others.

A few states, such as Massachusetts, allow a worker to receive both impairment and wage-loss benefits for the same injury, while other states, such as Texas and Maine, allow multiple benefits, but limit them to severe injuries with an impairment rating over some figure, such as 15 percent.

Finally, it should be remembered that permanent partial benefits are nearly always combined with temporary total benefits. Usually temporary total benefits are paid first until the medical condition stabilizes and the worker reaches maximum medical improvement. They are then followed by permanent partial benefits. In most states the permanent partial benefits are paid in addition to temporary total benefits, but a few, such as Kansas and Louisiana, deduct the temporary benefits from the permanent award.

8.7 Examples

The preceding sections have discussed the basic alternatives that are used for compensating permanent partial disability and some of the concepts that are used to describe these systems. It may be helpful to provide here a few examples of the way states actually compensate workers with permanent partial disabilities.

A word of caution is in order. The examples below are intended to be just that, examples of the various alternatives that can be used. It is beyond the scope of this chapter to present a detailed description of the system in any individual state. These examples will provide the reader with an understanding of the alternatives that are used. The reader should not, however, consider these rather simplified descriptions as a legal description of how the system functions in the individual states described.

8.7.1 Missouri

Missouri is an impairment state.[4] It has a schedule that covers injuries to the extremities, sight, and hearing. The schedule provides for the number of weeks payable for the loss of each such body part.

For example, the loss of a hand is listed for 175 weeks. If Ms. J was earning $400 per week and suffered an injury to her hand that resulted in a 25 percent loss of use of her hand, she would receive benefits at the rate of $266.67 ($400 × ⅔) per week for 43.75 weeks (175 × .25). The rating would be made and the period of payment would start after Ms. J reached the point of maximum medical improvement.

For *nonscheduled* injuries, that is, injuries to parts of the body not included on the list, Missouri asks physicians to rate the extent of the impairment as compared to the body as a whole. A whole person is rated at 400 weeks. Thus if Ms. K was earning $400 per week and had a severe back injury that resulted in an impairment equal to 15 percent of a whole person, she would receive benefits at the rate of $266.67 per week for 60 weeks (400 × .15).

Missouri is an example of a state that in theory applies a pure impairment approach, but seems unable to adhere to this extreme in practice. Ballantyne and Telles report that physicians do seem to take into consideration factors such as the age, education, and occupation of the injured worker when determining the extent of the impairment, even though the statute does not specify that they should.[5] This is facilitated by the fact that the vast majority of all permanent partial cases are resolved through an agreed upon lump-sum settlement rather than a decision by the state agency or courts.

8.7.2 *Wisconsin*

Wisconsin is a state that quite intentionally compensates benefits based on the degree of impairment under some circumstances and based on the loss of wage-earning capacity under other circumstances.[6] Workers who are rehired by the former employer at 85 percent or more of their preinjury wages receive *functional impairment* benefits, while workers who do not return to work, or who return to work at lower wages, receive higher, *earning capacity* benefits.

Functional impairment benefits are based on the amount of physical impairment. The rating is made by a physician according to guidelines published by the Wisconsin Workers' Compensation Division. The rating method is similar to that discussed above for Missouri except that the presence of detailed guidelines tends to result in more uniformity among physicians making ratings.

The rating of loss of earning capacity is usually done by vocational experts who consider not only the physical impairment, but also the worker's age, education, training, work experience, previous earnings, and the likelihood of future employment. There are no guidelines for the evaluation of earning capacity.

Ballantyne and Telles provide an example of a worker with a preinjury wage of $400 per week in 1992. If the worker returns to work at $340 or more per week (85 percent of $400), he or she receives only impairment benefits. Assuming a back injury with an impairment rating of 5 percent, the worker would be entitled to 50 weeks (5 percent of 1,000 weeks for the whole body) at the maximum weekly amount in 1992 of $144 for a total of $7,200. If, however, the worker did not return to work or returned to work at a lower wage, the same worker would likely receive a lost earning capacity rating of 25 percent. This would entitle the worker to benefits at the rate of $144 for 250 weeks (1,000 × . 25), which would result in a total payment of $36,000.

This duality in the payment formula results in a strong incentive for employers to offer jobs to injured workers. This is cited by

Table 8.1. Weeks of Permanent Partial Disability per Percentage of Disability in California

Range of Percentage of Permanent Disability Incurred	Number of Weeks of Benefits for Each Percentage of Disability Within Percentage Range
Under 10	3
10–19.75	4
20–24.75	5
25–29.75	6
30–49.75	7
50–69.75	8
70–79.75	9

Ballantyne and Telles as one of the reasons for the overall success of the Wisconsin workers' compensation system.

8.7.3 California

California is a state that bases all permanent partial benefits on a combined consideration of the extent of physical impairment and vocational factors such as the occupation and age of the injured employee.[7]

California is also a state that has a very broad schedule. The schedule purports to list every conceivable possibility and to indicate a percentage rating that a worker with a given disability should receive. The schedule also indicates formulas to be used in considering the effect of the worker's age and occupation.

The California schedule yields a percentage disability rating. This rating, however, is not directly translated into the number of weeks of benefits. It is felt that such a direct conversion results in the overcompensation of minor disabilities and the undercompensation of more serious disabilities. Accordingly, California pays more weeks of benefits for higher percentage disability ratings. The weeks assigned for the various ratings are listed in Table 8.1. Thus a worker with a 15 percent disability would receive three weeks of benefits for each percentage point under 10 and four weeks of disability for each percentage point between 10 and 15.

8.7.4 New York

New York serves as an example of a state that compensates some disabilities (scheduled losses) on the basis of the physical impairment and other disabilities (nonscheduled losses) on the basis of wage loss.[8] New York is also an example of a state that adjusts a worker's wage-loss benefits based upon a wage-earning capacity.

The schedule covers loss of eyesight, hearing, and the extremities. If a worker suffers this type of injury, the benefits are based upon the degree of physical impairment and paid according to the schedule. Thus, for example, if Ms. L suffered an injury that resulted in 25 percent loss of use of an arm, she would receive benefits for 78 weeks. (An arm is rated at 312 weeks and 78 is 25 percent of 312.) These scheduled benefits are paid regardless of whether the individual returns to work.

A worker who suffers an injury to some other part of his or her body, such as the back, receives wage-loss benefits. If, after reaching maximum medical improvement, he or she is unable to return to work because of the injury, benefits are paid at the rate of two-thirds of the wage loss. If an individual has not returned to work, the rate would be two-thirds of the preinjury earnings. If the worker has returned to work at a lower paying job, the rate is two-thirds of the difference. If the worker has returned to work at a job that pays wages equal to or greater than the preinjury earnings no benefits are paid. (The rate of benefits is, however, limited to the maximum, which is relatively low in New York. It was $400 per week for 1992.)

Benefits for nonscheduled injuries are limited by the individual's wage loss, but may be reduced by the individual's wage-earning capacity. Thus if Mr. M was injured while earning $400 per week and after maximum medical improvement had not returned to work, he might claim that he was entitled to benefits at the rate of $266.67 per week ($400 × ⅔). His employer, however, might be able to demonstrate that considering his physical condition, there were in fact many jobs that he could do which would pay $300 per week. If the judge found that Mr. M had a wage-earning capacity of $300, then his lost wage-earning capacity would only be equal to $100 ($400 − $300) and he would receive benefits at the rate of $66.67 per week.

Wage-loss benefits are payable for up to 18 years.

The situation in New York is further complicated by special benefits for major permanent partial disability. If the worker has an impairment that is greater than 50 percent of the arm, leg, foot, or hand, he or she receives the scheduled benefits based upon that loss and after that benefit is exhausted, may be entitled to receive wage-loss benefits.

8.7.5 Pennsylvania

Pennsylvania is an example of a state that pays nearly all benefits based upon the wage-loss concept and allows for the adjustment of the worker's benefits based on an earning capacity.[9]

Pennsylvania does not use the concept of maximum medical improvement. Instead, short-term and long-term disabilities are compensated in the same manner. If the individual is totally disabled, and has no income, he or she receives two-thirds of the preinjury wages. If the worker has a partial wage loss, he or she receives two-thirds of the difference. Total disability benefits can continue indefinitely, but a worker can receive no more than 500 weeks of partial disability benefits.

As in New York, a worker's benefits may be reduced if he or she has an earning capacity, even if the worker is not actually earning wages.

The one exception to the wage-loss approach in Pennsylvania is a rather limited schedule. As in most states, the schedule includes vision, hearing, and the extremities, but unlike most states, the schedule applies only if there is a total loss or total loss of use of one of these members. In those cases, the worker is paid according to the schedule. In all other cases, Pennsylvania workers are paid wage-loss benefits.

8.7.6 Michigan

Michigan is a state that attempts, according to the theory of its laws, to take a pure wage-loss approach.[10] It is only able to do this, however, by allowing a very high percentage of lump-sum settlements that resemble in many ways payments for impairment or loss of wage-earning capacity.

Like Pennsylvania, Michigan makes no distinction between short-term and long-term disabilities. The use of its schedule is even more restricted, applying only to amputations and loss of sight. All other benefits are paid on the basis of the worker's wage loss. If there is an actual wage loss attributable to the injury, benefits are paid. If there is no wage loss, there are no benefits. Thus assume Ms. N is an unskilled laborer and Mr. O is a human resource manager. Assume further that they each suffer a very severe back injury with permanent residual impairment. If Ms. N because of her occupation and lack of education is never able to return to work, she will receive benefits for the rest of her life. If Mr. O returns to work in five weeks, he will receive benefits for those five weeks and nothing more.

Unlike New York and Pennsylvania, Michigan does not consider a theoretical wage-earning capacity. (Although as this is being written, one case in the Michigan Court of Appeals has indicated that the court may be moving in that direction.[11]) Thus in Michigan, unlike in New York or Pennsylvania, the employer would be precluded from claiming that Ms. N's benefits should be reduced because she has the capacity to earn some estimated amount.

Michigan does allow lump-sum settlements called *redemptions*. It frequently happens that an employer disputes whether the worker continues to be disabled. These cases most often result in a compromise settlement. The compromise is negotiated on the basis of the likelihood that the worker will win and receive lifelong benefits or that the employer will win and the worker will receive no further benefits. But the negotiated payment greatly resembles permanent partial awards paid in states such as Missouri, Wisconsin, and California.

8.7.7 Nevada and Washington

Two states approach permanent partial disability in rather unique ways that deserve mention. In Nevada, an injured worker receives permanent partial disability benefits for five years regardless of the severity of the disability. Instead of varying the length of the payment period, the amount of each payment is adjusted. Each 1 percent of impairment of the whole person is compensated by a monthly payment equal to 0.6 percent of the worker's average monthly wage for a period of five years.

In the state of Washington, a whole person is considered to be worth $90,000 and the worker receives a percentage of that amount equal to the impairment rating. Thus, in Washington, the amount of impairment benefits does not depend on the worker's wages. Everyone's arm is worth the same amount.

8.8 Evaluations and Recommendations

What is the best system? Which combination of these factors is most generous to workers, costs the least, has the best incentives, and most equitably distributes benefits? This author is not about to make a recommendation. That will be left to others who are more daring than I. As discussed in chapter 16, I feel that the opportunity for real long-term improvements in workers' compensation most often lies at the firm and plant level, not in changing a basic system. Nevertheless, there are certainly advantages and disadvantages of the various approaches, and it is not unusual for state legislatures to want to reform their systems. Accordingly, I offer the following brief discussion concerning recommendations for the compensation of permanent partial impairment.

8.8.1 Larson

Arthur Larson has taken the most direct stand. He argued that most workers' compensation statutes were originally wage-loss systems and that the basic purpose of workers' compensation is to compensate the employment-related consequences of an employment-related injury. He argued that the wage-loss approach does this most clearly and directly and is, therefore, the more appropriate system.[12]

8.8.2 Berkowitz and Burton

As mentioned earlier, Monroe Berkowitz and John F. Burton, Jr., have conducted an extensive nationwide study of the way we compensate permanent disability. Their book, *Permanent Disability Benefits in Workers' Compensation*, contains an excellent analysis of the topic, as well as an evaluation of the system used in 10 states.[13]

They agree with Larson that wage loss should be a more important component than it usually is. Unlike Larson, however, they would keep some element of payment for physical impairment. They suggest a hybrid approach that would combine an impairment rating with the wage-loss concept.

Every worker who had at least a minimal permanent partial disability would receive an impairment rating from 1 to 100 percent. Berkowitz and Burton insist that the impairment rating must be made according to some clear guidelines such as the American Medical Association's *Guides to the Evaluation of Permanent Impairment*. They would use guidelines that cover all injuries, not a limited schedule. They would permit, but not insist upon, an adjustment of this schedule for vocational factors such as the worker's age, education, and work experience. If these factors were to be applied, however, they should be applied through an automatic formula, not through the discretion of a judge or rater. Like other commentators, Berkowitz and Burton feel that much of the problem in workers' compensation comes from the uncertainty or inconsistency in evaluation of disability.

After the expiration of impairment benefits, workers would be entitled to receive wage-loss benefits. The authors present a variety of different alternatives for adopting a wage-loss system. They also suggest the possibility that wage-loss benefits should be paid for a limited period of time by the carrier and thereafter assigned to a special fund financed by assessments on all carriers and self-insured employers.

This brief discussion does not do justice to the detailed proposal offered by Berkowitz and Burton. Anyone considering a basic change should examine their proposal in detail. It contains a number of variations on each option and ways in which the recommendations can be adopted to various degrees.

8.8.3 *The National Commission*

The National Commission did not make any specific recommendation for permanent partial disability, but did offer certain suggestions. It seems to suggest that there should be a combination of wage loss and impairment in most cases. In other words, a worker should be paid to some extent for both the employment-related and the non-employment-related consequences of an injury. More important, the payment for these two distinct types of consequences should be distinguished from each other. Thus, an assessment would be made of the physical impairment and a fixed sum paid based on that assessment regardless of when the worker returned to the job. In addition, the worker would be paid benefits based on the actual wage loss, if any, that was attributable to the injury. The right to wage-loss benefits might be limited to cases with an impairment of a certain degree of severity, say 20 percent. (If the National Commission proposal sounds strikingly similar to the Berkowitz-Burton idea, this should not be surprising since Burton was the chair of the Commission and Berkowitz was a consultant to it.)

8.8.4 Welch

The author would add one recommendation of his own. It is not a recommendation for the type of system to adopt, but rather a principle to be applied in designing reforms: the simpler the system, the better.

It is very tempting for consultants and experts to want to take the best elements from various systems already in existence and combine them into an even better system. The recommendations that consultants make to legislatures therefore tend to be rather complicated. The political process necessarily involves compromises and adjustments. This tends to further complicate the system that is enacted. Often the final result is an extremely complicated scheme that is difficult to understand, hard to administer, and needs lawyers to make it function.

If injured workers cannot easily understand their rights, they will turn to attorneys for advice. The more complicated the system, the more likely it is to have loopholes that employers, insurers, and workers will try to take advantage of. This will turn any scheme, no matter how well designed, into a more costly and time-consuming system. Accordingly, my advice is to "Keep it simple."

Notes

1. Berkowitz, Monroe, and Burton, John F., *Permanent Disability Benefits in Workers' Compensation* (Kalamazoo, Mich.: W.E. Upjohn Institute for Employment Research, 1987).

2. *Guides to the Evaluation of Permanent Impairment*, 3d ed. (Chicago: American Medical Association, 1988).
3. Boden, Leslie I., *The AMA Guides in Maryland: An Assessment* (Cambridge: Workers' Compensation Research Institute, 1992).
4. Ballantyne, Duncan S., and Telles, Carol A., *Workers' Compensation in Missouri: Administrative Inventory* (Cambridge: Workers' Compensation Research Institute, 1993); American Ins. Ass'n, *Workers' Compensation Law: State of Missouri* (Washington, D.C.: The American Insurance Association, 1992); Missouri Department of Labor and Industrial Relations, "Missouri Labor Laws and Regulations," *Workers' Compensation*, Vol. 6 (February 1991).
5. Ballantyne and Telles, *supra* note 4, at 24.
6. Ballantyne, Duncan S., and Telles, Carol A., *Workers' Compensation in Wisconsin: Administrative Inventory* (Cambridge: Workers' Compensation Research Institute, 1992), 16.
7. Barth, Peter S., and Telles, Carol A., *Workers' Compensation California: Administrative Inventory* (Cambridge: Workers' Compensation Research Institute, 1992).
8. Ballantyne, Duncan S., and Telles, Carol A., *Workers' Compensation in New York: Administrative Inventory* (Cambridge: Workers' Compensation Research Institute, 1992); American Ins. Ass'n, *Workers' Compensation Law: State of New York* (Washington, D.C.: The American Insurance Association, 1992).
9. Ballantyne, Duncan S., and Telles, Carol A., *Workers' Compensation in Pennsylvania: Administrative Inventory* (Cambridge: Workers' Compensation Research Institute, 1991).
10. Welch, Edward M., *Workers' Compensation in Michigan: Law and Practice* (Ann Arbor: Institute of Continuing Legal Education, 1993).
11. *Sobotka v. Chrysler Corp.*, 198 Mich. App. 455, 499 N.W.2d 777 (1993).
12. Larson §57.
13. Berkowitz and Burton, *supra* note 1.

Chapter 9

Disability Benefits

9.1 Introduction

Chapter 8 discussed how disability is assessed. Once it is determined that a Ms. A has a 50 percent disability or that she is totally disabled, how much does she get each week and for how long? This introduction will provide an overview of these issues and the remainder of the chapter will discuss them in some detail.

There is great variation among the states in the amount and duration of benefits, but in general the same process is used to make the determination. It begins with a determination of the worker's preinjury average weekly wage. A rate or percentage is applied to this to determine the benefit to be paid. Some states have a minimum rate and all have a maximum rate. In some cases the rate may depend on the number of dependents the worker is supporting.

In all states there is a waiting period for workers' compensation benefits. This ranges from three to seven days. The duration of benefits may depend on the type of system employed in the state (whether it is an impairment or wage-loss system) and on other factors.

Some states pay special cost of living allowances and other special benefits. A few states coordinate or reduce workers' compensation benefits based upon the receipt of other benefits.

Death benefits are usually calculated in a way similar to disability benefits. However, the question of dependency is more important in death cases, because if there are no dependents, often only a relatively small burial allowance is paid.

9.2 The Average Weekly Wage

In nearly all states the calculation of benefits begins with an attempt to define the worker's preinjury earnings. This is ordinarily called the average weekly wage. The period of time over which the "average" is calculated varies from state to state. It might be based upon the last 13 weeks, the last 6 months, or the last year. Some statutes use an actual mean for the entire period of time, while others base the calculation upon some formula such as the highest 39 of the last 52 weeks. Most states provide that if a reasonable assessment of the worker's wages cannot be derived by the formula, then the average weekly wage should be determined by reference to other workers performing the same or similar work. "Wages" ordinarily include all remuneration such as tips, bonuses, commissions, room and board, and overtime pay.

Fringe benefits such as contributions to a pension or group insurance plan are ordinarily not included in calculating the average weekly wage, although some states, such as Massachusetts, Michigan, and New York, include them to a limited extent.

If there has been a recent change in the employee's status or earnings, it may not be fair to calculate the average weekly wage based upon a fixed period of time in the past. Assume, for example, that Ms. B had worked as a laborer for most of the preceding year but had been promoted to a supervisor two weeks before her injury at a pay that was substantially higher than for laborers. Many courts would hold that her average weekly wage should be based upon the last two weeks rather than the entire preceding year.

If an employee is working part-time at the time of the injury, states will usually examine whether the part-time status was temporary or permanent and whether or not part-time status was typical for this job or this worker. If it was temporary and the worker ordinarily worked full-time and the job was ordinarily performed on a full-time basis, an adjustment may be made in establishing the average weekly wage.

Seasonal work sometimes presents problems for the calculation of the average weekly wage. Once the average weekly wage is established, the benefit formulas present in almost all acts require the payment for fixed periods of time, regardless of the seasonal nature of the work. However, some states allow an adjustment of the average weekly wage based upon the seasonal nature of the work.

Thus, assume Mr. C performed some seasonal work, such as farm work or construction, and ordinarily only worked six months a year. If he is found to have a certain percentage of disability, he will be entitled to benefits for, say, 200 weeks. These benefits will be paid for consecutive future weeks regardless of the season. If he was injured on the last day of the season and his average weekly wage is calculated over a period of the preceding six months, he will be paid the same benefits as a worker who was ordinarily employed all year long at the same pay rate. If, however, he was injured on the first day of the season, a calculation based upon the preceding six months would yield an exceptionally low average weekly wage. Accordingly, some states make special provisions for the calculation of benefits in the case of seasonal employment.

Questions also arise in the case of concurrent earnings. Assume Ms. D works 40 hours per week on one job and 10 hours per week on another. If she is injured on one of the jobs and cannot work on either, are her preinjury earnings in both jobs included in calculating the average weekly wage? States vary on whether to include the pre-injury wages on both jobs. Some states, such as Arizona and Georgia, include wages on both jobs only if the work was related or similar.[1] Thus, a janitor or night watchman who performed the same job for several establishments would be considered to have similar jobs, while an assembly worker who worked part-time as a life insurance salesperson would not.

A few states base the average weekly wage upon the wages in both jobs, but allow the employer responsible for the payment of benefits to be reimbursed to a certain extent from a special fund. (See section 13.3.)

It should be noted in all this that the goal in establishing an average weekly wage is to make some estimate of the earnings the worker would have received had it not been for the injury. In establishing the proper approach, a balance must be struck between mathematical formulas that are easy to apply, but may occasionally result in an inequity, and statutory provisions that strive for ultimate fairness, but that are difficult to administer and result in litigation.

9.3 The Basic Rate

Once the average weekly wage is determined, the weekly rate is set as a percentage of the average weekly wage. The most common figure is 66⅔ percent of the gross wages.

A few states pay benefits as a percentage (usually 80) of the "spendable earnings."[2] This is a newer approach. All other states base their calculation upon the worker's gross wages. Workers' compensation benefits are not subject to federal income tax (and usually not subject to state income tax). Accordingly, if a worker receives two-thirds of his or her gross income, this results in a figure that is significantly higher than two-thirds of his or her spendable earnings. Furthermore, tax rates are affected in different ways by a variety of factors that are probably not pertinent in determining the amount of workers' compensation benefits. These include things such as the number of dependents, whether one's spouse works, and the income tax bracket applied.

It should be the goal of workers' compensation to provide all workers approximately the same "replacement rate," that is, the same percentage of spendable income without regard to these extraneous factors. Research has demonstrated that a rate based upon a percentage of spendable income does a much better job of this than a rate based upon a percentage of gross wages.[3]

On the other hand, it is relatively easy to calculate the amount of gross earnings. The amount of spendable income is more difficult to determine. Ordinarily, this is done by adopting a series of tables published by the state agency which are by statute conclusive in determining the after-tax value for a worker with a given number of dependents at any specified wage rate. These tables must be generated each year. The result is a much more cumbersome process than a computation based upon gross wages.

A few states allow for a small increase in disability benefits if the worker has a dependent spouse or children.[4]

In most states the rate is the same for temporary total, permanent partial, and permanent total disability. See Table 9.1 (at pp. 110–11).

Nevada takes a unique approach to the rate of benefits for permanent partial disability. Whereas most states set the rate as a percentage of the worker's average weekly wage and vary the duration based upon the extent of disability, Nevada pays all permanent partially disabled workers for five years (or until age 70 if that occurs first), but varies the rate depending upon the extent of disability. Each 1 percent of impairment of a whole person entitles the worker to 6 percent of his or her average monthly wage.

9.4 Maximums and Minimums

Many states set a minimum level of benefits and all jurisdictions set a maximum level. Most often the maximums are established as a percentage of the state's average weekly wage for the preceding given year. In most states the maximum weekly compensation rate is equal to 100 percent of the state's average weekly wage or the average wage of all workers in the state. Table 9.2 (at pp. 112–14) lists the weekly maximum amount and the maximum as a percentage of the state's average weekly wage.

This does not mean that there is a cost of living adjustment in these states. It means instead that the maximum benefit for injuries occurring in a specific year is set based upon the state's average weekly wage at that time. Workers with injuries in prior years ordinarily do not receive increases. (See the discussion of cost of living allowances in section 9.8.)

Not all states have a minimum. Many states that do provide that the worker shall receive either the minimum amount or his or her average weekly wage, whichever is lower. Thus, if a state's minimum rate was $50 per week and Ms. E was earning $60 per week at the time of her injury, 66⅔ percent would give her a rate of $40 per week. However, the minimum would entitle her to $50 per week. If, however, her average weekly wage was only $25 per week, she would receive $25 as her benefit rate. Table 9.3 (at pp. 116–19) summarizes provisions governing minimum rates.

9.5 Commencement of Benefits

No jurisdiction allows the payment of benefits from the first day of disability. Instead, there is ordinarily a waiting period before any benefits are paid and then an additional period after which benefits are retroactively paid to the first day.

For example, a statute might provide that the worker does not receive any benefits for the first three days. If disability extends beyond the third day, he or she begins receiving benefits on the fourth day. If disability extends beyond ten days, then the employer must retroactively pay benefits for the first three days. The original waiting periods run from three to seven days and the extended period after which benefits are retroactively paid to the first day ranges from five days to four weeks. See Table 9.4 (at pp. 120–21).

9.6 Duration of Benefits

The duration of benefits depends on the type of benefit and the nature of the system used. Temporary total disability benefits ordinarily extend until the worker reaches maximum medical improvement. (See section 8.3.) As can be seen from Table 9.5 (at pp. 122–23), however, many states place a maximum limit on the number of weeks during which a worker may receive temporary total disability benefits.

As discussed in chapter 8, duration of benefits for permanent partial disability depends on the nature of the system used. In an impairment system, duration is usually adjusted to reflect the extent of the disability. (See subsection 8.5.2.) In a wage-loss system, benefits are ordinarily paid for as long as the worker is disabled (see subsection 8.5.3), but some states put a maximum limit on the number of weeks for which a worker may receive wage-loss benefits. Table 9.5 includes a listing of the maximum period for which a worker may receive benefits for a nonscheduled injury in an impairment state or for wage-loss benefits in a wage-loss state.

In most but not all states, benefits for permanent total disability are payable for life. Table 9.5 also lists the maximum duration of benefits for permanent total disability.

Table 9.1 Benefit Rates

| Jurisdiction | Percent of Worker's Wage | | |
	Temporary Total	Permanent Partial	Permanent Total
Alabama	66⅔	66⅔	66⅔
Alaska	80% SE	see note 1	80% SE
Arizona	66⅔	55	66⅔
Arkansas	66⅔	66⅔	66⅔
California	66⅔	66⅔	66⅔
Colorado	66⅔		66⅔
Connecticut	75% SE	75% SE	75% SE
Delaware	66⅔	66⅔	66⅔
District of Columbia	66⅔ or 80% SE, whichever is less	66⅔	66⅔ or 80% SE, whichever is less
Florida	66⅔	see note 2	66⅔
Georgia	66⅔	66⅔	66⅔
Hawaii	66⅔	66⅔	66⅔
Idaho	67	67	67
Illinois	66⅔	60	66⅔
Indiana	66⅔	66⅔	66⅔
Iowa	80% SE	80% SE	80% SE
Kansas	66⅔	66⅔	66⅔
Kentucky	66⅔	66⅔	66⅔
Louisiana	66⅔	66⅔	66⅔
Maine	80% of worker's after-tax earnings	80% of worker's after-tax earnings	80% SE
Maryland	66⅔	66⅔	66⅔
Massachusetts	60	60% of the difference between employee's AWW before injury and AWW after injury	66⅔
Michigan	80% SE	80% SE	80% SE
Minnesota	66⅔	66⅔	66⅔
Mississippi	66⅔	66⅔	66⅔
Missouri	66⅔	66⅔	66⅔
Montana	66⅔	66⅔ see note 3	66⅔
Nebraska	66⅔	66⅔	66⅔
Nevada	66⅔		66⅔
New Hampshire	66⅔	66⅔	66⅔
New Jersey	70	70	70
New Mexico	66⅔	66⅔	66⅔
New York	66⅔	66⅔	66⅔
North Carolina	66⅔	66⅔	66⅔
North Dakota	66⅔		66⅔
Ohio	72% for first 12 weeks; thereafter 66⅔%	see note 4	66⅔

continued

Table 9.1—*continued*

Jurisdiction	Percent of Worker's Wage		
	Temporary Total	Permanent Partial	Permanent Total
Oklahoma	70	70	70
Oregon	66⅔	66⅔	66⅔
Pennsylvania	66⅔	66⅔	66⅔
Rhode Island	75% SE	75% SE	75% SE
South Carolina	66⅔	66⅔	66⅔
South Dakota	66⅔	66⅔ (scheduled); 50 (nonscheduled)	66⅔
Tennessee	66⅔	66⅔	66⅔
Texas	70% of worker's earnings over $8.50 per hour; 75% for all others	70% of worker's earnings over $8.50 per hour; 75% for all others	75
Utah	66⅔	66⅔	66⅔
Vermont	66⅔	66⅔	66⅔
Virginia	66⅔	66⅔	66⅔
Washington	60–75	see note 5	60–75
West Virginia	70	70	70
Wisconsin	66⅔	66⅔	66⅔
Wyoming	66⅔ of actual monthly earnings	66⅔	
FECA	66⅔	66⅔–75	66⅔–75
LHWCA	66⅔	66⅔	66⅔

SE=Spendable Earnings
DOD=Duration of Disability
SAWW=State's Average Weekly Wage
FECA=Federal Employees' Compensation Act
LHWCA=Longshore & Harbor Workers' Compensation Act

[1] *Alaska:* Permanent partial disability benefits are determined by multiplying $135,000 by the employee's percentage of permanent partial impairment of the whole person and is payable in a single lump sum, unless the employee is enrolled in a vocational rehabilitation program. Compensation may not be discounted for any present value considerations.

[2] *Florida:* Section 440.15(3)(b)—Wage loss benefits are based on actual wages lost and are not subject to a minimum. Wage loss is equal to 80% of the difference between 80% of the employee's average monthly wage and the wage employee is able to earn after reaching maximum medical improvement, provided the monthly wage loss benefits shall not exceed 66⅔% of the employee's average monthly wage at the time of injury.

[3] *Montana:* Section 39-71-703—Wage loss benefits are determined by multiplying the percentage of impairment by 350 weeks not to exceed a permanent partial disability rating of 100 percent.

[4] *Ohio:* For unscheduled injuries (based on a percentage of PPD), weekly benefits are limited to ⅓ of the SAWW, for a portion of 200 weeks.

[5] *Washington:* Payments based on permanent physical impairment; in event award exceeds three times the State's average monthly wage, employee receives first payment equal to three times the State's average monthly wage with balance in monthly payments per temporary disability schedule plus 8 percent interest per annum on unpaid balance.

Source: State Workers' Compensation Laws, U.S. Department of Labor, Office of Workers' Compensation Programs, January 1994, Tables 6, 7, and 8.

Table 9.2. Maximum Benefits

Jurisdiction	Temporary Total		Permanent Partial		Permanent Total	
	Amount	Percent of SAWW	Amount	Percent of SAWW	Amount	Percent of SAWW
Alabama	$419.00	100	$220.00, see note 1	100	$419.00	110
Alaska	$700.00	N/A	see note 2	N/A	$700.00	N/A
Arizona	$323.10	N/A	$323.10	N/A	$323.10	N/A
Arkansas	$267.00	70	$200.00	N/A	$267.00	70
California	$336.00	66⅔	$148.00 (scheduled)	N/A	$336.00	66⅔
Colorado	$432.25	91	$150.00 (scheduled)	N/A	$432.25	91
			$120.00			
			(nonscheduled)			
Connecticut	$638.00	100	$529.00	100	$638.00	100
Delaware	$339.29	66⅔	$339.29	66⅔	$339.29	66⅔
District of Columbia	$679.17	100	$679.17	100	$679.14	100
Florida	$444.00	100	$444.00	100	$444.00	100
Georgia	$250.00	N/A	$250.00	N/A	$250.00	N/A
Hawaii	$481.00	100	$481.00	100	$481.00	100
Idaho	$351.00	90	$214.50	55	$351.00	90
Illinois	$712.92	133⅓	$384.73	N/A	$712.92	133⅓
Indiana	$394.00	N/A	$394.00	N/A	$394.00	N/A
Iowa	$797.00	200	$733.00	184	$797.00	200
Kansas	$313.00	75	$313.00	75	$313.00	75
Kentucky	$415.94	100	$311.96	75	$415.94	100
Louisiana	$319.00	75	$319.00	75	$319.00	75
Maine	$441.00	90	$441.00	90	$441.00	90

continued

State						
Maryland	$510.00	100	$383.00 (serious cases—250 weeks or more) $170.00 (nonserious cases—75 to 249 weeks) $94.20 (minor nonserious cases—1 to 74 weeks)	75 / 33⅓	$510.00	100
Massachusetts	$565.94	100	$424.46	75	$565.94	100
Michigan	$475.00	90	$475.00	90	$475.00	90
Minnesota	$508.20	105	$508.20	105	$508.20	105
Mississippi	$243.75	66⅔	$243.75	66⅔	$243.75	66⅔
Missouri	$470.06	105	$246.22	55	$470.06	105
Montana	$362.00	100	$181.00	50	$362.00	100
Nebraska	$265.00	N/A	$265.00	N/A	$265.00	N/A
Nevada	$432.39	100	$432.39	100	$432.39	100
New Hampshire	$709.50	150	$709.50	150	$709.50	150
New Jersey	$460.00	75	$460.00	75	$460.00	75
New Mexico	$333.02	85	$333.02	85	$333.02	85
New York	$400.00	N/A	$400.00	N/A	$400.00	N/A
North Carolina	$466.00	110	$466.00	110	$466.00	110
North Dakota	$358.00	100	$358.00	100	$358.00	100
Ohio	$482.00	100	$482.00	100	$482.00	100
Oklahoma	$307.00	75	$205.00	50	$307.00	75
Oregon	$478.95	100	$478.95	100	$478.95	100
Pennsylvania	$493.00	100	$493.00	100	$493.00	100
Rhode Island	$463.00	100	$463.00 (nonscheduled) $90 (scheduled)	100	$463.00	100
South Carolina	$410.26	100	$410.26	100	$410.26	100
South Dakota	$338.00	100	$338.00	100	$338.00	100
Tennessee	$355.97	N/A	$355.97	N/A	$355.97	N/A
Texas	$464.00	100	$325.00	70	$464.00	100

Table 9.2—continued

Jurisdiction	Temporary Total		Permanent Partial		Permanent Total	
	Amount	Percent of SAWW	Amount	Percent of SAWW	Amount	Percent of SAWW
Utah	$413.00	100	$275.00	66⅔	$351.00	85
Vermont	$644.00	150	$644.00	150	$644.00	150
Virginia	$451.00	100	$451.00	100	$451.00	100
Washington	$517.16	105% of state's monthly wage	see note 3	N/A	$517.16	105% of state's monthly wage
West Virginia	$420.33	100	$280.22	66⅔	$420.33	100
Wisconsin	$466.00	100	$158.00	N/A	$466.00	100
Wyoming	$413.00	100% of monthly wage	$275.00	66⅔% of monthly wage	$275.00	66⅔ of monthly wage
FECA	$1,248.88	See notes	$1,248.88	N/A	$1,248.88	N/A
LHWCA	$738.30	200% of NAWW	$738.30	200% of NAWW	$738.30	200% of NAWW

SE=Spendable Earnings
DOD=Duration of Disability
SAWW=State's Average Weekly Wage
NAWW=National Average Weekly Wage
FECA=Federal Employees' Compensation Act
LHWCA=Longshore & Harbor Workers' Compensation Act

[1] *Alabama:* Section 25-5-57—In case a scheduled permanent partial disability follows or accompanies a period of temporary total disability resulting from the same injury, the period of TTD shall not be deducted from the maximum number of weeks set for such partial disability; in case of nonscheduled PPD, such periods shall be deducted.

[2] *Alaska:* Permanent partial disability benefits are determined by multiplying $135,000 by the employee's percentage of permanent partial impairment of the whole person and is payable in a single lump sum, unless the employee is enrolled in a vocational rehabilitation program. Compensation may not be discounted for any present value considerations.

[3] *Washington:* Payments based on permanent physical impairment; in event award exceeds three times the State's average monthly wage, employee receives first payment equal to three times the State's average monthly wage with balance in monthly payments per temporary disability schedule plus 8 percent interest per annum on unpaid balance.

Source: State Workers' Compensation Laws, U.S. Department of Labor, Office of Workers' Compensation Programs, January 1994, Tables 6, 7, and 8.

9.7 Death Benefits

Table 9.6 (at pp. 124–140) summarizes death benefits paid by the various jurisdictions if a worker dies as the result of a work-related injury. Many states pay death benefits until a widow or widower remarries, at which point benefits ordinarily stop. Some, however, provide for the payment of a fixed amount or "dowry" at the time of remarriage. Most often this is an amount equal to two years of benefit payments. In addition, all states provide for the payment of a burial allowance in fatal cases. This ranges from $700 to $7,500. See Table 9.7 (at pp. 142–43).

Death benefits payable to children are ordinarily paid until the children reach age 18. Some states provide for payments indefinitely if the child is physically or mentally disabled.

If a worker dies and leaves no dependents, then ordinarily no death benefits other than the burial allowance are owing. Some states require employers to make a payment into a special fund in such cases.

9.8 Cost of Living Allowances

One of the biggest complaints of workers and organized labor is that workers' compensation programs rarely provide any protection against the effects of inflation. A worker's benefits are based on the wages he or she was receiving at the time of injury. One researcher has demonstrated that in the case of young workers with a long-term disability this means that as time goes by they receive a smaller and smaller portion of what they would have earned had they not been injured.[5] This results from two factors: (1) workers generally progress to higher paying jobs as time goes on and (2) inflation results in higher wages for all jobs.

Thus, a worker who is permanently and totally disabled is paid a benefit that is carefully calculated to represent an appropriate percentage of his or her wage at the time of the injury. As time goes by, however, the worker's former co-workers progress to higher paying jobs and the new people on the old job receive cost of living increases while his or her compensation rate remains fixed at a rate based on wages earned at the time of the injury.

Table 9.3. Minimum Benefits

Jurisdiction	Temporary Total	Permanent Partial	Permanent Total
Alabama	$115-27½% of SAWW, or worker's average wage if less.	$115-27½% of SAWW, or worker's average wage if less, for scheduled injuries.	$115-27½% of SAWW, or worker's average wage if less.
Alaska	$110, or $154 if employee shows proof of wages, or worker's spendable weekly wage if less.	$110, or $154 if employee shows proof of wages, or worker's spendable weekly wage if less.	$110, or $154 if the employee shows proof of wages, or worker's spendable weekly wage if less.
Arizona	Payable, but not statutorily prescribed.	Payable, but not statutorily prescribed.	Payable, but not statutorily prescribed.
Arkansas	$20	$20	$20
California	$126	$70	$126
Colorado			
Connecticut	$127.60-20% of SAWW, or an amount not to exceed 80% of worker's average wage if less.	$50	$127.60-20% of SAWW, or an amount not to exceed 80% of worker's average wage if less.
Delaware	$113.10-22⅔% of SAWW, or actual wage if less.	$113.10-22⅔% of SAWW, or actual wage if less, for scheduled injury.	$113.10-22⅔% of SAWW, or actual wage if less.
District of Columbia	$169.79-25% of SAWW.		$169.79-25% of SAWW.
Florida	$20 or actual wage if less.		$20 or actual wage if less.
Georgia	$25 or average wage if less.	$25 or average wage if less.	$25 or average wage if less.

116

State			
Hawaii	$120-25% of SAWW or worker's average wage if less, but not lower than $38.	$120-25% of SAWW, or worker's average wage if less, but not lower than $38.	$120-25% of SAWW, or worker's average wage if less, but not lower than $38.
Idaho	$175.50-45% of SAWW.		$175.50-45% of SAWW.
Illinois	$100.90 to $124.30 or worker's average wage if less, according to number of dependents.	$80.90-$96.90 or worker's average wage if less, according to number of dependents.	$267.35-50% of SAWW.
Indiana	$50 or worker's average wage if less.	Payable, but not statutorily prescribed.	$50 or worker's average wage if less.
Iowa	$139-35% of SAWW, or actual wage if less.	$132-35% of SAWW, or actual wage if less.	$139-35% of SAWW, or actual wage if less.
Kansas	$25		$25
Kentucky	$83.19-20% of SAWW.	Payable, but not statutorily prescribed.	$83.19-20% of SAWW.
Louisiana	$85-20% of SAWW, or actual wage if less.	Payable, but not statutorily prescribed.	$85-20% of SAWW, or actual wage if less.
Maine			
Maryland	$50 or actual wage if less.	$50 or actual wage if less.	$50 or worker's average wage if less.
Massachusetts	$113.19-20% of SAWW, or worker's average wage if less.	Payable, but not statutorily prescribed.	$113.19-20% of SAWW, or worker's average wage if less.
Michigan		$131.82-25% of SAWW for scheduled injury only.	$131.82-25% of SAWW.
Minnesota	$96.80-20% of SAWW or actual wage if less.	Payable, but not statutorily prescribed.	$96.80-20% of SAWW or actual wage if less.
Mississippi	$25		$25
Missouri	$40	$40	$40

continued

Table 9.3—*continued*

Jurisdiction	Temporary Total	Permanent Partial	Permanent Total
Montana	Payable, but not statutorily prescribed.	Payable, but not statutorily prescribed.	Payable, but not statutorily prescribed.
Nebraska	$49 or actual wage if less.	$49 or actual wage if less for scheduled injuries.	$49 or actual wage if less.
Nevada		Payable, but not statutorily prescribed.	
New Hampshire	$189.20-40% of SAWW not to exceed employee's after-tax earnings.	$189.20-40% of SAWW, not to exceed employee's after-tax earnings.	$189.20-40% of SAWW not to exceed employee's after-tax earnings.
New Jersey	$123-20% of SAWW.	$123-20% of SAWW.	$123-20% of SAWW.
New Mexico	$36 or actual wage if less.	$36 or actual wage if less for scheduled injuries.	$36 or actual wage if less.
New York	$40 or actual wage if less.	$40 or actual wage if less.	$40 or actual wage if less.
North Carolina	$30	$30 for scheduled injuries.	$30
North Dakota	$215-60% of SAWW, or employee's actual wage if less.		$215-60% of SAWW, or employee's actual wage if less, unless claimant has received PTD payments for more than 10 years.
Ohio	$160.00-33⅓% of SAWW or actual wage if less.		$241-50% of SAWW, or actual wage if less.
Oklahoma	$30 or actual wage if less.	$30 or actual wage if less.	$30 or actual wage if less.
Oregon	$50 or 90% of actual wage if less.	$25	$50 or 90% of actual wage if less.
Pennsylvania	$273.80-90% of SAWW, if less.		$273.80-90% of SAWW, if less.
Rhode Island			
South Carolina	$75 or average wage if less.	$75 or average wage if less.	$75 or average wage if less.

118

State			
South Dakota	$169-50% of SAWW, or worker's average wage if less.	$169 or worker's average wage if less.	$169-50% of SAWW, or worker's average wage if less.
Tennessee	$64.80	$64.80	$64.80
Texas	$70-15% of SAWW.	$70-15% of SAWW.	$70-15% of SAWW.
Utah	$45	$45 to $70 according to number of dependents but not more than the employee's AWW.	$45
Vermont	$215-50% of SAWW, or worker's average wage if less.	$215-50% of SAWW, or worker's average wage if less.	$215-50% of SAWW, or worker's average wage if less.
Virginia	$112.75-25% of SAWW, or employee's actual wage if less.	$112.75-25% of SAWW, or actual wage if less for scheduled injuries.	$112.75-25% of SAWW, or employee's actual wage if less.
Washington	$44.05 to $83.81 according to marital status and number of dependents.	Payable, but not statutorily prescribed.	$44.05 to $83.81 according to marital status and number of dependents.
West Virginia	$140.11-33⅓% of SAWW.	$140.11-33⅓% of SAWW.	$140.11-33⅓% of SAWW.
Wisconsin	$30 or actual wage if less.	$30 or actual wage if less.	$30 or actual wage if less.
Wyoming			
FECA	$193.01 or actual wage if less.	$193.01 or actual wage if less.	$193.01 or actual wage if less.
LHWCA	$184.58-50% of NAWW, or worker's actual wage if less.	$184.58-50% of NAWW, or actual wage if less.	$184.58-50% of NAWW, or worker's actual wage if less.

SAWW=State's Average Weekly Wage
NAWW=National Average Weekly Wage
FECA=Federal Employees' Compensation Act
LHWCA=Longshore & Harbor Workers' Compensation Act

Source: State Workers' Compensation Laws, U.S. Department of Labor, Office of Workers' Compensation Programs, January 1994, Tables 6, 7, and 8.

Table 9.4. Waiting Periods

Jurisdiction	Waiting Periods	Retroactive After
Alabama	3 days (TTD only)	21 days
Alaska	3 days	More than 28 days
Arizona	7 days	More than 2 weeks
Arkansas	7 days	2 weeks
California	3 days (TTD only)	14 days
Colorado	3 days	More than 2 weeks
Connecticut	3 days	7 days
Delaware	3 days	7 days, including date of injury
District of Columbia	3 days	More than 14 days
Florida	7 days	21 days or more
Georgia	7 days	21 consecutive days
Hawaii	3 days (TTD only)	10 days
Idaho	5 days	More than 2 weeks
Illinois	3 days (TTD only)	14 days or more
Indiana	7 days (TTD only)	More than 21 days
Iowa	3 days (TTD and PTD)	More than 14 days
Kansas	7 days (TTD and PPD)	3 consecutive weeks
Kentucky	7 days	More than 2 weeks
Louisiana	7 days	6 weeks
Maine	7 days	More than 14 days
Maryland	3 days	More than 14 days
Massachusetts	5 days	5 days
Michigan	7 days	2 weeks
Minnesota	3 days (TTD)	10 days
Mississippi	5 days	14 days
Missouri	3 days	More than 14 days
Montana	6 days	No provision
Nebraska	7 days	6 weeks
Nevada	5 days (temporary disability only)	5 or more cumulative days within a 20-day period

continued

In a wage-loss state an assembler might have to return to work as a sweeper because of a continuing disability. At first, he or she will be paid at a rate carefully designed to represent an appropriate percentage of the difference between the wages of the assembler at the time of the injury and the wages now earned as a sweeper. As time goes by, however, the sweeper receives increased wages based on increases in the cost of living. As a result, the difference between the current wage and the average weekly wage at the time of injury is less and benefits go down. Eventually, the

Table 9.4—*continued*

Jurisdiction	Waiting Periods	Retroactive After
New Hampshire	3 days	14 days or more
New Jersey	7 days	7 days
New Mexico	7 days	4 weeks
New York	7 days	More than 14 days
North Carolina	7 days	More than 21 days
North Dakota	4 days	5 days
Ohio	7 days	2 weeks (payment for waiting period applies only in total disability cases)
Oklahoma	7 days	21 days
Oregon	3 days (TTD only)	14 days
Pennsylvania	7 days	14 days or more
Rhode Island	3 days (TTD only)	More than 2 weeks
South Carolina	7 days	More than 14 days
South Dakota	7 days	7 consecutive days
Tennessee	7 days	14 days
Texas	7 days	4 weeks
Utah	3 days (TTD only)	More than 14 days
Vermont	3 days (total disability only)	10 days
Virginia	7 days	More than 3 weeks
Washington	3 days (TTD)	14 days
West Virginia	3 days	More than 7 days
Wisconsin	3 days	More than 7 days
Wyoming	3 days (TTD only)	More than 8 days
FECA	3 days (TTD only)	More than 14 days
LHWCA	3 days	More than 14 days

FECA=Federal Employees' Compensation Act
LHWCA=Longshore & Harbor Workers' Compensation Act
TTD=Temporary Total Disability
PTD=Permanent Total Disability
PPD=Permanent Partial Disability
Source: State Workers' Compensation Laws, U.S. Department of Labor, Office of Workers' Compensation Programs, January 1994, Table 14.

sweeper job catches up to the wages of the assembler at the time of the injury. At this point benefits stop and the worker receives nothing, even though he or she is still working at a lower paying job because of an industrial disability.

A number of states have some form of cost of living adjustment, but they are all limited to some degree and most are quite restricted. A cost of living allowance must be distinguished from a "flexible maximum" benefit. Many states set the maximum weekly benefit at the state's average weekly wage for the preceding year. In this

Table 9.5. Maximum Duration of Benefits

Jurisdiction	Temporary Total	Nonscheduled Permanent Partial	Permanent Total
Alabama	DOD	300 weeks	DOD
Alaska	DOD		DOD
Arizona	DOD	DOD	Life or DOD
Arkansas	450 weeks	450 weeks	DOD
California	DOD	619.25 weeks	Life
Colorado	DOD	208 weeks	Life
Connecticut	DOD	780 weeks	DOD
Delaware	DOD	300 weeks	DOD
District of Columbia	DOD	DOD	DOD
Florida	104 weeks	364 weeks	DOD
Georgia	400	NA	DOD
Hawaii	DOD	NA	DOD
Idaho	52 weeks, thereafter 67% of SAWW for DOD	500 weeks	52 weeks, thereafter 67% of SAWW for DOD
Illinois	DOD	DOD	Life
Indiana	500 weeks		500 weeks
Iowa	DOD	500 weeks	DOD
Kansas	DOD	415 weeks	DOD
Kentucky	DOD	425 weeks	DOD
Louisiana	DOD	520 weeks	DOD
Maine	DOD	260 weeks; DOD if impairment is in excess of 15%	DOD
Maryland	DOD	DOD	DOD
Massachusetts	156 weeks	260 weeks	156 weeks
Michigan	DOD	DOD	DOD
Minnesota	DOD		Life
Mississippi	450 weeks	450 weeks	450 weeks
Missouri	400 weeks	400 weeks	DOD
Montana	DOD	350 weeks	DOD

continued

122

Table 9.5.—continued

Jurisdiction	Temporary Total	Nonscheduled Permanent Partial	Permanent Total
Nebraska	DOD	300 weeks	DOD
Nevada	DOD	DOD	Life
New Hampshire	DOD	350 weeks	DOD
New Jersey	400 weeks	600 weeks	450 weeks
New Mexico	700 weeks	500 weeks	Life
New York	DOD	DOD	DOD
North Carolina	DOD	300 weeks	DOD
North Dakota	DOD	500 weeks	DOD
Ohio	DOD		Life
Oklahoma	300 weeks	500 weeks	DOD
Oregon	DOD	NA	DOD
Pennsylvania	DOD	500 weeks	DOD
Rhode Island	DOD	DOD	DOD
South Carolina	500 weeks	340 weeks	500 weeks
South Dakota	DOD	DOD	DOD
Tennessee	400 weeks	400 weeks	400 weeks
Texas	104 weeks	401 weeks	Life
Utah	312 weeks	312 weeks	Life
Vermont	DOD	330 weeks	DOD
Virginia	500 weeks	500 weeks	DOD
Washington	DOD		DOD
West Virginia	208 weeks	336 weeks	Life
Wisconsin	DOD	1000 weeks	Life
Wyoming	DOD	NA	257 weeks; benefits may be extended by the district court
FECA	DOD	DOD	DOD
LHWCA	DOD	DOD	DOD

DOD=Duration of Disability; NA=Not Available; FECA=Federal Employees' Compensation Act; LHWCA=Longshore & Harbor Workers' Compensation Act

Source: *State Workers' Compensation Laws*, U.S. Department of Labor, Office of Workers' Compensation Programs, January 1994, Table 6, 7, and 8.

Table 9.6. Death Benefits for Surviving Spouses and Children

| Jurisdiction | Percent of Worker's Wage | | Payments Per Week | | | Maximum Period[1] | Notes |
	Spouse only	Spouse & children	Minimum	Maximum	Percent of SAWW		
Alabama	50	66⅔	$115-27½% of SAWW, or worker's average wage if less.	$419.00	100	500 weeks	
Alaska	80% SE	80% SE	$110, or $154 if employee shows proof of wages, or worker's spendable weekly wage if less.	$700.00	N/A	After 5 and 8 years, a spouse's benefit payments are reduced; and terminated at 10 years unless spouse is permanently and totally disabled or has reached age 52. Children until age 19 or married.	Children receive benefits if full-time students regardless of age for first 4 years. Spouse receives 2-year lump sum upon remarriage. WC benefits subject to offsets under Social Security and an employer pension or profit sharing plan.

continued

124

State					Dependents	Notes
Arizona	35	66⅔	Payable, but not statutorily prescribed.	$145.40-$277.08	N/A	WW; children until 18 or married.	Children receive benefits beyond 18 if physically or mentally disabled, or until age 23 if full-time students.
Arkansas	35	66⅔	$20	$267.00	70	WW; children until 18 or married.	Spouse receives 2-year lump sum upon remarriage. Children receive benefits if beyond 18 if physically or mentally disabled, or until age 25 if full-time students.
California	66⅔	66⅔	$126	$336.00	66⅔	WW; children until 18.	Total amount payable is $115,000.
Colorado	66⅔	66⅔	$108.06-25% of the maximum benefit.	$432.25	91	WW; children until 18.	Two-year lump sum payable upon remarriage if there are no dependent children. Children are compensated beyond 18 if physically or mentally disabled, or until age 21 if full-time students. WC benefits are subject to Social Security benefit offsets, excluding widows 60 years of age and older.
Connecticut	75% SE	75% SE	$127.60-20% of SAWW, or an amount not to exceed 75% of worker's average wage if less.	$638.00	100	WW; children until 18.	Children receive benefits beyond 18 if physically or mentally disabled, or until age 22 if full-time students. WC benefits subject to Social Security benefit offsets.

continued

Table 9.6—*continued*

Jurisdiction	Percent of Worker's Wage		Payments Per Week			Maximum Period[1]	Notes
	Spouse only	Spouse & children	Minimum	Maximum	Percent of SAWW		
Delaware	66⅔	80	$113.10-22²⁄₉% of SAWW.	$339.29-$407.15	66⅔-80	WW; children until 18.	Two-year lump sum payable upon remarriage. Children are compensated until age 25 if full-time students.
District of Columbia	50	66⅔	$169.79-25% of SAWW.	$679.17	100	WW; children until 18.	Two-year lump sum payable upon remarriage. Children receive benefits beyond 18 if physically or mentally disabled, or until age 23 if full-time students.
Florida	50	66⅔	$20 or actual wage if less.	$444.00	100	WW; children until 18.	Lump sum compensation of 26 weeks payable upon remarriage. Children receive benefits beyond 18 if physically or mentally disabled, or until age 22 if full-time students. Total amount payable is $100,000.

126

State							
Georgia	66⅔	66⅔	$25 or average wage if less.	$250.00	N/A	400 weeks, or age 65 for a dependent spouse and a partial dependent, whichever is greater.	Total maximum of $100,000 applies to surviving spouse who is sole dependent at time of death, and where there are no other dependents for 1 year or less. Children receive benefits beyond 18 if physically or mentally disabled, or until age 22 if full-time students.
Hawaii	50	66⅔	$120-25% of SAWW, or worker's average wage if less, but not lower than $38.	$360.73-$481.00 according to no. of dependants.	100	WW; children until 18.	Total maximum payable for a spouse if 312 times the effective maximum weekly benefit rate. Two-year lump sum payable upon remarriage. Maximum amount does not apply to children incapable of self support.
Idaho	45	60	$175.50	$261.30	67	500 weeks	Upon remarriage, spouse receives either 180 weeks of compensation or balance of 500 weeks, whichever is less.

Table 9.6—*continued*

| Jurisdiction | Percent of Worker's Wage | | Payments Per Week | | | Maximum Period[1] | Notes |
	Spouse only	Spouse & children	Minimum	Maximum	Percent of SAWW		
Illinois	66⅔	66⅔	$267.35-50% of SAWW.	$712.92	133⅓	WW; children until 18, or for not less than 6 years if orphan child is under age 18.	Children receive benefits beyond age 18 if physically or mentally disabled. Two-year lump sum payable upon remarriage in cases where there are no children. Children may receive benefits until age 25 if full-time students. Total maximum payable in any case is $250,000 or 20 years of compensation, whichever is greater.
Indiana	66⅔	66⅔	$50 or worker's average wage if less.	$394.00	N/A	500 weeks	Children receive benefits beyond 21 if physically or mentally disabled. Two-year lump sum is payable upon remarriage in cases where there are no children or the remainder of compensation, whichever is smaller. Total maximum amount payable is $197,000. Increases to $214,000 effective 7/1/94.

continued

128

State						
Iowa	80 SE	80 SE	$139-35% of SAWW, or actual wage if less.	$797.00	200	WW; children until 18.	Two-year lump sum payable upon remarriage if no children. Children receive benefits beyond age 18 if physically or mentally disabled, or until age 25 if full-time students.
Kansas	66⅔	66⅔	$25	$313.00	75	WW; children until 18.	Surviving spouse receives a lump sum equal to 100 weeks of compensation upon remarriage. Children receive benefits beyond age 18 if physically or mentally disabled, or until age 23 if full-time students. Total maximum payable is $200,000, excluding dependent children. WC benefits subject to UI and Social Security benefit offsets.
Kentucky	50	75	$78.88-20% of SAWW.	$207.95-$311.96 according to no. of dependants.	75	WW; children until 18.	Children receive benefits beyond 18 if physically or mentally disabled, or until age 22 if full-time students. Two-year lump sum payable to surviving spouse upon remarriage.

129

Table 9.6—*continued*

Jurisdiction	Percent of Worker's Wage		Payments Per Week			Maximum Period[1]	Notes
	Spouse only	Spouse & children	Minimum	Maximum	Percent of SAWW		
Louisiana	32½	65	$85-20% of SAWW, or actual wage if less.	$319.00	75	WW; children until 18.	Two-year lump sum payable upon remarriage. Children receive benefits beyond age 18 if physically or mentally disabled or until age 23 if full-time students.
Maine	80% of worker's after tax earnings.	80% of worker's after tax earnings.		$441.00	90	500 weeks	Children receive benefits beyond age 18 if physically or mentally disabled. WC benefits subject to UI benefit offsets, excluding lump sum settlements.
Maryland	66⅔	66⅔	$50 or worker's average wage if less.	$510.00	100	WW; children until 18.	Two-year lump sum payable upon remarriage. Children receive benefits beyond age 18 if physically or mentally disabled, or until age 23 if full-time students. WC benefits may continue after a maximum of $45,000 has been paid, if there remain wholly dependent survivors.

continued

State							
Massachusetts	66⅔	66⅔	$110	$565.30	100	WW; children until 18.	Children receive benefits beyond age 18 if disabled, or regardless of age if full-time students. Dependent surviving spouses receive benefits during periods when they are not fully self-supporting. Total maximum payable may not exceed 250 times the SAWW in effect at time of injury. Additional $6 will be added per child if weekly benefits are below $150.
Michigan	80% SE	80% SE	$263.65–50% of SAWW.	$475.00	90	500 weeks	Children receive benefits until age 16, 18 if full-time student, or longer if disabled, notwithstanding the 500-week limit.
Minnesota	50	66⅔	Payable, but not statutorily prescribed.	$508.20	105	Surviving spouse only—10 years; surviving spouse with children—until last child is no longer dependent, plus 10 years; children until 18.	Children receive benefits beyond age 18 if disabled, or until age 25 if full-time students. WC benefits subject to Social Security benefit offsets.
Mississippi	35	66⅔	$25	$243.75	66⅔	450 weeks.	An additional sum of $250 is payable to widows. Children receive benefits beyond age 18 if disabled, or until age 23 if full-time students. Total maximum payable is $109,687.

continued

131

Table 9.6—continued

Jurisdiction	Percent of Worker's Wage		Payments Per Week			Maximum Period[1]	Notes
	Spouse only	Spouse & children	Minimum	Maximum	Percent of SAWW		
Missouri	66²/₃	66²/₃	$40	$470.06	105	WW; children until 18.	Two-year lump sum payable upon remarriage. Children receive benefits beyond age 18 if disabled, or until age 22 if full-time students, and beyond age 23 if on active duty in the Armed Forces.
Montana	66²/₃	66²/₃	$181.00-50% of SAWW, or actual if less.	$362.00	100	Surviving spouse-10 years; children until 18.	Children receive benefits beyond age 18 if disabled, or until age 22 if full-time students or if they are enrolled in an accredited apprenticeship program.
Nebraska	66²/₃	75	$49 or actual wage if less.	$265.00	N/A	WW; children until 18.	Two-year lump sum payable upon remarriage. Children receive benefits beyond age 18 if disabled, or until age 25 if full-time students. Maximum weekly benefit increases to $310, eff. 6/1/94, and to $350, eff. 1/1/95. Starting 1/1/96, maximum weekly benefit will be 100% of SAWW.

132

State							
Nevada	66⅔		66⅔	$432.39	100	WW; children until 18.	Two-year lump sum payable upon remarriage. Children receive benefits beyond age 18 if disabled, or until age 22 if full-time students.
New Hampshire	66⅔	$189.20-40% of SAWW not to exceed employee's after tax earnings.	66⅔	$709.50	150	WW; children until 18.	Children receive benefits beyond age 18 if disabled, or until age 25 if full-time students.
New Jersey	50	$123-20% of SAWW.	70	$460.00	75	WW; children until 18.	After 450 weeks of benefit payments, any earnings of surviving spouse will be deducted from future WC benefits payable to the surviving spouse. Surviving spouse receives $2,500 lump sum upon remarriage. Children receive benefits beyond age 18 if disabled. Supplemental benefits for death are subject to Social Security, black lung, or disability pension offsets.

Table 9.6—*continued*

| Jurisdiction | Percent of Worker's Wage | | Payments Per Week | | | Maximum Period[1] | Notes |
	Spouse only	Spouse & children	Minimum	Maximum	Percent of SAWW		
New Mexico	66⅔	66⅔	Payable, but not statutorily pre-scribed.	$333.02	85	700 weeks	Two-year lump-sum pay-able upon remarriage. Children receive benefits beyond age 18 if disabled or until age 23 if full-time students. Total maximum equals the sum of 700 multiplied by the maxi-mum weekly benefit pay-able at the time of injury.
New York	66⅔	66⅔	$40	$400.00	N/A	WW; children until 18.	Two-year lump sum pay-able upon remarriage. Children receive benefits beyond age 18 if disa-bled, or until age 23 if full-time students. WC payments subject to So-cial Security benefit offsets.
North Carolina	66⅔	66⅔	$30	$466.00	110	400 weeks	WC benefits are payable to a surviving spouse in-capable of self-support for life. Dependent chil-dren receive benefits be-yond the 400-week limit until age 18.

State						
North Dakota	66⅔	$115	66⅔	$210.00 plus $10 per week for each dependent child.	N/A	WW; children until 18. Children receive benefits beyond age 18 if disabled, or until age 23 if full-time students. Widows receive a $300 lump sum and a $100 sum for each dependent child. Total maximum payable is $197,000.
Ohio	66⅔	$241.00-50% of SAWW.	66⅔	$482.00	100	WW; children until 18. Two-year lump sum payable upon remarriage. Children receive benefits beyond 18 if disabled, or until age 25 if full-time students.
Oklahoma	50	75		$307.00	75	WW; children until 18. Two-year lump sum payable upon remarriage. Children receive benefits beyond 18 if disabled, or until age 23 if full-time students. Spouse receives lump sum of $10,000 and $2,500 for each child not to exceed $5,000.

continued

135

Table 9.6—*continued*

Jurisdiction	Percent of Worker's Wage		Payments Per Week			Maximum Period[1]	Notes
	Spouse only	Spouse & children	Minimum	Maximum	Percent of SAWW		
Oregon				$319.38-$638.58 according to no. of dependents.	133⅓	WW; children until 18.	Children receive benefits beyond 18 if disabled, or until age 23 if full-time students. Spouse receives 24 times the monthly benefit amount in a lump sum upon remarriage. Spouse receives $150 a month per child for each of two children, and $50 a month for each additional child, subject to the monthly maximum benefit. If the surviving spouse dies before all children are age 18, child under 18 receives $400 a month until age 18.
Pennsylvania	51	66⅔	$273.80-or 90% of SAWW if less.	$493.00	100	WW; children until 18.	Two-year lump sum payable to widows upon remarriage. Children receive benefits beyond 18 if disabled, or until age 23 if full-time students.

136

State						
Rhode Island	66⅔	80		$463.00 plus $20 for each dependent child.	100	WW; children until 18.	Children receive benefits beyond 18 if disabled, or until age 23 if full-time students.
South Carolina	66⅔	66⅔	$75 or worker's average wage if less.	$410.26	100	500 weeks	Two-year lump sum payable upon remarriage of spouse. Children receive benefits beyond 19 if disabled, or until age 23 if full-time students.
South Dakota	66⅔	66⅔	$169-50% of SAWW, or worker's average wage if less.	$338.00 plus $50 per month for each child.	100	WW; children until 18.	Two-year lump sum payable upon remarriage. Children receive benefits beyond 18 if disabled, or until age 22 if full-time students.
Tennessee	50	66⅔	$64.80	$355.97	N/A	WW; children until 18.	Children receive benefits beyond 18 if disabled, or until age 22 if full-time students. Total maximum amount payable is $142,388. Lump sum of $10,000 will be paid to decedent's estate when there are no dependents.
Texas	75	75	$68-15% of SAWW	$464.00	100	WW; children until 18.	Two-year lump sum payable upon remarriage. Children receive benefits beyond 18 if disabled, or until age 25 if full-time students.

continued

137

Table 9.6—*continued*

Jurisdiction	Percent of Worker's Wage		Payments Per Week			Maximum Period[1]	Notes
	Spouse only	Spouse & children	Minimum	Maximum	Percent of SAWW		
Utah	66⅔	66⅔	$45 to $70 according to no. of dependents.	$351.00	85	312 weeks	WC benefits may be extended if survivors remain wholly dependent. After 312 weeks, benefits to wholly dependent spouse become subject to Social Security benefit offsets. 52-week lump sum or remainder of award payable upon remarriage, whichever is less.
Vermont	66⅔	76⅔	$215-50% of SAWW.	$644.00	150	WW until age 62; children until 18.	Children receive benefits beyond age 18 if disabled or if full-time students.
Virginia	66⅔	66⅔	$112.75-25% of SAWW, or actual wage if less.	$451.00	100	500 weeks	Children receive benefits beyond age 18 if disabled, or until age 23 if full-time students.

138

State							
Washington	60	70	$44.05 to $83.81 according to no. of dependents.	$517.16	105% of state's *monthly* wage.	WW; children until 18.	Children receive benefits beyond age 18 if disabled, or until age 23 if full-time students. Lump sum of $1,600 becomes payable at time of death. Upon remarriage, surviving spouse is entitled to $7,500, or 50% of remaining annuity value, if less.
West Virginia	70	70	$140.11- 33⅓% of SAWW.	$420.33	100	WW; children until 18.	Children receive benefits beyond age 18 if disabled, until age 25 if full-time students.
Wisconsin	66⅔	See notes	$30 or actual wage, if less.	$466.00	100	300 weeks	Additional WC benefits are payable from the State Fund for dependent children under age 18 (10% of surviving spouse's benefit is the allowance made for each child.); and if child is over age 18 and disabled, benefits may continue for 15 years.
Wyoming				$275.00	66⅔% of *monthly* wage.	231 weeks	Children receive benefits until age 19 or beyond if disabled, but not to exceed age 21. Court may continue payment beyond 231 weeks at 33⅓% of SAWW.

Table 9.6—*continued*

Jurisdiction	Percent of Worker's Wage		Payments Per Week			Maximum Period[1]	Notes
	Spouse only	Spouse & children	Minimum	Maximum	Percent of SAWW		
FECA	50	75	$1,115.17, actual wage if less. Also see note 2.	$1,248.88	See notes.	WW; children until 18.	WC benefits are based on the pay of a specific grade level in the Federal Civil Service. Children receive benefits beyond age 18 if disabled, or until age 23 if full-time students.
LHWCA	50	66⅔	$180.29-50% of NAWW, or actual wage if less.	$738.30	N/A	WW; children until 18.	Children receive benefits beyond age 18 if disabled, or until age 23 if full-time students. (NAWW is $369.15)

SE=Spendable Earnings
SAWW=State's Average Weekly Wage
WW=Widow/Widowerhood[1]
FECA=Federal Employees' Compensation Act
LHWCA=Longshore & Harbor Workers' Compensation Act
NAWW=National Average Weekly Wage
[1] The term "widow/widowerhood" means the period until the death or remarriage of either surviving spouse.
[2] Minimum indicated is the absolute amount of compensation payable monthly for death.
Source: State Workers' Compensation Laws, U.S. Department of Labor, Office of Workers' Compensation Programs, January 1994, Table 12.

way the maximum benefit is adjusted each year in accordance with changes in the cost of living. Under such provisions, however, a worker injured in a given year is always limited by the maximum rate in effect for the year during which he or she was injured.

A true cost of living allowance allows the worker to receive an adjustment each year in accordance with changes in the cost of providing for oneself and one's family or in accordance with what the worker would have earned had he or she continued on the job. I am not aware of any jurisdiction that provides a comprehensive cost of living adjustment for all benefits. As Larson indicates, there is a variety of approaches with no clear pattern.[6] Some states limit the allowance to certain types of disability, most often permanent total disability. Some states limit it to workers with injuries occurring during a specific period of time. Some make annual adjustments, while others are more limited. In Michigan, for example, workers injured between 1965 and 1979 received a one-time increase effective January 1, 1982. In some states the employer is responsible for the payment of the increases, while in others the increases are paid by a special fund as discussed in chapter 13.

During the inflationary times of the 1970s there was a call for legislative attention to this problem. As inflation has slowed, this call has slackened somewhat, but we can expect to hear more about it in the future. It is a very difficult problem. Disabled workers who are already suffering a calculated loss of part of their earnings should not have the loss steadily increased because of extraneous factors such as inflation. At the same time, most solutions would impose on employers a liability that they cannot predict, cannot control, and which is virtually unlimited. They are obviously reluctant to accept this.

9.9 Relationship to Other Benefits

A disabled worker could potentially receive a variety of benefits in addition to workers' compensation including social security (retirement or disability), pension (retirement or disability), unemployment compensation, sick leave, group disability benefits through the employer, disability benefits from a private policy, and the results of a judgment against a third party in civil court. To

Table 9.7. Burial Allowances

Jurisdiction	Allowance
Alabama	$3,000
Alaska	$2,500
Arizona	$3,000
Arkansas	$6,000
California	$5,000
Colorado	$4,000
Connecticut	$4,000
Delaware	$ 700
District of Columbia	$5,000
Florida	$2,500
Georgia	$5,000
Hawaii	NA
Idaho	$6,000
Illinois	$4,200
Indiana	$6,000
Iowa	$5,000
Kansas	$3,300
Kentucky	$4,000
Louisiana	$3,000
Maine	$4,000
Maryland	$2,500
Massachusetts	$4,000
Michigan	$1,500
Minnesota	$7,500
Mississippi	$2,000
Missouri	$5,000
Montana	$1,400
Nebraska	$2,000
Nevada	$5,000

continued

what extent are, or should, these be coordinated with workers' compensation?

Most group disability insurance plans provided by employers do not cover work-related injuries. Thus, a worker receives benefits under one system or the other, but not both. Some such policies, however, cover worker-related injuries but provide for an offset so that if the group disability benefits would be higher, the worker can receive workers' compensation and a supplement from the disability policy. Assume that Mr. F was earning $500 per week before the injury and would be entitled to $400 per week under the group insurance policy and $350 under workers' compensation.

Table 9.7—*continued*

Jurisdiction	Allowance
New Hampshire	$5,000
New Jersey	$3,500
New Mexico	$3,000
New York	NA
North Carolina	$3,000
North Dakota	$2,500
Ohio	$3,200
Oklahoma	NA
Oregon	$3,000
Pennsylvania	$3,000
Rhode Island	$5,000
South Carolina	$2,500
South Dakota	$3,000
Tennessee	$4,500
Texas	$2,500
Utah	NA
Vermont	$2,000
Virginia	$5,000
Washington	$2,000
West Virginia	$3,500
Wisconsin	$4,000
Wyoming	$1,800
FECA	$ 800
LHWCA	$3,000

FECA=Federal Employees' Compensation Act
LHWCA=Longshore & Harbor Workers' Compensation Act
NA=Not Available
Source: *State Workers' Compensation Laws*, U.S. Department of Labor, Office of Workers' Compensation Programs, January 1994, Table 13.

Under most policies he would receive one benefit or the other depending on whether the injury was covered by workers' compensation. Under a policy with an offset, however, he would receive $400 from the group policy if the injury happened at home; if it happened at work, he would receive $350 in workers' compensation and $50 from the group policy.

It should be pointed out that when we are talking about an offset in group insurance or a pension plan, the result is ordinarily governed by the terms of the insurance contract or the pension plan and not by the workers' compensation law. When we are referring to a reduction in workers' compensation benefits, the outcome is determined by the provisions of the workers' compensation act. Thus, a company and a union could decide between themselves whether a pension benefit would be reduced for the receipt of workers' compensation benefits, but only the legislature could decide that workers' compensation benefits would be reduced because a worker received a pension.

In fact, a few pension plans do provide a reduction in pension benefits as the result of the receipt of workers' compensation. Those that do approach it in a variety of ways. Some provide a reduction in the pension only if it is a disability pension, others only if it is a retirement pension. Some provide an offset to the pension if the worker receives weekly workers' compensation benefits but not a lump sum, and others the opposite. The parties to a pension plan can negotiate virtually any type of arrangement they desire.

The Social Security Act does not provide any offset to retirement or survivor's benefits based on the receipt of workers' compensation. There is, however, an offset to social security *disability* benefits. The Social Security Act provides that workers' compensation and social security disability benefits combined should not exceed 80 percent of the individual's average current earnings at the time of the injury. If they do, the social security benefits are reduced. Until the early 1980s, the Act provided an alternative under which, if a state's workers' compensation law provided for a reduction of workers' compensation benefits, then the social security reduction would not apply. It is surprising that more states did not take advantage of this, since it allowed states to shift the cost of disabilities from local employers to federal taxes. The Social Security Act has since been changed and no new states are allowed to take advantage of this provision, although those that previously had it are allowed to continue.

State workers' compensation laws provide for a reduction, offset, or *coordination* of benefits under a variety of circumstances. (See Table 9.8 at pp. 146–47.) Social Security and Unemployment Insurance are the benefits most frequently offset. As mentioned above, some states offset social security disability benefits. Some offset social security retirement and other pension benefits, and some provide an offset for virtually any benefit to the extent that it is paid for by the employer.

Is this fair? Should there be a reduction? This is related to the issue of what it is we wish to compensate, which is discussed in subsection 8.6.2. If a state takes an impairment approach and pays benefits based on the amount of physical impairment, the worker would ordinarily receive workers' compensation benefits even if he or she returned to work. Under this type of system it is not logical to reduce workers' compensation benefits because a worker receives a wage replacement benefit in the form of a pension. If, however, a state has decided to base workers' compensation payments on the amount of wage-loss, then there should be an adjustment of some kind when some other source replaces part or all of the lost wages.

Another more pragmatic approach suggests that if costs have to be cut, this is perhaps the least painful way to do it. In many states, there is so much political pressure to reduce the cost of workers' compensation that legislatures are forced to cut benefits in one way or another. Given that situation, it is probably most appropriate to reduce the benefits of workers who have some other form of income.

It is important to examine how an offset is calculated. The offset can be calculated with respect to wages, a percentage of wages, or workers' compensation benefits. Assume that Ms. G was earning $500 per week before her injury and that she is now entitled to $350 per week in workers' compensation benefits and $200 per week in pension benefits. If we were going to coordinate with respect to wages, we would say that she cannot receive more than a total of $500 per week. We would subtract her $200 in pension benefits from the wages of $500 and say that her workers' compensation benefits should be reduced to $300.

Wages	$500
Other benefits	−200
Maximum WC benefit	$300

We could also say that the maximum combined benefit should be 80 percent of her wages. This would result in a workers' compensation rate of $200 per week in this example.

Wages ($500 × .80)	$400
Other benefits	−200
Maximum WC benefit	$200

Table 9.8. Offsets to Workers' Compensation Benefits

Jurisdiction	Benefits Which Result in an Offset
Alabama	
Alaska	SS
Arizona	
Arkansas	Public or private pension
California	
Colorado	SS, UI, Pension, other disability plans
Connecticut	SS
Delaware	
District of Columbia	SS
Florida	SS, UI
Georgia	
Hawaii	
Idaho	
Illinois	
Indiana	
Iowa	
Kansas	UI
Kentucky	
Louisiana	SS, UI
Maine	UI, any other benefits to the extent funded by the employer
Maryland	
Massachusetts	SS, UI
Michigan	SS, UI and others to the extent funded by the employer
Minnesota	SS after $25,000
Mississippi	
Missouri	
Montana	SS
Nebraska	
Nevada	

continued

Finally, we could coordinate directly against the workers' compensation benefit.

WC benefit	$350
Other benefit	−200
WC benefit paid	$150

This latter approach seems particularly harsh.

9.10 Disfigurement

Forty-four jurisdictions pay some form of benefit for disfigurement. These are summarized in Table 9.9 (at pp. 148–152).

Table 9.8. *continued*

Jurisdiction	Benefits Which Result in an Offset
New Hampshire	
New Jersey	Supplemental benefits for PTD subject to SS or disability pension benefit offsets
New Mexico	UI
New York	SS (for survivor's benfits)
North Carolina	UI
North Dakota	SS
Ohio	SS, other disability plans
Oklahoma	
Oregon	SS
Pennsylvania	
Rhode Island	
South Carolina	
South Dakota	
Tennessee	
Texas	
Utah	SS after 312 weeks
Vermont	
Virginia	
Washington	SS
West Virginia	SS, other disability plans
Wisconsin	SS
Wyoming	UI
FECA	
LHWCA	

SS=Social Security
UI=Unemployment Insurance
PTD=Permanent Total Disability
FECA=Federal Employees' Compensation Act
LHWCA=Longshore & Harbor Workers' Compensation Act
Source: State Workers' Compensation Laws, U.S. Department of Labor, Office of Workers' Compensation Programs, January 1994, Table 17.

Notes

1. See Larson §60.30.
2. Alaska, Connecticut, Iowa, Maine, Michigan, and under some circumstances, the District of Columbia and Rhode Island.
3. DeVol Roberts, Karen, *Income Replacement for Short-Term Disability* (Cambridge: Workers' Compensation Research Institute, 1985).
4. Arizona, Massachusetts, North Dakota, Rhode Island, Utah, Vermont; see Office of Workers' Compensation Programs, Employment Standards Administration, U.S. Dep't of Labor, *State Workers' Compensation Laws*, January, 1993.
5. DeVol Roberts, Karen, *Income Replacement for Long-Term Disability* (Cambridge: Workers' Compensation Research Institute, 1986).
6. Larson §60.60.

Table 9.9. Jurisdictions Providing Disfigurement Benefits

Jurisdiction	Nature of Disfigurement	Compensation Received	Maximum Period
Alabama	Serious, materially affecting employability.	66⅔ percent of employee's average weekly earnings.	100 weeks
Arizona	Permanent, about head or face, including injury to, or loss of, teeth.	55 percent of average monthly wages; in addition, the Commission may allow such sum as it deems just.	18 months
Arkansas	Serious and permanent facial or head.	Maximum $3,500; no award for disfigurement shall be entered until 12 months after injury.	
California		No set figure but the nature of the disfigurement shall be taken into account when determining the percentages of permanent disability.	
Colorado	Serious facial, head, or exposed body parts.	Maximum $2,000, in addition to accident benefits provided under the law.	
Connecticut	Permanent.	Compensation shall be awarded for disfigurement not caused solely by the loss of use of a member of the body.	208 weeks
Delaware	Permanent and serious to exposed parts of the human body.	66⅔ percent of employee's weekly wage.	150 weeks
District of Columbia	Serious facial, head, neck, or other exposed areas likely to handicap employment.	Maximum $3,500.	
Florida	Serious facial or head.	$250 for each percent of permanent impairment of the body as a whole from 1 to 10 percent; and $500 for each percent in excess of 10 percent.	

148

Hawaii	Scarring and other consequences caused by medical, surgical, and hospital treatment.	Maximum $15,000
Idaho		No set figure but effect on employment and nature of disfigurement shall be taken into account when determining the percentages of permanent disabilities less than total.
Illinois	Serious and permanent to hand, head, face, neck, arm, leg, below knee, or chest above axillary line.	60 percent of the employee's average weekly wage, except if benefits are otherwise payable for permanent disability. 150 weeks
Indiana	Permanent, which may impair the future usefulness or opportunities of the employee.	At discretion of Industrial Board, except where benefits are payable elsewhere. 200 weeks
Iowa	Permanent head or facial, which impairs future usefulness and earnings.	Determined by the Industrial Commissioner according to severity of disfigurement.
Kansas[1]		
Kentucky	Serious and permanent of face, head, neck or other exposed areas of the body that is likely to affect employment opportunities.	Proper and equitable scheduled benefits. Period for which benefits are payable is decided after maximum healing and restoration of function.
Louisiana	Serious and permanent.	At discretion of Court, not to exceed 66⅔ percent of employee's wages. 100 weeks
Maine	Serious facial or head; neck if affects earning capacity.	An amount not exceeding two-thirds of the state average weekly wage, multiplied by 50.
Maryland	For mutilations and others not specifically covered in schedule.	Determined at the discretion of the Workmen's Compensation Commission. 156 weeks

continued

Table 9.9—continued

Jurisdiction	Nature of Disfigurement	Compensation Received	Maximum Period
Massachusetts	Bodily.	Proper and equitable compensation not to exceed the State average weekly wage multiplied by 32; in addition to other compensation for disability.	
Minnesota	Disfigurement or scarring, not resulting from loss of a member or other scheduled injury affecting employability or advancement opportunity. Permanent partial disability under the schedule if resulting from burns.	66⅔ percent of the employee's daily wage at time of injury, subject to a maximum of 100 percent of the state average weekly wage.	90 weeks
Mississippi	Serious facial or head.	Maximum $2,000	
Missouri	Serious and permanent about the head, neck, and/or arms including the loss of use or the loss of a member.	No statutory figure.	40 weeks
Montana	Serious face, head, or neck.	Maximum $2,500	
New Mexico	Serious and permanent about the face or head.	Maximum $2,500	
New York	Serious facial, head, neck, or chest.	Maximum $20,000	
North Carolina	Serious facial or head, and body when no compensation payable under schedule of injuries.	Maximum $20,000	
North Dakota	Effect diminishes the ability of the employee to obtain employment.	No set figure but such disfigurement shall be included as permanent partial disability.	
Ohio	Serious facial or head which handicaps employment.	Maximum $5,000	

150

State	Body area	Compensation	Maximum period
Oklahoma	Serious and permanent.	Maximum $20,000	
Oregon		No set dollar amount; however, compensation is payable only if disfigurement results in certain psychological adjustment problems.	
Pennsylvania	Serious and permanent of head, face, or neck.	$66\frac{2}{3}$ percent of the employee's average weekly wage.	275 weeks
Rhode Island	Permanent bodily.	Proper and equitable compensation determined by the Workers' Compensation Commission.	500 weeks
South Carolina	Serious and permanent of face, head, neck or other area normally exposed in employment.	Proper and equitable benefits, unless benefits are otherwise payable for the loss, except that benefits shall be paid for serious burn and keloid scars in addition to other benefits.	50 weeks
South Dakota[2]			
Tennessee	Serious of the head, face or hands, so altering the personal appearance as to materially affect employability.	$66\frac{2}{3}$ percent of the employee's average weekly earnings; not to be awarded if compensated under any other provisions.	200 weeks
Texas	Any that will impair the future usefulness or occupational opportunities of the injured employee.	$66\frac{2}{3}$ percent of employee's average weekly wages not to exceed the maximum weekly benefit, multiplied by the percentage of incapacity.	300 weeks
Utah	Areas of the body not specifically covered in schedule.	Such period of compensation as the Commission shall deem equitable and in proportion as near as may be to compensation for specific loss as set forth in the schedule.	312 weeks

continued

Table 9.9—*continued*

Jurisdiction	Nature of Disfigurement	Compensation Received	Maximum Period
Vermont[3]			
Virginia	Severely marked of head, face, hands, arms, or legs.	66⅔ percent of employee's average weekly wages.	60 weeks
Wisconsin	Areas of the body that are exposed in the normal course of employment.	At the discretion of the Department of Industry, Labor and Human Relations, a sum not to exceed the employee's average annual earnings.	
Wyoming	Permanent of the face or head that affects earning capacity.	In proportion to the extent of the disfigurement plus an award based on two-thirds of the state's average weekly wage.	25 weeks
FECA	Serious of the face, head or neck of a character likely to handicap employment.	66⅔ percent of employee's monthly wage; in addition, proper and equitable benefits not to exceed $3,500.	
LHWCA	Serious of the face, head or neck of a character likely to handicap employment.	Maximum $3,500.	

[1] *Kansas:* When a disfigurement is a handicap in obtaining or retaining employment, compensation will be paid up to a maximum of 415 weeks.
[2] *South Dakota:* Compensation for permanent disfigurement shall be payable for a portion of 312 weeks which is represented by the percentage of permanent disfigurement that bears to the body as a whole.
[3] *Vermont:* Compensation and percentage of loss for permanent impairment of any physical function not specifically mentioned shall be determined by the Commissioner of Labor and Industry.
FECA=Federal Employees' Compensation Act
LHWCA=Longshore & Harbor Workers' Compensation Act
Source: State Workers' Compensation Laws, U.S. Department of Labor, Office of Workers' Compensation Programs, January 1994, Table 11.

Chapter 10

Health Care Benefits

10.1 Introduction

This chapter will deal with regulations and statutory provisions concerning health care benefits. (The options available to individual employers concerning the quality and cost of health care are discussed in chapter 24.) The Workers' Compensation Research Institute has conducted extensive research in this area. The tables in this chapter are based on *Medical Cost Containment in Workers' Compensation: A National Inventory*, 1992–1993, by Carol A. Telles, WCRI Cambridge, Massachusetts, 1993. They are reproduced with permission of WCRI.

10.2 Benefits Provided

All jurisdictions now provide virtually unlimited medical care for work-related injuries. Most statutes define "medical care" quite broadly and include medications, artificial limbs, glasses, special shoes, and psychiatric treatment. Nursing care is also ordinarily covered, but sometimes becomes controversial especially if a family member provides the care and seeks to be paid for the services.

Generally all types of providers are covered including medical doctors and osteopathic physicians. The vast majority of jurisdictions also cover treatment by chiropractic physicians. In recent years, however, there have been many complaints that these treatments are costly. Oregon amended its law in 1990 to greatly restrict a worker's freedom to select chiropractic care after the first 30 days.

Ordinarily, the carrier makes payment directly to the provider (doctor, hospital, or other medical provider). However, it sometimes happens that a worker pays the provider directly. This could happen for a variety of reasons. Perhaps the worker went to the doctor without prior authorization from the carrier, or perhaps the worker did not know that the injury was work-related when treatment started. In these cases the worker is reimbursed by the carrier.

The right to medical benefits is ordinarily not affected by the receipt of indemnity benefits. Thus, there is no waiting period for medical benefits and they can continue even after the payment of indemnity benefits has stopped. At least in theory, the right to medical benefits continues indefinitely in most states.

10.3 Choice of Physician or Provider

Table 10.1 summarizes laws concerning who chooses the treating doctor. A majority of states allow the worker to make the initial choice. A significant number, however, allow the employer or insurer to make the initial choice. A few allow the worker to choose from the physicians on a list made up by the employer. A few others require the worker to choose from a list provided by the state agency. In general, however, these lists are so broad as to provide virtual free choice.

A great many states place some sort of limit on the extent to which a worker can change providers. Most frequently this takes the form of a provision that the worker is free to make one unrestricted change and thereafter may change only with the approval of the employer or the state agency. A few states that give the employer the initial choice of physician allow the worker full freedom to change after a certain amount of time, say 10 or 30 days. Finally, some states allow the employer to require the worker to change physicians under certain circumstances.

A worker may arrange for his or her own treatment at the employer's expense if the employer fails to provide reasonable medical care. This is true even in states that give the employer the right to choose the provider.

Table 10.1. Restrictions on Initial Provider Choice and Change of Provider

Jurisdiction	Initial Choice	Employee Change	Employer Change
Alabama	Employer/insurer selects	Employer/insurer list	None allowed
Alaska	Employee selects	Once, then employer/ insurer approval	None allowed
Arizona	Employee or employer, self-insurer*	Employer of self-insured insurer, agency, or provider approval	None allowed
Arkansas	Employer/insurer selects	Once with agency approval	Agency approval
California	Employee or employer/self-insurer*	Once after 30 days, employer/insurer selects	Within 30 days; after 30 days with agency approval
Colorado	Employer/insurer selects	Employer/insurer approval	None allowed*
Connecticut	Employee selects*	Employer/insurer approval	None allowed
Delaware	Employee selects	Unrestricted	None allowed
District of Columbia	Employee selects*	Employer/insurer or agency approval*	None allowed
Florida	Employer/insurer selects	Employer/insurer approval	Agency approval
Georgia	Employer/insurer list, 4 physicians	Once from list	Agency approval
Hawaii	Employee selects	Once, then employer/insurer approval	None allowed
Idaho	Employer/insurer selects	Employer/insurer approval	Unrestricted
Illinois	Employee selects	Once, then employer/insurer approval	None allowed
Indiana	Employer/insurer selects	None allowed	Unrestricted
Iowa	Employer/insurer selects	Agency approval	Unrestricted
Kansas	Employer/insurer selects	None allowed	Unrestricted
Kentucky	Employee selects*	Unrestricted	With agency approval
Louisiana	Employee selects*	Employer/insurer approval*	None allowed
Maine	Employee selects*	Once, then employer/insurer or independent medical exam approval*	None allowed
Maryland	Employee selects	Unrestricted	None allowed
Massachusetts	Employee selects*	Once, then employer/insurer approval	None allowed
Michigan	Employer/insurer selects*	After first 10 days*	None allowed
Minnesota	Employee selects	Employer/insurer approval*	None allowed
Mississippi	Employee selects*	Once, then employer/insurer approval	None allowed

continued

155

Table 10.1—*continued*

Jurisdiction	Initial Choice	Employee Change	Employer Change
Missouri	Employer/insurer selects	None allowed	Unrestricted
Montana	Employee selects	Employer/insurer approval	None allowed
Nebraska	Employee selects	Once	None allowed
Nevada	Employee selects	Once within 90 days, then employer/insurer approval	Employee approval
New Hampshire	Employee selects	Unrestricted	None allowed
New Jersey	Employer/insurer selects	None allowed	Unrestricted
New Mexico	Employee or employer/insurer*	Once if employer selects initial providers; none if employee selects*	Once if employee selects initial provider; none if employer selects*
New York	Employee selects*	Unrestricted*	With agency approval
North Carolina	Employer/insurer selects	Employer/insurer approval	None allowed
North Dakota	Employee selects	State fund approval	None allowed
Ohio	Employee selects	Unrestricted*	None allowed
Oklahoma	Employee selects	Parties/agency approval	None allowed
Oregon	Employee selects*	Twice, then employer/insurer or agency approval*	None allowed
Pennsylvania	Employer/insurer list, 5 physicians*	First 14 days from list*	None allowed
Rhode Island	Employee selects	Unrestricted	None allowed
South Carolina	Employer/insurer selects	Employer/insurer or agency approval	Unrestricted
South Dakota	Employee selects	Employer/insurer approval	None allowed
Tennessee	Employer/insurer list, 3 or more physicians	Employer/insurer approval	Agency approval
Texas	Employee selects	Once, then agency or employer/insurer approval	None allowed
Utah	Employer/insurer selects	Once, then employer/insurer approval	None allowed
Vermont	Employer/insurer selects*	Unrestricted*	None allowed
Virginia	Employer/insurer list, 3 physicians per specialty	Employer/insurer or agency approval	None allowed

State			
Washington	Employee selects	Unrestricted*	None allowed
West Virginia	Employee selects	Unrestricted	None allowed
Wisconsin	Employee selects	Once, then employer/insurer approval	None allowed
Wyoming	Employee selects	State fund approval	None allowed

Arizona: Free initial employee choice for insured employers; self-insured companies have initial choice of provider.

California: The employer or insurer initially selects the treating physician unless the employee notifies the employer in writing of a personal physician who will be the treating physician in case of an accident.

Colorado: The employer or insurer cannot change the treating provider after the initial selection unless it believes unnecessary or inappropriate care has been provided. In that case, the employer or insurer can request a utilization review from the DWC; the DWC director can order a change if a panel of three providers recommends one.

Connecticut: The employee selects from a list of all licensed physicians.

District of Columbia: The employee chooses from an extensive agency list (licensed treating providers who apply) both initially and to change.

Louisiana: The employee has the choice of one physician per specialty; the employee needs the approval of the employer or insurer to change within the same specialty.

Maine: The employee has a choice of one provider per specialty. The employee needs the approval of the employer or insurer or an independent medical examiner to change within the same specialty.

Massachusetts: Effective December 23, 1991, if an insurer has entered into a PPO arrangement for health care services, the employee's first scheduled appointment may be required to be with a provider in the plan.

Minnesota: The employer or insurer selects within 10 days of injury: the employer can challenge an employee's change.

Mississippi: The employer or insurer approval is required for change after the employee has an ongoing relationship with a provider.

New Mexico: The employee's choice is limited to one provider and any other specialists to whom he or she is referred by the chosen physician. New Mexico: In September 1990, New Mexico passed a law that gives the employer or insurer the option to control provider choice either during the first sixty days following the injury or after this 60-day period.

New York: The employee selects from an extensive list of physicians developed by the agency.

Ohio: The employee must notify the agency of a change of provider. This notification is rarely used to restrict the employee's right to change providers.

Oregon: Managed-care organization contracts may have different rules about initial choice and changes by the employee.

Pennsylvania: The employer has the statutory right to restrict the employee to a list of five physicians for the first 14 days of treatment following an injury. If the employer does not have a list, the employee can select the treating provider.

Vermont: By statute the employer or the insurer has the right to choose, but in practice the employee often chooses. Respondents note a discernable trend toward greater exercise of employer or insurer choice. The employee also is supposed to provide a written notice of change of provider to the employer or insurer, but in practice, the employee often changes without notice.

Washington: By statute the self-insurer or the state fund must approve a change in provider; in practice the employee almost always changes providers without getting approval first. In specific circumstances, the self-insurer or the state fund may require the worker to select a new treating provider.

Source: Workers' Compensation Research Institute.

157

There is often a great deal of debate over the right to choose the doctor. Employers assert that because health care costs are rising so rapidly, they need to have control over the choice of physician.[1] Employees, on the other hand, assert that they should have a right to choose a treating doctor.

In reality, the legal right to choose may not be as important as it seems. In many cases where employers have the right to choose they fail to exercise it and simply allow the worker to make the choice. In many other circumstances where the worker has the right to control the choice, the employer often makes a suggestion as to who the worker should see, and most of the time, the worker accepts that suggestion. In some states, regardless of the legal rights involved, many physicians, especially specialists, will not see a patient unless some employer or insurance carrier agrees in advance to pay the bill.

While this issue is usually debated in terms of health care costs, there is another factor involved. In many jurisdictions the opinion of the treating doctor has special force in determinations concerning the extent of the worker's disability. This may be provided for by statute, or it may have developed over time as a common practice. In those states, the choice of physician has implications not only for the cost and quality of medical care, but also for the ultimate determination of the extent of disability and the amount of indemnity benefits.

Both parties should realize that in the long run, the most desirable outcome for all concerned is a prompt and complete recovery of health for the injured worker. To this end, both parties should work toward arrangements that will result in the highest quality of care.

The National Commission recommended "that the worker be permitted the initial selection of his physician, either from among all licensed physicians in the state or from a panel of physicians selected or approved by the workmen's compensation agency." (R 4.1.)

10.4 Third-Party Payers

If medical bills have been paid by a third party, such as a group health insurance plan, and it is later determined that they should have been paid by an employer, the third party is ordinarily allowed to recover reimbursement from the employer. It should be noted that federal law guarantees this right to the Medicare program.[2]

10.5 Refusal of Medical Treatment

An injured worker is expected to accept and take advantage of reasonable medical treatment and examinations. In theory, compensation can be denied if he or she refuses to do so. In practice, however, benefits are rarely denied on this basis. To deny benefits it must be shown that the treatment was likely to be successful, that there was little risk of harm, and that there are no special circumstances involving this particular worker.

Questions of whether a person must lose weight, carry out exercises, or stop smoking are often difficult ones. The courts have been reluctant to deny benefits on this basis. Surgery is another issue that sometimes arises. In general it will depend upon the risks of the surgery, the prognosis for improvement as a result, and the reasons for refusal. It is rare, however, that a worker is denied benefits for refusal to accept surgery.

10.6 Health Care Cost Controls

10.6.1 The Problem

In the late 1980s and early 1990s, much emphasis has been placed on controlling the cost of workers' compensation health care. It has been the subject of numerous programs and publications.[3] The data support this concern. We are all aware that health care costs are one of the fastest growing components of the consumer price index, but we may not realize that workers' compensation health care costs are going up even faster than health care costs in general. From 1985–1990, health care costs for all payers increased by 9.7 percent. During that same period, workers' compensation health care costs increased by 15.2 percent.[4]

Health care is also the fastest growing component of workers' compensation costs. Health care is growing faster than indemnity costs and its share of the total cost is increasing. Burton points out that between 1960 and 1984, health care costs increased from 33.6 percent of the workers' compensation dollar to 35.0 percent, and that between 1984 and 1990 it increased from 35.0 percent to 40.9 percent.[5]

There is also considerable evidence of cost shifting to workers' compensation. Over the years, the largest payers of health care benefits, such as Medicaid, Medicare, and Blue Cross, have introduced many strategies aimed at controlling costs. Workers' compensation has been a late comer to most of these techniques. It appears that as a result providers tend to seek increased reimbursement from the workers' compensation system in order to make up for decreased payment from other payers. For example, in many circumstances, Medicaid actually reimburses at a rate that is lower than the cost to doctors and hospitals providing the services. Blue Cross allows these providers to break even or make a very small profit. It is only natural that they would seek to make up for their losses on Medicaid patients by obtaining higher reimbursement from workers' compensation payments. While this may make economic sense from the point of view of providers, employers who pay for the workers' compensation system do not feel that it is appropriate.

Some remarkable studies based on data from Minnesota have documented the differences in payments.[6] Baker and Krueger conclude that on average workers' compensation payers are paying 110 percent more than Blue Cross for treatment of patients with the same diagnosis. It is important to note, however, that this level of differences did not persist across all diagnoses. Analysis of the data finds that the differences were biggest for back injuries. Thornquist found that charges for back injuries were 130 percent higher for workers' compensation claimants, but that charges for fractures were about the same.[7]

A certain part of this difference in cost is attributable to providers charging more to workers' compensation payers and to the fact that workers' compensation payers have been less rigorous in their attempts to control costs. There may, however, be other reasons for the differences. It may be that workers' compensation patients receive more aggressive treatment.

In the case of a non-work-related injury, Blue Cross is paying only for the health care costs. In the case of a work-related injury, an employer or its insurer is making weekly indemnity payments in addition to paying health care costs. Presumably, it is willing to pay higher medical costs if they result in better or more aggressive treatment that reduces the indemnity costs.

It is also significant that the greatest differences occur among diagnoses such as back injuries, in which the proper course of treatment is not clearly agreed upon. In the case of a fracture, there is almost universal agreement as to what the treatment protocol should be.

The parties should remember that reducing health care costs is not the ultimate goal in workers' compensation. The 60 percent of the workers' compensation dollars that go to indemnity benefits are still also important. If a higher quality of health care can result in a speedier or more complete recovery for the injured worker, then surely, from the worker's point of view, this is a better result than lower medical costs. A speedier and more complete recovery will also tend to lessen the indemnity costs, and therefore in most cases will be a preferable outcome for the employer. The parties formulating workers' compensation cost control strategies must examine carefully the extent to which workers' compensation health care costs are artificially inflated and the extent to which "you get what you pay for."

10.6.2 The Strategies

The following sections will summarize cost control strategies that have been attempted at the state level and briefly mention possible action at the national level. Chapter 24 deals with strategies that are available to individual employers and insurers.

The strategies used to control health care costs include controlling the choice of provider, medical fee schedules, hospital payment regulation, utilization review, and bill review. Table 10.2 summarizes the most common strategies used by the various states.

Controls on the choice of provider are often seen as one way of controlling health care costs and are included in Table 10.2.

Table 10.2. Common Cost Containment Strategies in Workers' Compensation

Jurisdiction	Limited Initial Provider Choice	Limited Provider Change	Medical Fee Schedule	Hospital Payment Regulation	Utilization Review	Bill Review
Alabama	x		x	x	†	†
Alaska		x	x			
Arizona*	x	x	x		x	x
Arkansas	x	x	x			
California*	x	x	x			
Colorado	x	x	x	x		
Connecticut		x		x		
Delaware						
District of Columbia					x	
Florida	x	x	x	x	x	x
Georgia	x	x	x	x		
Hawaii		x	x	x		
Idaho	x	x				
Illinois		x				
Indiana	x	x				
Iowa	x	x				
Kansas	x	x	†	†		†
Kentucky			x	†	x	†
Louisiana		x	†	†	†	
Maine*	†	x	x	x	x	
Maryland		x	x	x		
Massachusetts		x	x	x	†	
Michigan	x	x	x	x	x	x
Minnesota		x	x	x		
Mississippi		x	†		†	†
Missouri	x	x				
Montana		x	x	x		
Nebraska		x	x	x		

continued

162

State						
Nevada#			x	x	x	x
New Hampshire			†	†	†	†
New Jersey	x		x	x	x	x
New Mexico*	x		x	x	x	x
New York			x	x		
North Carolina	x		x	x	x	x
North Dakota#			x	x	x	x
Ohio#			x			x
Oklahoma			x	x		
Oregon	x		x	x	†	
Pennsylvania	x			x		
Rhode Island			†			x
South Carolina	x		x	x		x
South Dakota	x		x			
Tennessee	x		x		†	†
Texas	x		x	x	x	x
Utah	x		x	x	x	x
Vermont	x					
Virginia	x		x			
Washington#			x	x	x	x
West Virginia#			x	x	x	x
Wisconsin			x	x		
Wyoming#	x		x	x	x	x
TOTAL (excludes †)	22	41	32	28	15	13
Change from 1991–1992	+1	+1	+5	+6	+1	+0

* Arizona and California divide initial provider choice between the employer and the employee. In New Mexico, the employer or insurer can control provider choice and change during the 60 days following the injury or after that period. In Maine, effective January 1, 1993, the employer has the right to select a health care provider for the employee for the initial 10 days of medical care.

† Being developed.

Exclusive state fund.

Note: The table does not reflect strategies that the states have authorized, but rather strategies that the states have implemented.

Source: Workers' Compensation Research Institute.

Because they have broader implications for the entire system, they have been discussed above in section 10.3.

10.6.3 Fee Schedules

Fee schedules were one of the early strategies used by states to control workers' compensation health care costs. Twenty-five states now have some form of fee schedule. Generally, these cover medical and surgical services, radiology, anesthesia, chiropractic services, and physical and occupational therapy. Prescription drugs, home health care, medical equipment, and dental care are less often included. As will be discussed below, fee schedules are an important first step, but fee schedules alone will not control health care costs.

A fee schedule can be seen as a listing of individual fees, but to some extent, every fee schedule is also a *relative value scale*. It not only lists fees for individual procedures, but reflects the values of these procedures relative to each other. One approach that has been gaining acceptance is to use the fee schedules as purely relative value scales. If an office visit, for example, is worth one unit, a surgery might be seen as worth 10 units. Once a jurisdiction has adopted a relative value scale, it can then make adjustments for inflation by simply applying a multiplier to the entire scale. It could also make adjustments to the scale if it felt there were valid reasons for paying a higher rate in one part of the state than in another.

California has developed a relative value scale for workers' compensation, and it has been adopted to varying degrees by Arizona, Kentucky, Maine, Maryland, Montana, New York, Oklahoma, Oregon, Texas, Utah, Washington, and West Virginia. This does not mean that these states reimburse providers at the same rate as California, it means rather that they have adopted the same relative values for the various procedures.

Medicare has adopted a *resource-based* relative value scale. Rather than starting with the currently accepted relative values of various procedures, it worked with scholars to examine the resources necessary to provide each procedure. This included considerations such as the time involved, the amount of equipment needed, the training or specialization required, and even factors such as the potential malpractice costs associated with the procedure. The resulting resource-based relative value scale (RBRVS) was in some respects strikingly different from most schedules previously used. In general, the resource-based finding indicated that complicated and highly technical procedures were being overvalued, while the services of primary care practitioners were being undervalued. Accordingly, the Medicare schedule tends to compensate primary care physicians at a higher rate and surgeons at a lower rate than had previously been the case. In 1993, Pennsylvania adopted the Medicare resource-based relative value scale for its workers' compensation system. It chose, however, to reimburse providers at 13 percent above the Medicare rates. Colorado, Washington, and West Virginia have also adopted this scale at least to some degree.

A fee schedule must use some system for identifying the services provided. The American Medical Association publishes a set of procedural codes called *Physicians Current Procedural Terminology*. The listings in this publication are most often referred to as "CPT Codes." This listing is becoming widely accepted throughout the health care industry as the standard approach.

10.6.4 Hospital Fee Regulation

The regulation of hospital fees is usually approached somewhat differently from fees for other providers. Some states, such as California and Connecticut, have a schedule based on the number of days of admission for the procedure performed. New York and a few other states use diagnostic related groups (DRGs). These have been used widely by Medicaid and Medicare. Under this approach, a hospital is paid a certain amount for each diagnosis regardless of the length of the stay or the complications involved. It is thought that if the appropriate level is set for the average procedure, hospitals will be reimbursed appropriately overall and they will have an incentive to avoid overutilization.

Other jurisdictions, such as Oregon and Rhode Island, pay on a cost plus basis. In other words, they use some means to estimate what the hospital's costs were, then pay a set percentage above those costs. This approach, of course, notably lacks any incentive to reduce costs.

Finally, a number of states including Florida, Georgia, and Hawaii pay at a discount from charges. They might, for example, pay 85 percent of whatever amount the hospital bills.

The latter two approaches raise some obvious questions. How is it possible to accurately determine the costs of various procedures? If payments are based on a discount from charges, will not hospitals simply increase charges? These are clearly weaknesses in these approaches. The approaches are, however, widely used in the health care community in general.

10.6.5 Bill Review

Obviously, if a fee schedule sets a maximum amount for a certain procedure some steps must be taken to ensure that payments above that amount are not made. Some individual insurers and self-insured employers have reviewed bills for years, and as discussed in chapter 24, this method is becoming increasingly popular. A number of states have a statutory mandate that bill reviews be carried out by either the private payer (insurance company or self-insured employer) or the exclusive state workers' compensation fund. In a few states, bill reviews are conducted by the state workers' compensation agency. Table 10.3 lists state requirements.

10.6.6 Utilization Review

As mentioned earlier, fee schedules alone will not control costs. If the fee for an office visit is reduced from $50 to $35, but the physician begins seeing patients twice as often, costs will go up rather than down. If previously the charge for an office visit included bandages and antiseptic, but the provider now sends a separate bill for these items, costs will also go up. This latter approach is called *unbundling*. Thus, a fee schedule is effective only if it is accompanied by *utilization review*.

Utilization review is a step beyond bill review discussed above. A bill review looks to see that the appropriate fee is being paid for the listed procedure. Utilization review asks whether the specific procedure was appropriate for the situation involved. Individual insurers and self-insured employers are increasingly turning to various forms of utilization review. A number of states now require

Table 10.3. Bill Review for Proper Charges:
Type of Program by Jurisdiction

Jurisdiction	Private Payers Mandated	Workers' Compensation Administrative Agency	Review by Exclusive State Fund
Alabama		*	
Arkansas	x		
Florida	x	x	
Kansas		*	
Louisiana		*	
Michigan	x	x	
Mississippi		*	
Nevada	x		x
North Carolina		x	
North Dakota			x
Ohio			x
Oregon	x	x	
South Carolina	x	x	
Tennessee		*	
Texas		x	
Washington			x
West Virginia			x
Wyoming			x
TOTAL	6	6	6

* Developing

Note: The remaining 33 jurisdictions do not have or are not developing medical bill review for proper charges as defined in this report. Florida, Michigan, and Oregon review a sample of claims to ensure that payers are carrying out mandated bill review. The Nevada statute requires payers to review providers' bills. In South Carolina, payers are required to conduct bill review; the Workers' Compensation Commission reviews bills when the payer or provider questions the amount of an allowable charge.

Source: Workers' Compensation Research Institute.

utilization review to some extent. Generally, utilization review is not required in all cases, but, for example, in cases in which the costs are over $5,000, or cases in which there is an inpatient hospitalization. Table 10.4 lists the states that mandate some form of utilization review and indicates the criteria for cases that are reviewed and what is reviewed

Table 10.5 lists who is required to conduct the review. As can be seen, in some states the employer, insurer, or state fund conducts the review, while in a few, the workers' compensation agency carries out this activity. Generally, utilization review is retrospective, that is, the reviewer reviews the events after they have occurred. If they appear to have been inappropriate, payment may

Table 10.4. Characteristics of Utilization Review Programs

Jurisdiction	Review Criteria	What is Reviewed
Alabama		*
Arkansas	Over $5,000 in medical costs; all inpatient hospital cases	Retrospective, focusing on hospital length of stay, physician and chiropractic visits, and other provider visits
District of Columbia	All claims	Necessity, character, and sufficiency of services
Florida	Over $20,000 in medical costs; referred cases; random sample	Referred cases; medical necessity; services related to compensable injury
Louisiana	All nonemergency hospitalization and cases over $750 in medical costs	Necessity, advisability, and cost
Maine	*	
Massachusetts		*
Michigan	Over $5,000 in medical costs; all hospital cases; cases where care is "inappropriate, insufficient, or excessive"	Appropriateness
Mississippi	*	
Nevada	Inpatient surgery; procedures costing more than $200	Charges; preauthorization; referral
New Hampshire	*	*

168

New Jersey	All hospitalization	Appropriateness of inpatient treatment; correct DRG
New Mexico	Agency-designated outpatient cases; all hospitalization	Necessity; appropriateness of setting and treatment; hospital days
North Dakota	All claims	Appropriateness; relatedness to injury; hospital days
Ohio	After 90 days of temporary total disability; all hospitalization	Hospital days; provider visits; necessity; appropriateness; authorization
Oregon	*	*
Tennessee	*	*
Texas	All claims	Preauthorization; appropriateness and necessity; utilization patterns; length of disability
Utah	All hospitalization	Preadmission certification
Washington	All hospitalization; certain back and neck strains and sprains*	Preadmission certification; mandated outpatient surgery; treatment protocols; second opinions
West Virginia	All hospitalization; certain outpatient procedures	Hospital days; outpatient provider visits; inpatient/outpatient procedures; authorization
Wyoming	After 90 days of temporary total disability	#

* Developing
# Developing chiropractic and orthopedic guidelines
Source: Workers' Compensation Research Institute.

Table 10.5. Utilization Review: Type of Program by Jurisdiction

Jurisdiction*	Private Payers Mandated	Workers' Compensation Agency	Exclusive State Fund	Other
Alabama		†		
Arkansas	x			
District of Columbia	x			
Florida	x	x		
Louisiana		x		
Maine		†		
Massachusetts		†		
Michigan	x			
Mississippi		†		
Nevada	x		x	
New Hampshire		†		
New Jersey				All-payer DRGs
New Mexico		x		
North Dakota			x	
Ohio		†	x	
Oregon		†		
Tennessee		†		
Texas		x		
Utah		x		
Washington	x		x	
West Virginia			x	
Wyoming			x	

* The remaining 29 jurisdictions do not have or are not developing utilization review as defined in this report.
† Developing
Source: Workers' Compensation Research Institute.

be denied. As discussed in the next section, some states are moving toward precertification.

10.6.7 Precertification

As discussed in the preceding section, utilization review usually takes place after the service has been provided. Under precertification, a hospitalization or procedure must be approved by the employer or insurer before it is performed. Nevada, Texas, Utah, and Washington have moved toward some form of precertification. Employers advocate for this approach as the best way to control costs. Workers, however, sometimes see it as an infringement on their right to a free choice of provider.

10.6.8 Dispute Resolution

In the past, disputes over health care bills were generally handled in a cumbersome manner. If the employer or insurer felt the bill was too high, it refused to pay either the entire bill or the amount it thought was excessive. The doctor or hospital then would dun the worker. In some cases the worker would pay the balance voluntarily, while in others he or she would refuse and the provider would file an action in court to collect the balance owing. This approach is known as *balanced billing*. Often at this point, the employer or insurer would intercede and either assist the worker in defending the action filed by the provider or pay the balance it had previously questioned.

In addition to being cumbersome, time consuming, and costly, this approach put the worker in the middle of the dispute, which should have involved only the carrier and the provider. It tended to break down both the physician-patient relationship and the employer-employee relationship, both of which are important in achieving a recovery and return to work.

Most states are moving toward procedures that prohibit balanced billing and allow for the state agency to resolve disputes between the provider and the carrier, and where possible, do so without involving the worker. Generally, if the dispute concerns the proper reimbursement for a procedure, the worker need not be involved. If, however, the dispute concerns whether a procedure is appropriate, especially if it is a precertification review, the worker should have a right to be involved.

10.6.9 Managed Care

Managed care is currently fashionable in legislative reform efforts. When used by politicians, the term can refer to anything from fee schedules to requiring that workers be treated in a health maintenance organization (HMO).

The more highly developed approaches to managed care use some form of *managed care organization.* In general, this means that the employer or insurer enters into an agreement with a group of providers such as doctors and hospitals. Under the arrangement, the carrier agrees to require or encourage its injured workers to obtain treatment from this group of providers. In return for the increased volume of business the providers agree to reduce charges. Carriers are finding that it is often possible to contract with groups that will provide services at rates substantially lower than the state-mandated fee schedules.

In states in which the employer has complete or substantial control over the choice of provider, it is relatively easy for the employer to guarantee a larger volume of business in return for the reduced price, and to require that injured workers take advantage of the price reduction negotiated with selective providers. In states in which the worker has a relatively free choice of provider, these things are more difficult. Accordingly, a number of states, such as Connecticut and Oregon, that had given the employee relatively free choice are now creating exceptions under which an employee may be required to seek treatment through a managed care organization selected by the employer.

Representatives of workers sometimes claim that employers really want to use managed care organizations as a way to control employee choice of physician. One way to alleviate this dispute is to give employees, either directly or through their representatives, some say in the management of the managed care organization or in the choice of which managed care organization will be used.

10.6.10 Co-pays and Deductibles

Co-pays and deductibles are schemes under which the patient pays some portion of his or her health care bill. They are common in health care outside of the workers' compensation system, and some argue that they are one of the most effective means of controlling health care costs.[8]

Advocates for workers disagree. They argue that part of the basic tradeoff in creating the workers' compensation system was an assurance of full coverage of medical costs. They also question whether co-pays and deductibles actually reduce overall costs or merely shift these costs to the patient. Finally they question the assumption that workers will seek less, or less expensive, health care if they are paying for part of it. They argue that in today's system, the patient generally decides when to go to a doctor for the first time but thereafter follows the advice that he or she receives. Finally, there is concern that co-pays or deductibles may discourage workers from receiving early treatment that might reduce the need for more extensive care in the future.

In 1993 Florida became the first state to use co-pays. No state uses deductibles.

10.6.11 National Health Care

As this is being written, the United States is considering a complete overhaul of its system for providing health care to its citizens. There is considerable debate concerning the extent to which workers' compensation should be part of this system.

Workers' compensation accounts for only about 3 percent of the total health care expenditures in the United States. If the rest of the country develops some system for controlling health care costs, it is hard to imagine how the workers' compensation system would benefit by being completely outside of that system. As mentioned earlier there is considerable evidence that there is already cost shifting to workers' compensation. If workers' compensation is left out of the national plan, this cost shifting would likely increase.

On the other hand, there are reasons why we might wish to treat workers' compensation claimants differently from other patients. Assume Mr. A comes to the doctor with a sore, swollen ankle. In an attempt to reduce health care costs many payers such as Blue Cross have been attempting to educate physicians not to order an X-ray immediately. In the majority of cases, this individual will have only suffered a sprain, and will recover promptly without spending money on an X-ray. If he does not show improvement in a few days, an X-ray can be ordered at that time to discover if there is a fracture. If a fracture is found, appropriate measures can be taken. If, however, Mr. A was injured on the job, the workers' compensation carrier will be paying not only the health care benefits, but also indemnity benefits that will be based at least in part on the length of time that Mr. A is away from work. Under these circumstances, the workers' compensation carrier will generally encourage the doctor to order an X-ray immediately. This will be worth the additional cost if it reduces the wage-loss benefits. Accordingly, it is argued that it may be appropriate to provide different care to injured workers.

It is also asserted by many that the cost of workers' compensation creates an incentive for safety and the prevention of injuries. If workers' compensation health care is completely integrated into a national health care scheme, some of this incentive will be lost.

Finally there is the question of managing care. As discussed extensively in second part of this book, the way a claim is managed and the way a worker is treated has great impact on the potential recovery. If the management of the medical portion of a workers' compensation case is placed in a national health care system and completely separated from the rest of the management of the case, the quality is likely to deteriorate.

As discussed in sections 2.7 and 2.8, the prospects for combining workers' compensation with other systems have both good and bad implications that must be carefully considered.

Notes

1. Research on whether this actually reduces medical costs has produced mixed results. Durbin, D., and Appel, D., "The Impact of Fee Schedules and Employer Choice of Physician." *NCCI Digest*, Vol. 6, No. 3 (1991), 39–59; Pozzebon, Silvana, "Do Traditional Health Care Cost Containment Practices Really Work?" *John Burton's Workers' Compensation Monitor*, Vol. 6, No.3 (May/June 1993), 17–22.
2. 42 U.S.C. §1395y(b)(1).
3. For example: Victor, Richard, B., ed., *Medical Cost Containment in Workers' Compensation: Innovative Approaches* (Boston: Workers' Compensation Research Institute, 1987); Greenwood, Judith, and Taricco, Alfred, eds., *Workers' Compensation Health Care Cost Containment* (Horsham, Pa.: Edited by LRP Publications, 1992).

4. Telles, Carol A., *Medical Cost Containment in Workers' Compensation: A National Inventory 1992–1993* (Cambridge: Workers' Compensation Research Institute, 1993), 4.
5. Burton, John, F., Jr., "Workers' Compensation Costs, 1960–1992: The Increases, the Causes, the Consequences." *John Burton's Compensation Monitor,* Vol. 6, No. 2 (March/April 1993), 1–15.
6. Thornquist, Lisa, "Health Care Costs and Cost Containment in Minnesota's Workers' Compensation Program." *John Burton's Workers' Compensation Monitor,* Vol. 3, No. 3 (May/June 1990), 3–26; Baker, Lawrence C., and Krueger, Alan B., "24-Hour Coverage and Workers' Compensation Insurance," *Health Affairs,* vol. 12 (supplement 1993), 271–81.
7. Thornquist, *supra* note 6.
8. Pozzebon, Silvana, "Health Care Costs Containment: A Review on the Literature on Cost Sharing." *John Burton's Workers' Compensation Monitor,* Vol. 3, No. 4 (July/August 1990), 21–22.

Chapter 11

Vocational Rehabilitation

11.1 Introduction

It is almost axiomatic that vocational rehabilitation should be the ultimate goal of the entire workers' compensation system. If a counselor or other provider can help the individual to overcome the effects of his or her injury and return to work, the worker is nearly always better off both financially and psychologically. Even in the most generous jurisdictions, the amount workers receive in compensation benefits is little compared with the value of a job that a person can perform successfully for the rest of his or her life. At the same time, vocational rehabilitation is in the best interest of employers. The cost of vocational rehabilitation is quite small when compared to the cost of indemnity benefits and successful rehabilitation will nearly always reduce the exposure of employers to indemnity payments.

Because of these apparent advantages to both workers and employers, it became for a time customary for most studies of workers' compensation systems to conclude with a section advocating expanded and enhanced vocational rehabilitation programs. Unfortunately, the reality of the situation does not always coincide with this theory. Sometimes workers resist vocational rehabilitation for a variety of reasons, and sometimes employers see it as a waste of money. Both sides sometimes use vocational rehabilitation in inappropriate ways.

This chapter discusses the legal requirements governing vocational rehabilitation. Section 19.3 discusses practical implications for employers and insurers.[1]

11.2 What Is Vocational Rehabilitation?

One ordinarily envisions a situation in which a trained counselor, usually one with a master's degree in rehabilitation counseling, meets with the individual and conducts an evaluation. This might include a review of medical records, an interview, and perhaps psychological and other testing. Based upon the results of this evaluation, the counselor recommends a rehabilitation plan. This might include retraining and nearly always would involve the counselor providing information about the job market, the requirements for those jobs, and how they match the abilities and limitations of the individual. The counselor might assist the individual in applying for and obtaining a job. The counselor might also help the worker by teaching him or her how to fill out applications and by providing coaching regarding interviewing skills. If it was determined that retraining was necessary, the counselor might help the worker develop an appropriate plan.

Most experts agree and agencies require that there be a hierarchy of goals for vocational rehabilitation. These are often classified in different ways, but the general outcome is something similar to the following:

1. Return to work on the preinjury job with the same employer.
2. Return to work at the preinjury job with modifications at the same employer.
3. Return to work at a different job with the same employer.
4. Return to work at the same or a similar job with another employer.
5. Return to work at a different job with a different employer.
6. Short-term retraining to allow return to work at a different job with the same or a different employer.
7. Long-term reeducation to allow return to work in an entirely different occupation.

While most people would agree to this hierarchy, there are a great many disputes in its application. Typically, the worker seeks some type of retraining or reeducation, while the employer wants to emphasize immediate job placement.

Another issue concerns what should be the ultimate goal of vocational rehabilitation. Traditional rehabilitation programs predated those related to workers' compensation. They were directed toward individuals disabled from a variety of causes, many of whom were disabled from birth. Generally, the goal of these programs is to *maximize* the client's potential. In the workers' compensation setting, on the other hand, the employer usually believes that the goal should be a return to work as quickly as possible.

Assume, for example, that Mr. A did not finish high school and that he was working on a punch press when he lost a foot. Ms. X, a counselor, meets with Mr. A, conducts an interview and some preliminary testing. She discovers that although Mr. A did not finish high school, he is, in fact, quite intelligent and has the potential to succeed in a college program. At the same time, she recognizes that there are many other jobs in the community that Mr. A could perform without any retraining. She knows, in fact, of some employers who would hire Mr. A.

Mr. A will most likely realize his maximum potential if he goes to college, obtains a degree, and works in some managerial or professional area. He will have greater earnings and be able to do more to provide for himself and his family. He will also probably make a more valuable contribution to society. On the other hand, this is a rather costly program. With a very modest amount of job placement activity, the employer's losses could be substantially reduced by placing Mr. A in some routine assembly-type position as soon as possible. What is the appropriate course of vocational rehabilitation? Shouldn't we always strive to help individuals obtain their maximum potential? Is it fair to ask the employer to bear the cost of this man's college education when for a much smaller effort it can return him to approximately the same position he was in before the injury? In general, it is said that in workers' compensation the goal of vocational rehabilitation should be to restore the worker to the position he or she was in before the injury.

11.3 Benefits

Vocational rehabilitation benefits generally include fees paid to a counselor for testing and other forms of evaluation, and for assistance in placement activities. Benefits may also include tuition, travel expenses, and room and board if some form of training or education is deemed appropriate.

Generally, workers receive some sort of allowance during rehabilitation. This is most often paid at the same rate as temporary total disability benefits. In states that pay benefits based on an impairment rating, this benefit is usually paid in addition to those impairment benefits. In states that pay benefits based on a wage-loss, this benefit is usually paid in place of the wage-loss benefit.

Virtually all states put some limit on either the total amount paid or the number of weeks during which the benefit is available. Fifty-two weeks is a typical limitation. (See Table 11.1.)

11.4 Mandatory Vocational Rehabilitation

When describing the vocational rehabilitation system in a given state, the first question usually asked is, "Is vocational rehabilitation mandatory?" It is tempting to try to answer this question with a simple yes or no. It really should be broken down into four questions.

1. Can the worker be penalized if he or she refuses to accept vocational rehabilitation services if the employer offers them? (This question is sometimes stated, "Can the worker be forced to accept vocational rehabilitation services?" This, however, is the wrong question. The answer to this question is of course "no." No worker is forced to engage in vocational rehabilitation. However, many states provide that workers can be deprived of other benefits if they refuse to cooperate.)
2. Can an employer be forced to provide or pay for vocational rehabilitation services if the worker asks for them?
3. Can the state agency require both parties to participate in vocational rehabilitation services even though neither party seeks to?
4. If a state agency has the power described in (3) above, to what extent does it exercise it?

Table 11.1 includes a listing of the requirements placed on employers and workers. It is the best collection of information

Table 11.1. Vocational Rehabilitation

Jurisdiction	Rehabilitation Unit	Can Employer Be Required to Pay?	Penalty to Worker Who Refuses	Benefits During
Alabama	None	Yes	Suspended	TTD
Alaska	M	Yes	Suspended	TTD + $200/month
Arizona	None	Yes	Reduced or suspended	NA
Arkansas	None	Yes	Suspended	PPD + maintenance expenses
California	M	Yes	Suspended	TTD + maintenance expenses
Colorado	M	Special fund pays	Reduced or suspended	TTD
Connecticut	D	Disability benefits only	Suspended	80% of TTD
Delaware	None	Yes	Suspended	TTD
District of Columbia	M	Yes	Suspended	TTD + $50/week
Florida	D, M	Yes	Reduced	TTD
Georgia	M	Yes	Reduced or suspended	TTD
Hawaii	R, M	No	Reduced or suspended	TTD
Idaho	D	Special state fund pays	Reduced or suspended	TTD
Illinois	None	Yes	Reduced or suspended	TTD
Indiana	D	Yes	Suspended	NA
Iowa	R	Yes	None	TTD + $20/week
Kansas	R, M	Yes	Suspended	TTD
Kentucky	M	Yes	Reduced by 50%	Normal weekly compensation
Louisiana	NA	Yes	Reduced by 50%	TTD
Maine	D, M	Yes	Suspended	TTD + $35/week
Maryland	R	Yes	Suspended	TTD + $40/week
Massachusetts	R	Yes	Suspended	TTD
Michigan	D, R, M	Yes	Reduced	Wage-loss benefits

State				
Minnesota	M	Yes	Suspended	TTD
Mississippi	R	Special fund pays	Suspended	TTD + $10/week
Missouri	R	Yes	Reduced by 50%	TTD/TPD
Montana	R, M	Special fund pays	Suspended	TTD
Nebraska	D, R	TTD only, special fund pays balance	Reduced or suspended	TTD
Nevada	D, R, M	Yes	Suspended	TTD
New Hampshire	M	Yes	Suspended	TTD
New Jersey	None	Yes	Suspended	TTD
New Mexico	None	Yes	NA	TTD
New York	R	Special fund pays penalties to employees	None	TTD + $30/week
North Carolina	D	None	Suspended	NA
North Dakota	D	Yes	Suspended	Special allowance
Ohio	D	Yes	None	NA
Oklahoma	R, M	Yes	None	Normal weekly compensation
Oregon	M	Yes	Reduced, suspended, or forfeited	TTD
Pennsylvania	None	None	None	Not provided by statute
Rhode Island	D	Yes	Suspended	TTD or PPD
South Carolina	None	Yes	Suspended	TTD
South Dakota	None	Yes	None	TTD
Tennessee	None	No	Suspended	NA
Texas	None	No	None	NA
Utah	None	No	None	NA
Vermont	None	Yes	Suspended	TTD

continued

Table 11.1.—*continued*

Jurisdiction	Rehabilitation Unit	Can Employer Be Required to Pay?	Penalty to Worker Who Refuses	Benefits During
Virginia	None	Yes	Suspended	TTD
Washington	D, M	Yes	Reduced by 50%	TTD
West Virginia	R	Yes	None	TTD
Wisconsin	None	No	None	TTD
Wyoming	None	Yes	None	NA
FECA	R	Yes	Decreased	TTD + $200/month
LHWCA	R	Special fund	Suspended	TTD + $25/week

D: State rehabilitation unit provides direct rehabilitation services to claimants.
R: State rehabilitation unit refers claimants to state agencies or other private providers.
M: State rehabilitation unit monitors vocational rehabilitation cases.
TTD: Temporary Total Disability benefits
PTD: Permanent Total Disability benefits
PPD: Permanent Partial Disability benefits
TPD: Temporary Partial Disability benefits
NA: Not available
Source: State Workers' Compensation Laws, U.S. Department of Labor, Office of Workers' Compensation Programs, January 1994, Table 15.

available on this point. Within recent years several states including California, Colorado, and Washington have changed their system from one that was to some extent a mandatory system to one that is more nearly voluntary. Writing for the WCRI, John Gardner suggests that the best system is one in which the state agency monitors cases, identifies those that are appropriate for rehabilitation, and gently suggests to the parties that rehabilitation should be considered.[2]

11.5 Financing of Vocational Rehabilitation

As can be seen in Table 11.1, in a few states, the state vocational rehabilitation agency bears all the expenses of vocational rehabilitation. In approximately 10 more states, the costs are shared between the employer and the state vocational rehabilitation service. In about half of the states, employers are required to pay all the costs of vocational rehabilitation.

In a handful of states vocational rehabilitation is paid for by a state fund. In states in which there is an exclusive state fund, this simply means that the benefits are paid initially by the state fund. In effect, they are being paid by the employer and charged back through premiums. In a few states, however, there is a special fund in which an assessment is made on all employers, and vocational rehabilitation services are paid for out of a fund created from these assessments. See chapter 13.

11.6 Vocational Rehabilitation Providers

Virtually all states have a division of vocational rehabilitation that is entirely separate from their workers' compensation program and different from a vocational rehabilitation "unit" located within a workers' compensation agency. These state agencies are, to a large extent, funded by federal funds and are designed to serve all disabled individuals. In most cases their emphasis is not on work-related injuries.

As indicated in Table 11.1, in about two-thirds of the states, these agencies also provide rehabilitation services to workers injured on the job. In the majority of states the employer is required to reimburse the state agency for all or part of the cost of providing these services.

In about two-thirds of the jurisdictions vocational rehabilitation services are also provided by private rehabilitation agencies. In about 10 jurisdictions these private agencies are licensed or approved by the state workers' compensation agency.

Numerous issues arise concerning private vocational rehabilitation agencies. It is sometimes suggested that they tend to be biased and that they develop into pro-worker and pro-employer agencies. A pro-worker provider would be more likely to recommend expensive educational programs and perhaps testify for the worker concerning the extent of disability, whereas a pro-employer provider would emphasize immediate job placement and testify in favor of the employer. It seems likely that vocational rehabilitation agencies develop along the same pattern as medical providers and others. A few are extremely partisan in favor of either workers or employers, while the majority are in the middle trying conscientiously to do the best possible job for all concerned. They take a professional approach to their work and recognize that successful rehabilitation helps both employers and workers.

In many states the state vocational rehabilitation agency has an image or reputation of being more independent than private providers. This may or may not be deserved. In a few states the state agency is seen as an alternative, an agency to which an individual can be referred when the employer and worker cannot agree upon a private provider.

In most states the private providers and the state agency compete actively for the same type of referrals. In a few states, however, they serve different populations. This appears to be the case in New York. When the employer is actively interested in encouraging the rehabilitation of a worker, the individual is usually sent to a private provider. When the employer is not interested in participating in rehabilitation and the worker is left to seek help alone, he or she usually winds up being serviced by the state agency.

11.7 Vocational Rehabilitation Units

As can be seen from Table 11.1, approximately 35 state workers' compensation agencies have a vocational rehabilitation unit.

Most frequently, these units monitor the provision of vocational rehabilitation services. This may mean that they require parties to engage in vocational rehabilitation; it may mean that they simply encourage parties to participate; in some states it means that they approve or license private vocational rehabilitation providers.

In some states, rehabilitation units make referrals of workers to rehabilitation providers. In only a handful of states does the unit provide direct vocational rehabilitation services. This most often occurs in exclusive fund states when a distinction between a workers' compensation bureau and the state workers' compensation insurance fund is not always clearly drawn.

In a substantial number of states, the vocational rehabilitation unit is involved in dispute resolution concerning issues related to rehabilitation. It may act as a mediator, it may make recommendations, or it may act as a decision maker concerning this issue.

11.8 The Problems

In theory, vocational rehabilitation should work to everyone's advantage, but many problems arise. In some cases, workers refuse to cooperate. An early return to work or the gathering of skills that are valuable in the job market may reduce the award that the worker will receive from the workers' compensation system. Accordingly, some workers think it advantageous to resist rehabilitation until a final determination is made concerning the amount of benefits that will be awarded as a result of the injury.

A wise worker will see that in the long run he or she is better off to have a job, but we all often fail to see the long-term wisdom of decisions we make. Moreover, we do not make our best decisions when we are hurting, out of work, and in immediate financial peril. The choice of the worker may also depend on the advice he or she is receiving at the time.

It is unfortunately the case that both sides sometimes use rehabilitation in inappropriate ways. A worker may demand a substantial and costly rehabilitation program that will increase the potential cost to the employer thus enhancing the settlement value for the worker. On the other hand, most workers' compensation statutes provide a penalty, usually the termination of benefits, if the worker refuses to accept a reasonable vocational rehabilitation program. Accordingly, it is possible for an employer to offer a program that is undesirable and onerous to the worker. If the worker finds that he or she is deriving little benefit from the program and sees it as a degrading experience, he or she is likely to refuse to cooperate and the employer may then be able to reduce its liability.

Proponents of vocational rehabilitation point out that its cost is relatively small when compared to the cost of indemnity benefits that it can reduce. Others argue that the studies which show a high return to work rate often include many individuals who might have returned to work anyway. The only study that used a control group to compare the benefits of vocational rehabilitation with a group of people who received no such help did not support the conclusion that vocational rehabilitation was cost effective.[3] That study, however, did not account for appropriate selection of candidates for rehabilitation.

Conflicts also arise as to what is vocational rehabilitation as compared to simple claims management. Many claims adjusters will assert that "in the old days" they used to go out and sit down at the kitchen table with workers and do the same thing that today is called vocational rehabilitation. In this context, it should be remembered that the way costs are allocated has certain implications. This is especially true for insured employers, but may also have some impact on self-insurance programs. Ordinarily, the expenses of claims adjusting are treated as expenses of the insurance company and tend to reduce its profit margin. On the other hand, rehabilitation expenses are often considered part of the *loss*. They will thus often affect the employer's experience rating and raise premiums in subsequent years. In some situations they are passed on directly to the employer. Thus, it is to the advantage of the insurer, but not the employer, to have as many functions as possible be considered *vocational rehabilitation*.

There are other reasons for drawing a clear line between adjusting and vocational rehabilitation. Questions arise as to where a vocational rehabilitation provider's ultimate loyalty should lie. Should it lie with the employer or with the worker? Theoretically, in most situations the ultimate goal would be the same for both.

Practically, however, this is often not the case. Vocational rehabilitation providers are able to obtain the confidence of the individual and to learn a great deal about his or her situation. They may also be able to influence the worker on such crucial issues as whether it is appropriate to settle or compromise in a claim. It is generally believed that these are not appropriate functions of rehabilitation counseling. If such counseling is to be successful, the worker must be able to have confidence in the counselor. If the worker perceives that the counselor's primary loyalty is to the employer, the counselor will not be able to provide effective counseling to the worker. Accordingly, it is important to distinguish between what is vocational rehabilitation and what is claims adjusting.

The above problems are listed because it is important that everyone understand them and be prepared to avoid them. I want to emphasize, however, that as discussed in section 19.3, when done properly, in the right case, vocational rehabilitation can be the best possible solution for both the worker and the employer.

Notes

1. A broader discussion of vocational rehabilitation can be found in Berkowitz, Monroe, and Berkowitz, Edward D., "Rehabilitation in the Work Injury Program," *Rehabilitation Counseling Bulletin*, Vol. 34, No. 3 (March 1991), 182–96.
2. Gardner, John A., *Improving Vocational Rehabilitation Outcomes: Opportunities for Earlier Intervention* (Cambridge: Workers' Compensation Research Institute, 1988), 30–32.
3. Greenwood, Judith G., Wolf, Harvey J., and Pearson, John C., *et al.*, "Early Intervention in Low Back Disability Among Coal Miners in West Virginia: Negative Findings," *J. of Occupational Medicine*, Vol. 32, No. 10 (October 1990), 1047–52.

Chapter 12

Procedures and Administration

12.1 Introduction

This chapter will cover the procedures followed in ordinary undisputed cases, those followed in disputed cases, the time limits imposed, and the structure of state administrations. Reviews of any workers' compensation system often emphasize the disputed cases and the procedures for resolving disputes. It is important to remember that this represents a minority of the cases. In the states followed most closely by the NCCI, in over 80 percent of the cases the parties either had no dispute or resolved their differences without the need for attorneys.[1] Of course, it is the larger cases that tend to be controverted and the controversies are concentrated in certain areas such as permanent partial claims. Nevertheless, it is worth remembering that most cases go through the system without dispute or controversy. We hear a great many complaints about workers' compensation and indeed there is room for improvement, but the fact is that most of the time the system works quite well.

12.2 State Agency Administration

In the majority of states, the workers' compensation agency is located within a department of labor or a department of labor and industry. State workers' compensation agencies are referred to as workers' compensation divisions, bureaus, commissions, or boards. The older model is for a commission or board to supervise the administration of the act and to also act as an appellate body. Agencies that operate under this model are more likely to be referred to as a board or commission. The newer model is to have a bureau or division that is responsible for administration of the act and that is separate from the appellate board or commission.

A few states, such as Nebraska and Oklahoma, have what is called a Workers' Compensation Court. In these states, the hearing officers are members of the judicial branch of government. In general, these courts tend to have more independence from regulation by the legislature or the executive branch. The administrative agencies in these states have varying degrees of autonomy from the court. This situation is to be distinguished from states in which there is an industrial accident board, but the appeal from a decision of an accident board is to the courts of general jurisdiction where the case may be tried all over again before a jury. Generally, states have moved away from this alternative. In Texas for example, most cases ended up in local courts until 1990. Since then, the right to appeal to local courts has been greatly restricted. In Ohio, there are still some circumstances under which workers' compensation issues can get to a jury in a local court, but this alternative is rarely used.

Most states finance the operation of their state's agencies through either a tax based on the amount of premium charged or an assessment based upon the amount of benefits paid. Ohio bases its assessment on the amount of payroll paid by employers. This seems a less desirable alternative. In the other systems, the amount of the assessment is based at least indirectly on the amount of losses. Thus, employers that use the system most, pay the most, and the assessment at least theoretically creates a safety incentive.

In states with a premium tax, insurers are charged a tax that might equal 1 percent of all the premiums they collect. Presumably, this tax is passed on to their insured employers. In states that use a premium tax and allow self-insurance, some formula is used to estimate what the premium would be for self-insured employers.

States that use assessments base the amount collected on the amount paid out in benefits. The assessments are levied in the same manner against insurance companies and self-insured employers. The base upon which assessments are made might include only indemnity benefits or all benefits paid out.

Eleven states—Alabama, Alaska, California, Hawaii, Illinois, Indiana, Iowa, Maine, Michigan, Rhode Island, and South Dakota—finance their agency in whole or in part out of the general tax revenues of the state. Agencies that are funded by general tax revenues tend to be more subject to variations in state budgeting policies. Judith Greenwood has discussed various aspects of this issue in *John Burton's Workers' Compensation Monitor.*[2]

In general, members of boards and commissions and the chief administrator of the workers' compensation bureau or division are political appointees of the governor. Trial level judges are sometimes political appointees and sometimes members of the civil service system.

12.3 Procedures

12.3.1 Introduction

Like compensation for permanent partial disability, procedures are an area in which there is great variation among the states. There is a general scheme that is followed by most jurisdictions. The details, however, vary not only in the specific procedures that are followed, but even in the terms that are used to describe them.

It would be beyond the scope of this book to attempt to provide any detailed listings of which procedures are followed in specific states. We will, however, sketch a general overview of the basic structure that is followed, suggest some of the alternatives that are used at various points, and discuss some approaches that experts see as particularly good or troublesome.

This section will deal with procedures that are prescribed by law. The practices and procedures that are carried out by insurers and employers in the workplace are discussed in Part 3.

12.3.2 Overview of Procedures

When an injury occurs, the worker is expected to give notice to the employer and sometimes the worker is also required to make a claim for workers' compensation benefits. The employer then reports the injury to its state workers' compensation agency.

The carrier, an insurance company, or self-employed employer, pays benefits to the worker during his or her temporary total disability. At the end of that period, benefits may be terminated by the carrier acting alone or sometimes with the approval of the state agency. It is determined at this point whether the worker has any permanent residual impairment. Often there is none. The individual returns to work and that is the end of the claim. If the worker is found to have a permanent and total disability, those benefits are begun. If there is a permanent partial disability, a determination must be made (usually by the state agency) of the extent of that impairment. Then benefits are paid based on that determination.

Disputed cases usually begin with some party filing an application or petition for hearing with the state agency. Next there is some form of informal mediation or conference at which the parties are encouraged to attempt to reach an agreed-upon solution to the case. If this is not accomplished, a hearing is held before a workers' compensation hearing officer. Ordinarily, parties have a right to appeal from the hearing officer's decision to a board or a commission. Sometimes the scope of review is limited to only legal and not factual issues. If the parties are still dissatisfied, they may appeal to the courts of the state. Generally, however, the courts will only review legal issues.

Many states allow the parties to reach a compromise settlement. Generally these must be approved by the state agency. Many states allow the reopening of determinations and/or settlements for various reasons.

12.3.3 Notice, Claim, and Time Limitations

Most workers' compensation laws place two different reporting requirements upon the injured worker—one for giving *notice* of the injury and one for making a *claim* for benefits. The notice period is relatively short, usually a few weeks or a few months. The purpose is to enable the employer to provide medical treatment and to allow it to investigate the circumstances of the injury.

Often the fact that a supervisory employee saw the injury or was told of it is sufficient notice. In general, the failure to give notice within the prescribed time period will not defeat the worker's right to benefits if it can be shown that the employer actually knew the injury occurred.

Notice requirements are usually liberally interpreted by the courts. It is, however, usually not enough that some co-employee knew of the injury, or that the employer simply knew that the worker was "not feeling well." If the employer pays compensation benefits or provides medical care, it is usually assumed that this is sufficient evidence that the employer had notice of the injury.

Some statutes contain provisions that failure to give notice does not defeat a worker's right to benefits unless the employer was somehow prejudiced by not receiving the notice. Prejudice might occur if the seriousness of the injury could have been mitigated had the employer been able to offer immediate medical treatment or if the opportunity to investigate the facts surrounding the injury has now been lost.

A *claim* is a request or demand by the worker to be paid benefits. The time for making a claim is usually one or two years. The claim is usually made with the state administrative agency, but in some jurisdictions it is made directly with the employer. The purpose of a claim requirement is the same as any statute of limitations under the law, that is, to protect the employer against claims that are too old to be investigated and defended. (It should be noted that "claim" is used here to refer to a requirement that the worker ask the employer or its insurance carrier to pay workers' compensation benefits. Sometimes, however, "claim" is used to refer to the procedure by which a worker requests a hearing and initiates a formal contested case procedure with the state agency.)

The time period for giving notice or making a claim usually does not begin to run until the worker would reasonably recognize the seriousness of the injury or disease, and realize that it was or might have been caused by the employment. Assume, for example, that Mr. A worked in a chemical plant and became disabled as a result of bladder cancer. Assume further that five years after his last day of work he learned for the first time that bladder cancer may be caused by exposures to the chemicals with which he worked. He should not be precluded from filing a claim. The same might be true if he knew he was suffering from some problem, but it took the doctors a long time to arrive at the correct diagnosis.

If a worker is paid other benefits, such as group insurance or pension benefits, instead of workers' compensation benefits, the time for making a claim usually does not run so long as those benefits are being paid. Such a rule is necessary, because otherwise an employer could lull a worker into not making a claim for workers' compensation benefits by providing him or her with some other type of benefits until the claim period had passed. As in the case of most statutes of limitation, the mental or physical incompetence of the person involved will delay the running of the time period.

It should be noted that the claim requirement is a true statute of limitations in most but not all states. In a true statute of limitations, no request for hearing can be filed after the time period has run. In some states, such as Michigan, if the worker has made a claim with the employer he or she can request a hearing at any time in the future.

A few states have a "one-year back rule" or a "two-year back rule." These provide that even in circumstances under which the claim or notice period may be waived, the worker can only receive benefits for one year back from the date he or she made a claim.

As discussed below, most states require an employer to file a report of injury. A few states have requirements that the time period in which a worker must make a claim does not begin to run until the employer has reported the injury to the state agency.

The National Commission recommended "that the employee or his surviving dependents be required to give notice as soon as practical to the employer concerning the work-related impairment or death. This notice requirement would be met if the employer or his agency, such as an insurance carrier, has actual knowledge of the impairment or death, or if oral or written notice is given to the employer." (R 6.9.)

The commission further recommended "that for those injuries and diseases which must be reported to the workmen's compensation agency, the period allowed for employees to file claims not begin to run until the employer's notice of the work-related impairment or death is filed with the workmen's compensation agency." (R 6.11.)

Finally, the commission recommended "that the time limit for initiating a claim be three years after the date the claimant knows or, by exercise of reasonable diligence should have known, of the existence of the impairment and its possible relationship to his employment, or within three years after the employee first experiences a loss of wages which the employee knows, or by exercise of reasonable diligence should have known, was because of the work-related impairment. If benefits have been previously provided, the claim period should begin on the date benefits were last furnished." (R 6.13.)

12.3.4 Report

All states require that the employer *report* to the state agency any work-related injuries that result in time away from work longer than the waiting period for the payment of benefits as well as fatality cases and cases involving amputations. (See section 9.5 concerning the waiting period.) Some agencies also require the reporting of cases that involve medical treatment, but no lost time from work. Reporting an injury is generally the employer's responsibility, although sometimes insurance or service companies carry out this task for the employer. An insured employer must of course also report the injury to its insurance carrier.

12.3.5 Information and Assistance

There is great variation among the states in the extent to which an injured worker (or an employer) can obtain information and assistance from the state workers' compensation agency. In recent years, there is increasing agreement that it is appropriate for the state to provide information to injured workers, and in many cases to go a step further and provide informal dispute resolution procedures. Assume that Mr. B has been off work for a short period of time and has not received benefits. Many states now provide an 800 number that he can call. There is usually a person available to answer questions about the conditions under which he would be entitled to benefits. Sometimes that person will also call the carrier and make an inquiry as to why benefits have not been paid. This may result in an explanation to the worker as to why he or she is not entitled to benefits. Yet it can also prod the employer or insurance carrier and result in the voluntary payment of benefits. Often the person from the state agency learns that the insurance company is waiting for a report from the doctor. The worker can then call the doctor and encourage him or her to send in the report. This procedure results in resolution of a substantial number of disputes. It tends to be most successful in relatively smaller cases.

Occasionally, employers call for assistance from these programs, but generally it is workers who are directly helped. It might seem that such programs tend to unfairly help workers as opposed to employers. It is generally felt, however, that in the long run everyone benefits from such programs. Workers who are not able to get assistance from state agencies usually turn to attorneys for help. Because of their training and experience, attorneys tend to feel that the most appropriate way to solve any problem is through formal litigation. Accordingly, most employers feel that they would rather have the state agency help workers solve their minor problems than face litigation.

12.3.6 The Commencement of Compensation

If a carrier believes that the injury is compensable, it will begin the payment of temporary total disability benefits. If it believes the injury did not occur at work, or there is no disability, it will deny the claim. In some cases, it may need more time to conduct an investigation.

Some jurisdictions require that the carrier either accept or deny a claim within a certain period of time and provide penalties for carriers that do not act within this period of time or that unreasonably deny claims. Wisconsin, for example, requires that the carrier take action within 14 days.

In all states, carriers must report to the state agency that payments have begun and the amount of payments. They also report any later changes in the payment rate.

12.3.7 Termination of Temporary Total Benefits

In all states temporary total benefits stop when the worker has reached maximum medical improvement (section 8.3) or when he or she has returned to work. Some states, such as Wisconsin, allow termination of benefits when a worker refuses a job offer.

An important variation among the states is whether the carrier can terminate benefits unilaterally. In Pennsylvania for example, a carrier believing the worker has achieved maximum medical improvement cannot terminate benefits unless it obtains a signed agreement from the worker or is granted permission to terminate benefits by the state after a hearing. In Minnesota, the employer must notify the worker of its intention to discontinue benefits. If the employee objects and requests a conference, then the carrier must continue to pay benefits until that conference is held. (In both Pennsylvania and Minnesota, an employer may terminate benefits unilaterally if the worker has returned to work and is receiving pay equal to or greater than his or her prior wages.)

In New York, a conference must be held before benefits can be stopped, but an employer can suspend payment of benefits pending the conference. In states such as Missouri, Wisconsin, and Michigan, an employer who feels the worker has recovered may file a notice with the state agency explaining its reasons and unilaterally stop paying benefits. In those states nothing further happens unless the worker files a request for a hearing.

12.3.8 Determinations of Permanent Disability

If it is obvious to the carrier that the worker suffers a permanent and total disability, the parties will agree to this and begin paying appropriate benefits. If there is a disagreement over this issue, then the parties must resort to the dispute resolution procedures discussed below.

If the worker is entitled to or claims to be entitled to permanent partial disability benefits, some procedure must be in place to determine the extent of the disability. Generally, this determination must be approved to some extent by the state agency. In some states such as Wisconsin, the parties are often able to agree on a disability rating and submit their agreement for approval by the state agency. In other states, however, parties almost routinely resort to the use of attorneys and the formal dispute resolution procedures described below to resolve this issue.

12.3.9 Agency Intervention

There is great variation concerning the extent to which state workers' compensation agencies actively intervene in the supervision of cases. It is sometimes said that the state agency is "active" or "passive," depending on the extent of its intervention.

Wisconsin and Oregon are often cited as states in which active intervention by the state agency avoids disputes and keeps the system running well. In general, agencies in these states monitor claims in an attempt to identify problem cases (cases in which the employer is not paying promptly or appropriately) and actively intervene to resolve disputes or assist the worker when necessary. Overall, both employers and workers seem pleased with outcomes in these states.

New York and Missouri are seen as states in which the agency is rather active, yet its activities are less fruitful. They require the parties to attend numerous meetings and conferences, but these meetings and conferences do not seem to resolve or avoid disputes.

Michigan is an example of a state in which the agency is rather passive. Under Michigan law, an employer is generally free to terminate or reduce benefits as it sees fit. It must report this to the state, but the state does not take any action unless the worker asks for assistance, in which case the state agency will schedule a mediation or a formal hearing. In general, the parties are on their own and the state intervenes only if one party asks for assistance in resolving a dispute. This approach seems to work fairly well in Michigan, but in many other jurisdictions the lack of an active state agency seems to lead to unnecessary litigation.

It should be noted that the ability of the employer to unilaterally terminate benefits only applies to cases in which it has paid benefits voluntarily. If there has been a dispute about the payment of benefits, resulting in a hearing and an order that the carrier must pay benefits, all states require that the carrier continue to pay until the order has been carried out or until there has been another hearing and a new order.

12.4 Disputes

Workers' compensation systems were originally intended to be simple, self-executing systems that would avoid attorneys and formal dispute resolution procedures. Currently, however, we hear many complaints about the excessive amount of litigation in these systems. It is undoubtedly true that in many jurisdictions there is excessive litigation. At the same time it must be remembered that while litigation of workers' compensation claims has now become more complicated and costly than it once was, it is still generally much simpler and faster than litigation in civil courts. It also must be remembered that we are dealing with very difficult issues about the extent to which an individual suffers pain or is disabled. While we can and should take steps to reduce litigation, we will never completely eliminate disputes over these issues. As long as we are dealing with such individual human issues, there will always be disputes and we will always need judges and attorneys to resolve them.

Finally, it must also be remembered that most disputed cases involved good faith differences between the parties. There are certainly cases in which the employer or the worker is clearly right and the other side is fraudulent or unfair. In the majority of cases that go to trial, however, both parties genuinely believe that they are right and under our judicial system they are entitled to a day in court.

Chapter 21 views the handling of disputed cases from an employer's point of view. The following sections review the formal process set up by state laws and workers' compensation agencies.

12.4.1 Disputed Issues

In all jurisdictions, there are likely to be disputes concerning compensability, that is, concerning whether the injury happened at work or at home. In states that grant a permanent partial disability rating, the extent of that rating is often the most frequent topic of dispute. Finally in wage-loss states, there are frequent disputes over whether the individual's continuing loss of wages is the result of a work-caused disability, or whether it is now the result of other factors such as economic conditions or the worker's lack of effort in seeking employment. In most states, the same general procedures are followed regardless of the issue.

12.4.2 Initiating the Contested Case

In states in which an employer cannot terminate benefits without permission from the state agency, carriers initiate a substantial number of disputed cases by requesting a hearing on this issue. In most other circumstances, the employer denies or terminates benefits, and it is up to the worker to file an application or petition requesting a hearing. One of the biggest continuing differences between workers' compensation and civil courts is that these petitions or requests for a hearing are usually simple and informal compared to the pleadings that start other lawsuits. In some states the worker must serve or send the petition to the employer or carrier and in others the state agency takes care of that procedure.

12.4.3 Informal Conferences

In the last few years alternative dispute resolution has become popular in all judicial proceedings. It is thought that through mediation, arbitration, or other devices, many cases can be resolved rather than sent to a formal, time consuming, and costly trial. This approach is becoming increasingly popular in workers' compensation and indeed has proved to be helpful in many circumstances. Accordingly, today most states would have at least one mediation or informal conference before a case is set for trial. At the conference, the mediator, consultant, or other person conducting the conference will explore the issues and encourage the parties to seek an agreed-upon solution if possible. The person conducting the conference might also determine whether there has been an appropriate exchange of information between the parties, and in some instances, may be given the responsibility of determining whether the parties are ready for trial.

In some states, this person might be no more than a mediator, without authority to issue a decision or approve agreements. In others, the person conducting the conference may have the authority to approve an agreement reached between the parties or may make recommendations to the person who will eventually hold the formal hearing. In some states, the judges who hold the formal hearings also conduct the informal conferences. In some states, there may be only one such conference, while in others, there may be multiple conferences at one or more levels.

12.4.4 Formal Hearing

In all states there is some point at which the parties, usually represented by an attorney, go before a hearing officer who conducts a hearing with a certain degree of formality. During these hearings, a record is made of everything that is said and done, and although there may be an appeal beyond this hearing, this is usually the last opportunity for the parties to present factual evidence. In most jurisdictions, these are referred to as formal hearings, although a variety of other terms are used, and the parties who regularly practice workers' compensation cases may often simply call them a "trial." States give a variety of titles to the individuals who conduct these hearings. They may be called hearing referees, administrative law judges, magistrates, or commissioners, and they may be referred to as "judge," even though they have some other formal title.

These hearings are usually substantially less formal than those in civil courts. The hearing officers rarely wear robes, and generally the rules of evidence are relaxed. Although most cases turn on medical issues, it is now rare for a physician to appear and give "live" testimony. Most often, written reports from the physicians are submitted into evidence to be read by the hearing officer. A few states, such as Michigan, apply the strict rules of evidence and require that a medical report cannot be placed in evidence unless the opposing party has had an opportunity to cross-examine the physician. Even in these jurisdictions, however, the testimony of the physician is usually taken by deposition. This means that the attorneys for the parties, along with a court reporter, go to the doctor's office and take his or her testimony there. The testimony is then transcribed and submitted to the hearing officer in written form.

Frequently the injured worker is the only person who testifies at the hearing in a workers' compensation case. If, however, there are issues about an offer of return to work or how difficult a particular job was, the employer may present witnesses. In states such as Wisconsin, in which vocational issues are important, vocational experts may appear and testify.

Ordinarily, decisions are not issued "from the bench," but written by the hearing officer and mailed at a later date.

12.4.5 Resolution of Medical Issues

Most workers' compensation cases turn on medical issues. For example, whether the work over the years caused or increased Mr. C's arthritis, or the extent to which Mr. D is impaired. States differ greatly in the manner in which they resolve these issues. One approach is referred to by the WCRI as *dueling docs*. Each party hires one or more physicians (who has had no contact with the case other than examining the worker) to offer an opinion on the medical issues in question. Physicians who conduct these examinations usually fall somewhere along a spectrum. At the extreme ends are physicians whose opinions are very predictable. They are either sympathetic to workers, and are very likely to find severe disability that is invariably caused by work, or they are very skeptical and conservative, and likely to find little if any disability and rarely relate it to the employment. Toward the middle are physicians who tend to be a little more or less sympathetic to workers, but whose opinions are more objective and appear to be more responsive to the facts of the case.

Under a system involving dueling docs, the attorneys for both sides must carefully choose the physician to whom they will send the worker. Since all workers' compensation cases are decided by a relatively few judges, the judges tend to know the background and tendencies of the physicians who testify. Thus an attorney can send a worker to a doctor at one or the other end of the spectrum and be fairly certain of the outcome of the evaluation. The judge, however, is unlikely to believe that doctor. In the alternative, the attorney can send the worker to a physician who is slightly sympathetic to the attorney's point of view, but who is seen by the judge as much more credible. Under these circumstances, the attorney cannot predict with nearly as much confidence what the outcome of the physician's evaluation will be.

The Workers' Compensation Research Institute and others generally see this approach as time consuming, costly, and not particularly reliable in arriving at the proper outcome. They suggest that most of the time the judges "split the difference" between the opinions offered. Attorneys, on the other hand, argue that this is the basic approach taken by our adversarial legal system. Each party is given an opportunity to prove the case as best it can and the judge makes a determination based on the evidence in the record.

Another approach is to give special weight to the opinion of the treating physician. The court might begin, for example, with the presumption that the treating doctor's estimate of the extent of permanent partial disability is correct. The other parties then would have a special burden in persuading the hearing officer that some other rating was appropriate. The special weight given to the opinion of the treating physician may be prescribed by the statute or regulations or it may be a custom that has developed over time. Hearing officers may simply prefer hearing the opinion of a physician who has actually treated a patient rather than one hired solely for the purpose of litigation.

Putting special reliance on the opinion of the treating physician seems to work somewhat better than exclusive reliance on dueling docs. It tends, however, to create controversy about how and by whom the treating physician will be chosen. As discussed in section 10.3, it also tends to encourage parties to choose treating doctors on the basis of the kind of testimony they are likely to give rather than their capacity to help the worker recover.

Another approach is for the state agency to create a panel or list of physicians and to have the evaluation or determination made by a physician chosen from that list either by the state agency or by the parties. Oregon seems to be using this approach with some success. California, which has for many years been the epitome of a state using dueling docs, has recently enacted a very elaborate system involving "qualified medical examiners" and "agreed-upon medical examiners." It is too early to tell whether this system will work.

Wisconsin uses a rather unique approach, which appears to be successful in the cases in which it is applied. As noted earlier, in states that use dueling docs, it is common for the hearing officer to "split the difference." If the plaintiff has a physician who says the impairment rating should be 20 percent and the employer has a physician who says the employment rating should be 10 percent, the judge simply awards 15 percent and resolves the case. In certain cases in Wisconsin, the hearing officer is not allowed to split the difference, but instead must choose one of the ratings offered by the competing physicians. WCRI refers to this as "last offer litigation," drawing the analogy to last offer arbitration, which in some cases has proven successful in resolving labor disputes.

If the hearing officer is free to split the difference, then each physician has an incentive to make an extreme evaluation in the desired direction. If, however, the hearing officer must choose one of the evaluations, he or she will likely reject the most extreme evaluation. This creates an incentive for the physicians to be realistic and for the appraisals to be much closer together.[3]

Finally it should be mentioned that, as discussed in subsection 8.6.5, states that use impairment rating guidelines, either those published by the American Medical Association or guidelines published by the state itself, tend to find it easier to resolve disputes.

12.4.6 Agency Appeals

All jurisdictions allow some form of appeal beyond the formal hearing. Originally most states had a workers' compensation commission. The commissioners would travel around the state and act as hearing officers. If the parties disagreed with the original outcome, the case would be reviewed by the entire commission. This is still the case in a few states such as Indiana. Generally, however, the original hearing has now been delegated to an independent staff of hearing officers with an appeal to a board or commission.

In all states, the commission may review errors of law made by the hearing officer. There are differences among the states concerning the extent to which the board or commission may review factual determinations. At one extreme is a commission that has *de novo* review. This means that although the parties may not introduce new evidence, the commission is completely free to review the evidence and make a new determination without regard to the finding of the hearing officer. If the hearing officer chooses to believe the worker and Dr. X and rejects the testimony of the company and Dr. Y, a commission with de novo review is free to do the exact opposite.

At the other extreme would be a commission that reviewed only legal issues. Although, as discussed below, this is the common standard with regard to review by the courts, I do not know of any state that has gone quite this far with respect to the commission.

In an effort to reduce the number of appeals, shorten the time for the resolution of cases, and make the process simple, many states are now restricting to some degree the fact-finding authority of a commission or board. This might take the form of a standard directing the commission to adopt the factual findings of the hearing officer if they are supported by *substantial evidence*. This would mean that if the hearing officer believed Dr. X and rejected the testimony of Dr. Y, the commission could not reverse simply because it thought Dr. Y more credible. The commission could reverse, however, in a case in which the hearing officer refused to accept the testimony of Dr. Y, even though there was no contrary testimony in the record.

12.4.7 Appeal to the Courts

All states provide an appeal to the courts on legal issues. Sometimes the appeal begins with the local circuit court, but most often it begins with an intermediate court of appeals and ends with the state supreme court. A few states still allow the courts to review factual issues to a limited degree. Most limit appeals to the court to the question of whether the commission has conformed to the law.

12.4.8 Reopenings

There is considerable variance in whether a determination can be modified or reopened. In a wage-loss system the basic concept is to modify each week's payments based on what the worker actually earned, so reopening is usually quite liberal in wage-loss states, especially if there is a change in the worker's condition. In impairment states the idea is to make a prospective assessment of the worker's impairment. As one would expect, there is much less opportunity for modification in impairment states. However, nearly all impairment states allow for some type of reopening or modification. Any such modification must usually be approved by the state agency or commission, and often there is a time limit. Reopenings might be allowed within a certain time after the determination is made, usually from one to ten years. In a few states this time period runs from the point at which benefits stop.

The grounds for modification also vary among the jurisdictions. If Ms. E is determined to have a 40 percent impairment, she might be entitled to benefits for 300 weeks. Suppose she immediately went out and took a job that was just as physically demanding as her previous work and performed it with no difficulty. Should her employer be allowed to reopen the determination and show that the first assessment was a mistake? On the other hand, suppose she was found to be entitled to only a few weeks of benefits. If she is still severely impaired and unable to work several years later, should she be able to ask for a reopening? What if there is an actual change in her physical condition, suppose she takes a clearly documented medical change for the worse, or suppose a new treatment is developed that cures the condition, should reopening be allowed? Most states allow a reopening within a specified time period if there is new evidence which was not available at the time of the original hearing. Practically, in the situations described above, states are more likely to allow a reopening if Ms. E's condition is worse than previously thought than if the condition is not as bad as previously thought.

There are obviously some situations in which it seems just to allow reopenings. However, judicial efficiency would require that cases be closed as quickly and completely as possible. There are certain costs for an employer or insurance company in just keeping a file open, and there are advantages for Ms. E if she can put it all behind her and no longer worry about her case.

The reopenings described above apply to determinations made by the state agency or to agreements reached by the parties. It is generally much more difficult to reopen a settlement of the kind described in the following section.

12.5 Settlements

Settlement arrangements are referred to by a variety of names including "lump sum," "compromise and release," "C 'n R," "washout," "settlement," and "redemption." The extent to which compromised settlements should be allowed is often a controversial topic.

It is tempting for a purist to argue that if a worker is entitled to benefits, he or she should receive all the benefits provided by law. If a worker is not entitled to benefits, the employer should not be encouraged to pay some amount just to resolve litigation or a threat of litigation. It can also be argued that most of the "abuses" of the workers' compensation system are related to compromise settlements. Some contend that employers are tempted to deny or withhold payment in hopes that when a worker must hire an attorney and wait for the delays that are usually involved in litigation, he or she will be willing to take a reduced amount in settlement of the case. Others contend that employers are sometimes forced to pay a nuisance value or even a substantial settlement because when a case is litigated, there is always a risk that a worker will win and the company will be ordered to pay a very substantial amount. The purists argue that if settlements were not allowed, employers would dispute fewer cases and claimants' attorneys would be more careful in selecting the cases they file.

In favor of settlements, attorneys and administrators point to the practical consideration that in most states, a very large percentage (often over 90) of all disputed cases are resolved through a compromise. If these settlements were outlawed, the system in most states would collapse. It is also true that when the parties reach a settlement, both have agreed to it. Thus both parties are at least partially satisfied by the outcome. If a matter goes to trial and is decided by a judge, at least one side will "lose." Finally it must be recognized that compromise and settlement is a basic part of all other aspects of our legal and political systems. People are accustomed to it and expect it to be available.

There is great variation in the degree to which states allow or encourage settlements. No good categorization of how the states handle this issue is available. In the remainder of this subsection, however, we will discuss various alternatives.

If it has been finally and officially determined that Mr. F is entitled to benefits at the rate of $200 per week for 200 weeks, should he have to wait to receive the checks each week or should he be allowed to receive all of the money in a single lump-sum payment? Most states would allow this type of lump-sum payment, and in fact, it would be a common practice in most jurisdictions. Generally, however, there would be some discount for the time value of the money, that is, a recognition of the fact that whoever holds the money can earn interest on it over time.

What if Ms. G claims that she has a disability that entitles her to 200 weeks of benefits, and her employer claims that her disability only entitles her to benefits for 100 weeks? Should they be allowed, perhaps encouraged, to compromise with a payment of benefits for 150 weeks? Most, but not all, states allow this type of agreement.

In a wage-loss state such as Michigan, disputes frequently arise in which Mr. H claims that he is still disabled and entitled to an order of continuing benefits for an indefinite period in the future. His employer claims, on the other hand, that he has recovered and is not entitled to future benefits at all. It is common in these circumstances for the parties to agree to a settlement involving the payment of a lump sum equal to the amount of benefits that would have been paid over a period of anywhere from one to seven years. The amount of the payment is usually negotiated not on the degree of impairment, but on the likelihood that the employee will win and receive benefits for life or that the employer will win and be required to pay nothing. It can be argued that compromises are appropriate in these cases since the only alternatives available to the hearing officer are the two extreme choices, whereas there are many cases in which the appropriate result is somewhere in between. It can be argued, however, that allowing compromises in such a situation converts the wage-loss system to an impairment or loss of wage-earning capacity system. Most states with wage-loss systems do allow such compromises.

What if the question is over compensability—whether the injury happened at work or at home? If the injury happened at work, Mr. H is entitled to 200 weeks of benefits. If it happened at home, he is entitled to nothing. Should the parties be able to compromise by a payment of 100 weeks of benefits? Most states allow such a compromise. In theory, Mr. H is entitled to all or nothing, but for purely practical reasons, most states find it advantageous to allow the parties to dispose of these cases through a settlement.

Does a compromised settlement include a settlement of the worker's rights to medical and vocational rehabilitation benefits, or only the right to weekly payments? The states vary greatly on this. There is no clear rule. Some allow for a complete settlement and others do not a permit a settlement of the right to medical or vocational rehabilitation benefits.

Can settlements be reopened? A few states allow the reopening of agreed-upon settlements, but generally reopening of settlements are allowed much less frequently than the reopening of the awards discussed in subsection 12.4.8.

12.6 Attorney Involvement

Generally, both parties in disputed cases are represented by attorneys. A few states, such as Ohio, allow nonattorneys, such as union representatives or insurance company claims people, to take part in disputed cases. Individuals who are not attorneys are generally not allowed to represent parties on a fee for service basis.

Attorney fees charged to workers are nearly always subject to regulation by the state agency, while attorney fees charged to employers are rarely subject to such regulation. Ordinarily, attorneys representing insurance companies and employers charge for the time and services they provide. This can be on the basis of hourly charge or on the basis of a set fee for pretrials, medical depositions, and trials.

Attorneys representing workers ordinarily charge a contingent percentage fee. It is generally felt that individual employees would not be able to obtain quality representation on any other basis. Accordingly, if Mr. I was injured and denied benefits, he might go to Attorney Y, who would agree to represent him for a contingent fee of, say, 20 percent. Mr. I would not need to pay Attorney Y any money "up front." If Mr. I eventually received an award of $10,000, Attorney Y would receive a fee of $2,000 ($10,000 × 20 percent). As Attorney Y was preparing the case for trial, there may be substantial expenses incurred. These would primarily be related to obtaining reports from doctors or hospitals, paying physicians to examine the worker and to testify concerning the case, and for court reporter fees. Ordinarily, Attorney Y would pay these costs out of pocket and would seek reimbursement when the worker received an award. If the worker loses and there is no recovery, then Attorney Y will not receive any fee and will ordinarily not recover the costs incurred.

The fees permitted range from 15 to 33.33 percent. Some include a sliding scale such as 20 percent on the first $25,000 and 10 percent on any amount above that figure. Generally the percentage fee is based on the total amount that the worker recovers when the case is resolved. It can be argued, however, that it is more appropriate to pay a higher percentage and base it only on the extent to which the attorney has increased the recovery. In other words, if the employer had offered Ms. J 100 weeks of benefits, and at the conclusion of the case, Ms. J is awarded 200 weeks of benefits, should the fee be based on the 100 weeks in increased benefits, or the total payment of 200 weeks? While it can be argued that it is most appropriate to base it only on the 100 weeks, practically speaking, it is much simpler to base it on the 200 weeks and this is what is usually done.

Who pays the attorney fee? Is it deducted from the amount the worker receives, or is it added to the amount that the employer must pay? Thirty-five jurisdictions report that under at least some circumstances it may be added to the costs of the employer. This varies, however, from jurisdictions in which the employer routinely pays for all attorney fees, to those in which the employer is required to pay a portion of the attorney fees only upon an exceptional finding that it denied benefits in bad faith.

While all states theoretically monitor the claimant's attorney fees, the degree to which they actually monitor the fees varies from state to state. In some states, such as Texas and Wisconsin, an effort is made to adjust or reduce the percentage fee based on the amount of time and effort that was actually spent on the case. In at least one state, North Dakota, fees are based on an hourly rate rather than a percentage.

The contingent percentage fee has interesting implications for workers' compensation systems. If the fees are set at an appropriate rate, they allow individual workers to hire attorneys whose expertise and experience is on a par with attorneys hired by large employers and insurance companies. In theory this should create an appropriate balance in the adversary system.

Absent the contingent arrangement, very few workers would be able to hire an attorney on an hourly basis. If the rates are too high, however, this encourages litigation and results in a large bar of workers' compensation attorneys who are allowed to advertise for, and in some cases improperly solicit, workers' compensation claims. If the contingent fee is too low, it becomes difficult for injured workers to find adequate representation, or a situation develops in which workers' compensation attorneys can only make a profitable living by handling a very high volume of cases. WCRI suggests that this situation has in fact developed in California.[4] This emphasis on volume may work well with routine cases, but tends to encourage the filing of nuisance cases and discourage attorneys from taking difficult cases. This leaves the worker with a difficult or complicated case without access to counsel. In some highly unionized environments, unions will refer routine cases to attorneys only with the understanding that those attorneys will also accept the more difficult cases.

The contingent fee arrangement implies that there will be a number of cases which the worker will lose and in which the attorney will receive no fee. If the fee rate is appropriately set, this will be balanced out by substantial fees in the cases the attorney does win. This arrangement, however, creates some incentive for attorneys that may not be appropriate. There is an incentive to settle or compromise as many cases as possible, since this assures that in those cases, the attorney will receive at least some fee compared to receiving no fee if a case is tried and lost.

This system also has implications when attorneys become advocates for workers in legislative reform efforts. Workers should prefer systems in which there is a penalty or other disincentive for carriers to deny benefits in deserving cases. If a system were perfectly structured, carriers would deny benefits only when they clearly had no liability. This, however, would result in a system in which no workers, or very few, win their cases as a result of a hearing. This in turn would result in little or no fees for their attorneys. One author has suggested that attorneys prefer systems in which carriers are encouraged to deny benefits in cases in which the worker is likely to prevail, thus creating some "easy" cases in which attorneys can recover a significant fee and make up for their financial losses in the cases they lose.[5]

12.7 Penalties and Fines

Many states impose penalties on carriers for a failure to file reports in a timely fashion. A more significant question is whether there is any penalty for a carrier that arbitrarily refuses to pay benefits. Many states require the employer to pay all or a portion of the worker's attorney fees, and a few states, such as Wisconsin, allow the worker to recover additional benefits if it is shown that there was a bad faith refusal to pay or bad faith in some other part of the claims process.

It is argued that since workers are in a vulnerable situation, there should be some inducement for the carrier to pay appropriately. If the carrier can cut off benefits and force the worker to hire and pay an attorney and wait for a considerable time for an order that he or she should be paid, carriers will take advantage of the situation and force workers into unfair compromises. Employers counter that if there is a penalty for refusal to pay there should also be a penalty for claims that are filed in bad faith. Others counter that the worker is already at a disadvantage since he or she is usually out of work and out of money while the litigation goes on. The answer to who has the advantage obviously varies from state to state depending on whether the worker is paid while waiting and the amount of freedom the carrier has in terminating benefits.

12.8 Sources of Information

The comparison of workers' compensation procedures among the various jurisdictions is very difficult. While the basic format is the same, there is tremendous variation in the specific procedures and even in the names that are used to describe them. The Office of Workers' Compensation Programs of the Employment Standards Administration of the U.S. Department of Labor publishes *State Workers' Compensation Administrative Profiles*. The latest version, dated October 1992 and released in the summer of 1993, was carefully prepared and is by far the best source of information comparing the administration of all jurisdictions in the United States. Nevertheless, there is a certain amount of vagueness in the responses and a lack of consistency among the states.

The WCRI has published a series of administrative inventories describing the workers' compensation systems in various states. These involve considerable detail and analysis. At the time of writing however, they are only available for California, Connecticut,

Georgia, Maine, Minnesota, New York, Pennsylvania, Texas, Washington, and Wisconsin.

Most of the state agencies listed in Appendix A publish booklets that describe how their system works but most of these include very little detail.

Notes

1. National Council on Compensation Insurance, *Workers' Compensation Claim Characteristics* (Boca Raton, Fla.: NCCI, 1991).
2. Greenwood, Judith, "Who Should Bear the Burden?" *John Burton's Workers' Compensation Monitor,* Vol. 3, No. 2 (March/April 1990), 8–17.
3. Boden, Leslie I., *Reducing Litigation: Evidence from Wisconsin* (Cambridge: Workers' Compensation Research Institute, 1988); Ballantyne, Duncan S., and Telles, Carol A., *Workers' Compensation in Wisconsin: Administrative Inventory* (Cambridge: Workers' Compensation Research Institute, 1992).
4. Barth, Peter S., and Telles, Carol A., *Workers' Compensation in California: Administrative Inventory* (Cambridge: Workers' Compensation Research Institute, 1992).
5. Lewis, John H., *The Illinois Workers' Compensation System: A Report to the Governor* (Coconut Grove, Fla.: 1989).

Chapter 13

Special Funds

13.1 Introduction

Over the years, the states have created funds to deal with a variety of special circumstances. These funds either pay benefits to workers or reimburse employers or insurers when the special circumstances apply. The earliest and most common of these were *second* or *subsequent* injury funds. They will be discussed in some detail below. This chapter will also provide a brief discussion of the other types of funds that are used.

13.2 Second (Subsequent) Injury Funds

A special problem arises when a worker suffers from two successive disabilities, the combined result of which is more serious than either of the individual disabilities. For example, the loss of an eye is a much more serious matter to an individual who had previously lost the use of the other eye. Workers' compensation laws evolved before there were antidiscrimination statutes to protect disabled workers. In the older environment, this situation created a very troublesome problem. If the law provided that the company employing the worker at the time of the second injury was responsible to compensate the person for the full extent of the disability he or she suffered after the second injury, there would be a great incentive for employers to discriminate against disabled workers. On the other hand, if the employer is only responsible for the amount of disability that would have been caused by the second injury in the absence of the first disability, the worker would not be compensated for all of his or her loss.

Most states have dealt with this problem by the creation of a special fund often called a second or subsequent injury fund. The original purpose of these funds was to encourage the hiring of disabled workers by ensuring that if the worker is subsequently injured, the employer will be required to pay no more benefits than if the injury had occurred to a nondisabled worker. A more detailed discussion of special funds can be found in "Special Funds in Workers' Compensation," by John Burton and Lloyd Larson[1] and an article written by Roger Thompson for the International Association of Industrial Accident Boards and Commissions.[2]

13.2.1 Second Injury Funds After the ADA

As discussed in section 2.4, the Americans with Disabilities Act (ADA), now makes disability-based discrimination illegal. In view of this, do we still need second injury funds? It is certainly possible to argue that we do not. If the original purpose of the funds was to discourage discrimination and that discrimination is now illegal, it can be argued that the funds are outdated. There are, however, two considerations, one from the employer and one from the worker's point of view, which suggest they may still serve a purpose.

First, employment discrimination based on gender and race has been illegal since passage of the Civil Rights Act of 1964. Few people would argue, however, that such discrimination ended immediately. Indeed there still appears to be some discrimination based on these factors 30 years after the effective date of that law. Accordingly, it is unlikely that the enactment of the ADA will immediately eliminate all discrimination against people with disabilities. It thus may still be appropriate to provide an incentive to employers to hire workers with a disability.

Second, it is possible to argue that second injury funds help employers more than workers, that they really do not provide much incentive to hire anyone. What the funds do is relieve the burden on employers who choose to hire workers with disabilities rather than to make it more likely that any given employer will hire any given worker. From this point of view, it can be argued that employers need the protection of the funds even more now that they are required to hire such individuals.

What are states doing? Not a great deal. Minnesota abolished its fund in response to the ADA. It should be noted, however, that the Minnesota fund was not very popular, even before the ADA. Alabama also abolished its fund at about the same time, but attributes this to factors other than the ADA. Michigan greatly restricted the eligibility requirements for one of its funds in response to the ADA. Other states are taking a "wait and see" approach.

In this regard, one should bear in mind that these funds are basically insuring mechanisms. They spread the loss among all employers. Accordingly, in deciding whether these funds should be continued, the question is not whether employers in general will be relieved of responsibility for the payment of benefits in the types of cases involved. The question is whether the costs of those cases will be spread among all employers, rather than allocated to the individual employer involved in the injury.

13.2.2 Variations

There are many variations in the way second injury funds are handled. The following sections will describe the alternatives that are used. It should be noted that many states have one or more "subfunds," each of which pays benefits under a different set of circumstances.

13.2.3 Which Preexisting Conditions Are Covered?

There is considerable variation among the states as to the nature of the preexisting condition that qualifies an individual for second injury fund benefits. A few states, such as Pennsylvania, limit the application of second injury funds to loss of an arm, leg, or eye. In some states, such as Missouri, coverage is broad enough to include any permanent impairment; others, such as California, require that the preexisting condition result in a disability or that it be a hindrance or obstacle to obtaining employment.

Some funds are limited to payment for certain disabilities. One Michigan fund, for example, pays benefits only to workers whose prior condition involved an impairment of the back or heart, or who suffered from epilepsy or diabetes.

A few funds, such as one in Michigan, require that the employer must have had knowledge of the preexisting condition prior to the injury. The Michigan fund in fact requires that the existence of the condition be certified or registered with a state agency.

Generally funds do not require that the prior condition be work related. The incentive to hire people applies regardless of the source of the injury.

13.2.4 The Results Covered

Many questions arise concerning when a subsequent injury will be covered. Assume that Ms. A had a bad back before she was hired. If she later suffers a work-related injury to her back that is so severe that she cannot work again, most states would bring her within the coverage of the second injury fund. What if she suffered an injury to her leg which, in combination with the back injury, rendered her permanently and totally disabled? Suppose the second injury was to her arm and was disabling, but there was no interaction between the arm and back disabilities; would she be covered? Must she be permanently and totally disabled, or is it enough if she is a little more disabled than before? There are no uniform rules concerning any of these issues.

A few states, such as Pennsylvania, limit recovery to situations involving the loss of a second member such as an extremity or an eye. Some funds, such as one in Michigan, require that the subsequent loss constitute a permanent and total disability. Others, such as California, require that the disability be at or above a certain level and some, such as Missouri, cover any circumstance in which the combined effect of the preexisting condition and the second injury is substantially greater than if the second injury occurred without the preexisting condition. The latter is certainly a theoretically appropriate approach. The problem with it is that these matters are very difficult to measure and this approach can lead to uncertainty and litigation.

Two states, Michigan and Montana, provide benefits to workers who were previously certified as disabled under the system, regardless of whether there is any relationship between the preexisting condition and the resulting disability. Most other states require that there be a relationship between the prior and subsequent disability.

Larson points out that, in theory, the preexisting condition should in some way contribute to the extent of the subsequent *disability*, although there is no reason why the preexisting condition must be in any way related to the *injury*.[3] Assume that Mr. B suffers from a heart condition so severe that he cannot undergo surgery and that he subsequently incurs a hernia in the course of his employment. Assume further that the hernia is a minor problem easily remedied by surgery, but is a complete obstacle to employment if the worker is unable to undergo the surgery. This would be an appropriate case for the second injury fund. The fund is needed by the worker, because otherwise the employer would be reluctant to hire a person with this heart condition. The fund is needed by the employer, because it would be unfair to require it to pay for permanent and total disability to a man whose only industrial accident resulted in a mere hernia.

On the other hand, we can envision a worker suffering from heart disease and a bad back, both of which are severe disabilities, and potentially severe problems, but which do not in any way combine with one another to increase the extent of the disability. Under these circumstances Larson would argue that second injury fund benefits are not appropriate.

13.2.5 Employer Knowledge

Another question about second injury funds deals with whether the employer must have had knowledge of the preexisting condition. If the goal is to encourage the hiring of disabled workers, then the goal is accomplished only when the employer knows that a disability exists at the time the worker is hired or at least some time before the injury occurs. Some funds, such as one in Michigan, require that the disability be certified or registered in some way with the state agency. Others have varying provisions concerning whether employer knowledge is required and the extent to which it is required. Some states, such as California and Missouri, have no requirement of prior employer knowledge. Although the requirement of prior knowledge is consistent with the goal of the funds, it can result in many disputes and considerable litigation. Some states, such as New York, have decided that it is not worth the costs that result from these disputes and dropped that requirement.

13.2.6 Benefits

Usually the benefits paid by the second injury fund are limited to indemnity benefits, but a few, such as New York, include medical benefits. In most cases qualification for the second injury fund does not change the benefits received by the worker. It merely relieves some of the liability of the employer.

Most often the fund pays the difference between benefits payable for the resulting subsequent disability and the benefits that would have been payable had the worker only suffered the second injury. For example, if Mr. C suffers an injury that would ordinarily result in a 20 percent disability, but because of a preexisting condition the injury results in a 45 percent disability, the employer would be responsible for a 20 percent disability and the fund would pay the rest.

Another approach used, for example, in New York, is that the fund simply begins paying benefits at some arbitrary point, usually 104 weeks after disability begins.

The more common increased disability approach is theoretically more appropriate, but is more costly not only in terms of the benefits paid, but also in terms of administration.

In some states the employer continues to pay all the benefits to which the worker is entitled, but receives reimbursement from the fund. In other states the fund makes payments directly to the worker to the extent that the fund is liable.

13.2.7 Financing

Originally, many second injury funds were financed by required payments to the fund in death cases where there were no surviving dependents. In those cases a carrier would ordinarily not be required to pay any benefits except perhaps a burial allowance.

Under the original and many present statutes, employers are required to make payment to the second injury fund in those cases. A few states, such as Wisconsin, require a specified payment to the second injury fund in certain other types of cases such as amputations.

More recently, many states have adopted a provision requiring payment to the funds based upon a formula that estimates the future needs of the funds and then assesses self-insured employers and insurance carriers based on the benefits paid by those entities during the preceding year. For example, all insurance carriers and self-insured employers in a given state might be required to pay an amount to the fund equal to 1.5 percent of all the indemnity benefits they paid out during the preceding year. A few states, such as Florida, base assessments on insurance premiums rather than benefits paid. In these states, some estimate is made of what the premium would have been for a self-insured employer.

A few states use general fund tax revenues to pay some part of the liabilities of the second injury fund. It is argued that this is appropriate because the purpose of second injury funds is to encourage the hiring of workers and this goal extends beyond the basic issue of work-related injuries. On the other side, it is argued that workers' compensation programs should pay all the costs of work-related injuries.

It should be noted these funds operate on a "pay-as-you-go" basis. This means that each year they attempt to collect sufficient monies to meet their responsibilities during the coming year regardless of when the injuries occurred. This is different from the concept ordinarily used by insurance carriers in which during a given year, they attempt to collect sufficient premiums to cover all future losses attributable to that year.

13.2.8 Other Issues

A number of other questions arise concerning second injury funds. These involve primarily problems such as whether the funds have a right to participate in third-party litigation and/or recovery, and whether the statute of limitations and various other provisions of the act apply to the funds in the same way they apply to insurance companies and self-insured employers. It is often said that the fund's liability is "derivative" of the liability of the employer. This raises questions about the extent to which the fund can participate in litigation, the extent to which it can enter into settlements independently, whether it can take advantage of settlements entered into by the employer, and other issues.

13.3 Other Funds and Other Purposes

In addition to compensation for second injuries, special funds have been used in other circumstances where it appears that it would be fair to give benefits to the worker, but unfair to charge them to an employer. Some states have a single fund that performs several functions while others have several separate funds.

Special funds, for example, are used to pay a cost of living allowance to workers under certain circumstances. Often, as in Michigan, this is restricted to workers who suffer a permanent and total disability or, as in Wisconsin, to workers who were injured during some specified time in the past. A few states, such as New York, use funds to pay workers in cases that were once closed but which have now been reopened. And a few states, such as Oregon, finance vocational rehabilitation benefits from a special fund. See section 11.5.

In a number of states, special funds have been created to protect certain industries. Michigan, for example, has a fund that protects mining, foundries, and logging. Alaska has a fund that protects its fishing industry. In these cases the employer pays benefits up to a certain limit, either a dollar amount or a set number of weeks, and the fund pays benefits thereafter. Several states have special funds for asbestos-related disabilities.

Another use of special funds relates to concurrent employment. Assume Ms. D is earning 50 percent of her income from Employer X and 50 percent of her income from Employer Y. Assume further that she is injured while working for Employer X and is disabled from both jobs. From her point of view, her compensation ought to be based upon the wage loss or incapacity she suffers with respect to both jobs. From Employer X's point of view, however, it should not be required to pay benefits as the result of a loss in another employment. Furthermore, if Employer X is insured, the carrier has collected premiums only with regard to the wages paid while Ms. D was working for Employer X. One solution is to pay Ms. D all the benefits she has coming as a result of her loss on both jobs, to require Employer X to pay only those benefits related to its employment, and have the second injury fund pay the balance. New York and Michigan are examples of states that have such funds.

In some states, delays related to litigation have become a serious problem especially where appeals are concerned. A few states, such as Michigan, have provided that if a worker is awarded benefits at the trial level, the employer must begin paying those benefits. If the employer eventually prevails as the result of an appeal, it is reimbursed from a special fund.

Many states have guarantee funds for self-insured employers. These funds pay benefits to injured workers in the event a self-insured employer becomes insolvent. They are generally funded by assessments on self-insured employers. Virtually all states have a guarantee fund for insurance companies. Those funds, however, are administered by the state insurance commissioner or department, and cover all types of insurance.

A few states, such as New York and Montana, have uninsured employer funds. These funds pay benefits to workers injured while in the employ of uninsured employers. They are usually funded by assessments and penalties.

In a few states, such as Washington, the same board that administers or hears appeals concerning the workers' compensation program is also responsible for a crime victims' compensation fund. Those funds are not related to the workers' compensation program in any other way.

13.4 The National Commission Report

The National Commission recommended "that each state establish a second injury fund with broad coverage of preexisting impairments." (R 4.10.) The Commission also recommended "that the second injury fund be financed by charges against all carriers, state funds and self-insuring employers in proportion to the benefits paid by each, or by appropriations from general revenue or by both sources." (R 4.11.)

The Commission found a striking lack of awareness of second injury funds and recommended "that workers' compensation agencies publicize second injury funds to employees and employers and interpret eligibility requirements for the funds liberally in order to encourage employment of the physically disabled." (R 4.12.) Since the Commission report, this problem has generally remedied itself. In recent years, many funds are reporting increased utilization.

The Commission also recommended that special funds be available in the case of uninsured employers and insolvent carriers or insolvent self-insured employers (R 6.21) and that state funds be used to ease the effect of inflation upon workers. (R 6.22.)

Notes

1. Larson, Lloyd W., and Burton, John F., Jr., "Special Funds in Workers' Compensation," In *Workers' Compensation Benefits: Adequacy, Equity, and Efficiency,* John D. Worrall and David Appel, eds. (Ithaca, N.Y.: ILR Press, 1985).
2. Thompson, Roger, "A Current Review of Second Injury Funds," *IAIABC J.*(Summer 1987), 23–35.
3. Larson §59.32 (f) and (g).

Chapter 14

Security for Compensation: Requirements for Insurance and Self-Insurance

14.1 Overview

All jurisdictions except South Carolina and Texas require that every employer subject to the act make some provision to assure that it can pay claims should they occur. Table 14.1 lists the primary alternatives that are summarized in this overview and discussed in more detail throughout this chapter.

An employer may provide for the payment of workers' compensation through either insurance or self-insurance. Insurance may be through either a private insurance company or a state-sponsored insurance fund. As can be seen from Table 14.1 six states allow only their state fund to sell workers' compensation insurance while 18 have a state fund that competes with private insurers and the balance have only private insurance.

All states except North Dakota and Wyoming allow self-insurance. This does not mean that an employer can simply not buy insurance. It means that the company must apply and be approved for self-insurance status.

Since workers' compensation coverage is mandatory, most states take some responsibility for ensuring that every covered employer either obtains approval as a self-insurer or obtains insurance coverage. There is great variation among the states as to how

Table 14.1. Type of Law and Insurance Requirements for Private Employment

Jurisdiction	State Fund	Private Insurance	Individual Self-Insurance	Group Self-Insurance
Alabama		X	X	X
Alaska		X	X	
Arizona	X	X	X	
Arkansas		X	X	X
California	X	X	X	
Colorado	X	X	X	X
Connecticut		X	X	X
Delaware		X	X	
District of Columbia		X	X	
Florida		X	X	X
Georgia		X	X	X
Hawaii	X	X	X	X
Idaho	X	X	X	
Illinois		X	X	X
Indiana		X	X	
Iowa		X	X	X
Kansas		X	X	X
Kentucky		X	X	X
Louisiana	X	X	X	X
Maine[1]	X	X	X	X
Maryland	X	X	X	X
Massachusetts		X	X	
Michigan	X	X	X	X
Minnesota	X	X	X	X
Mississippi		X	X	X
Missouri		X	X	X
Montana	X	X	X	X
Nebraska		X	X	
Nevada	X		X	
New Hampshire		X	X	X
New Jersey[2]		X	X	
New Mexico		X	X	X
New York	X	X	X	X
North Carolina		X	X	X
North Dakota	X			
Ohio	X		X	
Oklahoma	X	X	X	X
Oregon	X	X	X	X
Pennsylvania	X	X	X	
Rhode Island		X	X	X
South Carolina		X	X	X

continued

Table 14.1.—*continued*

Jurisdiction	State Fund	Private Insurance	Individual Self-Insurance	Group Self-Insurance
South Dakota		X	X	X
Tennessee	X	X	X	X
Texas[3]	X	X	X	
Utah	X	X	X	
Vermont		X	X	
Virginia		X	X	X
Washington	X		X	X
West Virginia	X		X	
Wisconsin		X	X	
Wyoming[4]	X			
FECA	X		X	
LHWCA		X	X	

FECA=Federal Employees' Compensation Act
LHWCA=Longshore & Harbor Workers' Compensation Act
C=Competitive
E=Exclusive
N=No
[1] *Maine:* Two prerequisites to the operation of the fund are: (1) that on July 1, 1994, if the premium volume in the voluntary market is less than 20% of the total statewide premium volume or, if by December 31, 1995, it is less than 25%, the operations of the fund may be initiated, and (2) that there be an appropriation of no more than $20 million to start the fund, which is to be repaid over a 10-year period.
[2] *New Jersey:* Permits ten or more employers licensed by the State as hospitals to group self-insure.
[3] *Texas:* Provides for mandatory workers' compensation coverage under Title 25 of State Statutes regarding rules and regulations for "Carriers" (Article 911-A, Sec. II Motor Bus Transportation and Regulations by the Railroad Commission). Self-insurance coverage is approved for private employers, effective January 1, 1993.
[4] *Wyoming:* The law is compulsory for all employers engaged in extrahazardous occupations and elective for all other occupations.
Source: State Workers' Compensation Laws, U.S. Department of Labor, Office of Workers' Compensation Programs, January 1994, Table 1.

this is carried out, as well as the amount of effort devoted to enforcing compliance with the requirement. Some states, for example, maintain regular contact with other state agencies and are notified whenever a new business is started or a license is granted. They then follow up to determine if the new business has purchased insurance.

Some states require that every covered employer register with the workers' compensation agency and indicate its insurance carrier. In these states the cancellation of insurance is often effective only if the state is notified. Some state agencies have a substantial staff that continually makes efforts to monitor compliance with the statute and to identify employers that do not comply.

Most states provide some penalty for the failure to comply. Often it includes civil or even criminal penalties. In addition, a noncomplying employer may ordinarily not take advantage of the exclusive remedy provision of the workers' compensation act. Accordingly, a worker injured while in the employ of such a company can usually sue the company in civil court.

As discussed in section 13.3, a few states have a fund to cover injuries that happen to employees of uninsured employers.

14.2 Alternatives

14.2.1 Overview

An employer can finance its obligation to pay workers' compensation benefits to injured employees in several ways. This section will discuss the various alternatives. The following sections will explore in more detail certain aspects of insurance and self-insurance. Chapters 22 and 23 are devoted to discussions of shopping for insurance and how to get the best service from an insurance or service company.

14.2.2 Self-Insurance

All states except South Dakota and Wyoming allow self-insurance. Most very large employers choose this alternative. This is, of course, different from just not buying insurance. It means that the employer has obtained approval from the state agency, usually the workers' compensation agency, to be self-insured after making a showing of financial stability.

In self-insurance, the employer has responsibility for handling claims and administering the program (although as discussed in subsection 22.2.8, it can delegate this to a service company). The implications of self-insurance are discussed in more detail in section 22.2.

14.2.3 Retrospectively Rated Insurance

Some large employers purchase an insurance policy that is *retrospectively rated*. This means that the premium is adjusted to pass on to the employer the costs of the losses that occur plus a fee for servicing the claims. It might be said that it is a "costs plus" arrangement. Under a "retro" policy, the employer assumes much of the risk of the losses but little of the responsibility for handling claims—the insurance company has this responsibility.

The adjustments to the premium are made periodically after the close of the policy year. The rating is thus "retrospective."

The employer does not assume all the risk, because these policies generally include a minimum and maximum premium. In other words, the insurance company is going to charge something for issuing the policy even if there are no losses, and after losses reach a certain level, the insurance company will accept all responsibility. The parties might agree, for example, that losses occurring during one year of up to $1 million will be charged back to the employer, but that if losses exceed that, the insurer will bear the liability. Because of this arrangement these are sometimes called "high-low" policies. The insurer, of course, bases charges on how much of the risk it is taking.

Retrospectively rated insurance is in some ways similar to self-insurance. As compared to other types of insurance, employers with retrospectively rated policies have a much greater incentive to be concerned about safety and return to work programs because they bear the loss much more directly. Very large employers with sufficient bargaining power in the marketplace can often negotiate variations on the customary retrospective policies concerning the shifting of the risk and the management of claims. Some employers use this as a gradual transition to self-insurance.

14.2.4 Insurance With a Large Deductible

Large deductible workers' compensation insurance policies have become popular recently. Under such a policy, the employer is responsible for the losses up to an agreed-upon amount. The deductible may be on a per accident basis or an annual aggregate basis. For example, the parties might agree that the employer would pay the first $150,000 in each compensation case, or that the employer would pay the first $2 million for all cases arising out of a given policy year. In the first instance, the insurer would pay all losses over $150,000 in any one case. In the second instance, the insurer would pay all losses over $2 million that occurred in the policy year. It would also be possible to have a policy that included both a per accident and an aggregate deductible. Table 14.2 lists the states that allow large deductibles.

Insurance policies with large deductibles are similar in many ways to retrospectively rated policies discussed above. This includes the incentive for safety and return to work programs. In a deductible policy, however, the charges to the employer are more likely to be based on the amounts actually paid out rather than those that are "incurred" or "reserved."

As with retro policies, the insurer can be held liable to the workers for all amounts should the employer become insolvent and the insurer manages all claims and makes all payments. The deductible amounts are not paid directly by the employer to the workers or providers. The claims are managed and paid by the insurer just as in any other policy. The costs attributable to the deductible are then charged back to the employer. The "deductible" is, in some sense, really just a way of calculating the premium.

It is important to understand one way in which large deductible policies are different from other insurance. The deductible amount is not considered "premium" received by the insurer when calculating certain taxes and the responsibility for the residual market. As discussed below in subsection 14.3.4, in some states the residual market results in substantial losses. These are passed on to all insurers in the state based on how much premium they write. Large deductibles allow insurers to make it appear that their total premium is less.

Since losses from the assigned risk pool are passed on to insurers, based on the proportion of all premiums that they write, this strategy does not reduce the residual market burden. It merely shifts some of it from companies that write large deductibles to those that do not. It is generally large insurers who write coverage for large employers that are able to write large deductible policies. Smaller insurers who generally write coverage for small employers are not able to do this. Some suggest that large deductibles unfairly

Table 14.2. States That Allow Deductibles

States	Large Deductibles	Small Deductibles
Alabama	X	X
Alaska	X	
Colorado	X	X
Connecticut		X
Delaware		X
District of Columbia	X	
Florida	X	X
Georgia	X	X
Hawaii		X
Illinois	X	X
Indiana	X	X
Iowa	X	
Kansas		X
Kentucky	X	
Louisiana	X	
Maine	X	X
Maryland	X	
Michigan	X	
Minnesota	X	
Mississippi	X	
Montana		X
Nebraska		X
North Carolina	X	
New Mexico	X	X
New York		X
Oregon		X
Pennsylvania	X	
Rhode Island	X	X
South Dakota	X	X
Tennessee	X	
Texas	X	X

Source: *The Workers Compensation Guide*, International Risk Management Institute, Inc., Dallas (1992).

shift costs to small insurers and small businesses. While this is an important policy consideration for regulators, large deductibles are nevertheless an attractive alternative for employers who can qualify.

14.2.5 Insurance With a Small Deductible

The 19 states listed in Table 14.2 allow some form of small deductible. The deductible amounts are usually between $100 to $10,000 per accident. As with large deductibles, generally claims are handled by the insurer and all payments are made by it, but the costs of the deductible amounts are charged back to the employer. Depending on the state, the losses that are included in the deductible amounts may or may not be included when calculating the employer's experience modification. (Experience-rated insurance is discussed in subsection 14.2.7 below.)

14.2.6 "Ad Hoc" Deductibles

"Ad hoc" deductibles are illegal in most states and usually constitute a breach of the insurance contract. Nevertheless, there are undoubtedly some employers who, in what they hope will be small cases, pay the worker and/or health care provider directly. They do not report these cases to the insurer and thus the losses do not affect their experience rating.

Beside being illegal and a breach of contract, there are several practical problems with this practice. If the case is ever litigated and it comes out that the employer tried to cheat the system, the judge will be less sympathetic to it during a trial. If the employer lied to the insurance company about its losses, the judge will be less likely to believe the employer if it testifies that it offered a job to the worker or that its witnesses did not see an injury happen on the job. Also, an insurance company may be reluctant to renew a policy if it discovers that the employer has not been reporting losses as it agreed to under its policy.

Finally, as I say so often, the problem in workers' compensation is not the little cases or the big cases. It is the cases that should be small claims but turn into big ones. One of the things that an employer is paying for is good claims handling: fast action to take control of cases, make payment when appropriate, and get people back to work. If the employer pays the claim directly, it will be losing the help of the insurance company in doing all of this. It is also likely that it will be evident to the worker that something is going on that is not quite right. He or she will become suspicious and be more likely to consult an attorney.

14.2.7 Experience-Rated Insurance

The vast majority of employers have experience-rated policies. If the annual premiums are above about $4,000, the policy will most likely be experience rated. In fact, in most states, this is required. At its simplest, experience rating means that the premium is adjusted up or down based on the loss experience of the employer. The adjustment, however, is much less direct than for retrospective policies or policies with deductibles.

An experience modification formula has been published by the National Council on Compensation Insurance (NCCI). As discussed in section 3.5, NCCI is an organization sponsored by the insurance industry. The calculation of experience modifications is one of its primary missions. Most insurers in most states use the NCCI formula. The formulas used in other circumstances are generally based largely on the NCCI approach.

The formula considers losses for the three previous years. The "losses" are not the amounts paid out to workers and providers but the "incurred" losses, the amounts paid out plus the reserve, the insurance company's estimate of what the case will ultimately cost. In most states, the losses of individual employers are reported by all insurance companies to NCCI, which then calculates the experience modification factor for each employer. In a few states this is done at the state level. The losses are reported on a "unit statistical report."

The formula is rather complicated but two points should be emphasized:

1. The formula puts more weight on frequency than severity. Thus, an employer with three losses of $15,000 each will be penalized more than an employer with one loss of $45,000. It is felt that employers can do more to control whether injuries will occur than how serious they will be. This seems less clear today than it was in the past in view of the emphasis on return to work programs and other types of disability management. Indeed, NCCI recently modified the formula to put slightly more emphasis on severity. It should be noted that severity is not excluded from the calculations. The amount of each loss is a very important factor.
2. The losses of a small employer are given less weight than the losses of a large employer. The larger the base or sample the more "credible" will be a prediction based on past

experience. Thus, the formula includes factors that tend to increase or decrease the effects of past experience based on the size of the employer.

The formula results in an "experience modification factor." The manual, or base, premium rate is multiplied by this factor. Thus if an employer has an experience modification factor or "mod" of 1.20, its premium will be adjusted upward by 20 percent. Likewise a "mod" of .80 will result in a reduction of 20 percent. The calculation is always made by comparing the employers with others who have employees in the same job classifications. It thus compares each employer with others doing the same type of work. (The pricing of insurance is discussed in subsection 14.3.2.)

14.2.8 Non-Experience-Rated Insurance

This is basically the "all others" category. Employers that are too small to be experience rated—those with premiums under about $4,000 per year—purchase insurance policies for which the premiums are not adjusted based on the losses. The small employer is not experience rated because a single unusual accident could have too much impact on its rating.

14.2.9 Accident Funds

As discussed in section 14.4, in six states workers' compensation insurance is available only from state-run funds. Eighteen states offer either a state fund or private insurance. The policies offered by the state funds are similar to those offered by private insurers.

14.2.10 Group Self-Insurance

As shown in Table 14.1, 30 states allow group self-insurance funds. Most of the policies written by these groups are similar to experience-rated policies written by private insurance companies. There are, however, a few important differences.

A group of people who wish to start an insurance company must meet many requirements, one of which is to put up a "surplus."

This means that they must set aside a large sum of money to assure that they will be able to pay claims in the future. By contrast, group self-insurance funds are generally not required to have a surplus. Instead they are "assessable," that is, if the losses in any year are unexpectedly high, the fund may be required to assess all of the members an additional charge to cover the losses. In fact, in many states, all members of the group have a "joint and several liability" for all losses. This means that if the fund did not collect sufficient premiums and some members of the group had become insolvent or had gone out of business, the remaining members could be held responsible for all of the losses. In practice this rarely happens.

In many states, group funds are an attractive alternative, especially for smaller businesses. They offer good service at reasonable prices. They often put considerable emphasis on safety and cancel employers that do not comply with their safety standards.

Originally, and still in many states such as Michigan, funds were limited to employers in a single industry. The funds might, for example, be organized by a home builders association or a retailers group and be limited to the group's members. The fund would develop special knowledge of the issues involved in its industry and the peer pressure from others in the same industry could be used to encourage members to comply with safety requirements. These are called *homogeneous* funds. Today several states allow *heterogeneous* funds. In Florida, for example, a significant portion of all workers' compensation insurance is written by four large funds sponsored by statewide trade associations that are not limited to a single industry.

14.2.11 Assigned Risk Pool

As discussed below in subsection 14.3.4, if, because of its bad record or the unusual nature of its risk, an employer cannot find an insurer that will sell it insurance voluntarily, it can purchase insurance through an "assigned risk pool" or "residual market." (In 13 states the state accident fund is required to sell insurance to "all comers." See section 14.4.) Generally the policies available from the pool are of the same nature as those available in the voluntary market and described above. There may, however, be a "surcharge" on employers in the pool.

14.2.12 *"Offshore Captives" and "Fronting Arrangements"*

Sometimes an employer wants to bear all of the risk (or cannot find an insurer who will sell it insurance) but does not want to be self-insured. A single or small group of employers can create its own insurance company. The company is wholly owned by one or a few employers, and only writes insurance for those businesses. It is called a captive insurance company. Very often, these insurance companies do not meet the requirements to be licensed in any state. Accordingly, they are created offshore, typically in Bermuda.

Since these companies are not licensed to do business in any state, they generally enter into a fronting agreement with a licensed insurance company. The fronting company pays benefits and manages the claims, but, for a fee, passes the losses on to the captive. This may sound complicated and seem suspect, but these arrangements are not uncommon.

14.3 Insurance Issues

14.3.1 *The Unique Nature of Workers' Compensation Insurance*

Workers' compensation insurance is different from other insurance in that the provisions of the insurance policy and the liability of the insurer to the injured worker are spelled out by law. In other types of insurance an individual can contract with an insurance company for a variety of different types of coverage. He or she can purchase a disability policy that pays one-half of the worker's wage loss or 60 percent of the worker's wage loss. There can be a three-month waiting period or a two-year waiting period. Under workers' compensation policies, however, all the terms are spelled out by the applicable law. Within each state every policy is the same.

In addition, certain defenses that are ordinarily available to an insurance carrier are not available in the case of workers' compensation. For example, if a person or a business purchases a policy of insurance and makes fraudulent representations about the nature of the business, that might be enough to void some policies. In workers' compensation, however, it does not affect the insurance carrier's responsibility to injured workers. The insurance carrier may be able to recover from the employer for damages that it can attribute to the fraudulent representations, but it will be responsible to pay benefits to any workers who are injured. (If the insurance policy never actually took effect, the insurance company may be exempt from responsibility.)

The cancellation of a workers' compensation policy is also often governed by special rules. Generally a policy can be canceled only if the workers' compensation bureau or commission is notified.

Some states require that any policy of workers' compensation insurance cover all the activities of the insured business. Other states allow a company to insure only a specific location for a given business.

14.3.2 The Pricing of Insurance

Although there are numerous variations the same basic process is followed in setting rates in all jurisdictions. The first step in rate-making is to define job classifications. There are about 600 different classifications in the system used by NCCI. The vast majority of all workers, however, fall into substantially fewer classifications. In most states the majority of all insurance is written in less than 100 classifications. Some common classifications are:

- Officer Clerk
- Outside Sales
- Drivers NOC (not otherwise classified)
- Parcel Delivery
- Carpentry-Finished Work

In each state there is some form of data collection organization, usually the NCCI, which gathers information about the workers' compensation losses in each classification. When this information is aggregated, the data collection organization can tell how much premium would need to have been collected to cover the losses in each classification. This is usually divided by the amount of payroll in each classification to give a payroll rate. This is stated as a percentage of the payroll or as dollars of premium per $100 of payroll.

Usually a trend factor is added to take into account whether losses appear to be increasing or decreasing in that classification.

Next, a factor is added for adjustment expense. This includes the cost of sending out adjustors to investigate cases, legal defense, and similar costs.

The procedure and formulas vary slightly from state to state, but generally this results in an amount known as the "pure premium." Factors are then added to cover the general expenses of running an insurance company, the expenses of marketing insurance, and a factor for profit. This amount is then used by the organization to estimate the "manual rates" or base premium for each classification.

The rate-making authority is usually an insurance commission or individual commissioner. As mentioned, the data collection organization is most frequently the NCCI or a state organization which is funded and whose directors are appointed by the insurance industry. In most states this organization makes a proposal to the rate-making authority as to what the rates should be. The rate maker then reviews the proposal and sets rates.

In theory the rates are set at a level that is fair to both insurers and employers. It is fair to point out, however, that political considerations play some role in rate making. In most states insurance commissioners are either elected or appointed by a governor who is elected. Raising insurance premiums is not a popular thing to do. As discussed in subsection 14.3.5, NCCI and the insurance industry argue that rates are sometimes kept artificially low.

The manual rates are often only the starting point for the calculation of rates that are actually paid. As discussed in subsection 14.3.3, in states that allow competitive pricing, insurance companies are allowed to vary from these to whatever extent they wish. Even in many states that require all companies to charge the same manual rate, companies are often allowed to vary the rates actually charged through the use of *scheduled credits*, *deviations*, and other discounts that are given to employers when a policy is written and through dividends that are paid by mutual companies at the end of a policy period. Thus, as discussed in section 22.3, shopping for insurance is important.

14.3.3 Competitive Pricing

In recent years there has been a movement toward allowing the *competitive* pricing of insurance. Prior to 1980, all states had

Table 14.3. Jurisdictions That Allow Competitive Pricing of Workers' Compensation Insurance as of March 1993

Jurisdiction	Filing Requirements	Role of Rating Organization
Alabama	Prior Approval	Loss Costs
Colorado	Prior Approval	Loss Costs
Connecticut	Prior Approval	Loss Costs
District of Columbia	Prior Approval	Loss Costs
Georgia	File and Use	Rates/Loss Costs
Hawaii	Prior Approval	Loss Costs
Illinois	Use and File	Rates/Loss Costs
Kentucky	Use and File	Loss Costs
Louisiana	Prior Approval	Loss Costs
Maryland	File and Use	Loss Costs
Michigan	File and Use	Loss Costs
Minnesota	Use and File	Loss Costs
Montana	File and Use	Rates
New Mexico	Prior Approval	Loss Costs
Oregon	Prior Approval	Loss Costs
Rhode Island	Prior Approval	Loss Costs/Rates
South Carolina	Prior Approval	Loss Costs
Texas	File and Use	None
Utah	File and Use	Loss Costs
Vermont	Use and File	Rates/Loss Costs

Source: National Association of Insurance Commissioners.

systems of *administered* pricing under which all insurers charged basically the same rate. By 1993, the 20 states listed in Table 14.3 allowed competitive pricing, and several other states allowed insurers to deviate from published rates to some degree. In states with competitive pricing, the rates are not set uniformly. Instead each insurance company is free to set its own manual rates.

Even in states with competitive pricing, there is always some organization, such as the NCCI, which collects and disseminates data about losses in prior years that can be used to estimate losses in the future. The extent to which the organization refines the data and the procedures under which companies adopt their rates vary from state to state. All states require insurers to file their rates with the insurance commissioner. In some they may not implement a new set of rates until it is approved; in others they may file and use a set of rates without waiting for approval. In some states the data collection organization publishes only data on losses and does not try to estimate a final rate. This is sometimes referred to as the *loss cost* approach. In other cases the organization publishes final rates but insurers are free to use these rates or adopt a set of their own. Table 14.3 indicates for each jurisdiction whether prior approval is required and whether the organization publishes final rates or only loss cost information.

Often an insurance company will look at a loss cost figure provided by a state data collection organization and in addition use its own calculation based upon its "book of business." It will then attempt to estimate the premium rate that will create a profit and at the same time be low enough to bring in desirable new business.

Some argue that competitive pricing will allow insurance companies to charge prices that are too high, while others claim that competition will drive prices too low and we will see bankruptcies of insurance companies. So far neither seems to have happened in the states that have tried this approach. If fact, this approach seems to work quite well. It takes the political element out of rate making and generally results in rates that do not cause a large residual market.

14.3.4 The Residual Market (Assigned Risk Pools)

Since workers' compensation insurance is usually a precondition to doing business it is necessary that this insurance be available to all who need it. Private insurance companies, however, are not required to sell insurance to everyone who applies, so there must be some other mechanism to make insurance available. As discussed in section 14.4, in six states, workers' compensation insurance is available only from a state-sponsored insurance company or "fund." These insurers must "write all comers." In 11 additional states, there is a state fund that competes with private insurance companies but which is not allowed to turn down a risk. They are "the insurer of last resort." (See Table 14.8.)

In the remaining states, there is an "assigned risk pool" or "residual market." In most of these, it is managed by NCCI. The other states manage it on a state-by-state basis but often with actuarial help from NCCI.

The pools consist of employers that carriers do not want to insure. For the most part, these are employers with an unusually high number of injuries compared to other employers in the same industry. Also, some industries that are especially dangerous tend to have a high percentage of all their employers in the pool.

In the past, some people have alleged that the assigned risk pools had a disproportionate share of small employers. They claimed that insurance companies make more profit by writing insurance for large risks and that as a result they more frequently turn down smaller companies, which in turn puts more small employers in the assigned risk pool.

It does seem that some employers with unusual risks get placed in the pool even though they are not "bad" risks. Actuaries and underwriters attempt to predict the losses that will occur in each job classification and to set premiums to cover these losses, pay expenses, and make some profit. To make a reliable prediction, they need to know the experience of a large number of workers. Data are not available for jobs performed by only a few people. Insurance companies are reluctant to write coverage for employers who specialize in such activities and they then wind up in the pools. While data do not seem to be available, it would appear that this is a relatively small percentage of the employers in the pools.

Many assigned risk pools lose money. All of the combined NCCI pools are losing over $2 billion a year. Why? According to NCCI and the insurance industry, the premiums are simply not enough to cover the losses. Premiums are based on the "average" risk in each job classification. The assigned risk pools are populated by the worst risks in each classification.

To some extent, this is offset by the "modification factor," an increase or decrease in an employer's premium based on its past record. In some states, there is a "surcharge" of say 25 percent placed on employers in the assigned risk pools. In many cases, however, this does not seem to make up for the bad experience of the employers in these pools.

Who bears the loss? At least initially, the insurance companies. It is divided among all the companies that do business in each state based on their percentage of the market. If ABC Insurance Company writes 7% of the premiums in state X and the pool in that state has a loss of $10 million, then ABC Company must pay $700,000 into the pool (7% of $10 million).

Historically, the pools averaged between 4 and 12 percent of the market. At that rate, they were an annoyance but not a serious problem for the insurance industry. As can be seen from Table 14.4, this percentage has increased sharply. In 1993, 25 percent of the market in the NCCI states was in the assigned risk pool.

Table 14.4. Residual Market Share Pool Premium as a Percentage of Direct Written Premium

Calendar Year	Percent
1975	4.6
1976	7.7
1977	11.8
1978	12.7
1979	12.7
1980	12.0
1981	10.2
1982	8.0
1983	6.2
1984	5.5
1985	9.7
1986	16.3
1987	19.0
1988	19.6
1989	19.1
1990	21.0
1991	21.0
1992	24.7
1993	25.0

Source: National Council on Compensation Insurance, Inc.

Why is this happening? NCCI and the insurance industry would respond very quickly with "rate inadequacy." As discussed in subsection 14.3.2, in about 30 states, the law requires that all insurance companies use the same premium rates for workers' compensation insurance. These are set by the state, usually by an insurance commissioner. The industry claims that in many states the insurance commissioners have set rates that are too low. This makes it hard for companies to make a profit from writing workers' compensation insurance in those states.

At least at first, it is not impossible, only difficult, to make a profit. To do well, however, a company must write only "good risks," those employers that have especially good safety records. To do this, insurers turn down the marginal risks. Unable to buy insurance in the voluntary market, these companies are now forced into the assigned risk pool.

The insurance industry describes this as the "death spiral." As the pool grows, losses from the pool grow. An increasing amount of each insurer's resources must be devoted to paying for these losses. This makes it increasingly less desirable to write business in the voluntary market in those states, which in turn results in the denial of coverage to more employers, which further increases the size of the pool.

The increasing size of assigned risk pools has adverse consequences for everyone. Most immediately, it means that insurance companies lose money. It also means higher premiums for the larger number of employers that must purchase their insurance through the pool. It hurts other employers as well. As insurance companies are required to absorb increasing losses from the assigned risk pool, they seek to raise all of their rates to cover these losses. This results in "good" employers paying for the losses caused by "bad" employers.

Finally, there is at least an indirect potential that injured workers will suffer. In the rush to reduce costs and thus premiums, legislators sometimes find it easiest to reduce benefits or restrict eligibility. Of course, there are some who would say that this is what started the spiral in the first place and that a reduction in losses is the place to start.

How are these claims handled? The pool does not actually pay or defend the claims itself. Instead, they are assigned to insurance companies who agree to be "servicing carriers." In most states, this work is divided between six or seven companies. This activity has caused some controversy in itself. It is considered by some that the companies do not handle cases from the assigned risk pool in the same way they handle cases from their own customers. It is alleged that they do not provide as much in the way of safety services and that they do not investigate and defend these claims as vigorously. How can they be expected to defend these as well? After all, it is not their money.

Insurers vehemently deny this. They argue that they treat these claims exactly the same as all others. If it is not their money in the short run, they are responsible for the losses in the long run and so they do have an incentive to properly handle the claims. NCCI has recently instituted an elaborate set of procedures to reward servicing carriers that do a good job and punish those who do badly.[1]

How are carriers paid for handling these claims? They are paid a percentage of the premium. In a typical state, the servicing companies might be paid 30 percent of the premium as their fee for servicing the claims. This is a pretty good rate. While insurance companies must bear the losses of underwriting the assigned risk pool, those that service the pools generally make a profit from that activity.

While there is some dispute over what causes the problem, and much dispute over how to cure it, almost everyone would agree that it is a problem and a measure of the difficulties in a state's workers' compensation system. Table 14.5 shows the percentage of insurance premium that was in the residual pool in 1991 for each state for which data are available.

There is no consensus on how to solve this problem. NCCI and many insurance companies would argue that "rate adequacy" is the key. If insurance commissioners would approve fair rates, insurance companies could make a fair profit, then they would be anxious to voluntarily write business, and very few employers would have to resort to the residual market.

Another more specific approach is to increase the surcharges on the assigned risk pool. In that way, at least those companies in the pool would be paying their own way. Others say that this is just a symptom of more basic problems and that in some states the entire system needs to be reformed.

Competitive pricing is an approach that has been successful in some states and is being tried in others. As discussed in subsection 14.3.3, instead of having an insurance commissioner set a price that all insurance companies charge, let the companies charge whatever they want and the market will lead to a price that is fair for all concerned. If the price is "fair," insurers will want to sell insurance and fewer people will have to resort to the assigned risk pool.

14.3.5 Are Rates Adequate?

Are insurance premium rates too high, too low, or just right? An answer to that question is surely beyond the scope of this book but any discussion of workers' compensation insurance would be incomplete without at least a brief discussion of the issue. A thoughtful analysis by members of the staff of the National Association of Insurance Commissioners (NAIC) is found in "Market Conditions in Workers' Compensation Insurance: Interim Report" by Robert W. Klein, Erich C. Nordman, and Julienne L. Fritz.[2] The position

Table 14.5. Percentage of Premium in Assigned Risk Pool in 1992

Jurisdiction	Percent
Alabama	42.1
Alaska	17.0
Arizona	3.3
Arkansas	50.9
Connecticut	13.9
Delaware	14.3
District of Columbia	16.4
Florida	27.8
Georgia	24.5
Hawaii	12.5
Idaho	2.9
Illinois	13.5
Indiana	17.3
Iowa	17.4
Kansas	35.2
Kentucky	42.1
Louisiana	78.4
Maine	82.6
Massachusetts	64.7
Michigan	13.1
Mississippi	51.6
Missouri	32.5
Nebraska	20.5
New Hampshire	39.8
New Jersey	11.8
New Mexico	51.8
North Carolina	23.0
Oregon	7.7
Rhode Island	87.9
South Carolina	41.0
South Dakota	24.2
Tennessee	41.4
Vermont	40.8
Virginia	26.9

Source: National Council on Compensation Insurance, Inc.

of the insurance industry can be found in numerous publications of NCCI including its "1994 Issues Report."

Workers' compensation insurance premiums have gone up dramatically in the last several years (see Table 14.6) but the insurance industry maintains that they have not gone up fast enough or at least that they have not kept pace with increases in losses and costs. The industry usually presents this in terms of its *combined ratio*, the ratio of its benefit costs, expenses, and dividends compared to premiums received. As can be seen from Table 14.6, in

Table 14.6. Average Premium Rate Changes and Combined Ratios

Calendar Year	Change in Average Premium Rates	Workers' Compensation Insurance Combined Ratio
1980	2.9	101.4
1981	−2.1	102.8
1982	−1.4	103.9
1983	1.7	112.5
1984	.4	121.9
1985	11.5	118.8
1986	8.9	121.1
1987	9.6	117.6
1988	8.9	118.4
1989	6.1	118.2
1990	12.1	117.4
1991	7.4	122.6
1992	10.0	121.5
1993	2.5	109.5

Source: National Council on Compensation Insurance, Inc.

1992 that ratio stood at 121.5, which means a loss of 21 cents for every dollar of premium.

Casual observers often view these figures incredulously. If companies were really losing that much money on workers' compensation insurance, they would get out of the business. (In fact many companies are trying to get out of the business in some states.) The combined ratio, however, does not tell the whole story. It does not include return on investments or federal taxes. (Since insurance companies are required to set aside large amounts of money for future losses the return on investments is a very significant figure.)

When these factors are taken into consideration it does appear that insurers are making a profit in workers' compensation insurance but only a very small one. Table 14.7 compares the return on net worth of workers' compensation insurance to other lines of property/casualty insurance and other industries. As can be seen the profit is small and has been declining. Furthermore the NAIC report suggests that the industry may be underreserved, that companies may have set aside too little money to pay future losses attributable to recent policy years. If true, this will make the situation even worse.

What accounts for this situation? NCCI would respond very quickly with "rate suppression." Over the last several years insurance commissioners have approved amounts equal to less than

Table 14.7. Return on Net Worth

Calendar Year	Workers' Compensation	Prop/Casualty Insurance	Forbes All Industry	Fortune Service Industry
1985	13.7	9.6	12.7	12.8
1986	10.1	13.7	13.0	13.1
1987	9.8	16.8	13.6	11.5
1988	7.3	12.7	14.1	13.0
1989	7.0	10.5	14.4	12.3
1990	4.8	9.4	12.1	11.3
1991	2.4	9.8	9.9	11.3
1992	4.8	5.5	10.7	12.0

Source: National Council on Compensation Insurance, Inc.

half of the rate increases that NCCI has requested. The insurance commissioners would counter that the NCCI is an advocate for the insurance industry and that there is no reason to assume that its estimates are necessarily the correct ones. Commissioners have a duty to review the data and reach their own conclusions and this in fact they have done. Often it is their conclusion that the NCCI estimates are too high.

Commissioners also point out that competition plays a role here. Companies often use deviations and other competitive devices to sell insurance at rates that are even lower than the rates they claim are inadequate. Often this occurs when an insurance company is selling an employer a series of insurance policies including workers' compensation, liability, property damage, and other lines.

The figures above analyze workers' compensation as a separate line of insurance. Companies argue that this is the proper approach since it should be able to stand alone. It would be unfair they argue to expect other lines of insurance to support it. This is undoubtedly true but is also true that for large multiline companies workers' compensation insurance is often not sold alone. It is most often sold as part of a package that includes other lines. To the extent the companies intentionally take a loss on workers' compensation in order to sell some other more profitable line of insurance, it is not fair to say that workers' compensation should be able to stand alone and be profitable.

There is at present no resolution to this controversy but a couple of things can be pointed out. The losses are not uniform.

They vary from state to state and from company to company. In some states, such as Alaska, Indiana, Oregon, and Wisconsin, workers' compensation is a profitable line of insurance.

The NAIC report indicates that 36.2 percent of insurers had profits on workers' compensation in 1991 and 16.4 percent had profits of over 10 percent. How can some companies be profitable while the industry as a whole is doing so badly? Does this disprove the claim that rates are too low? There is not enough data to answer these questions but the profitable companies seen to have some things in common. They are usually small insurance companies that write only workers' compensation in one or only a few states. Some state insurance funds and many group self-insurance funds are also "profitable" when their performance is measured by insurance industry standards. They too only write one line of insurance and limit it to one state.

When asked why they do better, the managers of these companies most often say that it is because of the expertise they have developed. They have developed expertise in one line of insurance for one state. They are good at underwriting, at helping their insureds with safety and prevention, and at claims handling. Other insurance companies respond that to some extent the success of these companies is due to selective underwriting. They write or accept business only from the good risks and leave other insurance companies to insure the unsafe or uncooperative employers. These companies would respond by admitting that while they will not *continue* to insure an employer that does not have good safety practices, they will often take a chance on an employer with a bad record if it shows a sincere intention to improve. In fact some of these are known for taking companies out of the assigned risk pool.

It should also be noted that since these companies write only workers' compensation, they are never tempted to reduce prices on workers' compensation in order to sell some other line of insurance.

It should be noted that recently some states have improved their market by allowing competitive pricing as discussed in subsection 14.3.3. At least under competitive pricing the insurance industry cannot blame anyone but itself if prices are too low. This is not a panacea. If rates are presently too low, moving to competitive pricing will result in an increase in price, and competition has its dangers. However, a number of states, such as Michigan and Texas,

Table 14.8. State Workers' Compensation Insurance Funds

Jurisdiction	Competitive or Exclusive	Insurer of Last Resort
Arizona	C	
California	C	Y
Colorado	C	Y
Idaho	C	
Louisiana	C	Y
Maine	C	Y
Maryland	C	Y
Michigan	C	
Minnesota	C	
Montana	C	
Nevada	E	Y
New Mexico	C	
New York	C	Y
North Dakota	E	Y
Ohio	E	Y
Oklahoma	C	Y
Oregon	C	
Pennsylvania	C	Y
Rhode Island	C	Y
Texas	C	Y
Utah	C	Y
Washington	E	Y
West Virginia	E	Y
Wyoming	E	Y

C=Competitive
E=Exclusive
Source: American Association of State Compensation Insurance Funds.

have found competition to be an important part of workers' compensation reform.

Finally as can be seen from Tables 14.6 and 14.7 things seem to have begun to improve at insurance companies in recent years.

14.4 State Funds

When workers' compensation acts were first passed many states dealt with the issue of availability by creating a state workers' compensation insurance fund. Originally these were designed to ensure that some insurer would be willing to provide coverage to any employer. They have evolved considerably since then but still serve that function to a substantial extent.

As can be seen from Table 14.8, 24 states have such funds today. In six states the fund is exclusive. There is no private workers' compensation insurance in the state. In 18 states there is a competitive state fund. The fund was started by the state and is to varying degrees controlled by it but it competes with private insurers. In 11 of these states the fund is the insurer of last resort. It replaces an assigned risk pool and cannot turn away any employer.

It has been traditional for the insurance industry to oppose the existence of state funds as unfair competition by government, an intrusion into the free enterprise system. Advocates for the funds argue that most funds do not receive any subsidies, and in many states, the funds seem to be more profitable than private insurance companies. (The state funds do not actually keep a profit but return it to policyholders in the form of dividends or reduced premiums.) If government can effectively compete with private enterprise, why not let it?

Recently, the insurance industry has supported the creation of funds in states such as Maine and Texas in which a large portion of the premium was being written in the residual market. This usually has been done in conjunction with a move to competitive pricing.

Notes

1. National Council on Compensation Insurance, Inc., "Residual Market Charts a New Course," *Management Summary 1992.*
2. Kansas City: NAIC, July 9, 1993.

Chapter 15

Interstate Comparisons

15.1 Introduction

It is common in workers' compensation to want to make comparisons between states. As discussed in chapter 16, research shows that there is as much, if not more, difference among employers within the same state as there is from one state to another. Putting too much emphasis on interstate differences can lead employers to ignore the ability they have to influence their own workers' experience.

Nevertheless, because there is so much interest in the topic and because it is appropriate to look at interstate differences for the purpose of improving state systems, this chapter will examine a few ways of comparing states. It will look at comparisons based on cost, compliance with National Commission recommendations, and benefit levels.

There are many other comparisons that might be appropriate, such as the percentage of claims that result in disputes, or how long it takes to resolve disputes. Unfortunately, there is a dearth of information about workers' compensation that is comparable from state to state. There is some movement by the International Association of Industrial Accident Boards and Commissions (IAIABC) and others to improve this situation, but at this time very few areas allow reliable comparisons.

Table 15.1. Benefit Cost Rates 1991

Jurisdiction	Benefit Cost Rate		Change 1987–91	
	Rate	Ranking	Change	Ranking
Alabama	1.84	23	30.5	19
Alaska	1.99	20	−36.2	51
Arizona	1.40	37	37.3	13
Arkansas	1.72	25	17.8	37
California	2.23	12	33.5	14
Colorado	2.16	17	20.7	34
Connecticut	2.14	18	69.8	2
Delaware	1.27	40	25.7	25
Dist. of Columbia	0.69	51	−11.5	48
Florida	2.18	16	31.3	16
Georgia	1.53	31	27.5	24
Hawaii	2.22	14	29.1	21
Idaho	1.54	29	2.0	43
Illinois	1.52	32	31.0	17
Indiana	0.83	50	45.6	9
Iowa	1.06	47	24.7	27
Kansas	1.48	33	29.8	20
Kentucky	1.80	24	19.2	36
Louisiana	2.23	13	−23.4	50
Maine	4.72	1	39.6	11
Maryland	1.35	38	20.5	35
Massachusetts	2.38	9	77.6	1
Michigan	1.46	35	22.7	28
Minnesota	1.44	36	2.1	42
Mississippi	1.55	28	14.0	40
Missouri	1.31	39	45.6	10
Montana	3.35	4	−11.1	47

continued

15.2 Benefit Costs

Table 15.1 lists estimates of the dollars paid in workers' compensation benefits for every $100 of payroll in each state. The figures are for 1991, the latest year for which information is available. They include the amounts paid to workers in indemnity benefits and to health care providers for medical benefits. They do not include the costs of administering the system.

These data are gathered by the Social Security Administration. They are further analyzed and published in this form by the National Foundation for Unemployment Compensation and Workers' Compensation.

Table 15.1.—*continued*

Jurisdiction	Benefit Cost Rate		Change 1987–91	
	Rate	Ranking	Change	Ranking
Nebraska	1.09	45	21.1	31
Nevada	2.79	6	31.0	18
New Hampshire	2.41	7	63.9	3
New Jersey	1.09	46	32.9	15
New Mexico	2.41	8	21.1	32
New York	1.10	44	52.8	6
North Carolina	1.00	48	61.3	4
North Dakota	1.70	26	28.8	22
Ohio	2.14	19	16.3	38
Oklahoma	2.38	10	21.4	29
Oregon	2.25	11	−19.4	49
Pensylvania	2.20	15	52.8	7
Rhode Island	3.48	3	58.9	5
South Carolina	1.21	42	21.0	33
South Dakota	1.54	30	21.3	30
Tennessee	1.57	27	38.9	12
Texas	2.85	5	15.9	39
Utah	1.20	43	−6.2	45
Vermont	1.47	34	50.2	8
Virginia	0.95	49	25.0	26
Washington	1.86	22	−9.7	46
West Virginia	3.51	2	−5.4	44
Wisconsin	1.27	41	28.3	23
Wyoming	1.88	21	4.4	41
National Average	1.79		27.9	

Source: National Foundation for Unemployment Compensation and Workers' Compensation.

15.3 Compliance With the Recommendations of the National Commission

In 1972, the National Commission on State Workmen's Compensation Laws, which had been appointed by President Nixon, made a series of recommendations. Nineteen of these were deemed "essential." These 19 essential recommendations of the National Commission soon came to be recognized as a standard by which state workers' compensation laws could be measured.

Since 1972 the U.S. Department of Labor (USDOL) has monitored state compliance with these recommendations. Its findings, as of July 1, 1992, are listed in Table 15.2. Table 15.3 lists the recommendations. Some of the recommendations are broken down

Table 15.2. Compliance With Essential Recommendations of the National Commission

Alabama	13.00
Alaska	14.25
Arizona	12.00
Arkansas	8.50
California	11.00
Colorado	13.25
Connecticut	14.00
Delaware	12.00
District of Columbia	15.75
Florida	12.00
Georgia	9.75
Hawaii	14.75
Idaho	9.00
Illinois	15.00
Indiana	11.50
Iowa	15.50
Kansas	12.00
Kentucky	14.25
Louisiana	11.25
Maine	14.00
Maryland	14.25
Massachusetts	12.75
Michigan	9.75
Minnesota	12.50
Mississippi	7.25
Missouri	14.75
Montana	12.75

continued

into subparts. The USDOL counts these as one-half or one-fourth of a recommendation. Thus a state's compliance may be a fraction.

15.4 Benefits

While Table 15.1 lists the costs to employers, Table 15.4 examines the benefits paid to workers. Because there is so much variation in the forms of compensation provided by the states, it is difficult to make exact comparisons. Nevertheless, there is at least one approach that is generally accepted as a fair comparison. As described in sections 8.3, 9.3, and 9.4, temporary total benefits are those most frequently paid. Table 15.4 lists the rate at which they are paid and the maximum amount allowed. The latter is shown

Table 15.2.—*continued*

Nebraska	13.50
Nevada	14.75
New Hampshire	18.75
New Jersey	10.00
New Mexico	10.00
New York	10.75
North Carolina	13.75
North Dakota	13.50
Ohio	15.50
Oklahoma	10.75
Oregon	13.50
Pennsylvania	13.75
Rhode Island	13.50
South Carolina	11.50
South Dakota	13.25
Tennessee	9.00
Texas	12.50
Utah	12.00
Vermont	15.25
Virginia	11.75
Washington	13.75
West Virginia	14.75
Wisconsin	15.00
Wyoming	8.25
Average	12.66

Source: U.S. Department of Labor, Office of Workers' Compensation Programs, 1992.

as a dollar amount and as a percentage of the state's average weekly wage.

15.5 Insurance Market

As discussed in subsection 14.3.4, the percentage of premium that is in the assigned risk pool is often considered a measure of the health of a state's insurance market with a high percentage meaning an unhealthy market. Table 15.5 lists the percentage of premium in the assigned risk pool for states from which data are available.

Table 15.3. Essential Recommendations of the National Commission on State Workmen's Compensation Laws

R2.1	Coverage by workmen's compensation laws be compulsory and that no waivers be permitted. R2.1(a) Coverage is compulsory for private employments generally. R2.1(b) No waivers are permitted.
R2.2	Employers not be exempted from workmen's compensation coverage because of the number of their employees.
R2.4	A two-stage approach to the coverage of farmworkers. First, as of July 1, 1973, each agriculture employer who has an annual payroll that in total exceeds $1,000 be required to provide workmen's compensation coverage to all of his employees. As a second stage, as of July 1, 1975, farmworkers be covered on the same basis as all other employees.
R2.5	As of July 1, 1975, household workers and all casual workers be covered under workmen's compensation at least to the extent they are covered by Social Security.
R2.6	Workmen's compensation coverage be mandatory for all government employees.
R2.7	There be no exemptions for any class of employees, such as professional athletes or employees of charitable organizations.
R2.11	An employer or his survivor be given the choice of filing a workmen's compensation claim in the State where the injury or death occurred, or where the employment was principally localized, or where the employee was hired.
R2.13	All States provide full coverage for work-related diseases.
R3.7	Subject to the State's maximum weekly benefit, temporary total disability benefits be at least 66 2/3 percent of the worker's gross weekly wage.
R3.8	As of July 1, 1973, the maximum weekly benefit for temporary total disability be at least 66 2/3 percent of the State's average weekly wage, and that as of July 1, 1975, the maximum be at least 100 percent of the State's average weekly wage.
R3.11	The definition of permanent total disability used in most States be retained. However, in those few States which permit the payment of permanent total disability benefits to workers who retain substantial earning capacity, the benefit proposals be applicable only to those cases which meet the test of permanent total disability used in most States.

254

R3.12   Subject to the State's maximum weekly benefit, permanent total disability benefits be at least 66 2/3 percent of the worker's gross weekly wage.

R3.15   As of July 1, 1973, the maximum weekly benefit for permanent total disability be at least 66 2/3 percent of the State's average weekly wage, and that as of July 1, 1975, the maximum be at least 100 percent of the State's average weekly wage.

R3.17   Total disability benefits be paid for the duration of the worker's disability, or for life, without any limitations as to dollar amount or time.

R3.21   Subject to the State's maximum weekly benefit, death benefits be at least 66 2/3 percent of the worker's gross weekly wage.

R3.23   As of July 1, 1973, the maximum weekly death benefit be at least 66 2/3 percent of the State's average weekly wage, and that as of July 1, 1975, the maximum be at least 100 percent of the State's average weekly wage.

R3.25   (a) Death benefits be paid to a widow or widower for life or until remarriage, and (b) in the event of remarriage, two years' benefits be paid in a lump sum to the widow or widower. (c) Benefits for a dependent child be continued at least until the child reaches 18, or beyond such age if actually dependent, or (d) at least until age 25 if enrolled as a full-time student in any accredited educational institution.

R4.2   There be no statutory limits of time or dollar amount for medical care or physical rehabilitation services for any work-related impairment.

R4.4   The right to medical and physical rehabilitation benefits not terminate by the mere passage of time.

Source: Report of the National Commission on State Workmen's Compensation Laws, U.S. Government Printing Office, 1972.

255

Table 15.4. Temporary Total Disability Benefits

Jurisdiction	Rate	Maximum Amount	Percent of SAWW
Alabama	66⅔	$400.00	100
Alaska	80% SE	$700.00	N/A
Arizona	66⅔	$488.37	N/A
Arkansas	66⅔	$252.30	70
California	66⅔	$336.00	66⅔
Colorado	66⅔	$414.05	91
Connecticut	80% SE	$769.00	150
Delaware	66⅔	$327.83	66⅔
District of Columbia	66⅔ or 80% SE, whichever is less	$647.84	100
Florida	66⅔	$425.00	100
Georgia	66⅔	$250.00	N/A
Hawaii	66⅔	$460.00	100
Idaho	67	$335.70	90
Illinois	66⅔	$688.14	133⅓
Indiana	66⅔	$360.00	N/A
Iowa	80% SE	$755.00	200
Kansas	66⅔	$299.00	75
Kentucky	66⅔	$394.39	100
Louisiana	66⅔	$307.00	75
Maine	80% SE	$441.00	90
Maryland	66⅔	$494.00	100
Massachusetts	60	$543.30	100
Michigan	80% SE	$457.00	90
Minnesota	66⅔	$481.94	105
Mississippi	66⅔	$235.84	66⅔
Missouri	66⅔	$449.80	105
Montana	66⅔	$349.00	100
Nebraska	66⅔	$265.00	N/A
Nevada	66⅔	$432.39	100
New Hampshire	66⅔	$676.50	150
New Jersey	70	$431.00	75

continued

Table 15.4.—*continued*

Jurisdiction	Rate	Maximum Amount	Percent of SAWW
New Mexico	66⅔	$321.83	85
New York	66⅔	$400.00	N/A
North Carolina	66⅔	$442.00	110
North Dakota	66⅔	$343.00	100
Ohio	72% for first 12 weeks; thereafter 66⅔%	$460.00	100
Oklahoma	70	$277.00	75
Oregon	66⅔	$444.55	100
Pennsylvania	66⅔	$475.00	100
Rhode Island	66⅔	$440.00	100
South Carolina	66⅔	$393.06	100
South Dakota	66⅔	$321.00	100
Tennessee	66⅔	$318.24	N/A
Texas	70% of worker's earnings over $8.50 per hour; 75% for all others	$456.00	100
Utah	66⅔	$401.00	100
Vermont	66⅔	$611.00	150
Virginia	66⅔	$434.00	100
Washington	60–75	$460.46	100% of state's monthly wage
West Virginia	70	$405.44	100
Wisconsin	66⅔	$450.00	100
Wyoming	66⅔ of actual monthly earnings	$404.00	100% of monthly wage
FECA	66⅔	$1,248.88	See notes
LHWCA	66⅔	$721.14	200% of NAWW

NAWW=National Average Weekly Wage
SAWW=State's Average Weekly Wage
SE=Spendable Earnings
Source: State Workers' Compensation Laws, U.S. Department of Labor, Office of Workers' Compensation Programs, January 1993.

Table 15.5. Percentage of Premium in Assigned Risk Pool in 1992

Jurisdiction	Percent
Alabama	42.1
Alaska	17.0
Arizona	3.3
Arkansas	50.9
Connecticut	13.0
Delaware	14.3
District of Columbia	16.4
Florida	27.8
Georgia	24.5
Hawaii	12.5
Idaho	2.9
Illinois	13.5
Indiana	17.3
Iowa	17.4
Kansas	35.2
Kentucky	42.1
Louisiana	78.4
Maine	82.6
Massachusetts	64.7
Michigan	13.1
Mississippi	51.6
Missouri	32.5
Nebraska	20.5
New Hampshire	39.8
New Jersey	11.8
New Mexico	51.8
North Carolina	23.0
Oregon	7.7
Rhode Island	87.9
South Carolina	41.0
South Dakota	24.2
Tennessee	41.4
Vermont	40.8
Virginia	26.9

Source: National Council on Compensation Insurance, Inc.

Part 3

Microworkers' Compensation

Chapter 16

Microworkers' Compensation: Introduction

16.1 Introduction

Part 3 of this book takes a different approach from Part 2. This chapter will serve as an introduction to that approach. It will begin with a brief explanation of microworkers' compensation, discuss some research that documents the importance of this view of the system, and conclude with an explanation of the inventory that makes up most of the remainder of the book.

16.2 The Importance of Microworkers' Compensation

Part 2 focused on *macro*workers' compensation, the larger system, the legal rights and responsibilities of workers and employers, and how the system is administered by governmental workers' compensation agencies. This part focuses on what I call *micro*workers' compensation. Workers' compensation at the level of the company or firm. It focuses on things individual employers can do to improve their workers' compensation experience.

Those closest to the system, such as claims adjusters, attorneys, and others, have known for many years that some employers have fewer and smaller claims than others. They have also realized that there were things employers could do to reduce their exposure. Until recently, however, not much attention has been focused on these aspects of the workers' compensation system. Politicians, legislators, the media, and to some extent unions and higher management in many companies have always seen workers' compensation as a legal issue. If a worker is hurt, he or she hires an attorney and files a claim against the company. If costs are too high, the employer goes to the legislature and lobbies for changes in the law.

Recently, however, there has been an increasing awareness of the things that employers can do to change their workers' compensation experience and indeed an awareness that even if employers are successful in legislative reform, their individual problems will not be resolved until they deal with the situation in their own workplace. Workers' compensation is an anomaly in that it is an area in which employers look to government to solve their problem. In most areas, employers would feel they were in great difficulty indeed if the solution to their problems lay with government. They would much prefer to create their own solution whenever possible.

A number of factors have contributed to the increased emphasis on microworkers' compensation. One of the turning points was research conducted in Michigan. As mentioned above, many people have known for years that some employers did much better than others. No one had, however, documented how big the differences were. Indeed, there had never been scholarly research examining this issue to any significant extent. The research conducted in Michigan demonstrated that (1) there were significant differences among employers within the same industry and the same state, (2) many of the factors that accounted for the differences were within the control of employers, and (3) the differences among employers within the same industry were bigger than the differences among states.

16.3 Proof That it Makes a Difference: The Michigan Research

When I became director of the Bureau of Workers' Disability Compensation in Michigan in 1985, all of the emphasis was on interstate comparisons: how did Michigan compare with other Great Lake states, with the national average, and with our neighbor Indiana, which had always been the lowest cost state in the country. The assumption was that the most significant variable was the state legal systems. I wanted to determine if there were significant differences among employers within a single state, and if so, to what extent these differences were attributable to factors within the control of employers.

I was pleased to learn that H. Allan Hunt, Ph.D., of the W.E. Upjohn Institute for Employment Research in Kalamazoo, was also interested in these questions, as was Rochelle Habeck, Ph.D., of the Rehabilitation Counseling Program at Michigan State University. In 1987, we were able to arrange for a study sponsored by the Michigan Bureau and the Upjohn Institute. Michael J. Leahy, Ph.D., also of the Rehabilitation Counseling Program at Michigan State University, joined the study later.[1]

The study examined the workers' compensation experience of approximately 5,000 Michigan firms with 50 or more employees. It compared the number of claims closed in 1986 with the number of workers employed. We assumed that there would be substantial differences among employers in different industries. Accordingly, the study focused on the differences among employers within the same industry.

The study found remarkable differences among employers within the same industry. In fact, it found that these *intra*state differences were substantially greater than *inter*state differences. The National Foundation on Unemployment Compensation and Workers' Compensation reported that Michigan's costs were about two times those in Indiana. The difference between Indiana and Maine (the lowest and highest cost states) was about sixfold.[2] Because of limitations in the data available, we looked at frequency rather than cost, but there is clearly a relationship between the two. The Michigan study found that the "worst" Michigan employers had 10 times as many claims as the "best" Michigan employers. See figures 16.1 and 16.2.

The study examined 29 different industries and the tenfold difference was found in each of those industries. For example, in the transportation equipment manufacturing industry, 6 percent of the plants had fewer than one injury per 100 employees while 8 percent had 11 or more injuries per 100 employees. At the same time, 38 percent had fewer than 3 injuries per 100 employees while 15 percent had 9 or more injuries per 100 employees. See figure 16.3.

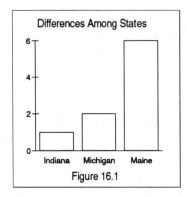

Figure 16.1

Figure 16.2

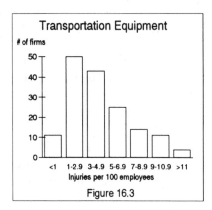

Figure 16.3

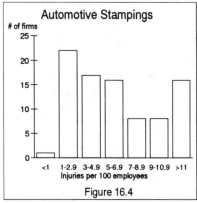

Figure 16.4

This industry analysis was based on the two-digit standard industrial classification (SIC) codes. To account for the difference in the work done within industries, the researchers broke some industries down into their four-digit SIC code. Thus, for example, fabricated metal products was broken down into subgroups such as auto stamping. The differences persisted. In auto stamping, 25 percent of the employers had fewer than 3 injuries per 100 employees while 18 percent had 11 or more injuries per 100 employees. There was as much variation at the four-digit industry level as at the two-digit level. See figure 16.4.

These large differences among employers within the same state are obviously not attributable to differences in the law. What factors do account for the differences? To answer this question, the researchers conducted a mail survey of the high and low frequency employers in four industries (food production, fabricated metals, transportation and equipment, and health services). The survey covered a number of areas but special attention was focused on three factors:

1. Safety and the prevention of accidents.
2. Management climate and culture.
3. Disability prevention and management.

The survey asked a series of questions in each category. When the responses from all of the questions in each category were taken together, each of these three categories was found to be a significant factor in differentiating between low and high frequency employers.

The specific items within each category that are statistically significant by themselves are:

1. *Safety and prevention of work-related accidents—*

- Monitoring and correcting unsafe behaviors on a systematic basis;
- Safety training for new and transferred employees;
- Modeling and attending to safe behaviors on the part of company leaders.

2. *Management climate and culture—*

- Using a profit or gainsharing program to stimulate and reward productivity of employees at all levels;
- Permitting employee participation in problem solving and decision making;
- Communicating from the bottom up as well as the top down.

3. *Disability prevention and management—*

- Providing wellness programs and fitness resources to promote employee health;
- Using light duty or modified work assignments to help restricted workers back to the job;
- Having procedures to monitor and encourage supervisors to assist in the return to work of injured workers;
- Providing employee assistance programs;
- Screening employees on a continuing basis for job-related health and disability risks.

In summary, the study demonstrated that those employers that most frequently engage in safety and prevention efforts, that tend to have an open managerial style and a corporate climate that shares decision making, and that make the most effort to prevent and manage disability are the employers most likely to have low workers' compensation claims.

More recently, the Michigan Department of Labor, the Upjohn Institute, and Michigan State University sponsored a replication of this research.[3] The results were announced in June of 1993. This version of the study looked at 220 employers in 8 industries and included detailed on-site visits of 32 firms. Once again, the researchers found a direct link to the number of lost time injuries and employer activities related to (1) safety diligence, (2) safety training, and (3) proactive return to work programs.

The most recent study phrased its results in terms of the reduction in the number of workers' compensation cases that appeared to result from a 10 percent increase in each of these practices. It found that a 10 percent increase in safety diligence resulted in a 13 percent decrease in workers' compensation cases. A 10 percent increase in safety training resulted in a 6.5 percent decrease in workers' compensation cases, and a similar increase in proactive return to work effort resulted in a 13.6 percent decrease in workers' compensation cases.

It seems clear then that there is much employers can do to lower their workers' compensation costs and reduce the injuries to their workers. The remainder of this book will be devoted to a review of these techniques.

16.4 The Format of Part 3

Most of the rest of this book is an inventory of ideas on how to improve an employer's workers' compensation program. It is a list of strategies that are used by employers that are the most successful in dealing with workers' compensation.

I have chosen to present this part in a question and answer format so that it will not only provide you with ideas, but will enable you to take stock of where you stand now, and measure your progress in the future. A word about how this format evolved is in order.

Part 3 of this book grew out of a series of seminars that I teach to employers for Michigan State University (MSU). The original intent was to present a system by which employers could evaluate their workers' compensation program. We had hoped to develop a system that would allow employers to rate their system and compare themselves to others.

We had some misgivings about this approach, however. For one reason, it would be hard to do this with any degree of validity. Moreover, it seemed to put the emphasis in the wrong place. After completing the first Michigan study described in the preceding section, I contacted the joint General Motors-UAW safety program team to see if their members would be interested in participating in a similar study, which would compare the safety and workers' compensation records at different General Motors plants. Both the GM and the UAW members of the team told me they were not interested in such an approach. "If you compare safety records," they said, "half of the people will discover they are above average and stop working on safety. No one should ever stop working on safety. The emphasis should not be on comparison, but on continuous improvement. Everyone should take stock of where they stand today and set goals for doing better tomorrow."

Continuous improvement is of course the approach that most successful American companies are now using to improve quality. There is no reason this approach cannot work equally well for workers' compensation.

Still, to gauge improvement, there must be some baseline measurement, some method for determining change. Accordingly, we have phrased most of the balance of this book as a series of questions that an employer can ask about its approach to various topics related to workers' compensation. You are, of course, free to use this in any way you like. You may prefer to use it simply as a series of suggestions that you can accept or reject as is appropriate to your own circumstances. On the other hand, you may actually treat it as an inventory and score yourself on the various subsections that are appropriate. You could then choose specific sections, and work to improve them over the next several months, after which you could again review the questions and measure your improvement.

16.4.1 Special Acknowledgments

The items in this inventory are drawn from a broad spectrum of experiences. Two sources, however, deserve particular acknowledgment. The first is a series of meetings that I held when developing the course for MSU. A number of people graciously agreed to meet with me and freely offered their suggestions for what employers could do to improve their workers' compensation systems. Many of those people are included in the acknowledgments at the beginning of this book.

The other source that I have found particularly helpful is the experience of the people who attend the various seminars and other programs I teach for MSU. As I review with them my collection of the best ideas for improving workers' compensation programs, they frequently share with me their stories of successful approaches to various problems. I am especially grateful for all of the things my students have taught me.

Notes

1. Habeck, Rochelle V., Hunt, H. Allan, and Leahy, Michael J., *et al.*, *Differences in Workers' Compensation Experience Among Michigan Employers* (Lansing, Mich.: Bureau of Workers' Disability Compensation, 1988); Habeck, Rochelle V., Leahy, Michael J., and Hunt, H. Allan, *et al.*, "Employer Factors Related to Workers' Compensation Claims and Disability Management," *Rehabilitation Counseling Bulletin* (March 1991), 210–242.
2. The Bulletin, a publication of the National Foundation for Unemployment Compensation and Workers' Compensation, June 1988.
3. Hunt, H. Allan, and Habeck, Rochelle V., The Michigan Disability Prevention Study (Kalamazoo, Mich.: W.E. Upjohn Institute for Employment Research, 1993).

Chapter 17

Safety and Prevention

17.1 Introduction

Nothing will reduce injuries and lower costs more than an effective safety program. It could be the topic of an entire book. This chapter will focus on a few highlights. It will begin with a discussion of the importance of the commitment of top management, then switch to a discussion of incentives for safety. It will make some suggestions for identifying potential problems, discuss some types of safety programs, review some suggestions concerning safety rules, and conclude with a few specific ideas.

17.2 Commitment

17.2.1 Does management understand how important safety is?

Workers' compensation costs can be dramatically reduced through an effective safety program. Still, in many companies, management does not recognize the importance of safety. J. Donald Millar, M.D., the former Director of the National Institute for Occupational Safety and Health, commented to the House Education and Labor Committee on November 21, 1991: "Society puts a high value on safe water, safe streets, and even safe sex, but not as yet on safe working conditions."

17.2.2 *Does management realize the potential payoff from a real commitment to safety?*

DuPont is frequently cited as an example of a company with a real commitment to safety. It has 100,000 employees in the United States and averages 30 lost time claims a year.

This figure is so good that some people refuse to believe it. I have cited it literally hundreds of times in talks to various groups. Often someone will come up to me at a break and say, "I used to work at DuPont." I wait, assuming that they are going to challenge my statement. Invariably they tell me, "It is a great place to work. You wouldn't believe how much emphasis they put on safety." Often they go on to tell some story that demonstrates the importance of safety at DuPont.

Some companies do put a tremendous emphasis on safety, and it pays off in fewer injuries and lower workers' compensation costs.

17.2.3 *Does management understand the importance of its commitment to safety?*

The one element that I see in every company with an outstanding safety program is a complete commitment from top management. You can make some gains without this commitment, but the companies that are able to make dramatic changes are those in which top management provides the leadership.

17.2.4 *What is done to convey the message that top management is committed to safety?*

While commitment of top management is a prerequisite to an effective safety program, that alone is not enough. Management must let all employees know of its commitment. Some suggestions for communicating this commitment are included in subsection 17.7.2.

17.2.5 *Is safety incorporated into corporate objectives, strategies, and policies?*

Safety has been listed as the number one corporate objective at DuPont for many years. One year in the 1980s DuPont decided not to number their corporate objectives. Quality, safety, and other items were on the list, but the objectives were not numbered and safety was not at the top of the list.

Injuries increased that year!

Is this possible? Does anyone really pay attention to corporate objectives? The next year DuPont put the numbers back on, safety was number one, and injuries went down.

17.2.6 *Do you provide adequate personnel and resources to safety programs?*

Of course, the ultimate test of management's commitment to safety is whether it is willing to devote resources to a safety program. These resources might include staff, materials such as protective clothing and equipment, and the time of line managers.

17.2.7 *Is management aware that a good safety program will also improve morale, production, and quality?*

Although safety programs cost money, there are many payoffs. The most clearly measurable payoff is reduced workers' compensation costs. As discussed in subsection 26.3.14, there are also less measurable payoffs, such as avoiding the loss of production that results from an injury. Many managers also report that the things that are necessary for a good safety program, such as attention by management to the needs of workers, a rethinking of processes, and opening channels of communication, also increase production and improve quality.

17.3 Incentives

17.3.1 *Is there some clear way in which managers and supervisors are held accountable for safety?*

Every employer should have some system. Examples of accountability are found in subsections 25.2.5, .6, and .7.

17.3.2 *Is safety part of everyone's performance appraisal?*

Companies that are serious about safety include safety as part of the performance appraisal of every employee.

17.3.3 *Do workers' compensation costs get charged back to departments or supervisors?*

If you charge the costs of work-related injuries to some corporate account, you take away the incentive for safety from the people who are in the best position to do something about it. The costs of work-related injuries should be passed down through the organization as far as possible. Of course, there must be some element of insurance. A first line supervisor cannot be charged with all the costs of a fatal injury that just happens to occur on his shift. On the other hand, supervisors who do not have time for safety in their areas might look at things differently if the cost of the workers' compensation case affected their bonuses. This is discussed further in subsection 25.2.6.

17.3.4 *Does workers' compensation loss data get back to departments or supervisors?*

As discussed in chapter 26, the collection of data is essential. It does no good, however, unless it gets to the people who can do something about the problem. There should be some regular system for sharing data and information with managers and hourly workers.

17.4 Identifying Potential Safety Problems

17.4.1 *Is there a system in place to identify potential safety problems?*

Every employer should have a comprehensive system in place. The items that follow cover a number of specific suggestions. You should review these, decide which ones are appropriate for your company, and then establish a formal policy outlining your system for identifying potential safety problems.

17.4.2 Following an injury, is there an investigation into its cause?

The occurrence of an injury is the surest evidence that a problem exists. After every injury, there should be a complete investigation to determine why it occurred and how similar injuries can be prevented in the future. Section 20.4 includes a more detailed discussion of the investigation of injuries.

17.4.3 Do you investigate a "near miss"?

It takes some effort to encourage reporting, but the most successful employers have systems that include the investigation of not only accidents but also situations that could have been accidents. These might include, for example, a slip and fall on a greasy floor, even though no one was injured; a metal chip flying away from a grinding machine, even though it did not strike the operator; or a forklift driver having to swerve to avoid hitting a worker at an intersection. Dealing with near misses literally allows you to avoid accidents before they happen.

17.4.4 Is an evaluation made of all lifting tasks?

Employers with high rates of back injuries sometimes find it necessary to go through their entire operation and look at every task that involves lifting. For each task they ask: Is this necessary? Is it dangerous? Can it be done in some better way? Because back injuries are so common, they are most frequently selected for this type of analysis. This approach, however, could be applied to any type of problem that occurs frequently.

17.4.5 Do you scrutinize employee complaints for signs of a safety problem?

Of course there is a lot of complaining in many workplaces, but when workers complain that a job is too hard or unpleasant, they may be warning you of a danger. In some cases they may not understand it or they may be reluctant to report the hazard.

Supervisors, however, should be alert to the possibility that unpopular jobs are potentially dangerous.

17.4.6 *Do you examine jobs with high absenteeism or turnover rates?*

What is the reason people do not like to work on these jobs? There may be a hazard that could lead to an injury.

17.4.7 *Do you look for workers modifying their jobs or tools?*

This is a sure sign of a problem. If Joe has rebuilt his work station with duct tape, there is something wrong. It may be a problem with the job, with the tools, or with Joe, but something should be done before it turns into a workers' compensation problem.

17.4.8 *Is there a system to ensure that changes in the workplace are evaluated for their potential dangers?*

Even if you fix all of your problems you cannot rest. A new machine or even rearrangement of a work area can throw everything off balance. The most effective employers have a formal system under which every change is evaluated for potential hazards.

17.4.9 *Do you listen to workers?*

The workers who are doing the job are in the best position to know about hazards and to suggest ways to remedy them. It is very important that management seek input from its employees concerning safety.

17.4.10 *Is there a way for a worker to report unsafe conditions without fear of reprisal?*

In today's workplace, it is tempting for employers to assume that workers complain about even ordinary circumstances and sue over everything that is at all unusual. But behind the few who complain all the time, there may be many who are actually afraid to report unsafe conditions.

Employers should have some system for anonymous or protected reporting of hazards. Some employers do this through safety committees or a suggestion system.

As discussed below, the best way to encourage reports of unsafe conditions is to establish a record of responding promptly and appropriately whenever hazards are reported.

17.4.11 *If you find a problem, do you fix it?*

It is not enough to find a problem. You must fix it. Generally this means that the maintenance department or a line supervisor is told of the situation and asked to remedy it. It is, of course, best if he or she is given specific instructions on how the situation should be fixed.

17.4.12 *Is there some follow-up to make sure that the unsafe condition is, in fact, corrected?*

It is not enough to simply suggest to the maintenance department or line supervisor that a problem should be corrected. The safety system should include some follow-up to make sure that the correction is actually carried out. See subsection 17.8.2 for a suggestion on how this might be done.

17.5 Programs

17.5.1 *Is your safety program designed to meet your specific needs?*

DuPont is a company that is often held up as an example of excellence in safety. When it first went into business over a hundred years ago its only business was the manufacture of explosives. It had a very simple safety program—the plant manager and his family lived on the premises.

Obviously, this will not work for everyone. The point is that every business has unique needs and problems and must design a program that fits its individual situation.

17.5.2 *Do you use any type of safety contest?*

The safety contest is one of the most common types of safety programs. For example, if the plant goes for one year without a lost time injury you raffle off a trip to Hawaii. The employer can design these contests or purchase packages from vendors.

This type of scheme has worked for many companies, but some safety experts question whether it is the best approach. It tends to encourage underreporting. Workers are encouraged by supervisors and co-workers not to report injuries or to charge them to group benefit plans. These contests also emphasize the negative. There is a reward if certain things do *not* happen. This is not the best way to modify behavior.

17.5.3 *Do you focus on hazards rather than injuries?*

Liberty Mutual Insurance Company and others have found that by counting *hazards* rather than injuries it is possible to focus on the positive rather than the negative. These programs attempt to identify all of the hazards in a workplace. (Hazards, of course, can include either physical conditions or behavior, the way a job is done.) Then a prize—a pizza party, a bonus, or whatever—is given to the department that has done the most to reduce hazards.

17.5.4 *Do you have an atmosphere in which workers are comfortable about reporting hazards?*

This relates back to many of the ideas discussed earlier concerning a commitment to safety and identifying problems. It bears repeating that it is essential for the employer to create an atmosphere in which workers are comfortable calling the attention of fellow workers or supervisors to even very minor hazards in the workplace.

17.5.5 Do you use teams to identify hazards?

One approach that is used by Liberty and others is to appoint a team for each department to identify all hazards. These might include a chair that is too high, a slippery spot on the floor, the way Jane bends over when she lifts, or any other hazard. After a team from each department or area has attempted to identify all of its own hazards, the teams move to a different department. The team from department A goes to department B while the team from department B goes to department C and so on. When all these evaluations are done, you have a clear list of the things you need to work on and a sound basis for a contest or any system of rewards.

17.5.6 Do you post your progress?

The typical prize-for-no-lost-time program posts big signs in prominent places noting the progress that has been made. Posting the progress in a positive reward system will have an even greater effect. One company was concerned that truckers were unloading without putting "chocks" under the wheels of the trucks. Instead of the usual sign, "It has been 163 days since we suffered a lost time injury," the sign over the stairway to the loading dock now reads, "It has been 163 days since we unloaded a truck without having the wheels chocked." As you can imagine, not many truckers go up the stairs without being sure that there are chocks under the wheels of their trucks.

17.5.7 Do you use some simple rewards?

Not all programs have to be complicated or formal. Some companies prefer simple, immediate rewards. One approach is to give out "slugs" that can be used in the coffee or soda machines. Following a training session on proper lifting techniques, all of the supervisors are given a supply of slugs. Whenever they see a worker lifting in the proper manner, they give him or her a slug.

17.5.8 *Do you have some form of safety committee?*

Every successful employer has some form of safety committee. There is some debate about whether these should be mandated by law. They can take many forms, but it seems essential to designate a group of people who are concerned about safety and monitor a company's progress in this area. I agree that a commitment from top management is more important than having a committee but I know of no employers that have a true commitment to safety and no committee.

17.5.9 *Is everyone involved?*

I was recently privileged to take part in a workers' compensation seminar in Boise, Idaho. I led a discussion on safety that turned to the question of committees. One participant told of how effective his company's committee was. Another complained that at his company the committee was totally ineffective, the workers did not report things to the committee, they did not trust the committee, and its recommendations were rarely followed.

The two participants began to explore the differences between the committees at the two companies. They seem very similar. Finally someone asked, "Who's on your committee?" The committee at the successful company included both managers and hourly workers, at the unsuccessful company it was all management.

Safety committees are far more likely to succeed if they include a substantial representation of hourly workers or the union if there is one.

17.5.10 *Do you have a "safety board?"*

I use the term "safety board" to refer to a committee that investigates accidents. It may be the same safety committee that performs other functions and should include both hourly workers and managers. Whenever an incident occurs, the worker and all appropriate supervisors explain to the committee what happened. This has many payoffs.

First, and this should be the top priority, the committee can decide what steps should be taken to ensure that similar incidents will not occur in the future. Second, managers are held accountable for safety. They report to the committee not only what can be done to avoid these incidents in the future, but why they allowed this to happen under their supervision. Workers are also held accountable if they were at fault. Finally, injured workers are given a forum to voice their concerns. During the years that I represented injured workers, I found that my clients would want to explain in great detail why the injury happened and how it could have been avoided. Because workers' compensation is a no-fault system, this was generally irrelevant, but I always listened patiently. Often I wondered if the employer ever listened to these stories and whether the worker would have come to an attorney if someone from the company had been willing to listen. An injured worker deserves a hearing about why the injury occurred. If the employer will not listen, there are lawyers who will.

17.6 Safety Rules and Standards

17.6.1 Do you have safety rules?

Virtually all employers have some set of safety rules.

17.6.2 Did everyone participate in setting up your rules?

Of course safety experts have an important role to play in writing the safety rules. So does management. The rules will, however, be more effective and you will have better compliance if line supervisors and hourly workers also take part in formulating them. In many companies, they are written by the safety committee described in 17.5.8 above.

17.6.3 Are they reviewed periodically?

Things change. Rules that seemed appropriate two years ago may be out of date today. There should be a regular review of all safety rules.

17.6.4 Are the rules reasonable?

It is possible to write a set of rules that are so strict that they would prevent all accidents. If they were followed, however, no one could do the job. Rules must be reasonable and must consider the way people really work. This is one reason it is important for the rules to be written by the people who will have to live with them.

17.6.5 Are the rules enforced?

Having involved everyone in the creation of the rules and having written rules that are realistic and reasonable, you are now in a position to enforce them strictly. The degree to which they are enforced will send a message about the importance you put on safety. If people are regularly disciplined for violating attendance rules but rarely for safety violations, it will send a message that attendance is more important than safety. Safety should be your most important objective.

Some states allow employers to deny workers' compensation benefits to an individual who was injured because of a violation of a safety rule. The employer, however, must be able to show that the rule was clearly announced and strictly enforced.

17.6.6 Do you comply with OSHA standards?

Compliance with standards published by the Occupational Safety and Health Administration (OSHA) and others should be the minimum elements of a safety program. There should be some system to monitor and ensure compliance.

17.7 Safety Training and Education

17.7.1 Do you have a comprehensive program of safety training and education?

Someone in a company should review all the needs and opportunities for teaching people about safety. This should include formal and informal education, short- and long-term projects, and monetary commitment. These then should be woven into a comprehensive overall strategy, which is reviewed periodically.

17.7.2 How do you communicate your company's commitment to safety?

As discussed in section 17.2, it is critical for the company to have an overall commitment to safety. This commitment must be communicated to everyone. There are many ways in which this is done. The obvious ways include mentioning it in employee booklets and including it in corporate goals.

There are other ways that are less obvious but more important. Do you enforce safety rules? Do you allow paid time for safety training? Do you budget for all necessary safety equipment? Do you buy tools that are designed with safety in mind? Like it or not, all of these things are part of your education program. They send a message about safety.

17.7.3 Do you communicate to all workers your company's safety goals and progress in meeting them?

Every safety program should include goals and a means of informing all employees of your progress in meeting them.

17.7.4 What training do you have for people who are new to their job?

Accidents are much more likely to occur when a person is new to his or her job. Safety training is especially important whenever a person starts a new job. This should include new hires and current employees who are transferring to a new job within the company.

17.7.5 Do you train workers on how to do their jobs without being injured?

Training should include not only how to avoid accidents, but how to do the job right. This is especially important with respect to repetitive trauma disorders. There are ways to do most jobs that will greatly reduce the likelihood of problems. You cannot assume that workers know the best way to do a job. Someone must show them.

17.7.6 Are there safety education programs for everyone?

Safety education should include everyone—managers, supervisors, and hourly workers.

17.7.7 Do you hold periodic informal safety meetings between supervisors and their employees?

In some places these are called "tail board" or "tool box" talks. For a few minutes every morning or once a week, "the crew" or any group of people spends five minutes reviewing the safety aspects of their jobs. These regular brief informal meetings can be more important than formal training.

17.7.8 Do you hold a safety review before you start any new job?

A number of companies have a policy that requires the supervisors to gather together all the workers before they start any new job or process. They spend a few minutes talking about the safest way to do it. They ask who has done it before, what safety problems were encountered, and plan how they will do it.

17.7.9 Do you have a "family safety night"?

Some employers bring in the families of their workers for a tour of the company facilities and a review of safety procedures. This reinforces for everyone the importance that the company puts on safety.

17.8 A Few Specifics

17.8.1 Are recommendations followed up?

We hear so often about new initiatives that have great potential but fail. Management is committed to safety or quality or "empowerment" and starts a new program, but after a few weeks or a few months, everything returns to "normal." Following up on recommendations is crucial to the success of a safety program.

If a safety committee makes a recommendation for a change or a worker notifies someone of an unsafe condition, everyone will be waiting to see what happens. If proper action is taken, it will add credibility to the program. If nothing happens, this will be seen as a signal that management is not really serious.

17.8.2 Is there a cost to not implementing a recommendation?

Most safety recommendations will require that someone—a supervisor, an engineer, or the maintenance department—spend some time and devote some resources to solving the problem. You want to make it easier to solve the problem than to ignore it.

One person told me that at her company, if a manager cannot comply with a recommendation, he or she must file a detailed written report within 72 hours explaining why not. This adds a cost to not complying.

17.8.3 Do you pay attention to routine tasks?

Many people are careful when they are doing unusual, dangerous jobs, but get careless when doing routine tasks. Workers need to be reminded of this.

17.8.4 Do you consider simple ergonomic solutions?

Ergonomics can be a sophisticated science, but it does not have to be. Sometimes it is just common sense. Do not overlook the simple solutions, like raising the height of a chair or rearranging a work station.

17.8.5 *Do you provide all the personal protective equipment that people need?*

I am speaking here of hard hats, gloves, masks, and so on. This seems so obvious that we should not need to mention it. Still, there are companies that complain about workers' compensation costs but that do not provide the most commonplace safety equipment.

17.8.6 *Is it easily available and comfortable to use?*

If workers are not using the equipment that you provide, ask if it is easy to get and use. A cheap mask that no one will wear is a waste of money. One that costs a little more but is comfortable to work in will repay you in the long run.

17.8.7 *Are all walking and working surfaces slip-resistant and free of grease and oil? Are travel routes clear of materials and wide enough? Are work and travel areas well lighted?*

Again, these things seem obvious, but there are a lot of employers who are paying workers' compensation for slips and falls that could have been avoided. Good housekeeping is an important component of any safety program.

17.8.8 *Are you concerned about auto safety?*

The most frequent cause of compensable deaths is vehicular accidents. You must educate your people about wearing seatbelts and should be buying cars with air bags and antilock brakes.

17.8.9 *Are workers rotated through jobs with a high exposure to repetitive trauma disorders?*

Employers frequently report that job rotation is a successful way of dealing with this common and serious problem.

Chapter 18

Disability Prevention

18.1 Introduction

The term *disability management* encompasses the preventive techniques discussed here and return to work programs discussed in chapter 19. I have chosen to focus separately in this chapter on the preventive aspect of disability management, which I call *disability prevention*.

18.2 Disability Prevention in General

18.2.1 "Put the right person in the right job." Can you do this under the ADA?

The Americans with Disabilities Act (ADA) is discussed in more detail in section 2.4, but a few comments are relevant here. For many years workers' compensation consultants have told employers "put the right worker in the right job." If this meant (1) give the little lady the hand work, (2) give the big guy the heavy lifting, and (3) never hire anyone with a record of a workers' compensation claim, that advice it is now clearly illegal.

On the other hand, there are circumstances where putting the right person in the right job may be appropriate. I had a woman in my class who was a supervisor at an assembly plant of an auto company. She had a job in her area in which the employee worked on the underside of a car while standing in a pit. Personnel sent her a man for this job who was six feet four inches tall. He kept bumping his head. So she sent him back saying he was too tall. In response they sent her a man who was five-nine. He could not do it either. He had to keep stretching and jumping. Finally they sent her a person who was just six feet and it worked out well.

Was this illegal discrimination? Probably not. These men were not disabled and thus not entitled to protection under the ADA. Moreover the decision made sense. These men were uncomfortable doing the job and did not object to the transfer.

Some people just fit better in some jobs. If the worker and the employer agree on a fit or lack of a fit, the ADA does not prohibit appropriate action. It does, however, prohibit certain assumptions that we used to make. Because of the ADA the rules have changed and are still evolving. It is not clear where this will all come out, but I would suggest the following:

- Do not make assumptions based on gender. This has been illegal since passage of the Civil Rights Act of 1964 and is a waste of resources. Work to stop it.
- Do not make assumptions based on apparent or assumed disability. Give the person a try. Attempt accommodation.
- In situations in which it is clear to both the employer and the worker that the job is not a "good fit" for this person try making adjustments. If that does not work try a reassignment. Most of the time there will be no problem.

18.2.2 Do you use a preemployment information service?

There are people who, for a price, will tell you if an applicant has ever had a workers' compensation claim. I do not recommend this. It is a violation of the ADA to ask an applicant if he or she has had a workers' compensation claim and it is a violation to refuse to hire a person because he or she has had a claim. It is possible to think of circumstances under which it would not necessarily be illegal to gather this information about an applicant but I do not think it is a good idea. If an applicant ever accused me of discrimination the last thing I would want to have in my files would be evidence that I paid someone to tell me if the applicant had filed a workers' compensation claim sometime in the past. Finally, the evidence is very weak that this is a reliable predictor of future problems.

18.2.3 *Have you given up on selection?*

You cannot discriminate based on gender, age, race, or disability but you can still choose the best applicant. Some employers tell me that they have simply given up on selection and take anyone who applies. Others, however, tell me that through drug screening and a good interview procedure, they are able to sort out the best candidates without illegal discrimination.

There are bad people in this world and you should not have to hire them. The new laws prevent you from discrimination based on some assumptions that were never valid in the first place and they perhaps make you work a little harder in the process but they do not prevent selection. If you hire bad people, they will be bad workers, and when they are hurt they will take advantage of the system. Time spent selecting the right workers will pay off.

18.2.4 *Do you educate workers about repetitive trauma disorders and encourage them to report early signs of problems?*

Employers who have dealt successfully with carpal tunnel syndrome and other repetitive trauma disorders usually use an approach that begins by educating workers about these problems and then encourages them to report the earliest signs of difficulty. Many employers are reluctant to attempt this approach and I am sometimes reluctant to suggest it but it seems to work.

When I have suggested this at seminars there are often people who say "Are you crazy? Go back and tell workers about a new type of claim they can make? We'd have a rash of claims." Other people tell me, "That might be a good idea but if I went back and suggested it, I'd be fired."

At recent meetings I have tried a different approach. I ask if there is any employer present who has tried this and inevitably there is someone who has and nearly always he or she reports that it worked. Generally the company did have an influx of claims at first, but they were mostly small claims and were easily resolved.

In the long run this approach cuts down on serious claims arising from these problems.

Generally people use a team that includes (1) an in-house human resource or claims person, (2) a therapist, usually someone trained in physical or occupational therapy, and (3) a physician. The human resource person manages the project for the employer. The therapist spends at least a few hours per week at the work site where he or she is available to see workers without delay, can observe the way the jobs are performed, and can coach workers in the best way to do the work. The physician acts a consultant in designing the project and sees patients as needed.

When a worker complains of a problem, it is important that there be an immediate response. Something must be done to relieve the symptoms. This might be a splint or brace as well as therapy or other measures. The work is also observed. Do we need to change the height of the chair, provide a rest for the wrist? Should job rotation be considered? Is coaching on how best to do the work appropriate? This process is not a simple solution. In addition to immediate action, there must be follow-up. There must be a check to see if things have improved. If they have not, something else must be tried. In the most serious cases, surgery and a transfer to nonrepetitive work is the last resort.

If repetitive trauma disorders are not a problem for you, you may not want to get into all of this, but many employers have told me that they found a solution to a serious problem in an approach similar to the one outlined above.

18.2.5 *Is there a simple procedure for a worker to request an accommodation without fear of retaliation?*

I think it is better to encourage workers to request a change in the work situation before they have a problem than to have them file a workers' compensation claim after an injury. Successful employers have a procedure that encourages everyone, not only people with disabilities, to notify management of things that can be done to make their jobs easier.

18.2.6 *Have you considered using "back belts?"*

Back belts are supports that workers wear around their waists to assist in lifting. They come in many forms and shapes. They are the latest fad. There is little serious research that documents why they work, and some medical experts question their efficacy. Some doctors warn that they should be used with caution by people who have high blood pressure. Others say that the effect is entirely psychological not physical. And everyone seems to agree that they should be used only in conjunction with training on how to lift.[1]

I agree with all of the above but virtually every employer I have talked with that has tried back belts has had a reduction in injuries. I agree that it is important that they be combined with training and their effect may only be to remind people to lift properly but they do seem to work.

18.3 Wellness

18.3.1 Do you have a wellness program to help your employees stay healthy?

Wellness programs will reduce workers' compensation costs. There is not much sophisticated research in this area, but many employers have done cost-benefit analyses that show that wellness programs are beneficial with respect to health care costs, even without considering workers' compensation.

18.3.2 Do you realize that a healthy work force will reduce workers' compensation costs?

There is a concept in public health that the health of the host will determine how it responds to any threat. A variety of things happen to all of us each day. If we are strong and healthy, we bounce back and it means nothing. If we are weak, we cannot resist or recover and it results in a disability.

Love, Medicine, and Miracles is a best selling book by Bernie S. Siegel, M.D.[2] Dr. Siegel is a cancer surgeon who believes fully in the traditional approach to the treatment of cancer. He noticed, however, what he called "exceptional patients." These people were able to survive cancers that killed most people. These were people who were exceptionally strong physically, psychologically, and spiritually.

In workers' compensation the problem cases we see are "exceptional patients" at the other end of the spectrum. We see people who are so weak physically, psychologically, and perhaps spiritually that they cannot recover from a strained back. We all hurt our backs from time to time but most of us get better in a few weeks. These people are disabled for months or perhaps never recover from minor injuries.

Helping people to be strong and healthy in the first place will reduce the effect of incidents that are bound to happen at work.

18.3.3 Do you have a program to help people stop smoking?

There is growing evidence that cigarette smoking is not only associated with heart and lung disease but that smokers are more likely to have back injuries.[3]

18.3.4 Can you justify the cost of wellness programs?

Don Tonti, formerly of the Walbro Company, puts it this way: No business would spend $1,000 on an office machine without setting aside some money or buying a contract for preventive maintenance. How much do we spend on the preventive maintenance of our employees? How much more do we have to lose if they "break down"?

18.3.5 What are some activities to be considered in a wellness program?

The following is a sample of activities often included in wellness programs:
- Health risk appraisal.
- Blood pressure screening, education, and follow-up.
- Exercise and fitness programs—anything from a fitness center to lunchtime walks.
- Exercise and stretch breaks.
- Smoking ban on company property.
- Smoking cessation programs.
- Seatbelt education.

- Weight management.
- Nutrition education.
- Cholesterol testing and counseling.
- Cancer education and detection.
- Back injury prevention programs.
- CPR and first aid training.
- Education on choosing health care services.
- Education on aging.
- A quiet place where employees can go to meditate or just relax.

18.3.6 *What are the basic considerations in designing your wellness program?*

A wellness program must

- Have support of top management.
- Have a corporate culture that supports or at least accepts these activities.
- Involve employees in planning and decision making.
- Reflect needs and values of the employee community.
- Have clear goals.
- Be a long-range program.
- Be convenient.
- Be truly voluntary.
- Keep records completely confidential.
- Not overpromise reults.
- Try to use local resources that are already available.
- Consider combining efforts with other business.
- Base reward on effort, not necessarily success, otherwise it may discriminate against individuals with a disability.
- Evaluate, revise, and fine tune the program regularly.

18.3.7 *Is employee health a stated goal of your company?*

If you are serious about it, it should be among your stated goals.

18.3.8 *Do you allow family participation in health activities?*

Workers with healthy families are more likely to be healthy themselves. Moreover, most employers pay for the illness of family members in one way or another. Thus, many employers find it worthwhile to offer various wellness and health programs to families of employees.

18.3.9 *Do you allow the use of company health facilities for non-work-related injuries?*

Some companies have exercise facilities but limit their use to rehabilitation for work-related injuries. Others give people with work-related injuries priority but allow any worker who wants to improve his or her health to use the facilities.

Don Tonti, formerly of the Walbro Company, relates that in Michigan there is generally one weekend in the spring that is the first time people can work in their garden, play baseball, or do other things that were not practical all winter. He says that on the Monday morning following such weekends his company used to experience an awful lot of sprains and strains. One year the company announced that its rehabilitation facility and athletic trainer would be available to workers for injuries that happen at home as well as on the job. On the first good weekend of that spring most of the injuries reported had happened at home.

18.3.10 *Do you allow or encourage drinking of alcoholic beverages at company functions?*

There are legal implications if an employer provides alcohol and health implications if the employer encourages its use. I think that, at least, employers should stop providing alcohol, even at holiday parties and picnics.

18.3.11 *Do you have an employee assistance program?*

Many employers provide employee assistance programs (EAPs). They were originally designed to help workers with drug- and alcohol-related problems. Today they often offer assistance with all types of emotional problems. They generally include confidential counseling and other services.

We do not have any good studies that document what portion of work-related injuries involve alcohol or substance abuse but I believe it is very high. Drug enforcement policies are of course important but assisting workers to quit will also pay off.

With an increasing concern by employers over stress claims, it is also important to help workers deal with stress, whatever the source. EAPs are one way in which employers help their workers deal with stress in a healthy manner.

18.3.12 *Where can you get more information about wellness programs?*

Wellness Councils of America, 7101 Newport Avenue, Suite 311, Omaha, NE 68152, (402) 572-3590.

18.4 Stress

18.4.1 *How common are mental stress cases in your area?*

Mental stress claims are an increasing problem. There is evidence that in some areas, such as Southern California, they constitute a substantial cost to the system. In most parts of the country, however, they constitute only a small fraction of the cases. The California situation has received much publicity but it may not apply to you. Check the facts in your area before you make assumptions.

18.4.2 *Do you understand the law that governs mental stress claims in your area?*

A few states are rather liberal in this area but most are not and there is a clear trend to restrict the compensability of mental stress cases. Section 2.3 covers this topic in more detail.

18.4.3 Do you investigate stress claims to the same extent as physical injuries?

Section 20.4 deals with the investigation of incidents that lead to claims. Some employers assume that while this may be appropriate for physical injuries it is not practical for mental stress claims. I would encourage you to apply the same procedures to all cases.

You may discover problem areas that are causing unnecessary stress. In finding and remedying these problems, you will also be documentating just how much stress there was for your use later if you decide to dispute the claim. Finally, as word gets around that you do these investigations, you will find that employees think twice about filing a stress claim unless there are real grounds for it.

18.4.4 Do you apply basic good claims handling techniques to stress claims?

The techniques discussed in chapter 20 are especially important in mental stress claims. Their use along with a good investigation should enable you to identify and cut off most outright fraud.

18.4.5 What do you do to reduce stress in your workplace?

As discussed in section 2.3, states differ greatly on whether these cases are compensable. Regardless of the law, an employer should do what it can to reduce the stress on its employees. This is, of course, easier said than done but some suggestions follow.

18.4.6 What steps do you take to reduce personal stress?

Experts point out that stress can come from the individual's personal experiences or from the organization. An employer may not be responsible for the stress that is unrelated to the job, but may nevertheless benefit by helping its employees to reduce such stress. The wellness programs discussed in section 18.3 are used by many employers to help individuals reduce or deal with stress.

18.4.7 What steps do you take to reduce organizational stress?

Presently, stress, its causes and remedies, are receiving much attention. In general I do not think this amounts to much more than good basic human resource management. The concepts discussed in section 25.3 should be of assistance in reducing stress in your organization.

18.4.8 Do you put special emphasis on employee assistance programs and harassment policies?

Good basic wellness and human resource management programs should go a long way toward reducing stress in the workplace. There are two specific programs that need to be emphasized. They are employee assistance programs and policies to eliminate racial and sexual harassment. EAPs are discussed in subsection 18.3.11 and harassment policies in subsection 25.3.9.

Notes

1. King, Beth J., "Research on Back Belts in Industry," *On Workers' Compensation*, Vol. 2, No. 5 (June 1993), 66–69.
2. Siegel, Bernie S., *Love, Medicine, and Miracles* (New York: Harper & Row, 1990).
3. Ryan, James, Zwerling, Craig, and Orav, Endel J., "Occupational Risks Associated with Cigarette Smoking: A Prospective Study," *American J. of Public Health*, Vol. 82, No. 1 (January 1992).

Chapter 19

Return to Work and Vocational Rehabilitation

19.1 Introduction

The goal in every workers' compensation claim should be the prompt return to work of the injured employee. This is good for the worker and saves money for the employer. In most cases it should happen without any problems or special effort, but sometimes it will need to be facilitated or even forced by the employer. In a few other cases, the help of a skilled rehabilitation counselor will be required. This chapter discusses employer-based return to work programs and the use by employers of vocational rehabilitation. Chapter 11 discussed the legal issues related to vocational rehabilitation.

19.2 Return to Work Programs

19.2.1 Do you realize that, after safety, this is the most important part of your workers' compensation program?

An early return to work is the healthiest outcome for a worker, and in almost all cases the least costly outcome for an employer.

In my experience as a claimants attorney, most employees start out wanting to return to work. When I would see workers during the first few weeks after an injury, they would invariably say that they wanted to go back to work. They would complain that "the walls are closing in on me," that they were "going crazy from just sitting around."

It is when these individuals sit around with nothing to do for three months, six months, or a year, that their attitude changes. They eventually begin to see themselves as "disabled," and a return to work becomes almost impossible.

More directly, an employer is always better off to have a person on the job engaged in productive activity in return for wages than to have the person at home drawing workers' compensation benefits.

19.2.2 Do you keep workers in the habit of coming to work?

As Roger Fries of the Accident Fund of Michigan puts it, "You have to keep them getting up every morning, taking a shower, and brushing their teeth." If the worker continues to feel that he or she is part of the work force and is never allowed to sit home and change his or her self-image to that of someone who is disabled, the disability is likely to be shorter for the worker, with lessened liability for the employer.

19.2.3 Do you attempt to find modified duty in the original work area?

Of course, persons who can return to their old job should do that immediately. If their limitations prevent them from doing so, however, then the first alternative should be an attempt to return to work that meets the restrictions and is closely related to their previous job.

19.2.4 Do you attempt to find other sources of light duty?

If no light duty is available where the employee previously worked, then other placements must be considered. Sometimes the workers' compensation department actually creates these positions. As another alternative, managers throughout the company are asked to notify the workers' compensation department of possible light duty jobs within their area. The workers' compensation department keeps a list or "bank" of such light duty jobs, and assigns workers to them as the need arises.

19.2.5 *Do you create financial incentives to accept workers with light duty?*

Most line managers are evaluated based on their production. Accepting a person back to work who has significant limitations may affect the manager's ability to meet his or her goals. One approach, as discussed in subsection 25.2.6, is to charge managers for all or part of the cost of the workers' compensation claim.

Another approach is to reward managers who find light duty positions. In some companies, if a manager accepts a worker with limitations, the salary is not charged to the manager's budget, but is instead charged to a special account set up within the human resource department.

19.2.6 *Do you limit the length of time that light duty is available?*

Most experts recommend that there should be a limitation placed on the amount of time that a worker can be placed in a special light duty position. Time limits used by employers vary between 60 days and 6 months. I would also suggest that the policy should not be absolute. It should be applied to the majority of situations, but an employer should be prepared for an occasional worker for whom a permanent light duty assignment may be appropriate.

19.2.7 *Have you considered a special work area or a transitional workshop?*

Many very large employers have found it effective to set aside a part of the operation as a transitional workshop. The work there might include washing gloves, sorting good parts out of scrap, cleaning tools, or a variety of functions.

19.2.8 *Are there people in your organization who think a worker should not return unless he or she is completely recovered?*

This has always been a bad policy. It has turned many minor injuries into long-term disabilities and sent many workers to lawyers. Now such a policy also violates the Americans with Disabilities

Act. The ADA clearly requires that employers at least consider the possibility of an accommodation. A blanket policy that says in effect "we do not accommodate" is a violation of the law. See also section 2.4.

19.2.9 Do you realize there may be apprehension on the part of both worker and management?

When I represented workers, I would often find myself telling a worker that he or she had been released to light duty and that the worker should go in and "give it a try." Very often their reply would indicate that they were afraid to do that. "The company will be out to get me. The least little thing I do, they will fire me." I would know that at the same time the lawyer on the other side of the case was calling the company and encouraging them to take the worker back on light duty. The company often replied, "We can't take him back. He'll be out to get us. The least little thing that happens, he will holler 'comp.'"

Both parties thought they were at a disadvantage. This is, of course, impossible. In fact, it is to the advantage of both sides if the worker returns.

19.2.10 Do you do something to make the return to work easier?

Steelcase is a manufacturer of office furniture in Western Michigan. It has an interesting approach to return to work. If a worker has been off for a significant time, he or she is called by the supervisor who says, "You are going to be released to come back to work next Tuesday. Come into the plant this Friday and have lunch with me."

The worker goes in and talks to the supervisor in a relaxed atmosphere, sees his or her co-workers, and views the job and work situation. This approach reduces the tension, eases the transition, and makes it much more likely that the return to work will be successful.

19.2.11 *Do you and others realize that if a worker has been off for even a few days, he or she will need some physical reconditioning?*

Assume that Mr. A does a job that includes vigorous activities involving his legs, arms, and back and that he injured his knee. If he is away from work for even a week, he will not only have problems with his knee, but he will have lost some of the strength in his arms and back.

To some extent this is inevitable, but it certainly highlights the importance of early return to work. In addition, the employer can help things by providing conditioning for the worker and being sensitive to the situation. Both the worker and the supervisor should be told that the individual will need to gradually work back to full performance. This may be even more important for older workers.

19.2.12 *Do you consider the best timing for a return to work?*

There are some physicians who never release a worker to return on a Monday and try instead for a Wednesday or Thursday. In that way, a worker does not have to "get through a whole week" but can have a rest after working two or three days.

19.2.13 *Do you keep the worker coming to the work site?*

Some employers think that it is valuable to keep the worker coming to the work site on a regular basis. The worker is kept in the habit of coming to work and the employer has a chance to see the worker and talk to him or her regularly. In this way, you can observe the worker's apparent health, answer questions that may arise, and generally keep in touch. Of course, this assumes that someone takes the time to talk to the worker when he or she comes in. (If you do not take the time, you are throwing away an opportunity.)

Can you *require* a worker to come in person to pick up his or her check? This will vary from state to state, but in every state you can *ask* the worker to come in. Some employers get too concerned with technicalities. If you simply ask, most workers will agree to come in. Of course, some common sense must be used here. If

Mr. B is in a body cast, it may not be reasonable to expect him to travel to the work site.

19.2.14 What is your state law regarding a refusal to accept an offer of work?

Many states allow an employer to terminate or reduce benefits if a worker refuses an offer of reasonable work. In other states, this is not specified in the statute, but the fact that a worker refused a job often leads a hearing officer to give a smaller award. In any case, it is important to know the specifics of the law in your state and understand how it is applied.

19.2.15 Are your policies aimed at denying benefits or at getting the person back to work?

The first goal of your return to work policy should be an actual return to the job. Cutting off benefits should become the goal only if that fails.

For example, in some states an employer can terminate benefits if the worker refuses a job offer, but the offer must be in writing and must include specific details about the job. I would not start by making the offer in that fashion. Start by making the offer in a way that is designed to get the worker to accept it. Usually this would be in an informal conversation that is part of an ongoing dialogue between the employer's representative and the worker. If such efforts fail, then send the formal written offer.

19.2.16 Do you have an overall plan in place before it is needed?

An *ad hoc* return to work attempt on a case-by-case basis is better than nothing, but a planned program is much more effective. The most effective employers have an announced policy that "if there is anything that a person can do, we will find a job."

19.2.17 Do you learn from the experiences of workers returning to light duty?

Often, workers who have been injured and return to light duty assignments are able to see things differently. They may be able to help you seek ergonomic improvements that are needed, and may even be able to help you improve the work flow.

19.2.18 Have you educated your workers about your policy?

People sometimes ask what form the offer of a light job should take. As discussed above, if you intend to use the offer or a refusal of the offer to cut off benefits, you should be aware of the specific requirements of your state, but as mentioned, your first goal should be a successful return to work.

If that is your goal and you have an announced policy, the form of the actual offer should not be important. Workers should know from the outset that if they are hurt, they will be offered light duty as soon as they are able to do it. They should be expecting the offer long before it is time to make it. The employer's representative should have begun talking about return to work as soon as the acute trauma was over.

19.2.19 Have you educated everyone about your return to work policy?

I often hear that return to work attempts fail because of lack of cooperation from foremen, physicians, or fellow workers. The key is education. Every supervisor should know that if a worker is injured, he or she will be expected to take that person back even if this requires job modification or light duty. If supervisors know that this is company policy before anything happens, they will be more willing to deal with it in specific situations.

The same is true with doctors. Chances are that many of the employers who send workers to an industrial clinic want to turn their back on the problem. The doctors are accustomed to employers who will not take people back unless they are completely recovered. (Yes, this is still true even though it may be a violation of the ADA.) If you are different, if you have an aggressive return to work policy, tell the doctors when you first agree to send patients to them and remind them often. They should modify their approach and consider this in their treatment plan. (If they do not, change doctors.)

Fellow workers can also cause serious problems when an individual returns to light duty. Very often, the only way to create a light duty job is to have someone else do some of the tasks that were part of the original job. These are usually the least desirable tasks. It is much easier to tell people in advance, "If someone gets hurt around here, we're all going to pitch in and help ease that person back into their job," than it is to say, "Your buddy got hurt, so you're going to have to do part of his job."

19.2.20 *If a person is placed on restricted work, does someone follow up to see that the restrictions are being observed by the supervisor and the worker?*

In the ideal company, every supervisor would have a commitment to disability management and it would be included in his or her performance appraisal. Most supervisors, however, are primarily concerned with production or whatever function is the primary objective of their department. The person responsible for workers' compensation needs to follow up to be sure that supervisors are observing the restrictions placed on the worker. Even the best supervisors need some reassurance from time to time.

In some cases it may also be necessary to check to see that the worker is not exceeding his or her limitations. Most of the time I would be inclined to encourage workers to expand their activities as quickly as is comfortable for them, but in some cases they should be held strictly to the limits that the physicians have placed on them.

Some companies use a physical therapist or athletic trainer as the follow-up person. They can be of special help in showing the worker how best to do the job within his or her limitations.

19.2.21 *If you have a special work area or special jobs, is the atmosphere designed to ease the person back into the work force?*

If you use a special workshop, the supervisor should be someone who is sensitive to the problems of returning workers. Often there will a period of psychological, as well as physical, adjustment.

19.2.22 Is the special work too nice?

The special job should not be so soft that the worker will never want to leave.

19.2.23 Is the special work designed to encourage employees to return to their regular job?

The workers' compensation manager for a hospital told me that she has a job she calls "potty patrol." For health and public relations purposes, it is very important that all of the toilets in the hospital are kept clean. Accordingly, she assigns workers with limitations the job of checking all the toilets. They are not required to clean them, only report if they need to be cleaned. The individual thus spends his or her entire day going from toilet to toilet, checking to see if they are clean. I am told that people do not usually stay on this job very long.

19.2.24 Do you exceed the limits of what is a reasonable return to work program?

One employer told me that she brings people in to "watch the clocks." Injured workers are told to sit in a room and watch the clocks to make sure they are going around. In another plant workers are literally carried into the shop and allowed to spend the day lying on a cot in the first aid room so that the plant is not charged with a lost work day. While "potty patrol" may be borderline, I think that both of these approaches clearly go beyond what is reasonable. Employers who use these techniques are asking for trouble, not solving problems.

Every light or special job should add at least some value to the ultimate goals of the company. The greater the value added, the better. This is true for several reasons: (1) workers will be more likely to accept and perform the work, (2) the state will be more likely to cut off or reduce benefits if the worker refuses, and (3) the company gets more value in return for its pay.

19.2.25 *Do you use "work hardening"?*

In response to employers who have said that it is impossible or impractical for them to deal with the limitations of individuals in the workplace, many hospitals and other providers now offer "work hardening" programs. These facilities create situations that simulate the employee's work station. Here, however, the individual can rest after working for a few hours or even only a few minutes if that is appropriate. There are therapists available to assist the worker and monitor his or her progress. A course of physical therapy or exercise may be blended into the simulated return to work. The worker is gradually brought up to full capacity.

These programs are expensive and some employers are reluctant to use them. They would prefer to bring the worker back to a real job and make the modifications there if at all possible. Others use work hardening, but only if they can be sure that a job will be available at the end of the program. Why go through all of this preparation if there is no job to offer the worker? Proponents of work hardening point out that it can be used to evaluate a worker's capacity even if no job is available.

I think these programs might be better accepted by workers if they had a different name. After all, who wants to be "hardened"?

19.3 Vocational Rehabilitation

19.3.1 *Have you considered vocational rehabilitation?*

In many cases it is appropriate to obtain assistance from a rehabilitation counselor in helping an individual return to work. The legal issues related to vocational rehabilitation were discussed in chapter 11. This section will discuss some practical suggestions for employers.

19.3.2 *Are you careful in selecting which cases should be referred for vocational rehabilitation?*

Vocational rehabilitation providers like to point out that the cost of rehabilitation is relatively small compared to the costs of workers' compensation benefits. They also point out that the vast majority of injured workers are "rehabilitated" in the sense that they return to work. Employers, on the other hand, tend to see vocational rehabilitation as an additional cost that they must pay on top of other workers' compensation benefits. The key is to use vocational rehabilitation in appropriate cases.

Assume Mr. C was a skilled electrician and suffered an injury which resulted in the amputation of all the fingers on one hand. He probably cannot return to his previous job as an electrician. He is, however, skilled, he is probably at least reasonably intelligent, he has probably earned a good wage as an electrician, and accordingly he should be motivated to return to productive employment.

At the same time, he probably has no idea where to turn. He does not know what alternatives are available to him, and he does not even know how to find out about them.

He needs someone who will sit down with him and review his medical situation to determine what his limitations and abilities are. Next, the person will probably review his school record. Does he do well in a formal educational setting? Would vocational training be more appropriate? This person should also have information about what training programs are available. Is there a local community college? Are there private schools that do a good job? Even more important, this person should understand the job market. If Mr. C graduates from a program at a community college, are there employers who will hire him? Finally, this person should get acquainted with Mr. C. He or she should understand Mr. C's preferences and attitudes. The person should not make a decision for Mr. C, but should guide Mr. C in choosing the right course. In short, Mr. C needs a rehabilitation counselor. This approach can make the rest of Mr. C's life much happier and more productive, and will, in all likelihood, greatly reduce the ultimate liability to Mr. C's employer.

Consider, on the other hand, Mr. D. He hurt his back while lifting in the course of employment. Most people with similar injuries have returned to work long ago. But Mr. D does not seem to get better. The doctors seem to think there is something wrong, but no one is quite sure what it is. Mr. D has been offered light work by his former employer. He has tried it several times but has not been successful. Will vocational rehabilitation help Mr. D? It may. There are certainly rehabilitation counselors who will tell you success stories about helping people like Mr. D, and success in a case like this can be very helpful to both the worker and the employer, but the odds are very much against success in this situation.

19.3.3 *Do you understand your legal obligations with respect to vocational rehabilitation?*

The laws vary greatly from state to state concerning vocational rehabilitation, and they are in a state of flux at this time. Chapter 11 reviewed the legal situation.

19.3.4 *Do you consider the timing of vocational rehabilitation?*

It is almost universally agreed that vocational rehabilitation will be more likely to succeed if it is begun early. If injured workers get in the habit of being disabled, if they divorce themselves from the labor force, if they stop seeing themselves as workers, it becomes harder to return them to any position.

On the other hand, an employer does not want to spend money on vocational rehabilitation for a worker who would return to work anyway. As mentioned above, it is important to select appropriate cases for vocational rehabilitation. Generally, some time must go by before it is clear which cases are appropriate. I would suggest that most cases should be evaluated for vocational rehabilitation between 90 to 120 days after the injury. In some of those cases, it will be clear at that time whether vocational rehabilitation activities should begin. In other cases, it may be appropriate at that point to postpone a decision about whether vocational rehabilitation is appropriate and to review the question again in another three or six months. This suggested timetable is only a guideline and should not preclude the immediate referral to vocational rehabilitation in cases such as Mr. C in item 19.3.2 above, when the need for this sort of help is obvious from the beginning.

19.3.5 *Do you have a system that ensures the consideration of vocational rehabilitation in every case?*

There should be some "flag" on your computer system or someplace on your checklist so that in every case after, say, 90 to

120 days, the claims person responsible for the case reviews the file and makes a determination whether (a) vocational rehabilitation is appropriate, (b) vocational rehabilitation is not appropriate, or (c) the case should be reviewed again in another 90 days to consider vocational rehabilitation.

19.3.6 Do you always consider return to work with the original employer first?

There is no question that return to work with the original employer is (1) easiest, (2) least expensive, and (3) most likely to be successful. This should always be the first alternative considered by both the claims person and the rehabilitation counselor.

19.3.7 Do you use outside rehabilitation counselors to assist in return to work with the original employer?

Many companies would not consider this. They feel that a return to work of their employees to their company should be their responsibility. Perhaps they have used a rehabilitation counselor to develop their return to work program, but once it is in place, they feel it should work without the need of outside assistance. They make referrals to rehabilitation counselors only after it has become clear that a return to work with the same employer is not possible.

Some employers, however, have been quite successful in taking a different approach. They have found that bringing in an outside rehabilitation counselor assists management at all levels in finding ways that an injured worker can return to a job within their company.

Neither approach is necessarily best; each employer must decide what will work for it.

19.3.8 Do you use vocational rehabilitation as a way to get responsibility off of your desk?

If a claims person is overworked with too many cases, and has several "problem cases" in which he or she is not making any progress, it might be tempting to refer some or all of these cases for vocational rehabilitation. It gets the file off your desk. Now you don't have to worry about it for a while. It is someone else's responsibility. The claims person can also assert that he or she has "done something about this file." The problem is that the case may not be appropriate for vocational rehabilitation.

It is also possible to use rehabilitation counseling firms for activities that are more probably considered claims adjustment. Under some circumstances, it may well be appropriate for a rehabilitation counselor to go to various physicians and obtain medical reports, to talk to the worker and obtain a detailed history, and to ask the worker about his or her plans for the future. Under other circumstances, however, it would be most appropriate for these activities to be done by the claims staff. Indeed, it would be cheaper and more efficient in some circumstances for these activities to be done by the claims staff rather than an outside rehabilitation counseling firm.

Risk managers should monitor the situation to ensure that neither their in-house staff nor an outside insurance or service company is referring to rehabilitation counselors activities that they should be doing. See also section 11.8 concerning the financial impact of this strategy.

19.3.9 *Do you really expect vocational rehabilitation to work if the individual is forced into it?*

In some states, such as Michigan, a worker's benefits can theoretically be terminated if he or she refuses to participate in vocational rehabilitation. This creates a temptation for employers to confront the worker in certain problem cases by offering vocational rehabilitation. If the worker refuses, his or her benefits may be stopped.

The employer should understand, however, that vocational rehabilitation is not very likely to be successful under these circumstances. It is possible to coerce Ms. E into going to school, but it is very difficult to coerce her into doing well in school, and it is impossible to coerce her into doing well on a job interview.

I recognize that there are cases in which an employer is sincerely attempting to do everything it can for the worker, and in which the worker is absolutely refusing to cooperate. In these circumstances, the employer needs some way to demonstrate to the state agency the worker's lack of motivation and refusal to cooperate. In a limited number of cases, attempts to force a worker into vocational rehabilitation may be the best, or indeed the only way to do this. I worry, however, that it is an abuse of vocational rehabilitation, which under other circumstances can be used effectively to the advantage of both the employer and the worker. If vocational rehabilitation comes to be viewed in your area as a tool that employers use to cut off benefits, then in the future, some workers who could benefit by vocational rehabilitation are likely to resist it when it is offered by an employer.

19.3.10 Do you require some showing of effort by a worker who wants expensive vocational rehabilitation?

Some workers start back to school on their own, or they seek out a rehabilitation counselor. They may come to you with a plan. They may have figured how long it will take, they may have a list of expenses, they may plan to invest some of their own money in their rehabilitation. They may have been to several colleges or schools and brought back catalogs and analyzed the programs. They may have talked to or observed people doing the job they aspire to. In other words, they may have put forth considerable effort, even before they ask you to finance their rehabilitation.

Other workers may simply come to you and say, "I want you to rehabilitate me." Obviously, people in the first category are more likely to be successful in their rehabilitation program.

19.3.11 Do you carefully select and monitor the performance of rehabilitation firms?

Before selecting a rehabilitation counseling firm, an employer or its insurance or service company should obtain bids from the various firms in the area. It should meet with and interview the counselors who are actually going to do the job. It should seek references from and consult with others who have used these firms.

Once a firm is hired, there should be some procedure for monitoring its performance. Are the charges running at the expected level? How does the actual success rate compare with earlier predictions?

19.3.12 *Have you checked on licensing and/or approval procedures?*

In some states, the workers' compensation agency approves vocational rehabilitation providers. Some states also license rehabilitation counselors. Licensing is ordinarily done by some agency within a department of education. In any case, if you are selecting a rehabilitation provider, you should begin by calling your state workers' compensation agency and asking if there is an approval or licensing procedure in your jurisdiction. If there is, you should be cautious about making referrals to firms that are not approved and/or licensed.

I say "be cautious" rather than saying one should never refer to an unlicensed provider. In some states, licensing is permissive or indicates a higher level of proficiency. In general, one should require the highest possible level of approval or licensing. There may, however, be circumstances under which a person who does not meet all the formal requirements can nevertheless be very helpful to an employer and its workers.

Chapter 20

Claims Handling

20.1 Introduction

Claims handling is, of course, the heart of any workers' compensation system. The following sections discuss various aspects of this process. Handling of disputed claims is discussed in chapter 21.

In an insured employer, most of these functions would be carried out by the insurance company. A self-insured employer might handle many of these functions itself or delegate all of them to a servicing company or third-party administrator (TPA). In any case, it is the employer who will pay if they are not done properly, and it is therefore the employer's responsibility to insist that they be done and be done well.

20.2 Claims Management

20.2.1 Do you as an employer accept the fact that there will be claims?

While we must do everything possible to avoid injuries, claims are inevitable. How does management react? It is amazing the number of managers who treat this as some kind of personal affront. If the matter is taken too personally by any of the parties involved—the supervisor, a manager, the owner, or the claims person—this will interfere with the company's ability to deal with the situation in a businesslike manner.

While the human element is very important in workers' compensation, management must be able to deal with these situations according to a plan and in a rational and logical manner.

20.2.2 *Do you have control of the claims process?*

The goal of good claims handling should be to take control of the process. If employers want to control costs, they must control the process. I often hear the complaint that at Company A workers' compensation is "out of control" or controlled by the claimants' attorneys or "the system." This chapter includes many suggestions that should contribute to your ability to take control.

20.2.3 *Do you have the trust of workers?*

In order to take control, you must have the trust of the workers. They must trust you personally and there must be a trusting attitude toward the company in general. This may be affected by things beyond your control, but you must nevertheless understand its importance.

20.2.4 *Does the workers' compensation department have the trust of management and others?*

The workers' compensation department must deal continually with line supervisors, top management, and providers, such as physicians. If it is going to take control of the process, it must have a reputation for credibility and trust with all of these people as well as hourly workers.

20.2.5 *When you discuss a file with anyone, are you always honest and realistic?*

How do you establish and maintain the trust of the people involved? Primarily by being honest. If they catch you lying once, they will never believe you again, but it is not enough to just be honest. You must also be *realistic* in your assessments. If you tell the supervisor "Jane will be back in a week or so," when it may well be a month, if you tell the doctor's office they will be paid in 10 days when it may be 60, if you tell a worker "This is a really easy job," when it is a little hard, you will never build trust.

20.2.6 *Does the person who handles claims have regular contact with the workplace?*

It sometimes happens that the person who is in charge of the claim is at some distance from the workplace. That person should be continually in touch with someone at the worksite. This might mean, for example, that a claims adjuster for an insurance company calls an employer once a week and visits every couple of months. For a large self-insured employer, this might mean that the "plant representative" is consulted by the claims manager before important decisions are made concerning a case. The exact situation will, of course, vary depending on the insurance relationship and the status of the claim. There should, for example, be more frequent contact at critical times such as immediately after an injury or before a return to work.

20.2.7 *How much is done by mail, phone, in person? Have you evaluated which means are most effective?*

It is, of course, much cheaper if the claims adjuster can sit at a desk all day long, but losses are likely to increase as the result of this savings in claims expense. The more personal contact the better. Still, not everything can be efficiently done in person. An employer working with its insurance or service company should evaluate its processes and determine the best way to approach the important element of claims handling.

20.2.8 *Do you distinguish properly between losses and items that are part of adjusting expenses?*

When a claims adjuster interviews an injured worker, this is generally treated by an insurance or service company as part of the adjusting expense. It is considered part of what was contracted for in return for the premium or fee negotiated with the employer.

When, however, a rehabilitation counselor and often a case manager interviews a client, this is considered a loss that will affect the premium of an insured employer and be charged directly to a self-insured employer.

It is important to reach an agreement concerning how these items will be handled when a contract is first made and to follow up to ensure that the agreement is carried out.

20.2.9 *Do you set and regularly update a return to work goal on every file?*

Most claims experts recommend that you set and regularly update a return to work goal in virtually every case. One company that I know of has a large board in its claims office, where it lists and regularly updates the return to work goal for each case. This keeps everyone's attention focused on the ultimate goal of claims handling, a successful return to work of the individual. This may, however, violate the worker's right to confidentiality if not done carefully.

20.2.10 *Do you use commercial publications to estimate the return to work date?*

There are commercial publications that will help you do this. They contain a list of diagnoses and an estimate of the average time off work that should result from each. I hesitate to recommend these, however. Some are based on empirical studies and some are merely the best estimates of people who claim to be experienced in such matters. If you use these, it is important that they be used only as a starting point and not as the final word on how long a disability should last. See subsection 24.2.25 for a further discussion.

20.2.11 *If you are going to pay, how fast do you pay?*

The vast majority of workers' compensation cases are small claims that last only a few weeks. In most of these the employer does not contest in any way the worker's right to benefits. Other cases start out as small claims and should stay that way but turn into costly problem cases. One of the things that causes small cases to become big ones is the aggravation a worker experiences when he or she must go for a long period of time with no paycheck and no workers' compensation benefit. If you are going to pay, pay promptly.

What is a reasonable time? How long could *you* go without a paycheck? Most experts say that a worker should have a check in hand in 14 days.

20.2.12 Do you have a system to determine what other benefits the worker is receiving and whether they are appropriate?

In a long and complicated case, it is possible that in addition to workers' compensation, an individual would also receive group disability benefits, group medical benefits, sick pay, pension benefits, ADC, social security disability or retirement benefits, or benefits from a credit disability insurance policy.

In some cases it is reasonable and logical that the worker get one or more of these benefits in addition to workers' compensation. In other cases the benefits are not compatible with workers' compensation and no one should receive both for the same disability. In some states an employer is entitled to take credit against workers' compensation for many of these benefits. (See section 9.9.) In any case, the presence of these will affect the worker's willingness to return to work and/or settle for a lump sum.

An employer can only deal with these matters if it knows what is going on. Every workers' compensation program should have a system to regularly monitor what other benefits the worker is receiving.

20.2.13 Do you review files for third-party subrogation?

As discussed in section 4.3, in most states a worker and an employer can recover in a civil action if a third party was responsible for the injury. This is ordinarily only practical in cases involving serious injuries, but in those cases it can allow the employer to recover nearly all its losses. At some point in every claim, shortly after the injury if possible, every open case should be reviewed to determine if there is the possibility for third-party subrogation.

20.2.14 Do you have a system to check for Second Injury Fund reimbursement?

Most states have some form of second or subsequent injury fund. (See chapter 13.) These funds assume part of the liability when a worker had some disability before being hired and suffers a later injury at work. Someone should take a look at every serious case to see if this might apply.

20.3 What Happens When an Injury Occurs

20.3.1 Do you recognize this as a critically important event?

What happens at the time of injury can set the tone for the entire claim. I often tell the story of the football player. When a football player is injured all the action stops. All the attention is focused on the injured player. He is reassured. The coach puts his arm around the player. If he is helped off the field, the crowd applauds. Contrast this to what happens in the industrial setting when someone comes to the supervisor and says, "Joe hurt his back." What does the supervisor say? Most likely something obscene! If a worker is treated badly at the time of the injury, he or she never forgets it.

20.3.2 Does the company response send a message that injuries are serious matters?

It may be tempting to minimize incidents, to "not make a big deal out of it." It is possible that making a big deal out of an injury encourages the worker to take some time off. On the other hand, it also sends several other messages: (1) accidents are unusual events, we do not expect them to happen; (2) we are concerned and care about you; (3) we are going to observe you and follow up on what happens to you; and (4) we are going to take charge of this situation and direct what happens.

20.3.3 Does the company response send a message that it is concerned about the worker's well-being, that the worker can trust the company to take care of things?

Some workers go to their lawyers before they go to first aid. Companies assume that when a man or woman is injured the first thing he or she thinks about is "How much money can I get out of this?" Whenever I have fallen or gotten hurt, I have thought about very different things such as: "Did anyone see me? Did I look stupid? Did I tear my pants? How will I get the car home?"

I suspect that most workers begin by thinking about rather mundane things. I also believe that the company's response can be an important factor in determining how the worker will ultimately react. If the worker is treated with genuine concern, he or she will respond by trusting the employer to help with treatment and return to work.

20.3.4 Have workers been educated about what to do when an injury occurs?

As will be discussed in section 27.3, it is important that workers be educated in advance about how they are expected to behave when an injury occurs. It is, of course, also important that this information be readily available to them again at the time they need it. One approach that some employers take is to have a pamphlet outlining the procedures to be followed in the case of a work-related injury. These are given to new employees and are also available throughout the workplace so that workers can have a new copy when the information becomes important to them.

20.3.5 Do you have a simple reporting procedure?

In order to start the claims management procedures it is essential that the insurance company or claims department be notified immediately. The Travelers Insurance Company has instituted an interesting procedure. It has an 800 number that can be given to every supervisor who works for an insured company. The supervisor then can report an injury directly to a central location, which starts the claims handling process. Some employers are reluctant to let supervisors communicate directly with an insurance company. That is a judgment call. It is essential, however, that there be some simple system for prompt reporting.

20.3.6 Do supervisors know what to report?

The more information the claims department has, the better. At the same time, first line supervisors have a lot to do, and filling out forms is probably not a high priority. You have to make it easy for them. Under the system developed by Travelers, each supervisor can be given a list of the questions that will be asked when he or she calls the 800 number. In this way, the supervisor is more likely to gather the necessary information and feels more comfortable when making the call.

20.3.7 Do you tell the doctor or hospital that a worker is coming?

If you send a worker to a doctor or hospital, call ahead and tell them that he or she is coming. First of all, this will get the billing straight. Furthermore, calling ahead sends messages to both the worker and provider. It tells the worker once again that you are concerned and want to help. It tells the provider that you will be following this case, that you want the worker to have good care, and that you will monitor the case and perhaps watch for overtreatment.

20.3.8 Does someone go with the worker to the doctor?

I think it is important that this be done wherever possible. For one thing, it may not be safe to let a man or woman who has just been injured drive alone to a doctor or a hospital. In addition, sending someone with the worker reinforces again the messages about concern and control that were mentioned in the previous section.

20.3.9 *Do you have a form that you send with the worker to the doctor or hospital?*

Many employers find it especially helpful to have a form that accompanies the worker to the health care provider. The form might include the following:

- An authorization to treat the person and bill the employer or insurer.
- Information on where to send the bill.
- A description of the employer's understanding of how the injury occurred. (The doctor might as well have both sides of the story from the very beginning.)
- A description of the report that the employer expects the doctor to provide. This should include the items you would like to have in the report and specifics about where the report should be sent.
- Information about your return to work policy. If you have a policy that you will find a job for any injured worker who can get into the plant, the health care provider should be informed of this at the outset of treatment.

20.3.10 *Do you help the worker deal with minor details?*

Someone should notify the workers' family if he or she will be late coming home. They should be told whether the injury is serious or not. If it is serious, it may be appropriate to help the family get to the hospital. Help with even minor details, such as getting the car home, will be greatly appreciated by the worker and may have paybacks for the employer when it comes time for a return to work.

20.3.11 *How soon does someone contact the worker to explain the process?*

It is very important that a contact be made as quickly as possible. This can be in person or by phone, and will usually come from the person who will be responsible for managing the claim. The claims person should explain the process to the worker, let him or her know what will happen next, and assure the worker that he or she can be contacted if there are any questions or problems. Taking control of the process requires that information and inquiries keep coming back to the claims department. If you do not answer the workers' questions, there are lawyers who will.

20.3.12 *Is something sent in writing to the worker?*

A written statement should not be a substitute for a personal contact, but it should be sent in addition to that contact. Many companies send a letter explaining the workers' rights and reminding them who to call in case of a question. The Casualty Insurance Company attaches to that letter a small plastic card that the worker can peel off and keep in his or her wallet. The card includes the worker's claim number and the phone number and address of the contact person. If the employer wants to take control, if it wants to keep inquiries and information coming back to it, it must structure the situation to make this likely to happen. Providing a card that the worker can take along wherever he or she goes is an excellent way of doing this.

20.4 Investigation of the Injury

20.4.1 *What are the purposes and priorities of the investigation?*

The purposes of an investigation are:

1. To provide help to the worker.
2. To prevent future injuries.
3. To verify the claim.

It is important that the purposes of the investigation be prioritized in this order. It is morally and ethically appropriate. Moreover, it will result in a better investigation. The success of the investigation depends on the cooperation of the injured worker and fellow employees. If the employer's first priority is to help the worker and the second priority is to prevent future injuries, the employer will obtain much better cooperation and will be in a better position to verify the claim.

20.4.2 *Have you clearly delineated who is responsible for the investigation?*

Some companies assign this responsibility to the safety director, while in others it is assigned to the workers' compensation department. In many companies, the responsibility is shared with line supervision. There is no single best way. It is important, however, that the employer's policies be clearly delineated so that everyone knows who is responsible.

20.4.3 *Do you investigate every injury as if it would be litigated?*

Some employers have the policy of doing the most complete and thorough possible investigation in every single case. Others argue that this is not efficient, that it is generally possible to tell from the beginning which will be the more serious cases, and that given limited resources, they should be allocated in the most efficient manner. This is an individual decision that must be made by each company given its circumstances. A woman who manages workers' compensation for a large retail chain told me, "In most places, we investigate only the more serious claims, but in California, we do a thorough investigation of everything."

20.4.4 *Are all witnesses interviewed?*

Typically, the witnesses might include the worker, the co-workers, supervisors, and outsiders such as customers or bystanders.

Erv Vahration, the former director of Michigan's Bureau of Workers' Disability Compensation, likes to say that very often the most important witness is the one who did not see anything. This is the person who says, "I worked next to him all day long and didn't see anything at all. If something had happened, surely I would've noticed." It is important to talk to every possible witness.

20.4.5 *Do you obtain written statements from witnesses?*

If you are preparing for litigation, the statements from witnesses should be written and signed. Some states have special requirements regarding statements taken from an injured worker. In Michigan, for example, the statement must include an acknowledgment from the worker that he or she has read and received a copy of the statement. Employers should check local law in this regard.

20.4.6 *Have you considered reenacting accidents?*

A workers' compensation manager for a large trucking firm told me that in his area (Southern California), they actually reenact every accident in which a worker is injured. They go to the scene of the injury and videotape this reenactment with the injured worker and others repeating step-by-step what happened.

20.4.7 *Do you appreciate the deterrent effect of a careful investigation?*

The kind of investigation described above is, of course, time consuming and costly. There is no question, however, that if workers see this happening in other cases, they will: (1) be more careful to avoid injuries, and (2) think twice before they consider filing a fraudulent claim.

20.5 Deciding Whether to Dispute a Claim

20.5.1 *Do you have a clear procedure for deciding which cases to dispute?*

For most employers, the vast majority of cases are relatively small and clearly compensable. There is, however, always a certain percentage of cases in which it is questionable whether the injury occurred in the course of the worker's employment. It is important to have a clearly defined procedure for deciding whether to accept or reject these claims. This should include a delineation of whose input is obtained and who is responsible for the ultimate decision.

20.5.2 How complete an investigation do you have?

As discussed in section 20.4 above, there should be a very thorough investigation of questionable claims. This investigation should be done before the decision to dispute a case is made.

20.5.3 Is there input from someone close to the incident?

Whether you are a large, self-insured corporation or a small insured employer, there is always the temptation to allow these decisions to be made by a claims person who is at some distance from the actual events. This may be the appropriate place for the ultimate decision to be made, but there should always be input from someone who is close to what happened.

20.5.4 What role does the medical provider play?

It is obvious that in many cases the opinion of the physician will be important. Many employers feel, however, that the doctor should not be put in the position of the ultimate decision maker. First, to some extent, these are economic and human resource decisions rather than pure medical decisions. Furthermore, it is important to maintain a good patient-doctor relationship. If the doctor is seen as a judge or decision maker, it will tend to break down this relationship.

20.5.5 In deciding to dispute a case, do you consider the human relations cost?

If it is a clearly noncompensable case, it should probably be denied regardless of the circumstances. There are, however, many borderline cases. They are judgment calls. In those cases, some consideration should be given to the human relations cost of denying a claim.

20.5.6 How big a deal will this case be?

Do you want to spend thousands of dollars on attorney fees to defend a case that only involves a few hundred dollars in medical benefits? As discussed below and in chapter 21, it is sometimes important to set a precedent. Most of the time, however, it is better to be pragmatic.

20.5.7 *If workers' compensation is denied, what will the worker receive in other benefits?*

For some companies with large benefit packages, the financial difference between receiving workers' compensation and other benefits is very small. Likewise, the difference in cost to the employer is very small. This is surely a factor to be weighed in considering the importance of disputing a workers' compensation claim.

20.5.8 *What effect will workers' compensation have on other benefits?*

Because of union contracts or company policies, a worker's seniority may continue to accrue while he or she is off on workers' compensation, while it will stop accruing if the worker is off on group disability benefits. Under these circumstances, a worker may be inclined to pursue a disputed case, even though the dollar difference between workers' compensation and group benefits is very small. This is again an important factor for all parties to consider.

20.5.9 *Do you consider how many cases you want to try when you decide how many cases you will dispute?*

As discussed in more detail in section 21.6 below, a decision to grant or deny a claim today may result in either the payment of benefits or a legal battle that the employer will have to live with for many years in the future. If an employer grants benefits in questionable cases, it will have a smaller number of litigated claims, and will be in a position to fight them more vigorously. If, on the other hand, an employer disputes all questionable claims, it will likely have a great deal of litigation, and may well be forced into settling a substantial portion of those claims.

20.5.10 What percentage of denied workers proceed to litigate the claim?

If a very large percentage of the denials are litigated, you are probably denying too many.

20.5.11 What percentage do you win?

If you lose a very substantial percentage of the cases you deny, you are wasting money on litigation and creating a bad human relations atmosphere. If, on the other hand, you are winning all the cases you deny, you should probably be "testing the water" and denying more.

20.5.12 Do you have a procedure to ensure that the front line decision makers get feedback on the ultimate results of the case?

Very often, litigated cases are handled by a department that is different and sometimes isolated from the people who handle the initial claims. It is important that the people making the initial decision get regular feedback on the outcome of individual claims they grant or deny, as well as data on the overall outcome of disputed claims.

20.5.13 Is the claims staff able to check with the litigation staff for advice?

If the claims staff is separate from the staff that litigates disputed cases, the claims staff should have easy access to the litigation staff in order to seek their input and advice.

20.5.14 If you deny a claim, do you tell the worker and explain the reasons?

This is hard to do. It is certainly a job that no one wants. Many companies escape it completely by simply sending a form letter. There are, however, several reasons why it is important for some representative of the company to personally meet with the worker and explain why his or her claim has been denied.

First, it is simply the decent thing to do. Second, you may obtain more information from the worker, which will allow for a reconsideration of the decision. Finally, giving the worker a clear explanation of how the decision was made, why the claim was denied, and granting one more "hearing" about his or her side of the case may prevent litigation. Presumably, you have a good reason for denying benefits. If you do not give the worker an explanation, he or she is much more likely to go to the state agency or to an attorney, and it is very likely that an attorney will view the case differently than the employer.

20.6 Follow-Up

20.6.1 Do you have a plan for handling a case from beginning to end?

In section 20.3 I talked about what should happen when an injury occurs. It is also important that you have a plan for the entire case, including regular follow-up.

20.6.2 Do you have some system to ensure that no file ever "falls through the cracks?"

The worst case scenario for an employer (and probably for the worker) is for someone to pull out a file and say, "We're paying this case and no one has looked at it for two years." This should never, never happen, but it does. Every company should have some system to prevent this.

20.6.3 Do you tell the worker what will happen next? What the procedures will be? What you expect?

You presumably have in mind a plan for how the claim should proceed, what the worker should do at each step, whom he or she should talk to, when and how often. How does the worker know what you expect? When and where have you given your employees this information? The employer must have some system for informing and continually reminding the worker of the appropriate procedures.

20.6.4 *Do you keep the supervisor informed?*

At some point you may need to ask the worker's supervisor to help you return this employee to his or her job. You should keep the supervisor informed of the progress of the claim. You must maintain a balance between confidentiality of medical records and keeping the supervisor posted on the worker's progress.

20.6.5 *Is there someone who will listen to what the worker has to say about what happened?*

Within reasonable limits, there should be someone representing the employer who keeps in touch with and is willing to listen to injured workers. If the employer does not have time to listen to the worker, there are plenty of lawyers who do.

20.6.6 *Do you protect your claims people from workers who will monopolize their time?*

In the 1991 movie *What About Bob?* (Touchstone Pictures), a patient follows his psychiatrist on a family vacation. I suspect there are claims people who have had nightmares about such things. While it is important to listen to workers, there is a limit. Claims people should be protected from the passive-dependent claimants who will monopolize their time.

20.6.7 *Do you protect your claims people from danger?*

It is funny to joke about the passive-dependant claimant who wants to talk to the claims person every day. There are also some claimants who are more seriously "sick" or perhaps just plain mean. In some cases, claims people are in real danger. Security should be provided to protect the claims staff under those circumstances.

20.6.8 Does the immediate supervisor visit the worker when he or she is off?

When I represented injured workers they would often say, "I was off for six weeks and no one came to see me." As a claimants' attorney I had a standard reply. I told them they were silly to think that the employer cared about them and foolish to have expected a visit.

More recently I have learned that there are many employers who see to it that the supervisor visits the worker. Do they do this because they "care" or because it saves money in the long run? I am not sure of the motivation, but I am convinced that it does save money.

20.6.9 Do you consider whether a supervisor visit is appropriate in a given case?

I have had employers tell me that there are parts of cities to which they would never send their supervisors and I am sure you can think of some supervisors you would not want to send out to talk to an injured worker. While this is a good general policy, thought must be given to how it is applied to each individual case.

20.6.10 Has someone told the supervisor what to say, how to act?

It is easy for us as workers' compensation or human resource people to tell supervisors to visit injured workers, but if we expect them to do that, we should help. A good way to start is by telling the injured worker: "I'm sorry to hear that you were hurt."

20.6.11 How often does a claims person contact the worker?

It is easy to put responsibility on supervisors. How are *you* doing in handling the claim? In the early stages there should be a contact at least once a week. Later on this can be stretched out somewhat, depending on the circumstances.

20.6.12 *Do you monitor the return to work date?*

As discussed in subsection 20.2.9, virtually every file should have a goal, a date by which you expect this man or woman to be back on the job. This goal should be monitored and updated regularly.

20.6.13 *Are wellness and employee assistance programs available to workers off because of disability?*

They may need them more now than ever. They are discussed in section 18.3.

20.7 Reserves

20.7.1 *Do you understand the role of "reserves"?*

Insurers place a reserve on every case. This represents someone's estimate of what the case will ultimately cost. As discussed in sections 14.3 and 22.3, depending on the insuring arrangement, these can have a substantial effect on the employer's premium. Reserves are not quite as important to self-insured employers, but for accounting purposes, self-insureds do set and maintain reserves on every case. These are then carried as liabilities on the balance sheet.

20.7.2 *What approach is used to set reserves?*

Estimating the ultimate cost of the case is much more an art than a science. It can be said that there are three approaches to setting reserves:

1. The worst case scenario—always estimating the highest possible cost.
2. Stairstepping—reserving a case at a relatively low amount in the beginning, and gradually increasing it to a more realistic amount as time goes on.
3. The actual best guess—initially setting the reserve and

continually revising it to represent the most accurate possible estimate of what the case will cost.

Virtually everyone agrees that the third approach is the most appropriate. It is, however, not always followed. Marketing and sales people for an insurance company will put pressure on the claims department to keep reserves low in order to keep the employer customers happy. Experienced claims managers have told me, for example, that if a back case comes into the office that they can identify immediately as a long-term problem claim, they will know that it will ultimately deserve a reserve of several hundred thousand dollars. They tell me, however, that the "front office" would never allow them to put such a high reserve on a case so early in the process. Instead, they would be required to start out with a lower reserve and gradually increase it as time went by and more information came into the file.

On the other hand, there is a temptation for claims handlers and defense attorneys to set a very high reserve on cases. The best way for the claims handler to look like a hero is to settle a case for an amount substantially less than the reserve. He or she then appears to have saved the company a great deal of money. This assumes, however, that the reserve was appropriate in the first place. Setting a high reserve on the case can make it easier for the claims handler to look good.

Reserves also have an effect on the financial status of insurance companies, and it is said that sometimes the reserving policies of the entire insurance industry vary from time to time, depending on various factors including the financial markets. It is generally thought that the industry has been underreserved for several years.

20.7.3 *To what extent do you question the reserving practices of your insurance or service company?*

This is a difficult judgment call. You are paying the insurance or service company for its expertise in claims handling, including its expertise in setting reserves. On the other hand, the various factors discussed above may result in inappropriate reserves, or reserves that work to the advantage of the insurance company, but not to that of the employer.

They are your employees and, depending on the insuring arrangement, it is to a large extent your money. An employer has a right to an explanation of how the insurance company arrived at the reserve figures. In addition, the insurance company should be seeking the employer's input in setting these reserves. Beyond that, the questioning of reserves becomes more a matter of the overall relationship between the employer and the insurer.

Most states have some theoretical procedure by which an insured employer can appeal to the insurance department over pricing disputes, which would include pricing disputes based on reserves. These procedures are, however, rarely used. It is probably more appropriate to review the reserving procedures at the time you renew your contract or policy. If there are on-going disputes between the employer and the insurance company over the reserves, it should be an important factor in deciding whether you wish to continue working with that company.

20.7.4 Do the reserves include a factor for the time value of money?

Insurance companies actually set aside money to pay future losses. The insurance company earns investment income on this money. Often, however, at the level of the claims staff, this is not considered. The reserves are discussed in terms of what the actual ultimate payout will be. A discount or adjustment is later made by the financial department of the insurance company. This is not necessarily inappropriate. It is important, however, that everyone understand what the process is.

20.7.5 Is there some system to ensure consistency of reserving practices?

Since there is a lot of "art" involved in setting reserves, it is possible for variations to develop in these practices among the various offices of a large insurance company, or a large self-insured employer. Many companies have a formal procedure by which a sample of cases from all offices is regularly reviewed by someone at the corporate level to ensure that reserving practices are consistent throughout the company.

20.7.6 *What system do you use to ensure that reserves are regularly reviewed?*

Most experts suggest that the reserves set on a case should be reviewed every time a significant event happens in that case, every time, for example, a doctor's report is received, every time the claims adjuster speaks to the worker, and surely every time there is an attempt to return to work. Even if there is no activity on a case, it should be reviewed periodically. All permanent partial disability cases should probably be reviewed at least quarterly. Even dormant total and permanent disability cases should be reviewed at least annually.

Insured employers should review the reserves set by the insurance company each time they receive a "loss run," that is, a status report on open cases prepared by the insurer.

20.7.7 *What system do you have to ensure that reserves are taken off a claim when the file is closed?*

When a file is closed, the reserves should be taken off or set to zero. This usually happens automatically. It is not unheard of, however, for an employer to discover that it is being charged for reserves on a case that has long since been settled. Every employer should have some system to ensure that this does not happen.

Chapter 21

Disputes

21.1 Introduction

Ideally, if an employer followed all the advice in this book, it would never have any disputes and this chapter would be unnecessary. Unfortunately, it never works that way in practice. In the area of workers' compensation, we are dealing with abstract and personal concepts such as "disability." While the strategies outlined in this book will help reduce litigation, they will never eliminate it. Workers' compensation is an area in which there will always be some disputes that will require sorting out by lawyers and judges.

It would be nice to think that the disputes in workers' compensation represent a dichotomy, either the employer is right or the worker is right. Unfortunately, it is not as simple as that. Most cases are part of a continuum, as illustrated in figure 21.1. At one end of the spectrum there are a certain number of cases that the employer will surely win. At the other end of the spectrum there are a certain number of cases that the worker will surely win. Next to these is a band of cases in which either the employer or the worker is most likely to win. Finally, in the center, there are a significant number of cases that are nearly "50-50." It is not clear from the law or the facts who will win.

Differences among laws and judges in the various jurisdictions may influence this scale. They may shift the entire scale to the left or to the right, but they will not change the fact that it is a continuum rather than a clear division between who is right and who is wrong.

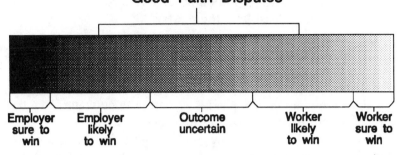

Figure 21.1

The Continuum of Disputes
Good Faith Disputes

| Employer sure to win | Employer likely to win | Outcome uncertain | Worker likely to win | Worker sure to win |

Finally, it is important to remember that the cases toward the center usually represent a good faith dispute. At the extremes, either employers or workers are doing what they can to beat the system. They are perhaps guilty of fraud. In the middle, however, both sides genuinely believe that they are right and that they are entitled to win. It is likely that both sides have reports from credible physicians who support their position. In dealing with the individuals involved in these cases, it is important for the parties to remember that they may be involved in a good faith dispute rather than a case in which they are surely right and the other side surely wrong.

This chapter will begin with a discussion of alternative dispute resolution procedures, turn next to attorneys, talk about hearings and appeals, and finally discuss settlements. This chapter discusses these matters from the employer's point of view. Chapter 12 described the procedures involved.

21.2 Alternative Dispute Resolution

21.2.1 Have you tried alternative dispute resolution procedures?

Alternative dispute resolution (ADR) has become popular recently in all areas of the law, including workers' compensation. These procedures are most often called mediation but sometimes referred to as informal hearings or conferences. Like most new approaches to solving problems, they have not always been as successful as their proponents had hoped. Nevertheless, they have substantial potential for workers' compensation. You should know which informal dispute resolution procedures are available in your jurisdiction, and at least give them a try.

21.2.2 *Do you understand that mediation allows you to keep control?*

Under mediation, the parties agree to the outcome. In a trial or hearing, the parties turn the final decision over to a hearing officer or judge. No matter how good the attorney, this means that when the proofs are finally closed, the final decision is out of your hands. In mediation, you retain control. In a trial, control is turned over to someone else.

21.2.3 *Do you understand that mediation is usually cheaper and faster?*

Mediation is usually so much cheaper and faster than the formal procedures that it is worth doing even if it only resolves a small percentage of the cases.

21.2.4 *Who do you send to mediation—claims people or attorneys?*

Because of certain changes in procedures and requirements, there was a period of time during which the Accident Fund of Michigan regularly sent attorneys to mediation hearings. During that time, it resolved about 23 percent of the cases at the mediation. Things then changed, and the Fund began to send the claims staff instead of attorneys to the mediation. After the change, the Fund found that they resolved 68 percent of the claims at mediation.

Some cynics would say that this happens because attorneys do not want to settle cases. They make more money if a formal trial is necessary. There may be some truth to this, but I believe there is another factor that operates as well. Because of their training and experience, attorneys generally have more faith in formal dispute resolution procedures. They are taught in law school that ultimate justice is more likely to be reached if a decision is based on the formal procedures and rules of evidence that have evolved over the years. Whether or not this is true is beyond the scope of this book. I would, however, make two points: (1) your attorneys may discourage you from using mediation, but try it anyway; and (2) if the rules of your jurisdiction allow it, try sending someone other than an attorney to represent you at mediation.

21.2.5 Do you use informal hearings to talk to the worker and get information?

The formality of workers' compensation proceedings varies from state to state. Generally, however, when an individual hires an attorney and files a lawsuit, the other party is, at least theoretically, prohibited from talking directly to the individual and asking him or her questions about the dispute. In civil courts, there are elaborate discovery mechanisms that allow one party to send written questions to the other, or to question the other party in a deposition. These discovery proceedings are generally not available in workers' compensation.

An informal hearing, however, generally involves a situation in which both parties sit down in a room and talk about the case. This very often provides the employer with an exceptional opportunity to ask the worker questions and to discover what the worker is likely to say at trial.

21.2.6 How much authority do you give the person who represents you at a mediation?

If you want to resolve a case, then the person representing you must have the authority to do so. This is true whether it is an attorney or a claims person. Obviously, there should be some limit to this. If in your judgment the case is worth between $10,000 and $20,000, you may want to give the person authority to go up to, say, $22,000. Under the circumstances, however, you would be wasting everyone's time to send to mediation someone who had the authority to settle a case for no more than $12,000.

21.2.7 Is there a procedure to ensure that before going to mediation, the claims people have carefully reviewed the file?

It seems like stating the obvious to say that you are most likely to do well at mediation if the person representing you has spent some time carefully reviewing the file in advance of the mediation hearing. Unfortunately, this is not always the case.

21.3 Attorneys

21.3.1 Do you set high ethical standards for your attorney?

There are honest lawyers, and you should insist on being represented by one.

Moreover, you want a lawyer who is honest with everyone. Be cautious about the attorney who tells you he or she will win by being tricky or deceitful. The person who will deceive or trick the other side will most likely also trick or deceive his or her clients.

You will be best served by an attorney who truthfully presents all of the facts in the light most favorable to you. There is a fine line between forceful advocacy, which presents the case in the way most favorable to a party, and fraud, which misrepresents the facts. A good lawyer should understand this distinction and should never violate it.

21.3.2 Will your attorney help you prepare a plan to deal with your overall workers' compensation strategy?

A good attorney should not only represent you in disputed cases, he or she should be willing to work with you to review all aspects of your workers' compensation program. You may want to assure yourself of this while seeking an attorney.

21.3.3 Does the attorney come to your workplace?

Like physicians who treat your workers, the attorney who represents you needs to have firsthand knowledge about the jobs the individual performed and the atmosphere in your facility. He or she should be willing to come to your workplace and observe the situation.

21.3.4 What percentage of trials does your attorney win?

Given the choice, would you prefer an attorney who wins 100 percent of the cases he or she tries, or an attorney who wins about 75 percent of the time? How would an attorney go about winning 100 percent of the time? Given the continuum in figure 21.1, the only way to win every case is to try only the cases at the extreme left end of the spectrum. What happens to the rest of the cases? The attorney settles them. How does the attorney settle them? By paying out your money. The attorney who wins 100 percent of the time is not willing to take chances. He or she is settling too often.

Some attorneys are literally afraid to try cases, or at least to try difficult cases. They push their clients to settle whenever possible. On the other hand, there are some attorneys who are afraid to settle cases. Making a settlement decision often involves more difficult judgments than a trial. As a result, some attorneys try more cases than they should.

I will discuss settlement strategy in section 21.6. You should, however, be wary of the attorneys at the extremes.

21.3.5 Are you able to choose your attorney?

Some insurance companies use "house counsel," that is, attorneys who are their full-time employees, while others contract the work out to independent law firms. Servicing companies generally use outside attorneys. Large, self-administered, self-insured employers sometimes use house counsel and sometimes use outside firms.

Your ability to choose an attorney will obviously depend on your situation. If you are a small insured employer, you will probably have to accept the attorney assigned to you by your insurance company. If you are large enough to have significant bargaining power with the company that sells you insurance, you may be able to insist that they hire certain law firms to represent you. If you are self-insured, you should be able to designate the firms you wish to have represent you.

In some situations, you may also wish to designate which attorney within the firm will handle your cases. Some law firms are reluctant to do this. Once again, your ability to insist upon it will depend on your size and bargaining power. You should understand that there is nothing unethical or improper, however, in making a request for an individual attorney.

21.3.6 Does your attorney keep you posted?

Your attorney should be sending to the insurance or servicing company at least a brief report after every significant event in the case. This would include such things as a pretrial hearing, a mediation, or the deposition of a medical witness. Copies of these should be passed on to the employer.

21.3.7 Do you supply your attorney with the information he or she needs?

It is easy to criticize attorneys for not being prepared, not doing a good job, or not keeping you informed. You must understand that their ability to represent you effectively depends to a very large extent on whether you provide them with the information they need in a timely manner.

21.3.8 How often do you reject your attorney's advice?

It is your money. At least if you are self-insured, you have the right to make the ultimate decision in every case. Nevertheless, you are paying your attorney for his or her expertise. If you are rejecting it too often, you should probably either reconsider your policies or change attorneys.

21.3.9 Do you spend too little money on attorneys?

In general, we need to reduce attorney involvement in the workers' compensation system. If an employer must pay out money, it is better that it go to the injured worker than to an attorney.

Sometimes, however, employers are too quick to settle. As will be discussed in section 21.6, it is sometimes appropriate to spend a substantial amount of money on attorney fees to establish a reputation or precedent rather than settle.

21.3.10 Can you talk reasonably with claimants attorneys?

There is a tendency among employers to see claimants attorneys as evil people who are "the problem" with the workers' compensation system. This stereotype may be appropriate for a small percentage of claimants attorneys, but most of them are reasonable people who are merely acting as advocates for injured workers. Listening to their point of view can tell you a great deal about individual cases, and perhaps a great deal about your relationship with your work force. You can learn from claimants attorneys. This author, after all, is a former claimants attorney.

21.4 Hearings

21.4.1 Do you have a system to ensure that everyone is prepared for hearings?

When the trial day comes, it is absolutely essential that everyone be prepared. If the attorney has asked for personnel records, they must be provided. If you plan to present witnesses, they must be available. Strive to be ready before the trial date.

In most states, a large percentage of the cases that are set for trial are actually settled rather than tried. It is a fact of our system that most cases are settled "on the courthouse steps" on the day of trial. It thus often seems like a waste of time to go through all the preparations when, in fact, most cases are not tried. Picture, however, the situation in which two attorneys sit down at a table and discuss settlement on the morning that a case is scheduled for trial. If one of those attorneys is fully prepared and ready to try the case, and the other is unprepared or unsure that witnesses are available, the attorney who is prepared has a tremendous advantage in the settlement negotiations. Be prepared.

21.4.2 Does someone from the employer go to the formal hearings?

Someone who works for the employer should attend the hearing in every important case. It gives the employer a face. The worker is virtually always present. When the judge sits down to decide the case, he or she is going to visualize an individual to whom he or she must say yes or no. The judge should also be visualizing an individual who represents an employer, a person who will receive either good or bad news.

The presence of someone from the employer is also likely to "keep things honest." When the worker takes the witness stand and begins to answer questions about how the injury occurred and how difficult the work is, the worker is less likely to be honest if he or she is the only one within miles who has a good understanding of the worksite.

In addition, questions often arise that cannot be anticipated. There is frequently a need for information that has not previously been gathered. If there is someone present from the employer, he or she may be able to deal with this situation. Finally, having someone present gives you an opportunity to observe the performance of your insurance or service company and your attorney.

Practices vary on the extent to which nonattorneys are expected to be present during settlement negotiations. In virtually every jurisdiction, however, the employer does have a right to have a representative present during a formal hearing.

21.4.3 Does someone from the insurance or service company go to the hearing?

Sometimes insurance or service companies merely send their attorneys to hearings, and no one from the claims staff attends. This may be appropriate in some circumstances, but it is often helpful to have a claims person present during the hearing.

21.4.4 What do you know about the judge?

If you are trying a substantial number of cases in any jurisdiction, you or your attorney should gather information about the reputation and record of the judge. Some are more sympathetic than others. Some have quirks. They may, for example, generally be sympathetic to workers but "have a thing" about heart cases. It is very important for you to know as much as you can about the judge with whom you are dealing.

21.4.5 *What do you know about the other attorney?*

As I mentioned earlier, some attorneys like to try cases and some attorneys are afraid to try cases. This is equally true of attorneys who represent workers. Knowing the other attorney's strengths and weaknesses is an important part of your trial strategy.

21.5 Appeals

21.5.1 *What percentage of cases do you appeal?*

In an administrative system, such as workers' compensation, appeals are relatively easy, and it is tempting to appeal a large percentage of the decisions. This, however, is not necessarily appropriate.

21.5.2 *What percentage of the appeals do you win?*

This is the best way to tell whether you are appealing too many cases. If you appeal 90 percent of the decisions you lose, but you win only 5 percent of the appeals, you are appealing too often.

21.5.3 *What is the cost of the appeal?*

Attorneys may be quick to tell you that it will not cost "too much" to file an appeal, and you might as well take another chance. It is easy for the person who is receiving the payment to say that the costs are not too high. There are other costs as well. There is a certain cost to keeping the file open for an additional period of time. It requires attention from your claims staff and it may be hurting your relationship with the individual employee involved, and with other employees. You should weigh all these costs against the likelihood that you will win when making your decision concerning appeals.

21.6 Settlements

21.6.1 What is your reputation for settlements?

If you are an employer of substantial size in your community, you will develop a reputation for settlements among workers, unions, and their attorneys.

Consider the claimants attorney, sitting in his or her office, when a worker comes in with a marginal case. There is some chance that the worker could prevail, but the odds are against it. If you have a reputation as someone who is "hard-nosed," who rarely ever settles cases, who will insist that the matter go to trial and demand that the worker prove every aspect of his or her claim, the attorney is likely to say, "I don't think I can help you." If, on the other hand, you have a reputation as a company that rarely tries cases, is always willing to settle, and will pay "something" to get rid of any case, the attorney is going to take the case and take a chance. To the extent possible, an employer should attempt to create a reputation that it does not easily settle cases.

21.6.2 What is your settlement strategy?

The appropriate settlement strategy is this: Try your winners and settle your losers. This is very easy to state, but difficult to implement. Often employers complain to me that they "lose every case they try." This should not happen. While data are hard to come by I doubt that there are many states in which employers in general lose more that 60 to 65 percent of the cases. You may think that this is pretty bad, but it is certainly not "all the cases." What is happening to people that seem to lose every case?

Consider the continuum of figure 21.1. At the left end are cases that the employer is sure to win and at the right are cases that certainly come out in favor of the worker. (I have in mind here cases with an either or answer such as whether the accident happened at home or at work, but a similar view could be taken of cases involving issues such as the percentage of impairment.) A company that never wins a case must not be trying any of its "sure winners," the cases at the far left of the spectrum. Attorneys for workers are willing to settle these for relatively small amounts and, since in reality no case is "100 percent," it is tempting to take these settlements. If you want to win once in a while, however, and if you want a reputation for not settling, then once in a while you have to say "no" to these cases and try them.

Also a company that loses a lot is probably trying cases on the right end of the spectrum. It must be trying some cases that it is almost certain to lose. These are the cases to settle, to compromise, to pay. The claimants attorney will want big money for these cases and there may be some cases that just do not seem "fair" to you, but if a realistic evaluation suggests that you will lose, you are better off to settle these cases.

Of course, at the same time you are pursuing this strategy, claimants attorneys will also be trying to settle their losers and try their winners. All things being equal, only cases in the middle of the spectrum will be tried and each side should win 50 percent of the time. All things are rarely equal, however. Some lawyers are better than others and some employers are more realistic than others in evaluating cases. You will be rewarded if you step back once in a while, review your win-loss record, and consider whether you are using the right settlement strategy.

21.6.3 *Do you realistically evaluate cases?*

The discussion about settlement strategy in the above section assumes a realistic evaluation of the cases. This means that your attorneys and claims people have properly evaluated the opinions of the doctors and other witnesses. It also means that you have realistically considered the law in your state. Settlement negotiation on the morning of a trial is not the time to argue that the law in your state is unfair. (It may be unfair but that is an argument for the legislature, not the trial judge.) The laws of a state and even the attitude of a judge can move the continuum to the left or right. You may want to do something about that later, but during settlement negotiations the only question should be where you stand on the realistic continuum that you are facing.

21.6.4 *Is your settlement strategy part of your overall policy?*

As discussed in subsection 20.5.9, the ability to insist upon a trial at the end of a long dispute may depend on the philosophy that was applied when a case was first filed. If the company takes the position that it will give the worker the benefit of the doubt and only deny cases in which the worker is clearly wrong, then when it gets to trial, the company will have primarily cases that are on the left end of the continuum in figure 21.1. It will be able to insist successfully on a trial of the cases.

If, on the other hand, an employer denies all questionable claims, then a higher percentage will be disputed, and the cases that reach the trial level will include many cases that are at or beyond the center of the spectrum. In this situation, a "no settlement" strategy is likely to lead to losses in a substantial number of the cases.

There is no simple answer here. Some employers prefer to take a hard stand at the outset of the claim and let the chips fall where they may; others prefer to take a more reasonable posture at the beginning of the case and a harder stand when it comes time to litigate. In any case, a settlement strategy does not develop on its own. The policies applied to settling litigated cases should be part of an overall claims handling strategy.

21.6.5 *What is the cost of the trial?*

There is a cost of trying cases. It includes not only the attorney fee, but also the time that will be required of your staff and any witnesses who will be called to testify. The costs may also involve a loss of goodwill on the part of the employee involved, and perhaps other employees as well. These costs should not be a reason to "cave in" and pay a settlement, but they should be taken into consideration.

21.6.6 *Do you let inappropriate factors affect your settlement decision?*

As mentioned above, I am not averse to trying a case in order to establish the employer's reputation. Often, however, cases get tried for silly reasons. Just because the foreman "never liked this guy," does not mean that the judge will not like the guy or that you will win the case. Sometimes an outsider, such as a claims person or attorney, is able to make a judgment divorced from the personal feelings that develop about an employee over a period of time. It is important to understand the personal or emotional factors that may be affecting your attitude about a case and to put them in perspective when making decisions.

21.6.7 How "big a deal" will this case be?

Some cases just do not matter much. They will not cost you much to settle, and they really will not have much affect on your reputation or operations. In those cases, it is better to settle than to try the case.

21.6.8 How much authority is given to the attorney?

It is the general practice that the ultimate authority for settling the case rests with a claims manager at the insurance or service company or the self-insured employer. A certain amount of authority is delegated to the attorney handling the hearing or settlement negotiations. Delegating the appropriate amount of authority is a delicate art. If the authority delegated is not nearly enough to settle the case, negotiations will break down, and you are likely to end up trying cases that you would have preferred to settle. On the other hand, it is sometimes an appropriate strategy to hold back some authority. Maybe your attorney will want to be able to say, "Oh, I can't pay that much without calling the home office." This is a common strategy and is often appropriate. It is essential, however, to have someone there, at the home office, who can answer the phone and give the proper amount of authority at the right time.

21.6.9 Do you want to include in a settlement a waiver of an ADA claim?

Section 2.4 discusses the Americans with Disabilities Act (ADA). Many workers' compensation cases may also include potential claims under the ADA. If you settle a case, you will certainly want to wrap up all possible disputes arising out of the injury. Accordingly, it would be desirable from the employer's point of view to obtain a settlement or waiver of any potential ADA claim at the same time a workers' compensation case is settled.

As this is being written, few issues have been litigated to completion under the ADA. It will be some time before we know what are the appropriate approaches under that Act. We can point out, however, that there is a long history of settling cases under Title VII of the Civil Rights Act. Accordingly, there probably can be an enforceable settlement of cases under the ADA. However, there must be some additional consideration or payment in exchange for the worker's waiver to make this settlement enforceable. In short, if you want a settlement of two claims, you probably have to pay a little more money.

At present, some employers seem to be taking the position that if, up to the time of settlement, the worker has never asserted any claim under the ADA, it may be the best strategy to "leave well enough alone" and not to raise the issue. This may be an appropriate strategy. Nevertheless, there have not been that many ADA lawsuits so far, and there may not be as many as people are expecting. It is too early to be certain how this will develop.

Finally, if there is, in fact, a claim pending before the Equal Employment Opportunity Commission, or a state civil rights agency, it is probably best to settle all the claims at once. To do this, all the parties and all the attorneys should be brought together at a single settlement conference, and everyone should understand that the settlement will be a final and complete resolution of all of the claims. If you cannot reach an agreement to settle the discrimination case, you may or may not wish to proceed with a settlement of the workers' compensation case. What is most important, however, is that everyone understand what is being settled and what is not.

Chapter 22

Insurance and Self-Insurance

22.1 Introduction

The following sections will explore in more detail the implications of self-insurance and the pricing of insurance. Chapter 23 will be devoted to a discussion of how to get the best service from an insurance or service company.

There are various ways an employer can finance its obligation to pay workers' compensation benefits to injured employees including self-insurance and various forms of insurance policies.[1] These were discussed in section 14.2. An employer should consider the options listed there and the issues discussed in this and the next chapter in deciding which alternative is best for it.

Since the 1980s, there have been steep increases in insurance premium rates. These have led many employers to consider self-insurance. We will begin this chapter with a discussion of the requirements of self-insurance and include a review of the pros and cons from the employer's perspective.

22.2 Self-Insurance

22.2.1 What are the requirements for self-insurance?

To be self-insured, an employer must apply to and be approved by the state. This responsibility may rest with the workers' compensation agency or, less often, the insurance commission. All states

349

except South Dakota and Wyoming allow self-insurance. There are differences among the states on the specific requirements but the general factors considered are:

Financial stability.   The agency will require evidence of the financial situation of the company. This will include traditional financial statements and perhaps other information.

Additional security.   The state may require additional security such as a bond, letter of credit, or excess insurance. By issuing a bond or letter of credit, an insurance company or bank, respectively, assures that a certain amount of money will be available to pay claims should the employer be unable to do so. Bonds were the traditional approach to this but the bond market became tight in the late 1980s and many states began accepting letters of credit. It is assumed, but not yet certainly established, that the obligation of a bank issuing a letter of credit will survive the bankruptcy of an employer. Excess insurance may also be required. It is discussed in subsection 22.2.7 below.

In some states, bonds, letters of credit, and/or excess insurance are required of all self-insured employers. In others, this requirement is at the discretion of the agency approving the application.

A state regulator can use the requirement of additional security to help assure that he or she has made the right decision concerning an application. If ABC Company applies for self-insurance and its financial situation is borderline, the regulator might require that it obtain a bond. The insurance company issuing the bond will then also look at the employer's financial situation. If it is also concerned about the employer's finances, it will refuse to issue a bond or require a very high fee and/or collateral.

Length of time in business.   In some states there is a requirement that an employer must have been in business for a certain amount of time, typically five years.

Claims record.   Some states examine an employer's claims handling record or require that an employer use an approved servicing company.

Safety record.   Most states also, at least nominally, look at the employer's safety record.

22.2.2 *Is any one of these more important than the others?*

I think so. The biggest concern of regulators is the financial ability of the employer to pay claims as they become due. If a company has enough assets, it can usually get approved. If it is not sound financially, the rest does not matter.

22.2.3 *Where can an employer get more information about specific requirements?*

Several organizations publish listings of the requirements. Towers Perrin, for example, has a publication entitled *Financing Workers' Compensation: Self-Insurance and Other Options.*[2] These provide a good general overview. If, however, you are serious about self-insurance, you should obtain information about the state's requirements directly from the state agency involved. These are listed in Appendix A.

22.2.4 *What are the benefits of self-insurance?*

Reduced costs.   The premiums paid by an insured employer to an insurance company cover not only losses and loss adjustment expense but must also cover premium taxes, insurance company overhead, brokerage fees, marketing costs, any burden from the residual market that is being charged back to the insurer, and insurance company profits. At least in theory, self-insured employers save these costs.

Cash flow.   Although this varies somewhat depending on the insurance arrangement, in general, an insured employer pays a premium during the current year, which will cover all losses resulting from injuries occurring during that year. The payment of these losses may actually take place over many years in the future. The insurance company has the use of the monies collected during the premium year, until the losses must be paid. As a self-insured employer, however, you can "pay as you go." (It should be noted, however, that a self-insured employer will have to carry a liability for future losses on its balance sheet.)

Escape from the fluctuations in the insurance market.   In some states there are substantial fluctuations in the insurance market. These affect both the price and availability of workers' compensation insurance. Once an employer is approved for self-insurance, it can, to some extent, escape from these fluctuations. It may, however, still have to deal with the availability and pricing of excess insurance.

More direct concern about safety and return to work.   When the costs of workers' compensation are being paid more directly by the employer, it is more likely to be concerned about, and to implement, high quality safety and return to work programs.

Better control over claims management.   A self-insured employer can apply its own philosophy to the management of claims. It can choose more directly which cases to pay and which to dispute. It can ensure that cases are paid promptly, when they should be paid, and fight fiercely when that is the appropriate alternative.

22.2.5 What are the disadvantages of self-insurance?

More responsibility.   Although the self-insured employer can control the claims process, it now has complete responsibility for this process. It can delegate some of the responsibility by hiring a service company, but ultimately, it is the responsibility of the employer, not the insurer. Along with this responsibility come numerous costs. These include the costs of hiring a third-party administrator (TPA) (see subsection 22.2.8), or the costs associated with having the employer's personnel manage these responsibilities.

Increased risk.   The most obvious disadvantage of self-insurance is that the employer now bears a larger share of the risk, although as discussed in subsection 22.2.7 below, it may lay off part of the risk.

The long tail.   The tradeoff for better cash flow is what is called "the long tail" of workers' compensation. Most of the people who are injured this year will return to work within a few months after the injury. Some, however, may still be drawing benefits several years from now, and a few may be drawing benefits 10, 20, or 30 years from now. If an employer is self-insured for a period of time, it must bear the responsibility for those cases, so long as they remain open.

The regulatory burden.   It is not easy to obtain approval as a self-insured employer. States require detailed disclosure of the employer's financial situation, and, as discussed above, may require additional security.

If an employer operates in numerous states, the burden is multiplied, since approval must be obtained separately in each jurisdiction. For this reason, some employers with a highly dispersed work force prefer retrospectively rated or large deductible policies. Employers that have a high concentration of workers in a few states and a smaller number of employees working throughout the country often become self-insured in those states where they have many workers, and purchase insurance for the rest of their operations.

The tax deductibility of reserves.   If an employer pays a premium to an insurance company, much of it is not paid to the worker until many years in the future. The entire premium, however, is deductible at the time it is paid. If a self-insured employer sets aside reserves for the payment of future benefits, they are not deductible until they are paid to the workers.

22.2.6 *Is any one of these criteria more important than the others?*

Although the potential cost savings is frequently cited as the most important advantage of self-insurance, I believe that the ability of an employer to take control of its own workers' compensation process is at least as important, if not more so. If an employer plans to become self-insured and intends to hire a servicing company to completely manage all of the claims, it might better use some other arrangement and escape some of the risk. The greatest advantage is being able to be certain that claims are handled more directly and in the manner desired by the employer.

This, of course, means that the employer will have to devote more resources in terms of the time of its own employees and managers to the handling of claims. Some of this responsibility may still be delegated to a servicing company, but an employer loses the biggest advantage of self-insurance if it does not take control of the process.

22.2.7 *Must a self-insured employer assume all of the risk?*

Most self-insured employers "lay off" part of the risk through excess insurance. These are sometimes called "stop loss" policies. There are both *specific* excess insurance and *aggregate* excess insurance.

Nearly all self-insured employers purchase *specific* excess insurance. Specific excess insurance provides a maximum amount that an employer will have to pay for one *occurrence*. Generally, insurance carriers want to set the *retention amount* at a level that will rarely be exceeded. Thus, for example, a self-insured employer might purchase specific excess insurance with a retention amount of $200,000. It would be rare that a single injury would result in a claim for more than that. If that does happen however, the excess carrier would reimburse the employer for any benefits paid that exceeded $200,000. An *occurrence* is usually defined broadly enough to cover the circumstances under which a roof caved in and killed five employees. Under those circumstances, the specific excess carrier would begin reimbursing the employer when the losses from all five individuals together totaled the retention amount.

In *aggregate* excess insurance, the retention amount is based on the total losses for all injuries for a given time period, usually a year. Thus a company might purchase aggregate excess insurance with a retention amount of $2 million for a policy year. If all of the losses resulting from injuries that occurred during that year exceed

$2 million, then the insurer reimburses the employer for any amounts in excess of $2 million.

22.2.8 Does a self-insured employer have to administer its own claims?

No. Many self-insured employers use a servicing company or a third-party administrator (TPA) to administer the claims. Generally, the largest self-insured employers are self-administered, while the majority use a servicing company. Even if an employer does use a TPA, it need not delegate all of the administration to the servicing company. The various possible arrangements are limited only by what the two parties can agree to.

An employer could, for example, delegate all claims handling to the TPA, but require that its adjusters meet regularly with the employer so that the employer has more direct and immediate impact on the policy decisions governing each claim. Or an employer and a servicing company could agree that the employer will do substantial parts of the claims handling, including referral to physicians, and arranging for return to work programs, but that the TPA will file forms with the state agency and handle litigated cases.

Since one of the primary advantages of self-insurance is the ability to take better control over the claims handling process, employers should be cautious not to lose this advantage by delegating everything to the TPA.

22.2.9 If you self-insure, be sure your name is on the checks.

Very often, the servicing company writes and mails the checks to the injured workers and the medical providers. Sometimes the checks are drawn on the service company's account, and sometimes the service company is given authority to draw checks on the employer's account. It is important, however, that when the worker (or the doctor) receives a check, it has the employer's name on it. The employer will want the worker's cooperation in the future. You are giving this person money. You should take credit for it.

22.3 Insurance Pricing

22.3.1 *Do you shop for the best deal on workers' compensation insurance?*

Every insured employer should shop carefully for the best deal on workers' compensation insurance. This should be treated like every other item that a company purchases.

22.3.2 *Do you understand the alternative forms of insurance?*

Section 14.2 describes the various alternatives. The remainder of this section will assume that your company has chosen some form of insurance.

22.3.3 *Do you shop for service as well as price?*

Workers' compensation premiums are ultimately determined by the amount of the losses. Good service can reduce the losses. In the long run, service may be more important than the immediate premium. Chapter 23 deals in more detail with service issues.

22.3.4 *How often do you reevaluate your insurance?*

Most policies are written on a yearly basis. Accordingly, it is probably appropriate to reevaluate the situation each year, to some extent. It would not be wise, however, to change carriers every year. First, there is a cost involved in getting acquainted with new people and becoming familiar with the procedures of a new company. Second, and more important for workers' compensation insurance, is the fact that the old carrier will continue to be responsible for handling claims that occurred during the policy years it was on the risk. Accordingly, an employer that changes insurers frequently will be required to deal with many different insurance companies. Third, insurers tend to pay more attention to claims from employers that they currently insure.

It is probably most appropriate to do a complete evaluation every two or three years, and to change only if there is an opportunity to significantly improve either the price or the quality of service.

22.3.5 Do you have a formal procedure for securing bids?

Some employers have formal procedures. They begin several months before the policy expires, with the employer sending out a standard quotation form that each bidder is expected to follow. The bids are evaluated according to the established procedures.

22.3.6 Do you allow time for the bidding process?

You should start the process at least three months before the expiration date of the policy. Since workers' compensation insurance is mandatory, the buyer is at a disadvantage in the marketplace if time is running short.

22.3.7 Is there coordination within your company between the person responsible for buying workers' compensation insurance and the people who administer the plan on a day-to-day basis?

I am always amazed at the number of companies in which the chief financial officer places workers' compensation insurance based on his or her relationship with a broker, without ever asking the human resource manager, or other people who must live with the policy on a day-by-day basis, whether or not the insurance company is providing good service. It is essential to coordinate between the individual or department that is purchasing the insurance and the individuals who must deal with it daily.

22.3.8 What does your broker or agent do to earn his or her fee?

A good agent or broker can do a great deal to help an employer with all of the issues raised in this chapter. Brokers and agents earn substantial fees by placing workers' compensation insurance.

It is only fair for an employer to demand service in return for those fees. A good broker should help its clients with all of the issues discussed in this chapter.

22.3.9 *What is the market for workers' compensation insurance in your state?*

As discussed in section 14.3, the market for workers' compensation insurance varies greatly from state to state. As this is being written, insurers are very reluctant to write workers' compensation insurance in Maine or Florida, but very willing to write such coverage in Michigan or Illinois. The state of the market depends on various factors that are discussed in section 14.3. As an individual purchaser, you may not be able to do anything about these factors. It is nevertheless important to know where you stand in the marketplace. If it is a buyers' market, you will certainly want to be aware of this. Of course if you are in a state with an exclusive state fund (see section 14.4) your only choices will be that fund or self-insurance.

22.3.10 *Does your state allow competitive pricing?*

As discussed in subsection 14.3.3, in some states there is administered pricing; that is, the insurance commissioner sets a schedule of rates for workers' compensation insurance and all carriers are expected to comply with it. Other states allow open market or competitive pricing, under which each insurance company is allowed to file its own schedule of rates. Obviously, a buyer needs to know the situation before he or she goes into the marketplace.

22.3.11 *To what extent does your state allow "deviations" or "scheduled credits"?*

Some states that have administered pricing nevertheless allow competition in the forms of deviations or scheduled credits, and all allow the payment of dividends. It is important to understand the extent to which these are allowed in your jurisdiction.

22.3.12 To what extent may you receive credits based on safety disability management or other subjective factors?

Many insurers will reward employers for these practices. To the extent that you are doing them, you should take advantage of the rewards. To the extent that the rewards would result in substantial savings, an employer should consider implementing or expanding such practices.

22.3.13 Do you use your good record to "sell" your company?

In some states insurers are reluctant to write workers' compensation insurance. If you have a good safety or return to work record, this will make you a more attractive client. Use this to sell your company to potential insurers.

22.3.14 Do you review your classifications regularly?

As discussed in section 14.3.2, insurance premiums are based on the classification of the work performed and employers' costs can be greatly affected by the assignment of payroll to these classifications. It is essential that an employer regularly review the classifications to which its payroll has been assigned. This can result in substantial savings.

22.3.15 Do you regularly review the reserves set on cases?

For an experience-rated employer and some retrospectively rated employers, the premium will be affected by the reserves set on open cases. Section 20.7 discusses how reserves are set. The point here is that regularly reviewing the reserves may help an employer reduce the price it pays for insurance.

The extent to which an employer wishes to question the reserves set by an insurance company is a matter that should be carefully considered. On the one hand, the employer is paying the insurer for its expertise in dealing with claims, including its expertise at setting reserves. On the other hand, an employer at least deserves an explanation of how the reserves are set, and an opportunity to ask for a more detailed review of the reserves in selected cases, if they seem inappropriate.

When a case is closed, the reserves should be removed. It is not unheard of to discover that an insurer has mistakenly failed to remove the reserves on closed cases in a timely manner.

22.3.16 *Have you considered installment payments?*

Very often, this is an option available to employers that will help with their cash flow situation.

22.3.17 *Are you careful not to include overtime premium in "payroll?"*

Generally, if an employer pays a premium rate for overtime work, the premium portion of the overtime pay should not be included in calculating payroll for the purpose of calculating insurance premiums. In other words, if a laborer receives $5 an hour for straight time, and $7.50 an hour for working overtime, the payroll reported to the insurance company should be only $5 per hour for all hours worked.

22.3.18 *Can you get a better price by combining the purchase of workers' compensation with the purchase of other insurance?*

Often insurance companies will give a better deal if the purchase of workers' compensation insurance is combined with the purchase of general liability and other types of insurance. There are, however, problems with this approach, as explained in the next item.

22.3.19 *Have you compromised on workers' compensation insurance as part of a "package deal?"*

As suggested in the previous item, sometimes the best price for insurance can be obtained by purchasing a package that includes workers' compensation, general liability, and other lines of insurance. Sometimes the quality of service from the workers' compensation carrier is compromised when such a purchase is made. This lack of service can result in higher losses, which will eventually cost more than is saved by purchasing the package. Accordingly, an employer must always weigh the tradeoffs between the best price and the best service.

Notes

1. For more information, see International Risk Management Institute, Inc., *The Workers Compensation Guide* (Dallas: IMRI, 1992); and Miccolis, Jerry A., ed., *Financing Workers' Compensation: Self-Insurance and Other Options* (Stamford, Conn.: Towers Perrin, 1992).
2. Miccolis, *supra* note 1.

Chapter 23

Dealing With Insurance and Service Companies

23.1 Introduction

This chapter covers selecting and dealing with insurance companies and service companies. An insured employer is purchasing both insurance protection and the servicing of claims. As discussed above and in chapter 14, the cost of workers' compensation insurance is almost always affected to one degree or another by the amount of the losses. The service obtained from an insurance company can affect these losses. Accordingly, obtaining a cheaper price on insurance this year, at the cost of good service, may increase the losses that are incurred, and thus the price that an employer pays for insurance, for several years in the future. Obtaining the best possible service from insurance companies is thus crucial.

As discussed in subsection 22.2.8, the majority of self-insured employers contract with a service company or third-party administrator (TPA) to administer all or part of their workers' compensation program. It is perhaps even more critical to obtain good service from a service company than from an insurance company because the employer is bearing a greater part of the risk.

Section 22.3 dealt with the pricing of insurance. This chapter talks about how to obtain the best service. It deals with strategies that are appropriate at the time a contract is made, and the ongoing relationship with the company. With regard to service, the considerations for service companies and insurance companies are about the same, and so they will be treated together.

23.2 Shopping

23.2.1 *Do you understand the marketplace?*

As discussed in subsection 22.3.9, the market for insurance differs greatly from state to state. In some states, such as Maine and Florida, it may be difficult to find a willing insurer. On the other hand, in states such as Michigan and Illinois, it may be a "buyers market" in which insurers will be competing for your business. Your broker or agent should be able to provide you with information about your position in the marketplace.

Administering the workers' compensation program for self-insured employers is a fast growing line of business. In general, if you are a self-insured employer looking for a third-party administrator, you will find many companies competing for your business, whatever your location.

23.2.2 *Do you realize that your ability to shop may be affected by your safety and return to work record?*

As discussed in subsection 22.3.12, insurance and service companies prefer to contract with employers who have good safety and return to work records. If you have a good record, you should use this as a bargaining tool. If you do not, you should review the discussions in chapters 17, 18, and 19 in order to improve your position.

23.2.3 *Will the company help you with safety, return to work, and other programs?*

It should be standard practice for an insurance company or service company to provide employers with training and assistance for safety and prevention. Many companies also provide similar services with respect to return to work and other programs.

23.2.4 *Is the company approved by the appropriate state agencies?*

The insurance commissioners in every state approve insurance companies. Except under the special circumstances described in subsection 14.2.12, you should not even consider dealing with an insurance company that is not approved.

Service companies are a much newer phenomenon, and their regulation is not nearly as well developed. In some states, however, the workers' compensation agency approves or in some other way certifies service companies. Where that is the case, an employer should deal only with approved companies.

23.2.5 *What is the relationship of the servicing company to the excess insurer?*

As mentioned in subsection 22.2.7, most self-insured employers have specific and/or aggregate excess insurance. Often, insurance companies will have one division that sells excess insurance and another that acts as a servicing company. These companies would like to sell you both of their services. During the late 1980s, the market for excess insurance became tight. It was not seen as a profitable line, and there were not many carriers who wanted to write excess insurance. At the same time, providing service to self-insured employers was seen as a very attractive and profitable business. Accordingly, some companies would write aggregate excess insurance only for employers with whom they had a contract to act as a service company.

As this is being written in 1994, providing services to self-insured employers is still seen as attractive, but there is also a reasonable market for excess insurance. Nevertheless, an employer may be able to obtain a better price for excess insurance if it is purchased from the same company that is acting as its service company. So long as there is a reasonable market for excess insurance, however, I would suggest that the service company be chosen based upon the service it will provide, not on whether it will result in a better price on excess insurance.

Some companies sell excess insurance, but do not do business as servicing companies. If an employer's excess carrier fits into that category, it may be in a position to provide an objective evaluation of service companies. Such an insurer deals with a variety of service companies, and is probably often called on to repair the mistakes made by those companies. It may thus be in a good position to give an employer advice about the choice of a service company.

If, however, the excess carrier also is in business or has a subsidiary that is in business as a service company, that fact should be taken into consideration when seeking such advice.

23.2.6 *Have you negotiated a goal or standard for your insurance or service company?*

Where possible it is a good idea when contracting with an insurance or service company to set certain goals. You might, for example, say:

- We want to reduce our losses by 10 percent, as compared to last year.
- In all undisputed cases, we want the first check to be in the mail in less than 14 days.
- We want the insurer to make personal contact with injured workers within two days.

Goals should be specific and measurable, and designed to fit your particular situation.

23.2.7 *Do you follow up on the goals?*

It is, of course, useless to have goals unless there is a follow-up procedure and a regular check to determine if they are being met.

23.3 Staff

23.3.1 *Do you understand the importance of the insurance company staff?*

It is the people who make a difference among insurance companies. You can generally rely on your state insurance regulator to ensure that the company is solvent and will be around to pay the losses as they come due. In workers' compensation, the terms of the insurance policies are dictated by law. Accordingly, when shopping for workers' compensation insurance, or a workers' compensation service company, there are really only two considerations: price and service. The service is ultimately determined by the people involved.

23.3.2 Did you meet with the claims staff before choosing an insurance or service company?

Most of these companies have a large marketing staff. These are all wonderful people, and they will give you the best possible image of their company. Once you sign the deal, however, you will not see them again until renewal time. You will instead be dealing with the claims staff. It is essential that you meet with the claims people before you choose the company.

23.3.3 Does the company have its own claims adjusting staff?

There are a few companies that sell workers' compensation insurance that do not have their own claims staff. Instead, they rely on other companies to adjust their claims. This is not desirable for workers' compensation insurance. One of the most important things you are buying from an insurance company is its skill at handling claims. If this is being delegated to a third party, you cannot be sure of the quality you are purchasing.

There is one exception to this. If you have small operations in rural areas, it may not be practical for the company to have its own adjusters available in every location. Under those circumstances, it may be acceptable for the insurer to delegate the claims adjusting to an outside company.

23.3.4 Does the claims handler specialize in workers' compensation?

You should expect that the people handling your workers' compensation claims will be experts and specialists in workers' compensation. Here again, it may be appropriate to expect an exception in rural, thinly populated areas, where there are just not enough workers' compensation claims to keep one person busy. In that circumstance, it may be more appropriate to use a local adjuster who handles several lines of insurance.

23.3.5 *What is the workload of a claims adjuster?*

In today's economy, insurance and service companies, like many other industries, are downsizing or rightsizing. This means there are fewer employees to provide service to the employer customers of these companies. This, in turn, means that what used to be done in person is now done by phone, and what used to be done by phone is now done by mail. While some of this seems inevitable, it lessens the quality of the claims handling.

Ideally, a workers' compensation adjuster should have a caseload of between 150 and 175 cases. In today's market, it is probably more practical to expect a claims adjuster to handle between 200 and 250 cases. Of course, this may vary, depending on the types of claims that are handled. In some companies, the adjusters handle all types of claims, whereas in others, assignments are divided and workers are specialized. An adjuster who handles only litigated permanent partial claims, for example, would be expected to have a much smaller caseload than an adjuster who handles undisputed temporary total claims.

Other things being equal, however, the company whose adjusters have a smaller caseload will provide better service.

23.3.6 *How much turnover is there among the claims people?*

I would like to be able to tell you that you should find an insurance company whose claims staff stays with it for the entire length of their career. This is, however, very unusual in the insurance industry. It is a profession where it is common for people to move from company to company. Nevertheless, other things being equal, a company where the claims people stay for long periods of time will probably provide you with better service.

23.4 Providing Information

23.4.1 *Do you get good information from your insurance or service company?*

As discussed in chapter 26, having good information is essential to the management of a workers' compensation program. One of the most important things you are buying from an insurance or service company is information about your program.

23.4.2 Do you get regular loss runs from your insurance company?

Loss runs are listings showing all the open cases, the amount that has been paid on those cases, and the reserves set for future losses in those cases. You should receive these on a regular basis, at least quarterly, and more often if you have a significant number of outstanding cases.

23.4.3 Does the insurance company give you anything more than regular loss runs?

Many insurance companies provide employers with much more information than routine loss runs. The information provided should be tailored to your specific needs. The amount of information the insurer is willing to provide will probably depend on how big and important a customer you are. If you are a small employer and only have one or two claims per year, you can probably not expect too much more than regular loss runs. If you employ thousands of people and have many open cases, you should expect your carrier to break down the data in many of the ways discussed in chapter 26.

23.4.4 Can you access the company's database?

Some companies provide their clients with a terminal, which will allow the employer to access the company's database. This allows the employer to have the most current information on individual claims. It may also allow the employer to query the database and obtain specialized reports.

23.4.5 Do you carefully review the data that are made available?

Of course, it does no good to obtain reams of data from the insurance or service company if you do not review and use the information.

23.4.6 Does the insurance or service company staff promptly return your phone calls?

This is the least you should expect. If a company will not answer questions and return calls, you should not deal with it. The insurance or service company should respond promptly and politely, not only to the risk manager who places the insurance, but to every person working for the employer who must deal with it.

23.5 Claims Handling

23.5.1 Do you insist on good claims handling practices from your insurer or service company?

An employer should expect its insurance company or service company to perform all the claims handling functions discussed in chapters 20 and 21. There are a few functions that seem especially important in choosing or dealing with these companies. They are discussed below.

23.5.2 Does the insurance or service company have the same claims philosophy as you?

You may feel that these are your employees and you wish to give them the benefit of the doubt and thus pay any questionable cases. You may, on the other hand, feel that, if allowed, your employees will abuse the workers' compensation system, that you want to adhere strictly to the law, and that you want to deny questionable cases. Under certain circumstances, either approach may be appropriate. It is essential, however, that the company handling your claims have or least be willing to adopt the philosophy you think is appropriate. This is especially important with regard to service companies for self-insured employers, since as discussed in subsection 22.2.6, one of the primary reasons for being self-insured is to ensure that your own philosophy is applied.

23.5.3 *How much is done by mail, on the phone, in person?*

With regard to claims handling this is especially important. There is a trend today to reduce staff and have less personal contact with injured workers. Doing this increases the likelihood that the worker will become worried and alienated, and weakens the relationship between the individual worker and the employer. When this happens, the worker is more likely to turn to a union or an attorney for advice and help. The employer then loses control of the claim, and costs increase. The more direct personal contact, the better.

23.5.4 *How fast does the carrier decide on compensability?*

It is essential to make prompt payment in undisputed cases. As I have said frequently here, the problem in workers' compensation is the injury that should have been a small claim, and turns into a big one. Prompt payment of the first check is one of the most important steps in avoiding this. How long could you go without a paycheck before you became nervous, concerned, and distrustful of the person or company that was supposed to make the payment? Fourteen days is usually considered a reasonable standard for mailing the first check.

23.5.5 *Does the insurance company seek your input regarding payment, reserves, and settlements?*

You are paying an insurance or service company for its expertise, and you should be willing to defer to it on most issues. At the same time, the service or insurance company should be seeking information from the employer concerning how the injury occurred and the individual worker involved. It is also reasonable to expect the insurance company to at least seek some input from the employer on crucial issues such as settlement and reserves.

23.5.6 *How often does the insurance or service company meet with you to review files?*

If you have more than a few open files, you should expect the insurance or service company representative to come to your place of business three or four times a year, sit down with you, and review the status of each case, and the plans for dealing with those cases in the future. If you are bigger and have more claims, you should expect more frequent, regular contact.

23.5.7 *Do you provide the insurance or service company with the information it needs on a timely basis?*

Employers should shop for and demand prompt, high quality service from insurance and service companies. You should also understand, however, that effective claims handling depends, in part, on the employer. The insurance or service company cannot send out the first check until the employer has sent in information about the workers' wages. It cannot investigate a claim until the employer has sent along basic information about how the injury occurred. It cannot prepare for a trial in a disputed case unless the employer has provided information that has been requested along the way. You must do your part.

23.5.8 *Do you have some system to monitor how well you cooperate with the insurance or service company?*

As suggested earlier, you should set standards to monitor the performance of the insurance or service company. You should set similar standards to monitor how well you, the employer, are cooperating with them.

Chapter 24

Health Care

24.1 Introduction

As discussed in chapter 10 and section 2.4, the health care situation in workers' compensation, and indeed in the country as a whole, is rapidly changing. There are, however, certain basic strategies that should be helpful to an employer in obtaining high quality health care at reasonable prices. Most of these strategies will be appropriate in any future system. They will be outlined in this chapter.

24.2 Choosing and Monitoring Providers

24.2.1 Do you understand that quality is more important than price?

We pay a great deal for medical care in this country, and as discussed in chapter 10 and section 24.3 below, we must take steps to reduce the costs. It is important to understand, however, that the quality of health care is very important to workers' compensation. The worker deserves to be healed as quickly and completely as possible. In workers' compensation, the employer also has an interest in quality because poor health care will lead to longer and more severe disability and an increase in indemnity costs.

372

24.2.2 *When choosing providers, do you consider that they set the tone for the entire claim?*

The worker generally sees a physician immediately following his or her injury. At that point, the worker is apprehensive and often in pain. If the physician and staff are rude, impatient, and skeptical of everything the worker says, this will set up an adversarial relationship that may last throughout the handling of the claim.

24.2.3 *Would you go to the company doctor if you were hurt? Would you send your children there?*

If the doctor is not of the same quality that you would demand for yourself and your family, you should not send your workers there.

24.2.4 *Do you ever go to the company doctor's office?*

It is important to go to the doctor's office. Is it clean and neat? How long do people have to wait? Are people treated politely?

I have been in industrial clinics where the plastic chairs in the waiting room were patched with duct tape, and where I had to walk through one examining room in which a patient was being treated to get to another room where I was to be treated. If I had been sent there by my employer, I would have thought, "Somebody went out and found the cheapest doctor around, and that's who they've sent me to."

You will only know about the office and its procedures if you actually go there.

24.2.5 *Do you choose a doctor whom the workers will want to continue to see?*

As discussed in section 10.3, some states give the employer considerable control over the choice of physician. In other states, the worker has complete choice of the physician, or may change after a certain period of time. Whatever the law, in practice, most of the time, when a worker is injured on the job, the employer suggests a physician or clinic, and the worker goes there, at least for the first visit. If the worker is treated professionally and politely, he or she will continue to treat with that physician. Many employers who argue for a change in the law giving them more control over the choice of physician could obtain the same result by choosing the right doctor under the systems that are presently available to them.

24.2.6 *What importance do you put on good care, versus good testimony?*

Some employers choose physicians because when they are later asked to give an opinion concerning the cause or extent of disability they will be an articulate advocate for the employer's point of view. This is not in itself a bad reason to choose a physician, but it should not be the primary consideration. You would be better off to have a physician who really helps the worker get well than to have a physician who will minimize the extent of disability, whatever the outcome.

24.2.7 *Do you evaluate in-house providers as well as outside providers?*

Some very large employers have "plant doctors." Many others at least have nurses available in first aid stations. These providers should be evaluated and held to the same standards as providers on the outside.

24.2.8 *Will the doctor listen to the workers?*

A physician who takes a few minutes to listen patiently to the workers' complaints will achieve better results than the impatient provider, regardless of his or her technical competencies. In these troubled days for health care in this country, we do not seem to put much emphasis on what was once called a "good bedside manner." It is, however, a valuable asset if you can find a provider who has it.

24.2.9 Will the provider give you the reports you need?

Today's workers' compensation system cannot function unless the health care provider sends reports promptly to the employer or insurer. If providers will not do this, you probably cannot continue to deal with them, no matter how good they are in other respects.

24.2.10 Do you send a form with the worker to the provider?

As discussed in subsection 20.3.9, when the worker first goes to a new health care provider, it is helpful to send along a form with information about the injury, about how the claim should be handled, and about what reporting you expect from the provider.

24.2.11 If you use a managed care organization, do you understand that it is only as good as the people involved?

As discussed in section 2.6, there is much debate today about "managed care" and various ways in which the provision of health care can be structured administratively. All the issues raised throughout this chapter should be applied to managed care organizations in the same way they would be applied to individual clinics or physicians.

24.2.12 How does the provider know what your jobs are like?

In many workers' compensation cases, at some time, the doctor or other provider is going to be asked to offer an opinion about whether the individual can return to work. This opinion will be based to a large extent on the providers' understanding of the nature of the work. How does the provider know what the work is like? Must the provider rely on the worker's description? It is best if the provider has clear, objective information about your jobs. The next few items suggest ways to accomplish this.

24.2.13 *Does the provider come to your workplace?*

Your ability to require this may, of course, depend on your size and the number of patients you refer. If you are sending a substantial amount of business to a doctor, you should expect that doctor to spend a couple of hours once or twice a year walking through your facility, watching people work, looking at the jobs, and gaining firsthand knowledge of what the work environment is like.

24.2.14 *Do you send videotapes or other information to the provider?*

Obviously, a physician cannot come to your shop to look at every job for every injured worker. A set of accurate, well-written job descriptions that you can pull out of a file and send to the doctor is very helpful. In important cases, however, it is much more effective to send a videotape of someone actually performing the job.

24.2.15 *Have providers been educated about the company needs and policies?*

As will be discussed in chapter 27, it is important to educate all providers about your company and its policies. As discussed in section 19.2, this is especially true if you have an aggressive return to work policy. If this is the case, you should be continually reminding all providers that you want to bring people back to work as quickly as possible, and that you will do everything necessary to find work within the employee's limitations.

24.2.16 *Have you considered a staff physical therapist, occupational therapist, or athletic trainer?*

For many years large employers have had a "plant nurse" who worked in the first aid room. Today, many companies are adding people from other specialties. A staff therapist can review jobs for potential improvement before people are injured. If the facilities are available, he or she can provide therapy to injured workers much more economically than an outside provider. Finally, a staff therapist can "coach" returning workers about the best way to perform their jobs.

24.2.17 *Are you swayed by the promotional activities of health care providers?*

This is a very competitive industry. There are providers who will invite the vice-president to their box at the ball game, or for a trip on their yacht. I think the workers' compensation manager who accompanies an injured worker to the clinic for treatment is in a better position to make a judgment about which providers should be used.

24.2.18 *Do you consult with your insurance company or service company about the choice of providers?*

These companies deal with a large number of providers, on behalf of a large number of employers. Their experience and expertise should be considered.

24.2.19 *Do you coordinate with other plans on the choice of providers?*

If the workers' compensation system for an employer sends 20 cases a year to a doctor, the health care system for the same employer may send a thousand workers or family members to a doctor in the same period of time. The people who manage the health care system should share their experience and information with the people who manage the workers' compensation system.

24.2.20 *Is the location convenient?*

I have talked a great deal about quality and service, but you should not overlook simple things, such as a convenient location.

24.2.21 *Will your health care providers help you in planning for prevention, wellness, and disability management?*

It is a definite plus if the physician or facility that treats your injured workers will also help you with plans for prevention, wellness, and disability management.

24.2.22 *After a worker has been seen by a provider, do you ask the worker how it went?*

It has become popular today for many providers of services, from auto mechanics to hospitals, to have a routine follow-up, in which they, by mail or phone, ask their customers if they were treated well. There is much that can be gained by asking workers how they were treated by the health care providers to whom you refer them. First, you will gain a great deal of information about the providers, and second, you will be showing interest and concern in the worker. This will help you when the time comes for a worker's return to the job.

24.2.23 *Do you use intensive case management?*

Case management was first developed to deal with catastrophic disabilities such as quadriplegia and AIDS. The case manager, usually a nurse, intensely follows the treatment of the patient involved. The manager develops expertise about the proper treatment for the problem involved, and also about the providers that are available in the specialty or geographic area. The manager helps make decisions about when it is better for a person to be in a long-term care facility or to pay nurses to visit the person in his or her home. The case manager may call the treating physician and gently suggest that other experts have found some different course of therapy to be very successful in such cases.

This approach has been so successful in dealing with catastrophic cases that many employers and insurers are using it in cases involving less severe disabilities.

Attorneys and other advocates for workers sometimes criticize this as an intrusion into the physician-patient relationship, and some doctors feel affronted by the intrusion of a nurse into their medical decisions.

I have been somewhat surprised, however, to find that many physicians welcome this outside help and guidance. An injured worker has to deal with a great many entities: the employer, the insurance company, often several doctors, hospitals, and/or therapists. The case manager becomes the contact or coordinator for all of these entities. In today's complicated medical environment, an injured worker needs someone to guide him or her through the maze.

24.2.24 How often do you use informal case management?

It is probably not efficient to hire a case manager for every on-the-job injury. Nevertheless, depending on the severity of the case, some elements of careful case management can be most helpful.

24.2.25 Do you use protocols or guidelines that suggest what care is appropriate?

Recently, a wide variety of publications and computer systems that predict the appropriate course of treatment for a given injury has become available. These range from treatment protocols published by organizations such as the American Academy of Orthopedic Surgeons, which provide a basic outline of appropriate treatment for specific diagnoses, to computer programs developed by former claims examiners. You enter certain information into the program, and it will tell you what type of treatment the doctor should provide, how long the worker will be off work, and even what the reserves should be in the case. Some of these programs are the result of empirical research, and others are not.

These programs are never more than guidelines. They cannot tell you how soon Mr. A will get well, nor can they tell you what kind of therapy the doctors should use in every case. They can, however, tell you how long the average person with this diagnosis should be expected to be away from work, and they can provide general guidelines for what treatment is appropriate. They are probably most helpful in telling you which cases demand special attention. If a person's length of disability exceeds the guidelines by a substantial amount, or if a physician consistently uses therapies that are not suggested, this does not tell you that the worker is faking or that the doctor is a bad physician, but it does tell you that these are situations that should be monitored more closely.

It is also important to ask who developed the guidelines. Was it an independent scholar, a recognized association, an insurance company or actuarial firm that has a profit motive but also a reputation to protect, or someone who just decided to do this?

Finally, consider the methods used to develop the guidelines. Has there been any empirical research? Have the issuers actually collected data showing that most people with this diagnosis will return to work in this amount of time? Has there been a controlled study showing that this course of therapy works better than others, or have people just made guesses about what is best?

If an employer understands these limitations, and uses the programs or publications as guidelines rather than strict rules, they can be helpful.

24.2.26 How long does a person continue treatment with a provider without improvement?

If a person goes back to the same provider, week after week, and receives the same treatment and does not improve, there is something wrong. This is true whether the provider is a chiropractor or an orthopedic surgeon.

24.3 Health Care Costs

24.3.1 Do you understand and implement your state's system for health care cost control?

As discussed in section 10.6, many states have implemented fee schedules and systems of utilization review that are designed to control health care costs. It is important that you understand the system that is in place in your jurisdiction.

24.3.2 *Can you do better than the state system?*

If the state has a fee schedule, do not allow this to become the "floor"; instead it should be the "ceiling." Many employers and insurers find that they are able to negotiate services for fees that are less than the maximum schedule. Of course, this depends on how reasonable the schedule is in your jurisdiction.

24.3.3 *Do you have your own schedule of what reasonable fees are?*

A large employer or insurer should probably develop its own internal fee schedule, at least with respect to the procedures that it most frequently encounters. This is most important in states that do not have fee schedules, but even in those that do, you should have a feeling of whether you can expect to do better than the official fees for common procedures.

24.3.4 *Do you understand that the bills or "charges" of health care providers are not absolute?*

We are in an environment where the "charge" or the face value of a bill of most doctors, hospitals, and other health care providers is not taken seriously by most large payers. Employers should attempt to negotiate favorable fee arrangements. Large self-insured employers should do this themselves or with the help of vendors that specialize in managed care or health care networks. Smaller employers should expect their insurers to do this for them.

24.3.5 *Do you have a system of utilization review?*

Utilization review can mean many things. At least, it means that someone looks at every bill to see that the proper code and price is assigned to the procedure that has been performed. It might also include a review to see if the proper reports have been received before a bill is paid. Beyond that, it might include a review to determine if the procedures performed were appropriate for the problems the worker was experiencing, and to determine if the length or number of procedures were appropriate for the given situation.

Review might also include a determination that the procedures were actually performed and that there is no duplicate billing for the same procedure.

24.3.6 Do you understand that utilization review is more important than the fee schedule?

If a state or an employer adopts a fee schedule that reduces the charge for an office visit from \$40 to \$30, and the provider responds by seeing workers twice as often, nothing has been gained. Accordingly, while a fee schedule may be the necessary first element, a fee schedule alone will not reduce costs.

In addition to monitoring an increase in frequency, utilization review should also guard against "procedure creep." This occurs when what was previously called an office visit is reclassified as an "intense" office visit, which can be billed at a higher fee. Finally, utilization review should guard against "unbundling," that is, where the doctor's fees previously included the price of gauze and antiseptic, the doctor now adds additional charges for these items.

24.3.7 Have you shopped concerning the best alternative for providing pharmaceuticals?

The market for pharmaceuticals is very competitive. In the past, it was not uncommon for employers and insurers to let the worker go to the corner drugstore and to reimburse him or her for whatever the druggist charged. This would not be wise today. Employers should shop around for the best service and price concerning pharmaceuticals. It is now not uncommon to purchase pharmaceuticals through the mail. This may not be appropriate for emergency or acute care, but if a worker is receiving a maintenance dose of a drug over a long period of time, it is probably the most efficient approach.

24.3.8 Have you considered a managed care organization?

As discussed in section 2.6, it is currently the fad in workers' compensation to use some form of managed care organization. This might range from a group of providers who have agreed to a small percentage discount in return for a larger volume of patients, to a formal structure in which a group of doctors and hospitals have agreed to provide all of the necessary care to the injured workers of a given employer for a given duration, in return for a payment of so many dollars "per head." These are often called *capitation* plans. A number of states have recently amended their laws to allow for such an approach. It is not yet clear if and to what extent they are more efficient than the more traditional approach. On the one hand, as mentioned above, these plans are no better than the people who provide the service. In the long run, these people are the most important consideration. At the same time it must be said that the entire system of health care in the United States seems to be moving toward this type of arrangement.

24.3.9 Do you watch for "self-referrals"?

A self-referral is a situation in which a physician refers a person to a treatment facility in which the physician has a financial interest, for example, a physical therapy center. Some physicians argue vehemently that this is appropriate under certain circumstances. They argue that they can choose the best therapists and more carefully monitor the care provided if they have control over the facility. There is some research, however, that suggests that patients receive more care and more expensive care when physicians refer to facilities they own.[1]

At the very least, an employer has a right to know if a physician is making self-referrals. If your company doctor is referring a great many people to the same physical therapist, or the same radiologist, you have a right to ask if that doctor has a financial interest in the facility to which he or she is making the referrals. If there is an ownership interest, you should watch the cases more closely. If the bills are no higher and the return to work rate is as good or better than the return to work rate of other providers, you probably have no reason to complain.

24.3.10 Do you send a copy of the bills to the worker?

I think this has interesting results. First, your workers probably have no idea how much you are spending on their health care. I expect they would be favorably impressed if they knew. Second, you need the cooperation of your workers in controlling health care costs. You cannot really expect this unless they know how high these costs are. Finally, I suspect that if you sent a copy of every bill to the worker involved, every once in a while, a worker would call you and say, "Hey, the doctor never did this."

Note

1. See, for example, Mitchell, Gene M., and Olden, Scott, "Physician Ownership of Physical Therapy Services," *JAMA* (Oct. 21, 1992), 2055–59.

Chapter 25

Management Issues

25.1 Introduction

This chapter deals with four management issues related to workers' compensation: (1) the understanding by and commitment from top corporate management that must be present for a successful workers' compensation program, (2) the ways in which human resource management impacts on workers' compensation, (3) labor-management relations involving unions, and (4) the management of the workers' compensation program itself.

25.2 Corporate Management

25.2.1 Does management understand that the workers' compensation staff is not the key to the workers' compensation program?

Knowing that most of my readers are workers' compensation managers, I hesitate a bit to say this, but it is true. Most of the things that influence injury rates and workers' compensation costs are controlled by corporate policies or front line supervisors. Workers' compensation managers can have only a marginal effect on the success of the program. It is important that top management understand this.

25.2.2 *Is top management committed to improving the workers' compensation situation?*

I encounter many managers who spend a lot of time complaining to the legislature about how bad workers' compensation is but only a few (although their numbers are increasing) who are committed to improving workers' compensation within their own company. As the research discussed in section 16.3 clearly indicates, employers can make a difference in their own workers' compensation experience. These changes, however, do not come easily. This book attempts to offer many specific suggestions. Many of them, however, will cost some money to implement. Management must understand that if it wishes to change its workers' compensation experience, it must be willing to devote some resources to doing so.

25.2.3 *What does management do to convey the message that it is committed?*

The commitment of management is not enough. Everyone must know that management thinks this is important. The most obvious way to send this message is to start allocating resources to this area. Other things also help, such as newsletters or bulletin boards to highlight information on workers' compensation, safety, or disability management.

25.2.4 *Does management regularly review workers' compensation data?*

I know workers' compensation managers who tell me that whenever they have a bad month, they get a call from someone at "corporate." It would be nice if they got a call when they had a good month too. It would be even better if "corporate" were to call the plant manager about workers' compensation. Still, any indication that someone in top management reads that data is a good sign.

25.2.5 *Are safety and disability management items in the appraisal or salary review of every manager?*

Safety and disability management are the keys to lowering workers' compensation costs. The performance or salary appraisal is how you tell people what is really important in your organization. Are you sending the message?

25.2.6 *Is the cost of workers' compensation losses passed down to plants, departments, supervisors?*

If all the cost of workers' compensation comes out of some corporate account, then no one but the comptroller has any incentive to do anything about it and he or she is not in a position to make any difference. If, on the other hand, workers' compensation affects the bonus of every supervisor, people who used to say "there's no light duty in my area" may now find a way to bring injured workers back to the job.

A word of caution is in order here. I advocate passing the costs of workers' compensation down the line as far as possible but some reason has to be applied. A small department cannot be expected to absorb all the costs of every injury. Typically, companies charge the whole costs to a plant and pass on only a percentage of the costs to the department involved. Some companies, for example, charge a department for 20 percent of the losses. Others charge some arbitrary amount, such as $5,000, for each lost time injury.

25.2.7 *If a manager saves on workers' compensation costs, does he or she get the money for the budget?*

Even if the costs are not charged directly, there are other ways to create incentives. When I worked for the State of Michigan, each bureau had a line item in its budget to cover workers' compensation costs but it meant nothing. If we exceeded it, there was no punishment and if we were under, there was no reward.

An employer can at least set a budget for workers' compensation and if there is a savings, let the manager use part of the money for extra help or new equipment.

25.2.8 Do you use other financial incentives?

Another approach is to have a fund at the corporate level that can be used to pay the wages of a person who temporarily returns to work at light duty. The supervisor who can get an extra worker at no cost to his or her budget will be more willing to find light duty.

25.2.9 Where does responsibility for safety, disability prevention, health care, other disability benefits, and workers' compensation come together? What is done to coordinate these programs?

These programs depend on much the same information and they all affect one another. Unfortunately, in some companies, they are not coordinated.

25.2.10 Do you use the size of the company as an excuse?

"We're too small to have a light duty program." "We're so big we cannot make exceptions to our rules." There are advantages and disadvantages to every size. Use the advantages and do not rely on excuses.

25.2.11 Is there a system to ensure that changes in the workplace are evaluated for their potential dangers?

Changes in the physical layout or work policies all have a potential effect on safety, disability management, and workers' compensation. There should be a requirement in place to consider these factors whenever a change is made.

25.2.12 How often is there a "bay-by-bay" survey of the workplace by the plant manager? Comptroller? Human resource manager? Risk manager? Workers' compensation manager? Medical staff? Safety director?

There are certain problems that can be solved only by "hands on" solutions. These include workers' compensation, safety, and disability management. If top management insists on staying in the front office, the problems will never be solved.

25.2.13 Do managers talk to people?

I toured a plant once with the plant manager and the human resource manager. We walked up and down every aisle in the plant. There were only about 175 employees and we walked past all of them. The amazing thing was that not one word was exchanged between the workers and either of these managers. They did not say "Hi." They did not say "How's the family." They did not say "Hey, you SOB." They simply did not talk to each other.

This company had tried all the traditional approaches to workers' compensation but nothing seemed to work. The problem was that management could not relate to its workers. It is my experience that good managers are always talking *and listening* to their people.

Sometimes the people running a company are simply bad managers. If that is the case, then specific strategies related to workers' compensation will only have a minimal effect.

25.3 Human Resource Management

25.3.1 Do you realize the importance of good human resource management?

When I was representing workers, occasionally one would ask me, "How do I know when my back is hurting so much that I shouldn't work?" This is, of course, a question that is very difficult for an attorney to answer. I think that most workers figure it out for themselves.

Mr. A wakes up in the morning and his back hurts. If he feels he has been dealt with fairly by his employer, if the foreman treats him with respect, if he has some discretion in how he does his job, if the place is clean and well lighted, he says, "My back hurts but I'll go in and give it a try." If, on the other hand, he feels he is not getting a fair deal, if the foreman is riding him all day, if his co-workers are continually teasing him, if the place is dark and dirty, he says, "My back hurts. I can't go to work today."

I am sure that many people will read the above scenario and say, "That's wrong. We shouldn't pay comp just because someone is unhappy." I agree, but we cannot ignore the reality of the situation. This is illustrated by the "Boeing Back Study."

Researchers did a prospective study of 3,000 workers at the Boeing company in Seattle.[1] The study measured everything it could about the workers and their jobs. It measured the workers' physical strength and their range of motion; it looked at x-rays; it asked about the jobs: how much lifting, bending, twisting. The doctors measured everything they could about the workers and the work, then they asked, "Do you like your job?"

The study then followed these workers for three years. As you can imagine the best predictor of who would have a new disabling back injury was whether the worker liked his or her job.

We may or may not have to pay benefits to all of these people but we do have to deal with the situation and good human resource management is the way to do it.

25.3.2 *Do you use "fraud" as an excuse?*

There is fraud in workers' compensation and we need to take legal measures to deal with it. (See section 2.2.) There are other things that happen, however, that cannot be dismissed by simply calling them "fraud."

There are cases in which Ms. B gets hurt at home on Saturday and comes in on Monday and claims to have been injured on the job. That and similar cases constitute real fraud and something must be done about them. I believe however, that these are a relatively small percentage of the cases. Much more common are cases in which Ms. C hurts her back on the job and we see it and do not doubt that it happened. The problem is that Ms. C does not get better. Everyone else recovers from a back strain in a few weeks but after many months Ms. C still cannot go back to work. We know that she got hurt, we just cannot understand why she does not get better.

I do not call this "fraud" and we will not solve the problem by hiring detectives to catch her not hurting. I am convinced, however, and the research discussed at 16.3 indicates, that we can reduce the frequency of these problems by good human resource management.

Someone has said that workers' compensation is like a hand grenade that a worker can throw at an employer. Of course we should defuse the hand grenade but some employers are also asking, "Why do my employees want to throw hand grenades at me?"

A few specific suggestions follow for improving the human resource climate of a workplace. These are suggested as only a few of many things that can be done.

25.3.3 Do you have programs to deal with family concerns such as day care?

Every claims person has had the following experience. Mr. D was injured and has been released to light duty. After meeting with doctors, personnel managers, front line supervisors, and expending much effort, the claims person has arranged for an appropriate light duty job for Mr. D to return to. The claims person calls on Mr. D and tells him, "I've found a job you can do. You start Monday." Mr. D looks confused and says, "I can't do that. Who'll take care of the kids?"

In most states this would not be an excuse and Mr. D would be penalized if he refused an offer of work. Nevertheless these situations must be dealt with. In today's world, day care is a problem that haunts many people. A work-related injury may "solve" this problem. I am not saying that the workers' compensation system should be used for this purpose but let me put it this way: if you are doing a cost benefit analysis of helping your employees with day care, consider that it will probably reduce your workers' compensation costs.

25.3.4 Does your company provide employees with channels of communication to dispel rumors and to enable employees to discuss problems?

Stress cases are a problem for many employers. (See also section 2.3.) Anything that reduces stress in the workplace is helpful to workers' compensation as well as quality and productivity.

25.3.5 *Are employees given opportunities for growth and development through training or educational programs?*

These, of course, are programs that must be evaluated on their own merits. I would just suggest that anything that helps to build a long-term commitment to your company will also reduce workers' compensation costs.

25.3.6 *Do you use profit-sharing, gainsharing plans, employee stock ownership plans, or other alternative reward systems?*

The research discussed in section 16.3 specifically found such plans to be a factor in reducing the number of workers' claims.

25.3.7 *Do you allow workers flexibility in the way they do their jobs?*

Other research has identified this as an important factor in determining the length of a disability.[2]

25.3.8 *Do you consider the effect of human resource policies on workers' compensation?*

Sometimes policy changes can have unintended effects on workers' compensation. One company was interested in the concept of "pay for knowledge" and allocating reward based on group effort. It initiated a policy that members of work groups would be given a bonus based on the variety of jobs that everyone in the group was qualified to perform.

On its face this seemed like a good policy but it created a tremendous disincentive for the group to welcome back an injured worker who was restricted in what he or she could do. Some adjustment had to be made.

25.3.9 *Do you have strong policies designed to prevent harassment?*

Strict policies designed to prevent racial and sexual harassment are essential. There is more of this going on than we like to admit. Employers have moral and legal obligations to prevent such harassment. Preventing it will also save money.

Reducing harassment will reduce stress claims. Stress claims are a growing problem for employers (see section 2.3) and this is one important way to deal with them. Controlling harassment will reduce other claims as well.

Many employers assume today that every worker files a complaint about everything that happens. This is true for some people but not for everyone. There are many people in the workplace who are continually harassed and who never complain. They do, however, find other ways to deal with the situation. The woman whose foreman is continually making dirty remarks to her might never file a complaint but when she hurts her back she will never get better.

Strong policies against all types of harassment will pay off for workers and management alike.

25.3.10 *Do you adhere to good hiring practices?*

The Americans with Disabilities Act (ADA) and other factors may have made good hiring more difficult but it is still possible to hire good workers and turn down the bad ones. As discussed in subsection 18.2.3, if you are not careful about your hiring practices, you will pay for it in many ways including workers' compensation.

25.4 Unions

25.4.1 *Do you use the union as an excuse?*

"I'd do all that return to work stuff but the union would never let me" is a statement I often hear. Frequently it is an excuse rather than the real reason things are not being done.

25.4.2 *Have you asked the union to help with safety, disability prevention, and workers' compensation?*

Many who assume that the union will not help have never asked. Ask. You might be surprised.

25.4.3 *Did you bring the union in at the planning stage?*

If the union leadership is allowed to take part in the planning of the program they are more likely to accept it than if it is handed to them as something they must accept or reject. Furthermore, you might be surprised to find that the union has some valuable suggestions to contribute. After all, you are looking for programs the workers will accept and use.

25.4.4 *Do you realize that you have a legal obligation to bargain over wages, hours, and terms and conditions of employment?*

It may not be appropriate in the item above to say "allow" the union to take part in the planning. Many of the things we talk about here involve changes in the wages, hours, and working conditions of your employees. If you have a union, you have a legal obligation to bargain with it over these matters.

25.4.5 *Do you realize the importance that organized labor places on seniority?*

Some of the strategies we are talking about require exceptions to the seniority system. To many employers, seniority is a nuisance and making exceptions is no big deal. This is not the case with unions. To them seniority is very important. Do not treat this matter lightly. Many unions do agree to make exceptions to seniority. They want to help their brothers and sisters who are disabled. The point is that when management asks the union to make exceptions to seniority it should treat it as a serious matter.

25.4.6 *Have you considered limited exceptions to seniority, for example, light duty of no more than 60 days, or only five people on special assignment at one time?*

This will not only make it easier for the union to agree, it may be a good policy in itself. Emphasis should be placed on the temporary nature of light duty assignments. There should be a limit to their duration even where a union is not involved. I would add, however, that you should be prepared to make exceptions. You may encounter a person who everybody agrees needs a permanent light duty job.

Can you do this under the ADA? I think you can, if the limits are justifiable. It may well be that an accommodation that lasts more than 60 days is unreasonable or that it would be an undue hardship to have more than, say, 5 percent of the work force on special assignment at one time. See also section 2.4.

25.4.7 *Have you talked to the union about the ADA?*

The ADA provides a strong incentive, indeed it legally requires employers to make accommodations under many circumstances. I expect that in most union settings when a worker files a lawsuit based on the ADA it will be against both the union and the employer, because any alleged discrimination is likely to have been caused at least in part by the union contract and its application. Both the union and the employer should be interested in accommodation and return to work programs because they are good for business and good for the worker. Where that is not a sufficient motivation, however, perhaps one or both parties can be motivated by the threat of lawsuits.

25.4.8 *Have you explained to the union the importance of workers' compensation?*

It may be that your local union officials only hear about workers' compensation from apparently deserving members who have been denied benefits. If this is a big cost for your company, if there are many apparently inappropriate claims, take time to explain this to the union and show them the figures. Of course this must fit properly into your overall bargaining strategy with the union.

25.4.9 *Is workers' compensation the victim of labor management disputes?*

In some circumstances a rash of workers' compensation cases is a symptom of a bad labor management atmosphere. If that is the case, there is very little that can be done on the workers' compensation side to solve the problem. The basic labor management side of the problem must be resolved first.

25.4.10 *What is the relationship between the union and the local workers' compensation attorneys?*

In many areas local unions have favorite lawyers to whom they refer members. If the union gets a "kickback," this is illegal and unethical. Otherwise it is perfectly acceptable. In fact, if the lawyer is good and is reasonable to deal with, it may be to the company's advantage. There is probably not much an employer can do about this situation but it is important to understand it and know if it exists.

25.5 Management of Workers' Compensation

25.5.1 *Do you practice what you preach?*

I have said repeatedly in this chapter that good management practices are the key to workers' compensation. How well managed is your workers' compensation department? Do you use the techniques you preach to others?

25.5.2 *Are you, the employer (not your insurance company or service company), in control of your workers' compensation program?*

Techniques for doing this are discussed in more detail in chapters 20 and 23 on claims management and dealing with insurance companies. The point here is that they are your workers and it is your money and you, the employer, should be in control. You should set the tone, establish the policy, and make the important decisions.

25.5.3 *Do you (the workers' compensation department) have a system to recognize and reward the people or departments that are doing well?*

I said in section 25.2 that costs should be passed down and that safety and disability management should be in everyone's performance appraisal. If management will not do this, the workers' compensation department should do what it can to encourage good practices.

You can at least publish a list showing the record of each department for each month. (Not the names of injured workers, of course, but total dollars spent or dollars per hour worked or some other figure discussed in section 26.3 below.) You can also try periodically giving a certificate to the best department. There are many computer programs that generate certificates. People tell me they have been surprised at the effect these seemingly simple things have.

25.5.4 *Do you involve employees (all workers, the workers' compensation staff) in planning the improvements in your program?*

Participatory management is not just something for line managers. If you are going to preach this for others you must do it within your own staff. In seeking to improve the workers' compensation program, ask for suggestions from all hourly workers and all members of the workers' compensation team.

25.5.5 *Do you have a plan?*

Workers' compensation is a multifaceted problem. It is a battle that must be fought on many fronts at once. It is tempting to just jump in and start battling. It is a wise approach, however, to stop for a minute and lay out a plan. Know where you are going and what your priorities are. For example, you might choose two or three sections from this book as areas you are going to work on.

25.5.6 *Does your plan have goals and a target date?*

You must set specific goals and have a timetable for reaching them. Otherwise evaluation will be impossible.

25.5.7 *Does your plan include a commitment of time, money, and people?*

You need resources to solve any problem. Your plan should include a realistic estimate of what you will need. This might include money for safety training, a computer to analyze data, personnel to investigate claims, or any number of things. The details will vary from company to company, but before you start any plan, you must consider the resources that you will need.

25.5.8 *Do you have a regular procedure for evaluating your workers' compensation operation?*

Once a month or once a quarter someone should review your progress toward the goals that were established in any plan.

25.5.9 *Do you review policies as well as numbers?*

Most people review numbers and we will discuss that in some detail in chapter 26. Once in a while, however, you should review all of your policies. Are they out of date? Are they followed? Do people know what they are?

25.5.10 *Do you audit files?*

Some companies have a policy of periodically auditing all or a sample of their files. They completely review these files to see if they are being handled properly and in accordance with company policies. Many self-insured employers and insurance companies do this internally. It is also possible to hire an outside adjusting company to audit your files. Some self-insured employers do this to monitor the performance of their third-party administrator.

25.5.11 *What portion of your time do you spend on unusual as opposed to frequent cases? Does the cost justify it?*

Many workers' compensation people tell me that they spend most of their time on a few difficult cases. To some extent this is inevitable, but be careful to review the situation periodically. If more time were spent "up front" on apparently small cases, would it prevent them from becoming big cases later on?

25.5.12 *Do you see the state agency as your enemy or as a resource?*

Ideally the state agency should be a resource to work with employers. To some extent this is a function of the agency, its people, and its budget, but most relationships are subject to adjustment by both parties. If you have a good relationship, work to keep it that way. If you do not, it may be worth some effort to improve it. Successful employers find that it is well worth the time they spend getting acquainted with and establishing a good relationship with the mediator, judge, or other state official with whom they have to deal.

25.5.13 *Do you spend time exchanging sarcastic letters with the state, the union, anyone?*

This is very tempting in a field such as workers' compensation but it is rarely productive. Sometimes you need to write the letter but not mail it.

25.5.14 *Are you enthusiastic?*

You can accomplish nothing without enthusiasm. A real commitment to and belief in what you are trying to do will spread to everyone.

Notes

1. Bigos, Stanley J., Battie, Michele C., and Spengler, Dan M., *et al.*, "A Prospective Study of Work Perceptions and Psychosocial Factors Affecting the Report of Back Injury," *Spine*, Vol. 16, No. 1 (1991), 1–6.
2. Yelin, Edward, "The Myth of Malingering: Why Individuals Withdraw From Work in the Presence of Illness," *The Milbank Q.*, Vol. 64, No. 4 (1986), 622–49.

Chapter 26

Knowing Where You Stand: Data Collection and Analysis

26.1 Introduction

If an employer plans to improve its workers' compensation experience or any other part of its operation, it must have data. Data are necessary to measure improvement. Data will tell where the problems are, where attention should be focused, and where you will get the biggest payoff for the time and money you invest. The following stories will illustrate this.

Most General Motors plants have joint UAW-GM ergonomics teams. In one such plant, the team calculated that the biggest problem was carpal tunnel syndrome and that it was being caused by a type of air gun that was being used throughout the plant. The team went to the plant manager and asked him to replace these with air guns with a better design. The manager was sympathetic but replied that it would cost $1.5 million to replace all of these air guns and that he simply did not have the budget to do this. The team went back and further analyzed their data. They found that 80 percent of the injuries were occurring on only 20 percent of the jobs. They were then able to go back to the plant manager and say that, while in the long run he should replace all of the air guns, he could start by replacing only 20 percent of them. This would be within his budgetary limitations, prevent most of the injuries, and result in significant savings.

Another story comes from a large national food company. It had one division in which there were eight identical plants. When the corporation hired a new national safety director, he was surprised to notice that the plants had very different safety records. Some had very high injury rates while others had very low rates. This seemed strange since all the plants performed the same operations with the same equipment and had similar work forces. When he looked back over the years, he noticed that the high incidence rates varied over time. The plants that had high rates today had much lower rates a few years ago, and those with low rates today had high rates a few years ago. He could see no explanation for this and was puzzling over it at lunch one day when the corporation's salaried personnel director told him, "You know that division has an interesting policy. All the plant managers are moved every two years." The safety director went back and reviewed his data. He found that the high injury rates were following a few managers from plant to plant.

This chapter will first look at means of making comparisons between employers and then turn to a discussion of how employers should collect and analyze data related to workers' compensation.

26.2 Comparison With Others

In section 16.3 I emphasized the futility of always comparing one employer with another, and pointed out that it is much more important to strive for continuous improvement than to be satisfied with being above average. Nevertheless, I realize that many employers want to know how well they are doing in comparison with their competitors. This section will look at some ways of making comparisons between employers.

A couple of words of caution are in order. First, do not be satisfied with an above-average performance or be discouraged with a low comparative performance. The important thing is improvement. Regardless of where you stand today, set a goal and work to improve in the future.

Second, bear in mind that workers' compensation data are very imprecise. There are many variations from state to state and company to company. Comparisons based on the sources discussed here are rough guides at best.

26.2.1 *What is your experience modification factor?*

Subsection 14.2.7 discusses how modification factors are calculated for experience-rated employers. This is probably the best comparative measure of an employer's workers' compensation experience. It is based on workers' compensation losses in comparison with other employers whose employees do similar work (work in the same job classifications).

A rating of 1 means that you are at the average. I sometimes ask my graduate students the following exam question: "True or false: In a dangerous industry the average employer will have an experience rating of greater than 1."

The answer is "false," but it is tempting to say that since there will be more injuries in a dangerous industry the experience factor should be higher. The factor is constructed to make comparisons of employers with workers in the same job classifications. It measures how far a given employer deviates from average. The average is always set at one.

Thus, if you have a modification factor (sometimes called a "mod" or "rating") of 1.20, you are not doing well and are paying a 20 percent additional premium as a penalty for your poor record. If, however, you have a rating of .80, you are doing well and have had your premium reduced by 20 percent as a reward. Ratings sometimes go over 2.00 or 3.00 and I have seen them as low as .16. These are exceptional cases.

Remember that you cannot blame a high rating on bad state law or biased judges. The experience modification factor compares you to other employers in the same job classification in the same state. If you have a high rating, it means that other employers operating under the same conditions are doing better than you are.

There are many limitations to this means of comparison. A rating of 1.20 does not mean that you have had 20 percent more injuries or 20 percent higher costs. As discussed in subsection 14.2.7, the rating is based on a complicated formula designed by actuaries and underwriters. Its purpose is to determine how your rates should be adjusted to account for your record. It puts more emphasis on frequency than severity. Thus, an employer with 10 losses of $5,000 will have a higher rating than one with one $50,000 loss.

The rating is based on your losses for the three previous policy years. Thus, if my policy year starts on July 1 and I have several severe injuries in July, the injuries will not affect my rating until the next year. On the other hand, if I institute a safety program, it will not show up in my rating until a new policy year starts and my previous record will continue to affect my rating to some extent for three years after that.

Even given these limitations, the experience modification factor is the simplest and most direct way to make comparisons between employers. If you are an experience-rated employer, your experience modification factor should be readily available to you from your insurance company or agent. If you are too small to be experience rated, the information is probably not of value. Small employers are not experience rated because their rating would be influenced too much by random events. The single unusual accident would have too much impact on their rating.

As explained in subsection 14.2.3, for large retrospectively rated employers, the premium is not usually based directly on the experience modification factor, but the insurer probably calculates the factor and should make it available. Most self-insured employers have a policy of aggregate excess insurance. The insurer on that policy often calculates a modification factor and should be willing to make it available. In some states, such as Florida, the workers' compensation bureau calculates the modification factor for all self-insured employers to determine what premium they would have paid so that they can be assessed a premium tax. It may be a questionable approach to assessing taxes, but it nevertheless provides a modification factor to self-insured employers.

26.2.2 How does your OSHA record compare with others in your industry?

Summaries of Occupational Safety and Health Act (OSHA) data published by the Bureau of Labor Statistic (BLS) are another source of comparison. This information is national rather than state specific, is based on OSHA logs that may be less accurate than workers' compensation data, and is not always up to date. It is, however broken down by Standard Industrial Classifications (SIC)

Figure 26.1

Industry [1]	SIC code [2]	1991 Annual average employment (thousands) [3]	Incidence rates per 100 full-time workers [4]							
			Total cases [5]		Lost workday cases		Nonfatal cases without lost workdays		Lost workdays	
			1990	1991	1990	1991	1990	1991	1990	1991
Private industry [6]		90,573.8	8.8	8.4	4.1	3.9	4.7	4.5	84.0	86.5
Agriculture, forestry, and fishing [6]		1,257.9	11.6	10.8	5.9	5.4	5.7	5.3	112.2	108.3
Agricultural production [6]	01-02	n.a.	13.0	11.8	6.5	5.8	6.5	6.0	121.0	116.3
Agricultural services	07	n.a.	10.5	9.9	5.4	5.2	5.1	4.7	104.7	101.2
Forestry	08	n.a.	13.3	13.5	5.4	5.6	7.8	7.9	116.6	106.6
Fishing, hunting, and trapping	09	n.a.	6.0	6.7	3.9	4.0	2.0	2.6	87.9	114.7
Mining [7]		690.3	8.3	7.4	5.0	4.5	3.3	2.8	119.5	129.6
Metal mining [7]	10	56.2	6.8	6.5	4.1	3.9	2.7	2.6	61.7	82.0
Coal mining [7]	12	135.1	10.8	11.1	8.2	8.3	2.6	2.8	141.7	187.6
Oil and gas extraction	13	394.1	8.0	6.4	4.2	3.5	3.8	2.9	137.8	133.8
Crude petroleum and natural gas	131	191.3	2.8	2.4	1.4	1.1	1.3	1.2	40.7	30.1
Oil and gas field services	138	197.9	12.8	10.0	6.7	5.6	6.1	4.4	228.3	227.9
Nonmetallic minerals, except fuels [7]	14	104.9	7.1	7.0	4.2	4.1	2.9	2.8	61.8	74.1
Construction		4,684.6	14.2	13.0	6.7	6.1	7.5	6.9	147.9	148.1
General building contractors	15	1,151.8	13.4	12.0	6.4	5.5	6.9	6.4	137.6	132.0
Residential building construction	152	564.2	11.1	9.7	6.1	4.9	5.0	4.9	132.1	122.5
Operative builders	153	31.7	6.2	7.7	2.7	3.7	3.6	4.0	49.3	78.7
Nonresidential building construction	154	556.0	15.9	14.2	7.0	6.2	8.9	8.0	148.2	143.4
Heavy construction, except building	16	728.5	13.8	12.8	6.3	6.0	7.5	6.8	144.6	160.1
Highway and street construction	161	219.3	14.0	13.6	6.5	6.2	7.5	7.4	149.7	176.6
Heavy construction, except highway	162	509.2	13.7	12.4	6.2	5.9	7.5	6.5	142.3	153.2
Special trade contractors	17	2,804.3	14.7	13.5	6.9	6.3	7.8	7.1	153.1	151.3
Plumbing, heating, air-conditioning	171	614.7	15.7	14.1	6.6	5.8	9.1	8.3	124.6	133.8
Painting and paper hanging	172	159.2	9.3	9.9	5.3	5.7	4.0	4.2	153.7	165.4
Electrical work	173	517.8	13.4	12.6	5.2	5.1	8.2	7.5	106.3	107.5
Masonry, stonework, and plastering	174	416.1	17.1	14.7	8.7	7.5	8.4	7.1	200.5	189.8
Carpentry and floor work	175	176.2	13.1	13.2	7.0	7.0	6.0	6.2	141.7	156.2
Roofing, siding, and sheet metal work	176	191.5	18.0	16.7	9.7	8.9	8.4	7.8	253.2	245.7
Concrete work	177	n.a.	13.3	11.9	7.2	6.4	6.1	5.5	134.3	146.5
Water well drilling	178	n.a.	13.5	12.0	6.9	6.8	6.6	5.1	215.0	163.4
Miscellaneous special trade contractors	179	n.a.	14.6	13.4	7.0	6.3	7.6	7.0	171.6	153.2
Manufacturing		18,454.2	13.2	12.7	5.8	5.6	7.3	7.1	120.7	121.5
Durable goods		10,601.9	14.2	13.6	6.0	5.7	8.2	7.9	123.3	122.9
Lumber and wood products	24	678.9	18.1	16.8	8.8	8.3	9.2	8.5	172.5	172.0
Logging	241	78.1	17.5	15.9	10.8	10.0	6.6	5.8	281.0	279.5
Sawmills and planing mills	242	184.2	18.1	17.3	8.8	8.4	9.2	8.9	177.7	172.8
Sawmills and planing mills, general	2421	148.9	18.0	17.3	8.9	8.6	9.2	8.7	181.3	178.3
Hardwood dimension and flooring mills	2426	32.6	17.7	16.7	8.4	7.2	9.3	9.5	149.2	132.1
Special product sawmills, n.e.c.	2429	n.a.	25.2	25.1	14.5	14.2	10.7	10.9	347.5	374.5
Millwork, plywood and structural members	243	236.9	17.7	16.1	8.2	7.7	9.4	8.4	145.4	153.8
Millwork	2431	99.1	19.4	17.0	8.8	7.9	10.6	9.1	149.0	162.8
Wood kitchen cabinets	2434	64.9	14.5	14.5	6.9	6.8	7.6	7.7	121.1	124.3
Hardwood veneer and plywood	2435	22.3	17.8	15.2	7.7	7.4	10.1	7.8	137.7	162.5
Softwood veneer and plywood	2436	27.7	13.5	12.2	6.4	5.7	7.1	6.5	153.5	129.5
Structural wood members, n.e.c.	2439	n.a.	24.5	22.9	12.4	12.0	12.1	10.9	193.3	219.9
Wood containers	244	44.0	17.8	16.7	9.9	9.7	7.8	7.1	181.7	181.6
Nailed wood boxes and shook	2441	n.a.	18.8	17.1	10.6	9.5	8.3	7.6	183.7	175.6
Wood pallets and skids	2448	n.a.	17.6	16.8	10.1	10.0	7.5	6.8	185.7	201.1
Wood containers, n.e.c.	2449	n.a.	17.9	16.2	9.1	8.2	8.8	8.1	165.9	103.5
Wood buildings and mobile homes	245	55.2	25.5	23.1	10.9	10.3	14.6	12.8	174.5	177.1
Mobile homes	2451	38.2	25.4	22.9	10.3	9.5	15.1	13.5	172.9	158.5
Prefabricated wood buildings	2452	n.a.	25.8	23.5	12.2	12.2	13.6	11.3	178.0	218.9

codes, which are more familiar to many people than the insurance classifications used in the experience-rating formula.

A page from the publication "Occupational Injuries and Illnesses in the United States by Industry, 1991" is reproduced in figure 26.1. This publication provides information about the number of OSHA reportable cases, cases involving lost work days, and the lost work days by industrial classification.

Thus, an employer could look at SIC code 154 "nonresidential building construction," a subcategory of "general building contractors," which is in turn a category of "construction." It would find that during 1991 there were 14.2 OSHA reportable cases for every 100 full-time workers. (It should be noted that this refers to full-time equivalent workers. Two people who worked half time would be counted as one full-time worker.) Of these 14.2 cases, 6.2 resulted in some lost time from work while 8.0 did not. The total lost work days attributable to those 6.2 cases was 143.4.

Comparing yourself to these OSHA averages provides a rough approximation at best, but it is a relatively simple way of seeing how you are doing in comparison to your competitors. Figure 26.2 lists the regional offices from which this and other BLS publications can be obtained.

26.2.3 *Do you make informal comparisons?*

Sometimes the most important comparison is with the business down the street. Usually hard data are not available to make comparisons, but informal discussions can be valuable. As discussed in section 27.4 below, workers' compensation suffers from a lack of networking. Other professionals, accountants or electrical engineers, for example, belong to societies or professional groups. Often there are local chapters with regular meetings. It is much harder to find such groups that deal with workers' compensation.

There are many safety groups of one form or another. The Risk and Insurance Management Society (RIMS) often has local groups. And some manufacturers associations and chambers of commerce sponsor programs on workers' compensation. All of these groups are important sources of data about workers' compensation. They should be sought out and used to the greatest extent possible.

26.3 An Information System

26.3.1 *Do you have a comprehensive program for data collection and analysis?*

Comprehensive does not necessarily mean huge. Of course, the more information you collect the more ways you will be able

Figure 26.2

Bureau of Labor Statistics
Regional Offices

Region I
  1 Congress Street, 10th Floor
  Boston, MA 02114-2023
  Phone: (617) 565-2327

Region II
  Room 808
  201 Varick Street
  New York, NY 10014-4811
  Phone: (212) 337-2400

Region III
  3535 Market Street
  P.O. Box 13309
  Philadelphia, PA 19101-3309
  Phone: (215) 596-1154

Region IV
  1371 Peachtree Street, N.E.
  Atlanta, GA 30367-2302
  Phone: (404) 347-4416

Region V
  9th Floor
  Federal Office Building
  230 S. Dearborn Street
  Chicago, IL 60604-1595
  Phone: (312) 353-1880

Region VI
  Federal Building
  525 Griffin Street, Room 221
  Dallas, TX 75202-5028
  Phone: (214) 767-6970

Regions VII and VIII
  911 Walnut Street
  Kansas City, MO 64106-2009
  Phone: (816) 426-2481

Regions IX and X
  71 Stevenson Street
  P.O. Box 193766
  San Francisco, CA 94119-3766
  Phone: (415) 744-6600

to look at your situation but, at least at first, the goal need not be to have the biggest system. The starting place is to have a *system.* Someone must step back and ask, "What data do we have now? How do we use it? What additional data can we collect? How much will it cost? How will we use it? What information would be the most useful to us?"

Data systems tend to just grow up. People collect the information that is easiest to collect or that someone else tells them they have to collect, but they never use the information they have or fail to collect the information they need most.

The point here is that each employer must have a plan for what workers' compensation information it will collect and how it will be used.

26.3.2 Do you use information about the number of lost time injuries and lost days?

OSHA requires that every employer collect this information yet many workers' compensation departments fail to use it. As mentioned in subsection 26.2.2, it is one of the easiest sources of comparison with others. It can also provide a measure of change over time. Do not overlook these rather simple sources of data that may already be available.

26.3.3 Can you break your data down by division, plant, department, shift, supervisor, job?

The resources available to all of us are limited. We must concentrate our efforts where they will do the most to avoid the effects of injuries and reduce costs. To properly focus our attention, we must know where the problems are. We must have data to do this.

The extent to which you will need to break down information will depend on the size and structure of your company, but the more you can break down your data the better you will be able to focus your attention in ways that will provide the biggest payoff.

26.3.4 Do you know where your money is going?

How much is going to workers, doctors, hospitals, physical therapists, lawyers, the insurance or service company? Here again the more you can break down your costs, the better you can control them.

26.3.5 *Do you know what type of cases are costing you the most?*

Generally, injuries of short duration (temporary total cases) are the most frequent, and severe injuries (permanent total cases) are the most costly. In most states, however, and for most employers the largest amount of money goes to the injuries that fall between these extremes (permanent partial cases). How much of your money goes to each type of case? What is your average cost per case? You should have this information.

26.3.6 *Do you know what type of injury is costing the most money?*

How much of your cost goes to back injuries, slip and fall cases, carpal tunnel syndrome, and stress cases? Often employers are concerned about a few stress cases and the fact that carpal tunnel syndrome is increasing faster than other categories, yet by far most of their money is still going to back injuries. Knowing this will help you focus your attention on the most important areas.

26.3.7 *Are loss statistics viewed as a function of size, production units, hours of work, payroll, revenues?*

Generally loss data are presented as fractions. Dollars of loss per dollars of payroll is the most common approach. Sometimes the number of injuries or the number of lost work days is used as the numerator and sometimes the number of employees or number of hours worked is used as the denominator.

Especially if you are going to make comparisons, it is appropriate to use fractions. This it true for comparisons with different departments or for the same department over different periods of time. Be creative, however, in choosing the numbers you use.

Consider using as the denominator the number of units produced, patients treated, customers waited on, dollars of sales, profit, or any other reasonable number. Sometimes a new perspective will help you see where you need to focus your attention. For example, you might say that the company spends $50 on workers' compensation for each air conditioner that it produces or it has two lost time injuries for every 1,000 customers who come into the store. Often this will be more effective in getting the attention of top management or line supervisors.

26.3.8 Do you know how workers' compensation costs compare to sales and profits?

One approach that workers' compensation and safety managers have found effective is to compare workers' compensation costs to sales and profits.

Assume that you have a plan that will reduce workers' compensation costs by $100,000. All other things being equal, profits will increase by that amount if it is successful. Assume also that your company makes a profit equal to 5 percent of sales. The company would have to increase sales by $2 million to increase profits by $100,000. The investment needed to increase sales by $2 million is probably much bigger than the amount needed to improve a safety, disability management, or claims program enough to save $100,000. Yet many companies are more willing to spend the money on sales.

26.3.9 Do you distinguish between losses from the current year and payments attributable to prior years?

If you had 100 injuries in 1990, it is likely that 70 to 80 of those cases were closed within that year and 10 to 15 of the cases were closed within the next one or two years. There were, however, probably a few cases that lasted up to five years and maybe one or two that will go on for 10 to 20 years. These latter cases are, of course, the most expensive.

Viewed differently, this means that of the money you paid out in 1993 some went for injuries that occurred during that year, some went for injuries that occurred in the last few years, and some part of it may have gone for injuries that occurred many years ago.

If you are told that your costs for 1993 were $500,000, what does that mean? It may mean that you paid out a total of $500,000 during that calendar year for all injuries regardless of when they occurred, or it may mean that during that policy year you incurred losses that are expected to cost a total of $500,000 when they are all resolved. (*Incurred losses* generally include money already paid out and reserves for future payments.)

Both figures are important and useful. It is essential, however, that you know what you are talking about. Consider the safety director who promises management that he or she can cut losses by $10,000 per year through an accident prevention program. If management is looking at figures based on all dollars paid out in a given year it will be a long while before the safety director can deliver on that promise.

26.3.10 To what extent are loss data based on reserves?

If a case has been closed, the loss data should include only costs actually paid out. If a case is still open, loss data, especially policy year loss data, probably include the reserves—an estimate of the amount the case will cost in the future. This is a necessary and important part of the process. It should be noted, however, that the setting of reserves is more of an art than a science and that reserving policies may vary from adjuster to adjuster, from company to company, and from year to year. In evaluating any loss data, this should all be considered. (See section 20.7 for a further discussion of reserves.)

26.3.11 How much data do you get from your insurance or service company?

At the very least you should get a "loss run" every few months. This should describe in some detail all of the open cases and include information about the reserves in each case, your premium and how it was calculated. If you have several open cases, you should get information about their status quarterly.

The bigger the premium, the more service you can demand from your insurance or service company. This is appropriate because a large employer needs some formal way to collect and analyze data. Many large employers receive all the information discussed in this chapter from their insurance or service company.

26.3.12 Do you have access to your insurance or service company's database?

Some large employers have computer terminals with which they can obtain information from their carrier's database. (Only in very carefully prescribed circumstances would an employer enter information into the database.) Most commonly, this access would allow the employer to view the records in individual cases, but sometimes it might include the ability to construct queries and gather sets of data.

26.3.13 Is your system too sophisticated to be useful, too simple to do the job?

Every data collection system must be designed to fit the needs of the company. If you have only three employees, a simple file folder will assist you to remember who got hurt and how. If you have 100,000 employees, you should have one or more people who spend all their time collecting and analyzing these data.

Many vendors sell software for this purpose. In many cases, this may be the best approach. In others, you may wish to design something to fit your own needs or, as mentioned above, rely on information provided by your carrier.

26.3.14 Do you consider the hidden costs of injuries?

The easily collected data do not tell the whole story. What about the down time, the lost production, the loss in quality? Injured workers must be replaced. The replacement workers need training and ordinarily will need some time before they are up to the same level of production and quality as the experienced worker.

If claims are not handled properly, an injury often causes resentment between the worker and the company, or among fellow workers. The cost of this loss of morale is just one of many hidden factors.

I heard a mechanical contractor talk about a job site on which he had 20 people working. He said an injury had occurred there and that it cost him $3,500 even though none of his employees was involved. When the injury occurred, all the workers stopped doing their jobs and ran to help. When the ambulance came, they stopped again and stood around while the ambulance crew tended to the injured worker. The man was not seriously injured and returned to the job site later in the day. Again, time was lost as the people asked how he was.

Good safety and disability management practices will pay back much more than just the savings in workers' compensation costs. Some effort should be made to account for these.

26.4 Injury Data

Table 26.1 lists the data that would ideally be maintained on each case. This information would be stored in a database so it could be retrieved and analyzed based on any item. This is ideal but it is a goal toward which each employer should strive.

26.5 Correlation of Data

26.5.1 *Is there some central control or at least coordination of data related to workers' compensation?*

It is not unusual to find employers that collect much of these data but never "bring it together." This is of course a serious mistake.

26.5.2 *Do you compare workers' compensation and safety data?*

At the least, data from these two programs should be compared and coordinated. Chances are that the workers' compensation data can tell the safety people more about where the hazards are than the OSHA records can, and the safety people can do more to control workers' compensation costs than anyone else in the company. Still, there are many companies in which these two departments are separate and do not even share data.

Table 26.1. Injury Data

Name
Date of birth
Social Security number
Gender
Marital status
Dependents
Phone
Address
Date of hire
State in which hired
Date of injury
Date of death
State of injury
County
Nature of injury (sprain, fracture, etc.)
Body part affected
Source of injury (machines, hand tools, buildings, etc.)
Type of injury (fall, struck by, overexertion, repeated trauma)
Witnesses
Job classification (insurance class or company classification)
Work process involved
Industry
Division
Plant or location
Department
Supervisor
Job
Time of day
Shift
Health care providers

continued

26.5.3 Does workers' compensation share data with other departments that deal with health care and disability?

At locations that have high workers' compensation costs, are group disability and health care costs also high or is it more typical to have one high and the other low? If group disability and health care costs are low where workers' compensation costs are high, it may be a question of shifting the costs from one system to another. If this is the case, you will want to ask if there is something in the system that encourages such shifting. For example, are some hospitals or clinics charging more for the same treatment if it involves workers' compensation and is there a legitimate reason for this?

Table 26.1.—*continued*

Heath care costs
Date employer first notified
Who was notified, by whom?
Date employer workers' compensation department notified
Date insurance company or service company notified
Date state agency notified
State case number
Average weekly wage
Benefit rate
Other benefits lost
Other benefits received
Offset for other benefits
Date disability started
Date of first payment
Projected return to work date
Date case closed
Date of maximum medical improvement
Impairment rating
Lost days
Benefits paid
Reserves
Vocational rehabilitation activity
Subrogation?
Defense attorney, firm
Claimant attorney, firm
Judge
Costs of litigation
Settlement
Date of hearings
Appealed

How does the total cost of workers' compensation compare to health care, to other disability programs, to pension costs? Sharing data with the appropriate departments may help answer these questions.

26.5.4 Do you compare workers' compensation data to labor relations data?

If workers' compensation costs are high only in departments that have a high grievance rate or high absenteeism, it may be simply a symptom of something else that is going on. If that is the case, you will not solve the problem by changing the workers' compensation system.

26.5.5 *Do you compare workers' compensation data to production and quality data?*

The chances are that the departments and plants that have the lowest workers' compensation costs also do the best in terms of production and quality. What is the cause and what is the effect? I believe that if an employer uses the ideas in this book to reduce workers' compensation cost, it will also see an improvement in quality and production. As the workers' compensation manager you may want to have production and quality data available to make such comparisons.

Chapter 27

Education

27.1 Introduction

I must admit that being a college professor, teacher of extension courses, and author and publisher of a magazine, I am a bit biased in this regard, but I believe that education is a key element in any successful workers' compensation program.

27.2 The Parties to Be Educated

27.2.1 Management

As discussed in section 25.2, much of the success of a workers' compensation program depends on a commitment from top management. Accordingly, top managers must be educated so that they will understand what is needed in a successful workers' compensation program and be motivated to supply the needed elements.

27.2.2 Line Supervisors

In areas such as safety, return to work, and follow-up after an injury, the key person is often the injured worker's immediate supervisor. It is essential to educate these people about the key role they play, what they can do to make the system work better, and why this is important to the company.

417

27.2.3 Workers

Of course, the education of workers about many of the topics discussed in the next section is essential.

27.2.4 Families of Workers

Safety efforts, as well as return to work programs, will be more effective if they are understood by not only the workers, but the workers' families as well.

27.2.5 Providers of Workers' Compensation Related Services

The providers you deal with must also be educated. If, for example, you have instituted an early return to work program (see section 19.2) in which you will endeavor to find a job for any worker capable of getting to the plant, it is essential that the physicians treating your employees understand that you have such a program. Many of the employers they deal with may not be willing to take people back while they have some limitation. If you have a special policy, and are serious about it, you must inform medical providers.

27.2.6 All Vendors to Your Company

In recent years, many American companies have realized that in order to provide quality products and services to their customers, they must demand quality from their suppliers. The same principle applies in areas such as safety. Your purchasing department should, for example, inform all vendors that your company insists on an ergonomic design for all tools it purchases.

27.2.7 The Workers' Compensation Staff

Finally, as discussed below, it is essential that the workers' compensation staff be continually educated and updated on topics related to their functions.

27.3 Education in Practice

27.3.1 How do employees know what you expect from them as part of your workers' compensation policies?

Every workers' compensation manager that I know has in his or her mind the detailed scenario of what should happen when an individual is injured. How do workers know what that scenario is? Obviously they will not know unless someone has told them and reminded them frequently.

27.3.2 Do you give every worker a written statement of your workers' compensation policies?

It is essential to attempt to educate workers about safety, workers' compensation, and return to work programs before they become injured. Accordingly, every new hire should be given a statement concerning the company's policies on workers' compensation. This should be in addition to a separate statement concerning safety. The workers' compensation policy statement should contain information about the procedure to be followed when a worker is injured and some basic information about how your state's workers' compensation program works. If you have a return to work program, include a specific statement emphasizing that you will find work for injured individuals as soon as it is possible for them to return to work. The policy statement should also tell workers where to report injuries, what to do in the case of an emergency, and what health care providers you would like them to use.

27.3.3 Is your statement of workers' compensation policies regularly updated?

Things change. Insurance carriers change. Phone numbers change. The specifics of your policy may change. It is essential that you review your policies regularly (once a year, at least) and provide updated copies to all employees.

27.3.4 Can workers get a new copy of the policies when it becomes important to them?

Let's be realistic. Most of those nice policy statements discussed above are probably in the trunk of someone's car, unread. Companies should make sure that new copies are available whenever they are needed.

27.3.5 What do you do to remind workers about your policies?

Many companies highlight the most important aspects of their policies (for example, the availability of light duty as part of return to work programs) through bulletin boards, newsletters, or regular meetings with employees.

27.3.6 Have you educated your workers about how health care providers were chosen?

If you have carefully chosen doctors, hospitals, and other health care providers because of their high quality, you should tell your workers about this.

27.3.7 Have you educated employees about what to do in case there is some type of general emergency in the plant, such as a fire or flood?

This should be a regular part of your safety and workers' compensation program.

27.3.8 Do you provide first aid training to supervisors?

It is essential that there be a number of people throughout your workplace who are able to provide first aid and CPR when necessary. Some employers train all supervisors in these skills. Note, however, that new regulations concerning exposure to blood borne pathogens now require more extensive training of first aid workers. Thus it may be appropriate to be more selective in choosing who receives this training.

27.3.9 *Do workers understand the role of the employer, the insurer, the service company, and the state?*

Many workers think that everything is decided and administered by a state agency, even though, in fact, most of the decisions about their situation are made by either the employer or an insurance company. Depending on the situation in your company and your jurisdiction, you should let workers know what role the employer, the insurance company, the state, and other individuals play in their receipt of benefits.

27.3.10 *Do workers know that the money for injuries ultimately comes from the employer?*

Under most circumstances, either directly or indirectly, virtually all the money for workers' compensation benefits comes from the employer rather than the state, an insurance company, or third-party administrator. Do your employees understand this? If you have not told them, how would they know?

Many employees actually believe that workers' compensation benefits come from the state. They say they are "on state compensation." I have heard others say, "My employer paid premiums to the insurance company; I might as well take advantage of it."

Workers will be much quicker to cheat an insurance company than to cheat their employer. As discussed in subsection 3.4.1, much of the money for workers' compensation may ultimately come from workers themselves in the form of lower wages. Some may question this economic analysis, but at least employers should let workers know that workers' compensation has a direct effect on the profitability of the company. If, as suggested in subsection 25.2.6, workers' compensation losses are passed down to the plant or department, it may be appropriate to inform workers about this as well.

27.3.11 *If you expect supervisors to help with workers' compensation, have you told them why it is important?*

Many companies today claim that workers' compensation costs are pushing them toward insolvency. If this is in fact the case, and you expect first-line supervisors to help you deal with workers' compensation problems, you should inform them of the situation and show them the facts. It may even be wise to show them specifically the total workers' compensation costs for the company, the division, or the facility. When supervisors understand this, they may be more willing to find light duty jobs for an injured worker you wish to return to the plant.

27.3.12 *Have you educated supervisors on how they can help?*

Safety training is, of course, essential. Other types of training may be helpful as well. In subsection 20.6.8, I suggested that first-line supervisors should call or visit injured employees when they are away from work. People in our society, however, may be uncomfortable about calling on people. Spend a few minutes telling them why this is important, and suggesting what they should say and how they should act when they make the call. "I'm sorry to hear that you were hurt," is always a good way to start.

27.3.13 *Do your actions speak louder than your words?*

If in fact you've shopped around for the cheapest doctors in town, do not waste your time telling your workers you have chosen high quality providers. They will know that it is not true the first time they visit the doctor's office. Do not waste time educating workers about the importance of safety if the company will not invest in safety equipment. The best way to educate workers is through examples and actions.

27.3.14 *Do you have any formal education programs for management or supervisors?*

Many companies have regular training programs for supervisors or managers. This might be a session that lasts one day and occurs once a year, in which supervisors and managers are reminded of or updated concerning the company's workers' compensation policies.

27.4 Education of the Workers' Compensation Department

27.4.1 *What training program do you have for people who are new to your workers' compensation department?*

One large company has a 50-hour training program that it uses to train individuals who are new to the workers' compensation department. These could be individuals hired from outside directly into the workers' compensation department or individuals transferred to that department from other parts of the company. This is one of the most comprehensive approaches that I know of. Every company, however, should have some organized program for educating people new to the workers' compensation staff about not only forms and procedures but about philosophies and attitudes as well.

27.4.2 *What do you do to update your workers' compensation staff?*

Some companies have annual training sessions, or retreats, which are used to update their workers' compensation staff. Others use different methods, some of which are discussed below.

27.4.3 *What do you do to keep informed of legal developments?*

A few states have publications that regularly cover legal developments in those jurisdictions. These are too diverse for evaluation here. Some of the programs discussed below also deal with legal issues. Another approach would be to invite the attorneys handling your workers' compensation claims to regularly spend some time updating your staff on recent legal developments.

27.4.4 *Do you subscribe to any publications?*

Section 3.5 lists a few of the many publications that deal with workers' compensation.

27.4.5 *Do you belong to any national or state workers' compensation association?*

There is not much "networking" in workers' compensation. If we were accountants or attorneys or physicians, we would belong to associations that regularly had meetings on the national, state, and local level. As noted in subsection 26.2.3, there are some safety and risk insurance management societies (RIMS, for example) that meet regularly and deal in part with workers' compensation. It is very rare, however, for there to be a workers' compensation organization at the local or even state level. The organizations that do exist are discussed in section 3.5. Many employers find membership in those organizations very rewarding.

27.4.6 *Do you attend regular meetings or conventions about workers' compensation?*

As discussed in section 3.5, some associations have annual meetings or conventions. There are also some for-profit enterprises that sponsor such meetings. The value of these meetings varies from sponsor to sponsor and may also vary from year to year. Since there is so little networking in workers' compensation many employers find it valuable to take advantage of whatever is available.

27.4.7 *Do you talk regularly to workers' compensation people in similar companies about what they are doing?*

It would be very valuable to know what other employers in your town, neighborhood, or industry are doing in worker's compensation, which doctors they find to be the most successful, which attorneys they find to be the most honest, which insurance companies provide the best service. As mentioned, workers' compensation is an area in which there seem to be relatively fewer opportunities for sharing information. Employers should to take advantage of all opportunities that are available.

27.4.8 How knowledgeable are the workers' compensation people in your company regarding safety, health care, long-term disability, and pension benefits in your company?

All of these items are necessarily closely related in every company. In some companies, however, responsibility for them is diffused among various departments. There should be some regular way for people with responsibilities for all these programs to share information and ideas.

27.4.9 Do you educate your workers' compensation staff about the other functions of the company?

Unless you are an insurer, workers' compensation is probably only of minor importance to the overall company. You should not allow the view of the workers' compensation staff to be so narrow that they are unable to put their program in perspective. When I meet with individuals in the workplace, it is usually to talk about workers' compensation. I am most impressed, however, by those who first want to remind me about the new engine they are about to introduce, tell me that I have probably drunk from their plastic cups at a football game, or point out that my wife and daughters are surely impressed by their fine line of clothing. An understanding of and loyalty to the ultimate goals of the organization must come first. The workers' compensation program should be a means to those ends, not an end in itself.

27.4.10 Do you have a system for helping the workers' compensation staff deal with the stresses of their employment?

In workers' compensation, we only see people during the worst time in their lives. If Ms. A goes for years supporting herself and her family by the strength of her back or the agility of her hands, and then suffers a serious injury, she will likely have two or three years in which everything "goes to hell." In all likelihood, something will go wrong with the claim. Benefits will be late; perhaps there will be a dispute; she will run short of money; she will be shifted from one doctor to another; she will be in pain. In the majority of cases, after some period of time, Ms. A will recover and return to being a healthful worker and reliable provider for her family. She will probably remain in that healthy role for the rest of her life. Workers' compensation staff, however, will only see her during that year or two when everything is going wrong. This makes workers' compensation a very difficult job.

Every company should have some way to allow the workers' compensation staff to relieve its tensions, to share common problems, to talk and perhaps even joke about what is going on.

Part 4

Medical Issues

Chapter 28

Medical Aspects of Back Injuries

by M. Melissa Moon, D.O.*

28.1 Introduction

Low back pain is a significant problem in the general adult
population, impacting many aspects of society. The lifetime incidence of low back pain for adults has been reported to be anywhere
from 48.8 percent to 69.9 percent. Among chronic conditions, physician visits related to back pain are second only to those for heart
disease. Low back surgery is the third most common type of surgery
performed nationwide.

Anyone involved in workers' compensation is well aware of
the enormity of the cost of low back pain. In the 25 to 44 year old
age group, the most common reason for a decrease in work capacity
is low back pain. In the United States almost 40 percent of workers'
compensation dollars go to low back claims. The appropriate diagnosis and treatment of low back injuries, with an awareness of the

*M. Melissa Moon, D.O., is a Diplomate of the American Board of Physical
Medicine and Rehabilitation. Her residency was in Physical Medicine and Rehabil-
itation at the University of Michigan Medical Center, Ann Arbor, Michigan.
She received her Doctor of Osteopathic Medicine in 1987 from Michigan State
University and her Bachelor of Science in 1981, also from Michigan State Univer-
sity. She now practices with Rehabilitation Medicine Consultants, P.C., 702 W.
Lake Lansing Rd., Ste. 4, East Lansing, MI 48823, Tel: (517) 336-9090, Fax: (517)
336-0053.

workers' compensation environment, is essential for effective and efficient case management.

This chapter is designed to supply an overview of the medical aspects of low back pain and injuries for nonmedical professionals involved in the management of injured employees. The reader is encouraged to investigate the references if further detail is desired. Excellent, comprehensive writings on this subject are readily available. A brief listing is offered at the end of the chapter.

28.2 Anatomy

Like the human body in general, the human back is impressive in its multifunctional design. The spine serves as the attachment of numerous muscles, tendons, and ligaments to support the limbs, head, and organs. Its bony elements protect the irreplaceable and incredibly delicate spinal cord body. The back is required to withstand great forces while allowing amazing flexibility. However, as the statistics on back injuries show, all too often the demands placed on the back surpass its abilities, thus resulting in pain and disability.

There are many factors that can add to the likelihood of back failure, many of which are present in the working population. As with many medical conditions, age plays a significant role. In the back degenerative changes have been shown to begin as early as age 30. Personal habits such as obesity, smoking, and a sedentary lifestyle can add stress to the back. However, even in a physically fit, healthy individual the back will retaliate when asked to execute a move that is biomechanically incorrect or lifting that is too heavy or repeated too often. To understand back injuries, a basic understanding of the components of the back is helpful.

The vertebrae, or bones of the back, serve as the primary weight-bearing structures. Stacked one upon the other there are five regions. The cervical region consists of seven of the smallest vertebrae, which are numbered from C1 through C7. The cervical spine supports the skull and normally will form a mild lordotic (forward) curve (figure 28.1). The shape of the cervical vertebrae allows the maximum amount of mobility. The 12 vertebrae below the cervical region are much less mobile, and are referred to as

Figure 28.1

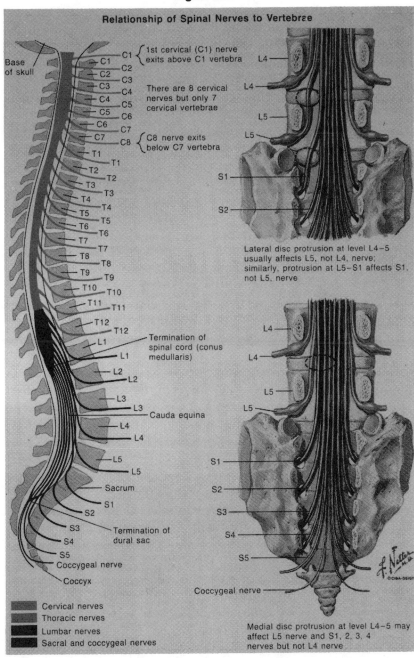

Relationship of Spinal Nerves to Vertebrae

1st cervical (C1) nerve exits above C1 vertebra

There are 8 cervical nerves but only 7 cervical vertebrae

C8 nerve exits below C7 vertebra

Termination of spinal cord (conus medullaris)

Cauda equina

Termination of dural sac

Cervical nerves
Thoracic nerves
Lumbar nerves
Sacral and coccygeal nerves

Lateral disc protrusion at level L4–5 usually affects L5, not L4, nerve; similarly, protrusion at L5–S1 affects S1, not L5, nerve

Medial disc protrusion at level L4–5 may affect L5 nerve and S1, 2, 3, 4 nerves but not L4 nerve

Source: Ciba-Geigy, "Low Back Pain," *Clinical Symposia,* Vol. 39, No. 6 (1987), plate 2. Copyright 1987 by Ciba-Geigy. Reprinted with permission.

431

the thoracic or dorsal vertebrae. These are numbered as T1 through T12 (or D1 through D12). The opposite curve in the thoracic area is referred to as kyphotic. The five largest vertebrae make up the lumbar (L1 through L5) or low back region. More motion is allowed in this region and the lordotic curve of the cervical spine is repeated. The fifth lumbar vertebrae, or L5, rests upon the sacrum. This large somewhat flat, almost triangular bone articulates (or attaches) with the low back and indirectly to the legs via the pelvic bones. The tip of the sacrum is where the tail bone or coccyx is found. This is a structure of little use in humans, serving mainly as an attachment for ligaments. It is sometimes a source of pain.

The anterior portion (or front) of the spine is composed of vertebrae and the intervertebral discs. Together these structures serve as the major weight-bearing structures of the spine. The posterior (or back) elements of the spine protect the delicate spinal cord. The posterior elements form an arch around the spinal cord and include structures referred to as the pedicles, the laminae (removed in a laminectomy), the facet joint, the spinous process (the palpable midline bump), and the two transverse processes to either side (figure 28.2).

In between the strong bony vertebral bodies is a softer shock absorbent disc. The tough outer fibers of the disc are named the annulus fibrosis and are arranged in laminated layers, almost like a steel belted tire. This arrangement offers the maximum amount of strength but extreme forces can cause the fibers to tear. The annulus fibrosis surrounds a softer gel-like center, the nucleus pulposus. This material has a high water content, which begins to dehydrate around age 30. Under pressure the gel will herniate (or pass) through any small tears or rents in the annulus fibrosis. Thus the herniated or ruptured disc. This is referred to as a herniated nucleus pulposus or HNP. This painful, inflammatory situation is detectible by physical exam, CT (CAT scans), or MR (magnetic resonance) scans and is often treated with surgery. The tears in the annulus can occur at the time of the herniation, as a result of a singular huge force. More commonly, the tears in the annulus occur over time as a result of a combination of age and the accumulated physical stress of everyday life. In this situation a herniation of the soft nucleus pulposus through the tough annulus fibrosis

Figure 28.2

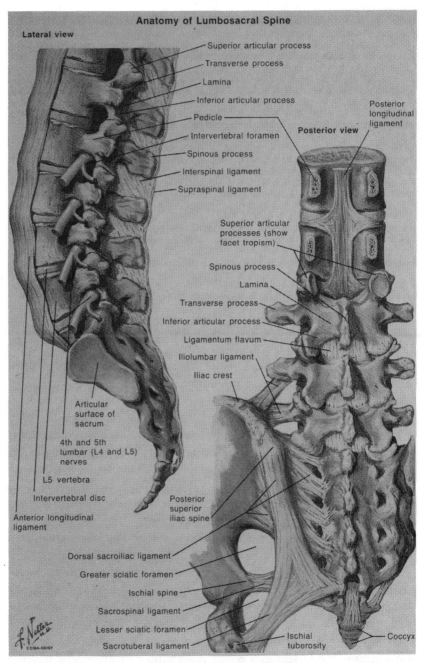

Anatomy of Lumbosacral Spine

Lateral view

- Superior articular process
- Transverse process
- Lamina
- Inferior articular process
- Pedicle
- Intervertebral foramen
- Spinous process
- Interspinal ligament
- Supraspinal ligament

Posterior longitudinal ligament

Posterior view

Superior articular processes (show facet tropism)

Spinous process
Lamina
Transverse process
Inferior articular process
Ligamentum flavum
Iliolumbar ligament
Iliac crest

Articular surface of sacrum

4th and 5th lumbar (L4 and L5) nerves

L5 vertebra

Intervertebral disc

Posterior superior iliac spine

Anterior longitudinal ligament

Dorsal sacroiliac ligament
Greater sciatic foramen
Ischial spine
Sacrospinal ligament
Lesser sciatic foramen
Sacrotuberal ligament

Ischial tuberosity

Coccyx

Source: Ciba-Geigy, "Low Back Pain," *Clinical Symposia,* Vol. 39, No. 6 (1987), plate 1. Copyright 1987 by Ciba-Geigy. Reprinted with permission.

433

may result from a seemingly trivial, and often forgotten, maneuver.

The spinal cord is the connection between the brain and the rest of the body. Spinal nerves branch from the spinal cord and exit to connect with the structures of the body. These spinal nerves pass out of a small canal or foramen (canals) in the bony posterior elements of the spine. In the low back these nerves are named for the vertebral body they pass beneath (i.e., L1–L5). In the sacral region the nerves are referred to as S1–S5 and pass through small foramen in the sacrum itself. These spinal nerves connect or innervate predictable muscles and areas of sensation of the leg. Injury to the spinal nerves as they leave the spinal cord and exit the spine is termed a radiculopathy. A radiculopathy can occur at any level (the most common involving L4, L5, or S1) and results in fairly predictable symptoms. These symptoms include pain, weakness and/or numbness in specific muscles or regions of the legs. The area of sensation represented by each specific spinal nerve is reproducible and predictable and referred to as a dermatome. Nondermatomal symptoms do not follow this predictable pattern and therefore do not support the diagnosis of a radiculopathy or spinal nerve root lesion in the back. A radiculopathy can result from a herniated disc or other sources including degeneration of the spine and bone spurs.

The sciatic nerve is a very large nerve that runs from the low back to the knee region, supplying branches to the skin and muscles of the leg. The nerve is mainly composed of fibers originating from L4, L5, and S1. The term sciatica is used to describe the symptoms of leg pain and numbness that follow the course of the nerve and may represent irritation of or damage to the nerve itself or the nerve roots that compose the sciatic nerve.

Myriad muscles, ligaments, and tendons support and move the vertebrae and discs. These are also an important source of low back pain. With incorrectly applied or excessive forces these structures can tear (or sprain), resulting in pain, swelling, and abnormal movement as these structures are well supplied with pain-sensing nerve fibers. The muscles and other soft tissues of the back are important in normal smooth motion of the back and extremities. Back pain can result from injury to these soft tissues and is referred to as musculoskeletal or mechanical low back pain, lumbago, or lumbar strain. This musculoskeletal low back pain is very prevalent in the work force and is often difficult to objectify.

The successful treatment of low back pain often hinges on active involvement and commitment by the patient in a rehabilitation program.

28.3 Sources of Low Back Pain

Even a partial list of the possible diagnoses that can present as low back pain can be overwhelming. This list can become quite manageable when restricted to the most common causes of low back pain in the work force.

Understanding the existence and significance of degeneration of the lumbar spine is essential to understanding the diagnosis of low back pain. Cadaver studies have shown that after the age of 30 there is slowly progressive degeneration of the structures of the back. This is evidenced by a documented change of the chemical composition of the disc. The nucleus pulposus becomes dehydrated, the annulus fibrosis becomes stiffer, often resulting in tears in the fibers and laminae. X-rays can reveal changes in the vertebrae, such as "lipping," or disc space narrowing. Imaging studies such as CT and magnetic resonance imaging may reveal diffuse bulging or frank herniation of the disc. This diffuse degeneration can be found in totally asymptomatic individuals. Therefore a diagnosis cannot be based on imaging studies alone. Especially in work-related cases, history and physical findings must be interpreted in consideration of the imaging studies before a cause of the low back pain can be identified.

28.3.1 Lumbar Disc Disease

As previously outlined, the lumbar disc is a shock absorbing structure located between the vertebral bodies in the anterior portion of the spine. As a result of excessive or disadvantageous forces, the soft inner nucleus pulposus can pass through or "herniate" through the outer annulus fibrosis. This will cause inflammation and/or compression of pain sensitive structures.

The injured individual will often, but not always, recall the inciting activity or event. Usually the pain will increase with time but may be disabling from the onset. In classic lumbar radiculopathy (or nerve root irritation), leg pain and/or numbness (i.e., sciatica) will be greater than back pain.

Important physical findings include asymmetrical or absent reflexes at the knee, ankle, or hamstring muscles, numbness in a predictable dermatomal pattern, weakness in predictable muscles as well as limitations in the motion of the lumbar spine. The straight leg raise test is felt to reflect a herniated disc and is considered positive when pain radiates down the back of the leg when the straight leg is raised with the patient lying on his or her back.

Diagnostic testing is used to help substantiate the diagnosis of a herniated disc. Plain x-rays are generally not helpful in the evaluation of the lumbar disc. However, x-rays will offer some information about the condition of the vertebrae. CT and MR scans have some limitations but in general offer good structural information about the lumbar spine and intervertebral discs. The MR scan is felt to be more sensitive for the evaluation of herniated disc in the lumbar spine than the CT scan but is not always available or tolerated by patients. Myelography involves the injection of a die into the spinal canal and offers more information about the specific anatomy. Electromyography and nerve conduction studies (EMG/NCS) are often used to determine if there is nerve damage present and to help pinpoint the level of the nerve and disc involved. EMG/NCS is helpful for prognosis and in considering the various treatment options.

Appropriate treatment for a herniated disc runs the gambit from a short course of physical therapy and medications to spinal surgery. Up to 7 to 10 days of bed rest is appropriate acutely, with gentle return to mobility as tolerated. The time off work is not necessarily shorter with the nonsurgical approach. Depending on the job, time off work for a herniated disc will be at least four to eight weeks with postoperative convalescence at least that long. Patients may have permanent restriction from heavy physical labor after a herniated disc.

A posterior herniation of a disc on rare occasions can cause compression on the end of the spinal cord. This may result in loss of bowel and bladder control and is a neurosurgical emergency.

28.3.2 *Musculoskeletal Low Back Pain or Lumbar Strains and Sprains*

Mechanical or musculoskeletal low back pain, lumbago, or lumbar sprain all generally refer to the same pathology. This is back pain as the result of an injury to the muscles, tendons, ligaments, and soft tissues of the low back. This is a common cause of low back pain in the industrial setting; however, the onset can be the result of a trivial, often forgotten, maneuver as well as a strenuous event. The patient with musculoskeletal low back pain will complain of aching or stabbing pains in the low back, either symmetrically or off to one side at the sacroiliac joint region or buttock. Numbness and shooting leg pain are typically not present although patients may notice thigh pain. Agility is often compromised, sleep may be impaired, and often time off work is required.

No more than two days of bed rest is recommended with musculoskeletal low back injuries. Slow mobilization including stretching and gentle exercises are prescribed. Muscle relaxants and/or nonsteroidal anti-inflammatory medications can be used for a short time. If the pain is quite severe, low doses of narcotic medication such as codeine are also used for a brief time. Generally muscle strains will resolve within two weeks. If they do not, then manipulation or two to six weeks of physical therapy may help speed up the recovery. Physical therapy will be successful only if the patient is actively involved in the process. Long-term success depends on a commitment on the part of the patient to major life-style changes. These may include weight loss and a fairly stringent adherence to a stretching and conditioning program at least three times a week forever! Individuals prone to musculoskeletal low back pain will decrease the frequency and intensity of the inevitable episodes with an appropriate home exercise program. The patients also benefit from the cardiovascular fitness and improved sleep that generally accompanies an exercise program. There may be some long-term limitations for the heavy laborer.

Back schools are a popular way to supply the education that is helpful in reinforcing the need for long-term commitment to a home exercise program. The back schools are usually organized by physical therapists, and are offered to individuals with many different types of back pain. Strengthening and conditioning programs can also be developed and implemented by personal trainers and exercise physiologists once the acute injury has diminished.

Orthotics (braces) such as a lumbosacral corset (low back brace) can assist with pain reduction for return to work, but should not be used routinely for the long term.

The piriformis syndrome is another source of musculoskeletal low back pain. This refers to pathology of one of the hip muscles that can cause irritation of the sciatic nerve and therefore leg and low back or pelvic pain. Treatment options include manipulation in conjunction with exercise and injection of steroids.

Musculoskeletal low back pain can also result from an asymmetry of the legs or pelvis. This will usually respond to mobilization or manipulative treatment by a physical therapist, physician, or chiropractor, and must be followed up with strict adherence to an exercise program.

28.3.3 Facet Joint Arthritis

Arthritis or inflammation of the facet joints will also cause low back pain. The facet joints are part of the posterior elements of the spine and result from the articulation between the vertebrae. As a result of degenerative forces upon these joints, pain and inflammation will occur. The complaints are usually confined to the low back or thigh region and increase with posterior extension of the low back. Treatment includes strengthening of the muscles of the lower back and abdomen, heat or ice and nonsteroidal anti-inflammatory medication. Facet joint injections of a steroid to block inflammation can also be effective in decreasing pain and disability.

28.3.4 Spinal Stenosis

Degenerative changes of the bones and soft tissues that make up the back can cause narrowing of the spinal canal, which contains the spinal cord. Low back pain and leg pain can result. This is typically worse when standing erect or walking. Although a conservative approach with physical therapy may be helpful, it may also be quite limited by the degenerative changes. Surgery can be performed to widen the canal; however, pain can continue despite the surgery as a result of the degenerative process.

28.3.5 Fractures

Just like any other bone in the body, fractures can occur in the vertebrae. Usually the onset of the pain is immediate and may be the result of severe trauma. A spinal fracture can result in a spinal cord injury often causing weakness or paralysis and severe disability. More often a compression fracture of the body of the vertebrae occurs, usually in abnormal bone and as a result of fairly trivial forces. Compression fractures of the vertebrae are most common in the elderly population, related to osteoporotic (thin and weak) bones. Therefore compression fractures are not often a cause of industrial back pain. Braces, strengthening, and surgery are the treatment options.

28.3.6 Miscellaneous Causes of Low Back Pain

Other causes of low back pain are rarely pertinent when considering work-related low back pain. These would include tumors, infections of the bones or discs, connective tissue disease including Rheumatoid Arthritis and Ankylosing Spondylitis, and congenital malformations of the spine.

28.4 Chronic Pain

By definition chronic pain of any type is pain which is disabling, recalcitrant to treatment, and lasting more than six months. In individuals limited by chronic pain, often the only option is a chronic pain program. There are many different types of chronic pain programs with different approaches to pain. A program with a procedure focus may include many injections, often by an anesthesiologist trained in pain treatment. Injections may often be successful and in general are tolerated fairly well by the patient. Treatment for chronic pain should always include a multidisciplinary approach with a focus on return to a more normal lifestyle and a strong psychological component. A chronic pain program may be costly and time consuming but can also offer hope to a population with multiple failures and limited options.

28.5 Medications

Most individuals with low back pain will use medications to decrease pain at some point. For lower level pain, over-the-counter medications including acetaminophen and ibuprophen will offer quite a bit of relief. Prescription medications used for acute and severe pain include stronger nonsteroidal anti-inflammatory medications (NSAIDs) or narcotic medications. In rare cases, individuals are hospitalized for treatment of severe pain with intravenous medications. Muscle relaxant medications are often used and offer the most relief when used for a short period of time with the onset of the pain. A short course of oral steroids (usually prednisone) may help to decrease the pain associated with a herniated disc. Medications to assist with sleep are appropriate and helpful when the pain becomes chronic and interferes with sleep. A pain clinic will offer a variety of injections or alternative oral medications for individuals with chronic pain. Long-term use of narcotic medications is rarely appropriate because of the potential for addiction.

28.6 Diagnostic Tests

The history supplied by the patient and the physical exam will lead the treating physician to a probable diagnosis. If a structural problem is suspected further testing may be appropriate. Plain x-rays of the back will supply information mainly about the alignment and integrity of the bones. Degeneration of the spine may be revealed as well as other pathology including fractures, tumors, or congenital abnormalities. Plain x-rays may also give helpful information about surrounding structures that can create pain which is referred to the low back. CT scans will give greater detail of the structures of the back. MR or magnetic resonance scan is a newer development and not available in all communities. The MR imaging (MRI) is generally the preferred test for the evaluation of the low back including the intervertebral discs. Individuals with claustrophobia or metal implants will not be considered for an MRI. Myelographic evaluation of the back will supply more information of the position of the structures of the back and is often performed as part surgical evaluation. Bone scans are not routinely a part of the evaluation of the low back but can give helpful information about the integrity of the bones. Blood tests are not routinely performed for the work-up of low back pain but may be necessary if there is concern about a connective tissue or rheumatologic disorder or other medical conditions including kidney disease. Nerve conduction testing and electromyography (NCV/EMG) yield essential information about the health of the nerves and muscle and the presence of nerve damage or a radiculopathy.

In general, low back pain is common in the adult population and therefore prevalent in the working population. Workers' compensation claims are often related to low back pain and injury. As previously cited, there are many causes of low back pain; however, in the working population a certain few types of low back pain seem to dominate. Low back pain can be difficult to treat resulting in excessive disability and time off from work. Treatment of the worker with recalcitrant low back pain requires cooperation and communication among physician, patient, therapist, case manager, and employer. Fortunately, the majority of adult low back pain is self-limiting and responds well to conservative treatment.

Selected Bibliography

Brown, Mark D., and Rydevik, Bjorn L., eds., "Causes and Cure of Low Back Pain and Sciatica," *The Orthopedic Clinics of N. Am.*, Vol. 22, No. 2 (Philadelphia: W.B. Saunders, April 1991), 263–82; 315–26.

Calliet, Rene, *Low Back Pain Syndrome*, 4th ed. (*Pain Series*) (Philadelphia: F.A. Davis, 1988).

Evaluation of Low Back Pain; "My Back Hurts," *Postgraduate Medicine*, Vol. 84, No. 3 (September 1988), 107.

Frymoyer, John W., "Medical Progress: Back Pain and Sciatica," *New England J. of Medicine*, Vol. 318, No. 5 (1988), 291.

Guyer, Richard D., "Lumbar Disc Disease," *Spine: State of the Art Reviews*, Vol. 3, No. 1 (Philadelphia: Hanley & Belfus, January 1989).

Hoppenfeld, Stanley, *Physical Examination of the Spine and Extremities* (Norwalk, Conn.: Appleton-Century-Crofts, 1976).

Jenkins, David B., *Hollinshead's Functional Anatomy of the Limbs and Back*, 6th ed. (Philadelphia: W.B. Saunders, 1991).

Kraft, George H., and Herring, Stanley A., eds., "Low Back Pain," *Physical Medicine and Rehabilitation Clinics of N. Am.* (Philadelphia: W.B. Saunders, February 1991).

Pope, Malcolm, Anderson, Gunnar, B., and Frymoyer, John W., "Occupational Low Back Pain: Assessment, Treatment and Prevention" (St. Louis: Mosby Year Book, 1991).

Conferences

Eleventh Annual Occupational Low Back Pain Conference: The University of Michigan Center for Occupational Health and Safety Engineering, October 29–30, 1990.

Chapter 29

Carpal Tunnel Syndrome and Upper Extremity Cumulative Trauma Disorders

by Dean S. Louis, M.D.*

29.1 Introduction

Carpal tunnel syndrome is a clinical condition that has received increasing publicity in the popular press. The focus of this chapter is to describe this entity, including historical perspectives, the pertinent anatomy, the signs and symptoms associated with the condition, diagnostic studies, and treatment options. In addition to this, a discussion of a few allied conditions will be included.

29.2 Anatomy

The carpal tunnel is an anatomical location in the middle of the palm between the bulky muscles at the base of the thumb and those at the base of the little finger. The tunnel is less than two

*Dean S. Louis, M.D., is Professor of Surgery, Chief, Orthopaedic Hand Service, University of Michigan Hospitals. He is Board Certified by the American Board of Orthopedic Surgery with a Certificate of Added Qualification in Hand Surgery. He has published numerous articles. He can be reached at the University of Michigan Hospital, Ann Arbor, MI 48109-0328, Tel: (313) 936-5200, Fax: (313) 764-9159.

Figure 29.1

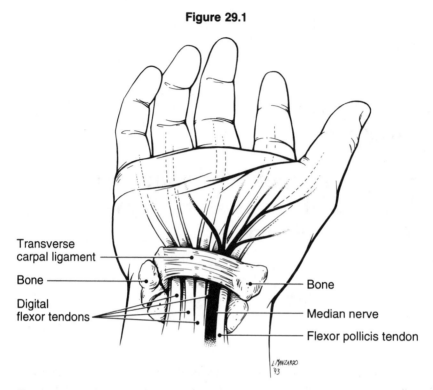

Transverse
carpal ligament

Bone

Digital
flexor tendons

Bone

Median nerve

Flexor pollicis tendon

L. MANZARRO '83

This artist's depiction of the carpal tunnel and its contents shows the median nerve in black, coursing beneath the transverse carpal ligament accompanied by the flexor tendons to the thumb and the fingers.

inches long. Its transverse dimension is no greater. In effect, this anatomical area is a tunnel through which 10 structures pass. The 10 structures include those tendons that flex the fingers and the thumb, and the median nerve that is responsible for motor control to some of the thumb muscles and for supplying sensibility to the thumb, the index, the long, and one-half of the ring finger. The anatomical boundaries of the carpal tunnel are formed on three sides by the bones of the wrist and the remaining side of the tunnel is formed by a stout ligament (figure 29.1).

The median nerve in this configuration is the victim, and if you will, a witness to the events that occur in the carpal tunnel. It is a victim because when the contents of this tunnel increase, or when the volume of the tunnel decreases, the median nerve, which is the softest structure in the tunnel, has pressure exerted upon it on a purely mechanical basis—thus it becomes the victim. It becomes a witness because when increasing pressure is placed upon it for one of the two reasons mentioned above, the person who is so affected will experience numbness and tingling in the sensory distribution of the nerve as previously described.

29.3 The Syndrome

A syndrome exists when a series of signs and symptoms occur together that indicate a certain condition. In the case of the carpal tunnel syndrome, symptoms usually predominate over the physical signs. Symptoms that generally occur are numbness and tingling in the median nerve distribution, pain in the hand or the wrist, awakening at night, and radiation of the discomfort into the forearm, elbow, and sometimes even the shoulder. The physical signs that may accompany this are usually only evident in far advanced cases. These include swelling just at the level where the hand meets the forearm. Also the muscles that arise at the base of the thumb may demonstrate wasting or atrophy. It is extremely important to note that this syndrome may have many different causes and so the treatment must be specific and directed toward the cause of the syndrome in the individual patient. Experience has shown that some causes are much more frequent than others. It is important, therefore, to recognize that the treatment program that is appropriate for one person may not be appropriate for another.

The following is a partial list of conditions that may be associated with the carpal tunnel syndrome:

1. Trauma, such as wrist fractures,
2. Diabetes,
3. Hypothyroidism,
4. Rheumatoid Arthritis,
5. Severe kidney disease, and
6. Pregnancy.

In addition, other conditions may produce symptoms and physical findings that are similar to the carpal tunnel syndrome, but they are in fact separate entities that must be managed entirely differently.

Examples of this are compression of the median nerve in the forearm, certain tumors involving the lung, certain neurological diseases, as well as osteoarthritis involving the neck.

Observations relating to compression of the median nerve being responsible for wasting of the muscles of the thumb were made as early as 1857. However, the clinical condition we now see only became prominent in the medical literature during the 1960s. There are now over 6,000 references in the medical literature regarding this condition, involving descriptions of larger series of cases treated by various methods including surgery, injections, splinting, descriptions of anatomical variations within the carpal tunnel itself, as well as descriptions of newer techniques for treatment, and complications associated with the treatment of this condition. In recent years, the carpal tunnel syndrome seems to have reached epidemic proportions, particularly in the workplace. It has been associated with work-related activities in a variety of situations. Some of the occupations involved are word processing, meat cutting, dental hygiene, industries where vibrating tools are used, telegraphers, and garment workers.

Highly forceful and highly repetitive activities have been identified as work characteristics common to the occupations that predispose individuals to develop the carpal tunnel syndrome. It is of interest that some individuals can perform a given job which has these characteristics of forcefulness and repetitiveness and yet they will never develop the carpal tunnel syndrome. On the other hand, another individual, after a brief exposure to the same job, will develop the full blown symptom complex.

The differences in these two situations are probably related to anatomical differences that have yet to be precisely calculated. It is known, for example, that the dimensions of the carpal tunnel in women are smaller than those of men. Yet the quandary still exists. Some women exposed to the same job will develop carpal tunnel syndrome while others will not. The relationship of the carpal tunnel syndrome to work environment has become a matter of great controversy. This is particularly true because of workers' compensation laws which state that a condition is compensable if it is "caused or aggravated by" a person's work. When a physician takes an in-depth work history from a patient who has symptoms of the carpal tunnel syndrome, it is important that the work task

Figure 29.2

This is an actual surgical photograph of the carpal tunnel after the ligament (black arrow) has been divided. The orientation of this picture is the same as the artist's diagram with the thumb to the right side of the illustration. The open arrow is on the thickened tenosynovial tissue. The median nerve is located between the two arrows.

be broken down into individual cycles forming the basis for the work and that the number of times the cycle is repeated during a work day be noted. In addition, the amount of rest incorporated during the work day or the total number of breaks is also a critical issue in obtaining such a history. Frequently, individuals perform repetitive activities that may represent over 10,000 separate hand and wrist motions during an eight-hour day. In response to such repetition, the lining around the tendons in the carpal tunnels (the tenosynovium) responds by thickening (figure 29.2). In response to rest, this thickened tissue may resolve, thus pressure placed on the median nerve may be diminished and the symptoms of the carpal tunnel syndrome may resolve.

In someone who has the early phases of the carpal tunnel syndrome, it is not unusual when taking a history to find out that the symptoms have resolved during the evening or on the weekends when the individual is not working, and at times when he or she is on vacation or otherwise away from the work environment and not involved in strenuous hand-intensive activities. It is important to note that where individuals have physically active avocational lives that involve repetitive use of their hands and wrists, such as racquetball, tennis, and squash, to name a few, such activities tend to compound their repetitive circumstances at work.

29.4 Examination

A physician's examination of a patient suspected of having the carpal tunnel syndrome will include an extensive history and physical examination of the involved extremity, and usually some additional studies will be indicated. The two that are most frequently done are X-ray examination of the hand and the wrist, and studies of muscle and nerve function (which are collectively known as EMG and nerve conduction studies, or electrophysiologic studies of nerve and muscle function). These studies demonstrate when there has been impairment of nerve or muscle function. A variety of other tests may be performed, but these are the ones most frequently used.

29.5 Treatment

Treatment of the carpal tunnel syndrome is patient specific. There is no universal solution to the problem. The following comments are meant to be general and generic and reflect the author's bias based upon his experience. If an individual has developed the carpal tunnel syndrome in relationship to his or her work, the most reasonable and logical solution for that individual would be to change the nature of the workplace, to change the way in which he or she performs work-related tasks, to add sufficient rest periods in an effort to diminish the continued repetitive stress and allow the tissues to rest and recover.

There are a variety of other treatment modalities that may assist or alleviate the symptoms of the carpal tunnel syndrome. These include eliminating avocational stressers, as described above, and the use of splints at night. Local steroid injections may have some benefit on a limited basis, and the use of noncortisone containing anti-inflammatory medium may also be of some benefit.

It has been my experience and that of other hand surgeons that persons who have the carpal tunnel syndrome related to work will generally not do well following surgery unless they return to some less hand-intensive occupation. Most individuals who return to the same forceful and repetitive jobs will have a recurrence of their symptoms following a brief period of relief. For those individuals where a definite job modification has been made so that they have been removed from the highly forceful and repetitive environment, surgery may be helpful if their symptoms persist. Although past teachings suggested that the carpal tunnel syndrome was a surgical disease, that was at a time when the patients we were seeing were predominantly women who were not involved in repetitive occupational tasks and who uniformly responded well to the surgical approach. The patients that we see today have a far different response to surgery. The equation for management of the patient with the carpal tunnel syndrome that applied 30 years ago is no longer applicable in light of the changing workplace and the increase in repetitive jobs. The old equation of carpal tunnel symptoms + abnormal electrophysiologic tests = surgery = complete relief is no longer a balanced equation. When surgery is indicated, the findings may be dramatic.

29.6 Other Cumulative Trauma Disorders

Although the carpal tunnel syndrome is far and away the most commonly seen cumulative trauma disorder, other areas of the body may be subject to repetitive stress and localized symptoms. These include flexor tendons in the hand where trigger fingers may occur, the inside and outside areas of the elbow (the epicondyles) which may result in medial or lateral epicondylitis, the muscles about the shoulder (the rotator cuff), and the wrist flexor and extensor tendons. It is a fairly common experience that when one takes up a new activity, such as running, tennis, golf, or any sort of conditioning program, there will be musculoskeletal aches and pain as a result of using previously unstressed muscles and tendons. Individual tolerances to such activities vary and it is not surprising that the person who assumes an occupational endeavor that requires repetitive use of muscle, tendon, and ligament complexes that have been previously underutilized may develop complaints in these areas. In general, the philosophy that relates to management of a patient with early carpal tunnel syndrome is also appropriate. Work history, analysis of the job, the postures that are assumed as well as cycle times and durations of work activities must be analyzed. In a very broad and general way, most of these conditions may be effectively treated by rest, activity restriction, appropriate conditioning programs, and occasionally medication. Some of these situations may pursue a prolonged and chronic course with slow resolution over time.

Selected Bibliography

American Academy of Orthopaedic Surgeons, *Data on Volume and Changes for Medicare Services by Orthopaedic Surgeons, 1986–1988,* American Academy of Orthopaedic Surgeons, Center for Research (December 1990), 27.

Armstrong, T.J., Foulkes, J., and Joseph, B.S., *et al.,* "An investigation of cumulative trauma disorders in a poultry processing plant." *Am. Ind. Hyg. Assoc. J.,* 43:103 (1982).

Bigos, S.J., Battie, M.C., and Spengler, D.M., *et al.,* "A Longitudinal prospective study of industrial back injury reporting." Paper presented at the American Academy of Orthopaedic Surgeons, 58th annual meeting, Anaheim, Cal., March 7, 1991.

Birkbeck, M.Q., and Beer, T.C., "Occupation in relation to the carpal tunnel syndrome." *Rheumatol Rehab.* 14:218 (1975).

Brown, P., "The role of motivation in the recovery of the hand." In M. Kasdan, *Occupational Hand and Upper Extremity Injuries and Diseases* (Philadelphia: Hanley and Belfus, 1991), 1.

Cannon, B.W., and Love, J.G., "Tardy median palsy: median neuritis: median thenar neuritis amenable to surgery." *Surgery* 20:210 (1946).

Cannon, L.J., Bernacki, E.J., and Walter, S.D., "Personal and occupational factors associated with carpal tunnel syndrome." *J. Occup. Med.,* 23:255 (1981).

Centers for Disease Control, "Occupational disease surveillance: carpal tunnel syndrome." *Morbidity and Mortality Weekly Rep.* 38:485 (1989).

Centers for Disease Control, "Occupational disease surveillance: carpal tunnel syndrome." *J.A.M.A.* 262:88 (1989).

Dimberg, L., Olafsson, A., and Stefansson, E., *et al.,* "The correlation between work environment and the occurrence of cervicobrachial symptoms." *J. Occup. Med.* 31:447 (1989).

Finkel, M.L., "The effects of repeated mechanical trauma in the meat industry." *Am. J. Ind. Med.* 8:375 (1985).

Gelberman, R.H., Ronson, D., and Weissman, M.H., "Results of a prospective trial of steroid injection and splinting." *J. Bone Joint Surg.* 62A:1181 (1980).

Gelberman, R.H., Hergenmoeder, P.T., and Hargens, A.R., *et al.*, "Sensibility testing in peripheral nerve compression syndromes: An experimental study in humans." *J. Bone Joint Surg.* 65A:632 (1983).

Gellman, H., Chandler, D.R., and Perasek, J., *et al.*, "Carpal tunnel syndrome in paraplegic patients." *J. Bone Joint Surg.* 70A:517 (1988).

Green, D.P., "Diagnostic and therapeutic value of carpal tunnel injection." *J. Hand Surg.* 9:850 (1989).

Grundberg, A.B., "Carpal tunnel decompression in spite of a normal electromyography." *J. Hand Surg.* 8:348 (1983).

Hadler, N.M., "Occupational illness: the issue of causality." *J. Occup. Med.* 26:587 (1984).

———. "Work related disorders of the upper extremity: Part I. Cumulative trauma disorders: A critical review." *Occupational Problems in Medical Practice* 4:1 (1989).

———. "Cumulative trauma disorders: An iatrogenic concept." *J. Occup. Med.* 32:38 (1990).

Hocking, B., "Epidemiologic aspects of repetition strain injury in Telecom Australia." *Med. J. Aust.* 147:218 (1987).

Ireland, D., "Psychological and physical aspects of occupational arm pain." *J. Hand Surg.* 13B:5 (1988).

Jones, B.F., and Scott, F.A., "Carpal tunnel release: The effect of workers' compensation on clinical outcome." Paper presented at the American Academy of Orthopaedic Surgeons, 58th annual meeting, Anaheim, Cal., March 7, 1991.

Lipscomb, P.R., In R.M. Szabo, *Nerve Compression Syndromes, Diagnosis and Treatment* (Thorofare, N.J.: Slack, Inc., 1989), 1.

Louis, D.S., Greene, T.L., and Noellert, R.C., "Complications of carpal tunnel syndrome." *J. Neurosurg.*, 62:352 (1985).

MacDonald, R.I., Lichtman, D.M., and Hanlon, J.J., *et al.*, "Complications of surgical release for carpal tunnel syndrome." *J. Hand Surg.* 3:70 (1978).

Marie, P., and Foix, C., "Atrophie isole de l'eminence thenar d'origine nevritique: role du ligament annulaire anterieur du carpe dans la pathologenie de la lesion." *Rev. Neurol.* 26:647 (1913).

Margolis, W., and Kraus, J.F., "The prevalence of carpal tunnel syndrome symptoms in female supermarket checkers." *J. Occup. Med.* 29:953 (1987).

Masear, V.R., Hayes, J.M., and Hyde, A.G., "An industrial cause of carpal tunnel syndrome." *J. Hand Surg.* 11A:222 (1986).

Morse, L.H., "Repetitive motions: Musculoskeletal problems in the microelectronics industry." *State of the Art Reviews: Occupational Medicine* 1:167 (1986).

Nancollas, M.P., Peimer, C.A., and Wheeler, D.R., "Long term results of carpal tunnel release." Paper presented at the American Academy of Orthopaedic Surgeons, 58th annual meeting, Anaheim, Cal., March 7, 1991.

Paget, J., *Lectures on Surgical Pathology.* 1st ed. (Philadelphia: Lindsay and Blakiston, 1854), 42.

Phalen, G.S., "The carpal tunnel syndrome: Seventeen years' experience in diagnosis and treatment of six hundred fifty-four hands." *J. Bone Joint Surg.* 48A:211 (1966).

Posch, J.L., and Marcotte, D.R., "Carpal tunnel syndrome: An analysis of 1201 cases." *Orthop. Rev.* 5:25 (1976).

Punnett, L., Robins, J.M., and Wegman, D.H., *et al.*, "Soft tissue disorders in the upper limbs of female garment workers." *Scand. J. Work Environ. Health* 11:417 (1985).

Schwind, F., Ventura, M., and Posteek, J.L., "Idiopathic carpal tunnel syndrome: Histologic study of flexor tendon synovium." *J. Hand Surg.* 15A:497 (1990).

Silverstein, B., "The prevalence of upper extremity cumulative trauma disorders in industry." Ph.D. Dissertation, University of Michigan, 1985.

Szabo, R.M., and Chidgey, L.K., "Stress carpal tunnel pressures in patients with carpal tunnel syndrome and normal patients." *J. Hand Surg.* 14A:624 (1989).

Thomas, P.K., and Fullerton, P.M., "Nerve fiber size in the carpal tunnel syndrome." *J. Neurol. Neurosurg. Psych.* 26:520 (1963).

Appendix

Workers' Compensation Agencies

Alabama
Workers' Compensation Division
Department of Industrial
Relations
Industrial Relations Building
Montgomery, AL 36130
(205) 242–2868
FAX (205) 240–3267

Alaska
Workers' Compensation Division
Department of Labor
P.O. Box 25512
Juneau, AK 99802–5512
(907) 465–2790
FAX (907) 465–2797

Arizona
Industrial Commission
800 West Washington
P.O. Box 19070
Phoenix, AZ 85005–9070
(602) 542–4411

Arkansas
Workers' Compensation
Commission
Justice Building
625 Marshall Street
Little Rock, AR 72201

(501) 682–3930
FAX (501) 682–2777

California
Department of Industrial
Relations
Division of Workers'
Compensation
455 Golden Gate Avenue
Room 5182, 5th Floor
San Francisco, CA 94102
(415) 703–5161
FAX (415) 703–3971

Workers' Compensation Appeal
Board
455 Golden Gate Avenue
Room 2178
San Francisco, CA 94102
(415) 703–4942

Colorado
Division of Workers'
Compensation
Department of Labor &
Employment
Chancery Building
1120 Lincoln Street, 14th Floor
Denver, CO 80203
(303) 764–4325
FAX (303) 894–2973

454   *Employer's Guide to Workers' Compensation*

Industrial Claims Appeals Board
1120 Lincoln Street, 14th Floor
Denver, CO 80203
(303) 894–2378

Connecticut
Workers' Compensation
    Commission
1890 Dixwell Avenue
Hamden, CT 06514
(203) 789–7783
FAX (203) 789–7375

Delaware
Industrial Accident Board
State Office Building, 6th Floor
820 North French Street
Wilimington, DE 19801
(302) 577–2884
FAX (302) 577–3750

District of Columbia
Department of Employment
    Services
Office of Workers' Compensation
P.O. Box 56098
Washington, DC 20011
(202) 576–6265

Florida
Division of Workers'
    Compensation
Department of Labor &
    Employment Security
Forrest Building, Suite 301
2728 Centerview Drive
Tallahassee, FL 32399–0680
(904) 488–2514
FAX (904) 922–6779

Georgia
Board of Workers' Compensation
South Tower, Suite 1000
One CNN Center
Atlanta, GA 30303–2788
(404) 656–3875
FAX (404) 656–7768

Hawaii
Disability Compensation Division
Department of Labor & Industrial
    Relations
830 Punchbowl Street, Room 209
Honolulu, HI 96813
(808) 586–9151

Labor & Industrial Relations
    Appeal Board
888 Miliani Street, Room 400
Honolulu, HI 98613
(808) 586–8600

Idaho
Industrial Commission
317 Main Street
Boise, ID 83720
(208) 334–6000
FAX (208) 334–2321

Illinois
Industrial Commission
100 West Randolph Street, Suite
    8–200
Chicago, IL 60601
(312) 814–6500

Indiana
Workers' Compensation Board
Room W196 Government Center
    South
402 West Washington Street
Indianapolis, IN 46204
(317) 232–3808
FAX (317) 233–5493

Iowa
Division of Industrial Services
Department of Employment
    Services
1000 East Grand Avenue
Des Moines, IA 50319
(515) 281–5934
FAX (515) 281–6501

Kansas
Division of Workers'
    Compensation
Department of Human Resources
600 Merchant Bank Tower
800 SW Jackson
Topeka, KS 66612–1227
(913) 296–3441
FAX (913) 296–0839

Kentucky
Workers' Compensation Board
Perimeter Park West, Building C
1270 Louisville Road
Frankfort, KY 40601
(502) 564–5550

Louisiana
Department of Employment &
    Training
Office of Workers' Compensation
1001 North 23rd Street
P.O. Box 94040
Baton Rouge, LA 70804–9040
(504) 342–7555
FAX (504) 342–6555

Maine
Workers' Compensation
    Commission
State House Station 27
Augusta, ME 04333–0027
(207) 287–3751
FAX (207) 287–7198

Maryland
Workers' Compensation
    Commission
6 North Liberty Street
Baltimore, MD 21201–3785
(410) 333–4700
FAX (410) 333–8122

Massachusetts
Department of Industrial
    Accidents
600 Washington Street

Boston, MA 02111
(617) 727–4900
FAX (617) 727–6477

Michigan
Bureau of Workers' Disability
    Compensation
Department of Labor
201 North Washington Square,
    2nd Floor
P.O. Box 30016
Lansing, MI 48909
(517) 373–3490

Workers' Compensation Board of
    Magistrates
201 North Washington Square,
    2nd Floor
P.O. Box 30016
Lansing, MI 48909
(517) 335–0643

Workers' Compensation Appellate
    Commission
201 North Washington Square,
    2nd Floor
P.O. Box 30015
Lansing, MI 48909
(517) 335–5828

Minnesota
Workers' Compensation Division
Department of Labor & Industry
443 Lafayette Road North
St. Paul, MN 55101
(612) 296–6107
FAX (612) 296–9634

Workers' Compensation Court of
    Appeals
775 Landmark Towers
345 St. Peter Street
St. Paul, MN 55102
(612) 296–6526

Mississippi
Workers' Compensation
    Commission

P.O. Box 5300
1428 Lakeland Drive
Jackson, MS 39216
(601) 987–4200

Missouri

Department of Labor & Industrial
  Relations
Division of Workers'
  Compensation
P.O. Box 599
3315 West Truman Boulevard
Jefferson City, MO 65102
(314) 751–4231

Labor & Industrial Relations
  Commission
P.O. Box 599
3315 West Truman Boulevard
Jefferson City, MO 65102
(314) 751–2461

Montana

State Compensation Mutual
  Insurance Fund
5 South Last Chance Gulch
Helena, MT 59604–8011
(406) 444–6500

Workers' Compensation Court
P.O. Box 537
47 North Last Chance Gulch
Helena, MT 59624
(406) 444–6520

Employee Relations Division
Department of Labor & Industry
P.O. Box 1728
Helena, MT 59624
(406) 444–3022

Nebraska

Workers' Compensation Court
P.O. Box 98908
State House, 13th Floor
Lincoln, NE 68509–8908
(402) 471–2568
FAX (402) 471–2700

Nevada

State Industrial Insurance System
515 East Musser Street
Carson City, NV 68509–8908
(702) 687–5220
FAX (702) 687–3946

Department of Industrial
  Relations
1390 South Curry Street
Carson City, NV 89710
(702) 687–3032

New Hampshire

Department of Labor
95 Pleasant Street
Concord, NH 03301
(603) 271–3176

New Jersey

Division of Workers'
  Compensation
Department of Labor
Call Number 381
Trenton, NJ 08625
(609) 292–2516

New Mexico

Workers' Compensation
  Administration
P.O. Box 27198
Albuquerque, NM 87125–7198
(505) 841–6000
FAX (505) 841–6009

New York

Workers' Compensation Board
180 Livingston Street
Brooklyn, NY 11248
(718) 802–6600
FAX (718) 834–3705

North Carolina

Industrial Commission
Dobbs Building
430 North Salisbury Street
Raleigh, NC 27611
(919) 733–4820

North Dakota
Workers' Compensation Bureau
500 East Front Avenue
Bismark, ND 58504–5685
(701) 224–3800
FAX (701) 224–3820

Ohio
Bureau of Workers' Compensation
30 West Spring Street
Columbus, OH 43215
(614) 466–1000

Industrial Commission of Ohio
30 West Spring Street
William Green Building
Columbus, OH 43215
(614) 466–6136

Oklahoma
Workers' Compensation Court
1915 North Stiles
Oklahoma City, OK 73105
(405) 557–7600
FAX (405) 557–7683

Oregon
Department of Insurance &
    Finance
21 Labor & Industries Building
Salem, OR 97310
(503) 378–3304

Workers' Compensation Division
Labor & Industries Building
Salem, OR 97310
(503) 378–3304

Workers' Compensation Board
480 Church Street South East
Salem, OR 97310
(503) 378–4283

Pennsylvania
Bureau of Workers' Compensation
Department of Labor & Industry
1171 South Cameron Street,
    Room 103

Harrisburg, PA 17104–2502
(717) 783–5421

Workmen's Compensation Appeal
    Board
1171 South Cameron Street,
    Room 305
Harrisburg, PA 17104–2511
(717) 783–7838

Rhode Island
Workers' Compensation Court
One Dorrance Plaza
Providence, RI 02903
(401) 277–3097
FAX (401) 421–3123

Department of Labor, Workers'
    Compensation Division
610 Manton Avenue
Providence, RI 02907
(401) 272–0700
FAX (401) 277–2127

South Carolina
Workers' Compensation
    Commission
P.O. Box 1715
1612 Marion Street
Columbia, SC 29202–1715
(803) 737–5700
FAX (803) 737–5768

South Dakota
Department of Labor
Division of Labor & Management
Kneip Building, 3rd Floor
700 Governors Drive
Pierre, SD 57501–2277
(605) 773–3681
FAX (605) 773–4211

Tennessee
Workers' Compensation Division
Department of Labor
501 Union Building
Second Floor

Nashville, TN 37243–0661
(615) 741–2395

Texas
Workers' Compensation
    Commission
4000 IH 35 South
Austin, TX 78704–7491
(512) 448–7900

Utah
Industrial Commission of Utah
P.O. Box 146600
160 East 300 South, 3rd Floor
Salt Lake City, UT 84114–6600
(801) 530–6880
FAX (801) 530–6804

Vermont
Department of Labor & Industry
National Life Building
Drawer 20
Montpelier, VT 05620
(802) 828–2286
FAX (802) 828–2195

Workers' Compensation Division
State Office Building
120 State Street
Montpelier, VT 05602
(802) 828–2286
FAX (802) 828–2195

Virginia
Industrial Commission
P.O. Box 1794
1000 DMV Drive
Richmond, VA 23220
(804) 367–8633

Washington
Department of Labor &
    Industries
Labor & Industries Building
P.O. Box 44000
Olympia, WA 98504–4000
(206) 956–5800

Board of Industrial Insurance
    Appeals
P.O. Box 42401
2430 Chandler Court SW
Olympia, WA 98504–2401
(206) 753–6823
FAX (206) 586–5611

West Virginia
Bureau of Employment Programs
Workers' Compensation Fund
P.O. Box 3824
Charleston, WV 25338–3824
(304) 558–0475

Workers' Compensation Appeal
    Board
601 Morris Street, Room 419
Charleston, WV 25301–1416
(304) 558–3375

Wisconsin
Workers' Compensation Division
Department of Industry, Labor &
    Human Relations
P.O. Box 7901
Madison, WI 53707
(608) 266–1340

Labor & Industry Review
    Commission
P.O. Box 8126
Madison, WI 53708
(608) 266–9850

Wyoming
Workers' Compensation Division
122 West 25th Street, 2nd Floor
East Wing, Herschler Building
Cheyenne, WY 82002
(307) 777–7441
FAX (307) 777–5946

**United States Department of
    Labor**
Employment Standards
    Administration

Washington, DC 20210
(202) 219–6692

Office of Workers' Compensation
  Programs
(202) 219–6692

Division of Planning & Standards
(202) 219–6692

Division of Coal Mine Workers'
  Compensation
(202) 219–6692

Division of Federal Employees'
  Compensation
(202) 219–7552

Division of Longshore and Harbor
  Workers' Compensation
(202) 219–8572

Branch of Workers' Compensation
  Studies
(202) 219–9560

Index

This index is alphabetized word-by-word (i.e., "Bill reviews" precedes "Billing").

J

K

About the Author

Edward M. Welch is a member of the faculty of the School of Labor and Industrial Relations at Michigan State University. From 1985 through 1990, he was Director of Michigan's Bureau of Workers' Disability Compensation. Before that he was a claimants' attorney.

Ed Welch serves as secretary to a Labor/Management Discussion Group on Workers' Compensation, which is co-chaired by the National Association of Manufacturers and the AFL-CIO. He was elected a charter member for workers' compensation of the National Academy of Social Insurance. He has served as Vice President of the International Association of Industrial Accident Boards and Commissions. In 1990 he received the outstanding achievement award in workers' compensation that is presented annually by the National Association of Manufacturers, the Alliance of American Insurers, and the American Insurance Association.

Ed Welch has published many books and articles. He is best known for his ability to take complicated issues related to workers' compensation and explain them in a simple, straightforward manner. He is publisher of *On Workers' Compensation*, a magazine with 10 issues yearly whose coverage includes articles on both the overall system and employer-level approaches to workers' compensation.